COLLEGE STUDENT DEVELOPMENT

Wendy K. Killam, PhD, LPC, CRC, NCC, is a professor in the Department of Human Services at Stephen F. Austin State University. Her research interests include college student adjustment, wellness throughout the life span, issues faced by older adults, and issues faced by veterans and military families. She enjoys working with college students and, in addition to working as a counselor educator, has worked in student affairs.

Suzanne Degges-White, PhD, LPC, LMHC, NCC, is a licensed counselor and professor and chair of the Department of Counseling, Adult and Higher Education at Northern Illinois University. She is the coauthor of three books that all touch on the ways in which relationships play out across life. These include her most recent book, *Toxic Friendships: Knowing the Rules and Dealing With the Friends Who Break Them* (2015); *Mothers and Daughters: Living, Loving, and Learning Over a Lifetime* (2014); and *Friends Forever: How Girls and Women Forge Lasting Relationships* (2011). Suzanne has also coedited four books addressing clinical counseling practice and innovative counseling interventions.

COLLEGE STUDENT DEVELOPMENT

Applying Theory to Practice on the Diverse Campus

Wendy K. Killam, PhD, LPC, CRC, NCC
Suzanne Degges-White, PhD, LPC, LMHC, NCC

Editors

SPRINGER PUBLISHING COMPANY
NEW YORK

Copyright © 2017 Springer Publishing Company, LLC

All rights reserved.

No part of this publication may be reproduced, stored in a retrieval system, or transmitted in any form or by any means, electronic, mechanical, photocopying, recording, or otherwise, without the prior permission of Springer Publishing Company, LLC, or authorization through payment of the appropriate fees to the Copyright Clearance Center, Inc., 222 Rosewood Drive, Danvers, MA 01923, 978-750-8400, fax 978-646-8600, info@copyright.com or on the Web at www.copyright.com.

Springer Publishing Company, LLC
11 West 42nd Street
New York, NY 10036
www.springerpub.com

Acquisitions Editor: Nancy S. Hale
Compositor: Newgen KnowledgeWorks

ISBN: 9780826118073
e-book ISBN: 9780826118165

Instructor's Materials: Qualified instructors may request supplements by e-mailing textbook@springerpub.com
Instructor's Manual ISBN: 9780826117946
Instructor's PowerPoints ISBN: 9780826119834

17 18 19 20 21/ 5 4 3 2 1

The author and the publisher of this Work have made every effort to use sources believed to be reliable to provide information that is accurate and compatible with the standards generally accepted at the time of publication. The author and publisher shall not be liable for any special, consequential, or exemplary damages resulting, in whole or in part, from the readers' use of, or reliance on, the information contained in this book. The publisher has no responsibility for the persistence or accuracy of URLs for external or third-party Internet websites referred to in this publication and does not guarantee that any content on such websites is, or will remain, accurate or appropriate.

Library of Congress Cataloging-in-Publication Data
Names: Killam, Wendy K., editor. | Degges-White, Suzanne, editor.
Title: College student development : applying theory to practice on the
   diverse campus / Wendy K. Killam, PhD, LPC, CRC, NCC,
   Suzanne Degges-White, PhD, LPC, LMHC, NCC, editors.
Description: New York : Springer Publishing Company, LLC, [2017]
Identifiers: LCCN 2017002725 | ISBN 9780826118073 (paper back)
Subjects: LCSH: College student development programs—United States—Case
   studies. | Student affairs services—Social aspects—United States.
Classification: LCC LB2343.4 .C64 2017 | DDC 378.1/980973—dc23
LC record available at https://lccn.loc.gov/2017002725

Contact us to receive discount rates on bulk purchases.
We can also customize our books to meet your needs.
For more information please contact: sales@springerpub.com

Printed in the United States of America by Gasch Printing.

*We dedicate this book to all of the student affairs professionals
who devote themselves to the guidance and support of their students
in their efforts to reach their full potentials.
It is our desire that this book provides student affairs professionals
with beneficial knowledge and new perspectives related to
student development theories so that they feel better prepared
to serve their diverse student bodies.*

CONTENTS

Contributors xiii
Preface xvii
Acknowledgments xxi

PART I: INTRODUCTION AND FOUNDATIONS

1. **Introduction to Student Affairs and Student Development Issues**   1
   Wendy K. Killam and Suzanne Degges-White

   History of Student Affairs   1
   Student Needs   2
   Family Support   3
   Wellness   3
   Education Cost and College Affordability   5
   Academic Readiness   6
   Nontraditional College Students   6
   Implications for Student Affairs Professionals   8
   Importance of Using Theories   9
   Conclusion   10

2. **Diversity and Sociocultural Theories of Learning and Development**   13
   Carrie A. Kortegast

   Case Vignette: Hope and Juan   13
   Overview and Description of Sociocultural Theories   14
   History and Development of Sociocultural Theories   14
   Application of the Theory   18
   Case Vignette Wrap-Up: Hope and Juan   19
   Case Vignette 1 for Reader Reflection: Courtney   19
   Case Vignette 2 for Reader Reflection: Sade   20

PART II: THEORIES OF DEVELOPMENT AS APPLIED TO COLLEGE STUDENTS

3. **Schlossberg's Transition Theory**   23
   Susan R. Barclay

   Case Vignette: Reynaldo   23
   Overview and Description of the Theory   23
   History and Development of the Theory   28
   Application Within Student Affairs   30
   Case Vignette Wrap-Up: Reynaldo   31
   Case Vignette 1 for Reader Reflection: Alex   32
   Case Vignette 2 for Reader Reflection: Hyun   33

4. **Erikson's Theory of Psychosocial Development**   35
   Suzanne Degges-White

   Case Vignette: Nehal   35
   Overview of Erikson's Theory of Psychosocial Development   36
   Application of the Theory Within Student Affairs   40
   Conclusion   45
   Case Vignette Wrap-Up: Nehal   45
   Case Vignette 1 for Reader Reflection: Maribel   46
   Case Vignette 2 for Reader Reflection: Mitch   46

5. **Perry's Theory of Moral Development**   49
   Ian S. Turnage-Butterbaugh, Waleed Sami, and Ricardo Phipps

   Case Vignette: Fatima   49
   History and Development of the Theory   50
   Overview and Description of the Theory   51
   Overview of Perry's Development Schema   52
   Deflections From Growth and Development   54
   Application of the Theory Within Student Affairs   54
   Implications for Student Affairs Professionals   57
   Case Vignette Wrap-Up: Fatima   59
   Case Vignette 1 for Reader Reflection: Tina   60
   Case Vignette 2 for Reader Reflection: Brendan   61

6. **Theories of Moral Development**   65
   Rebekah Reysen, Mandy Perryman, and Ricardo Phipps

   Case Vignette: Madison   65
   Moral Development on Campus   66
   Exploring Madison's Positioning Within Kohlberg's Schema   69
   Exploring Madison's Positioning Within Gilligan's Schema   71
   Case Vignette Wrap-Up: Madison   72
   Case Vignette 1 for Reader Reflection: Selective Community Interests   72
   Case Vignette 2 for Reader Reflection: Town Versus Gown   73

7. **Kolb's Theory of Experiential Learning**   75
   Kathryn S. Jaekel

   Case Vignette: Maria   75
   Overview and Description of Experiential
      Learning Theory   75
   History and Development of ELT   76
   Application of the Theory Within Student Affairs   78
   Case Vignette Wrap-Up: Maria   79
   Case Vignette 1 for Reader Reflection: Steve   80
   Case Vignette 2 for Reader Reflection: Cora   80

8. **Personality Types Based on the Myers–Briggs Type Indicator**   83
   Christine Borzumato-Gainey

   Case Vignette: Rebecca, an Introvert Sensing Thinking Judging (ISTJ)   83
   Overview and Description of the Theory Behind the Myers–
      Briggs Type Indicator   84
   Application of the Theory Within Student Affairs   86
   Conclusion   87
   Case Vignette Wrap-Up: Rebecca   88
   Case Vignette 1 for Reader Reflection: Makayla   88
   Case Vignette 2 for Reader Reflection: Michael   89

PART III: IDENTITY DEVELOPMENT IN COLLEGE STUDENTS

9. **Overview of Identity Development in Young Adulthood**   91
   Suzanne Maniss

   Case Vignette: Sofia   91
   Challenges to Identity Development   92
   Factors That Influence Identity Development   92
   Overview of Relevant Theories   93
   Psychosocial Development Theories   93
   Social Identity Development Theories   95
   Case Vignette Wrap-Up: Sofia   97
   Case Vignette 1 for Reader Reflection: Jeff   97
   Case Vignette 2 for Reader Reflection: Leon   98

10. **Chickering's Theory and the Seven Vectors of Development**   101
    Suzanna M. Wise

    Case Vignette: Jonah   101
    Overview and Description of Chickering's Theory   102
    History and Development of Chickering's Theory   105
    Application of Chickering's Theory   106
    Case Vignette Wrap-Up: Jonah   107
    Case Vignette 1 for Reader Reflection: Michelle   108
    Case Vignette 2 for Reader Reflection: Taylor   109

11. **Black and Biracial Identity Development Theories**   111
    Ricardo Phipps

    Case Vignette: Jamaal   111
    History and Development of Black Identity Development Theories   113
    History and Development of Biracial/Multiracial Identity
        Development Theories   115
    Application of Theories Within Student Affairs   117
    Case Vignette Wrap-Up: Jamaal   119
    Case Vignette 1 for Reader Reflection: Lalita   119
    Case Vignette 2 for Reader Reflection: Tiffany and Fumalaya   120

12. **Other Theories of Minority Identity Development**   123
    Jesus Cisneros

    Case Vignette: William   123
    Overview and Description of Minority Identity
        Development Theories   124
    History and Development of the Theories   131
    Implications for Student Affairs Practitioners   131
    Case Vignette Wrap-Up: William   132
    Case Vignette 1 for Reader Reflection: Julia   133
    Case Vignette 2 for Reader Reflection: Mark   133

13. **White Identity Development**   135
    Ian S. Turnage-Butterbaugh

    Case Vignette: Craig   135
    History and Development of White Identity Development Theories   136
    Overview and Description of White Identity Development Theory   136
    Application of the Theory Within Student Affairs   141
    Implications for Helping Professionals on a College Campus   142
    Case Vignette Wrap-Up: Craig   144
    Case Vignette 1 for Reader Reflection: Students Wrestling With Guilt   145
    Case Vignette 2 for Reader Reflection: White Students Responding
        to a Hate Crime   146

14. **Lesbian, Gay, Bisexual, Trans, and Queer Identity Development**   149
    Christian D. Chan, Adrienne N. Erby, Laura Boyd Farmer, and Amanda R. Friday

    Case Vignette: Marcus   149
    Theoretical Foundations of Identity Development   150
    Applications of the Theories Within Student Affairs   153
    Multicultural Student Services and Affairs   153
    College Counseling and Mental Health   155
    Connecting the Vignette and Student Affairs   156
    Case Vignette Wrap-Up: Marcus   156
    Case Vignette 1 for Reader Reflection: Vada   157
    Case Vignette 2 for Reader Reflection: Ty   157

15. **Disability and Identity Development** 161
Yuleinys A. Castillo

    Case Vignette: Melanie 161
    Overview 161
    Disability Identity Models 164
    Disability Identity in Student Affairs Services 167
    Case Vignette Wrap-Up: Melanie 170
    Case Vignette 1 for Reader Reflection: Paloma 171
    Case Vignette 2 for Reader Reflection: Aurelio 171

PART IV: FACTORS IMPACTING SELECTION OF MAJORS AND CAREERS

16. **College Major and Career Choice** 175
Wendy K. Killam, Suzanna M. Wise, and Bill Weber

    Case Vignette: Brooklyn 175
    Major and Career Indecision 175
    Developmental Factors 176
    Factors Influencing Decision Making 177
    Career Theories and Assessments 181
    Conclusion 182
    Case Vignette Wrap-Up: Brooklyn 182
    Case Vignette 1 for Reader Reflection: Melissa 182
    Case Vignette 2 for Reader Reflection: Sanjay 183

17. **Holland's Theory of Career Development** 187
Kevin Stoltz

    Case Vignette: Tyreka 187
    Overview of Holland's Theory 188
    History and Development of Holland's Theory 190
    Conclusion 192
    Case Vignette Wrap-Up: Tyreka 192
    Case Vignette 1 for Reader Reflection: Brent 194
    Case Vignette 2 for Reader Reflection: Demetrius 194

18. **Bronfenbrenner's Ecological Systems Theory** 197
Nathan C. D. Perron

    Case Vignette: Jose 197
    Overview and Description of Bronfenbrenner's Theory 198
    History and Development of Bronfenbrenner's Theory 202
    Bronfenbrenner's Theory Applied to Student Development 203
    Case Vignette Wrap-Up: Jose 205
    Case Vignette 1 for Reader Reflection: Phet 206
    Case Vignette 2 for Reader Reflection: Ashley 207

19. **Bringing Student Groups Together: Understanding Group Theory**   211
    Lucy Parker

    Case Vignette: Kaelyn   *211*
    Overview and Description of Group Theory   *212*
    Looking at Student and Group Development Through a
        Multicultural Lens   *217*
    History and Development of Group Theory   *218*
    Application of Group Theory Within Student Affairs   *219*
    Case Vignette Wrap-Up: Kaelyn   *220*
    Case Vignette 1 for Reader Reflection: Ahmed   *220*
    Case Vignette 2 for Reader Reflection: Judy   *221*
    Helpful Resources   *221*

20. **Theory as the Language of Student Affairs Professionals**   223
    Adam Gregory

    Case Vignette: Akio   *223*
    The Role of Student Affairs   *224*
    Review of the Historical Context of Student Affairs   *224*
    Student Affairs and Theory   *225*
    Using Theory as a Language   *226*
    Current Trends in Student Affairs   *227*
    Talking Across Campus: Monthly "Movie Nights"   *228*
    Future Trends   *231*
    Case Vignette Wrap-Up: Akio   *231*
    Case Vignette 1 for Reader Reflection: Amy   *232*
    Case Vignette 2 for Reader Reflection: Jasmine   *233*

Index   237

CONTRIBUTORS

Susan R. Barclay, PhD, NCC, LPC, ACS, GCDF-I
Assistant Professor and Program Coordinator
College Student Personnel Services and Administration
Department of Leadership Studies
University of Central Arkansas
Conway, Arkansas

Christine Borzumato-Gainey, PhD, LPC
Counselor and Adjunct Instructor
Elon University Counseling Center and Human Services Studies Department
Elon University
Elon, North Carolina

Yuleinys A. Castillo, PhD, CRC, LPC
Assistant Professor
Department of Counselor Education and Rehabilitative Services
Stephen F. Austin University
Nacogdoches, Texas

Christian D. Chan, MA, NCC
Doctoral Student in Counseling
Counseling and Human Development
The George Washington University
Washington, DC

Jesus Cisneros, PhD
Assistant Professor
Leadership Studies
University of Central Arkansas
Conway, Arkansas

Suzanne Degges-White, PhD, LPC, LMHC, NCC
Professor and Chair
Department of Counseling, Adult and Higher Education
Northern Illinois University
DeKalb, Illinois

Adrienne N. Erby, PhD, NCC
Lecturer
Counselor Education Program Coordinator
Lecturer and Interim Director of the George E. Hill Center
Department of Counseling and Higher Education
The Gladys W. and David H. Patton College of Education
Ohio University
Athens, Ohio

Laura Boyd Farmer, PhD, LPC, ACS
Assistant Professor of Counselor Education
Leadership, Counseling and Research
Virginia Tech
Blacksburg, Virginia

Amanda R. Friday, MEd
Graduate Assistant and Doctoral Student in Counseling
Counseling and Human Development
The George Washington University
Washington, DC

Adam Gregory, MA, MSEd
Doctoral Student and Graduate Assistant
Department of Counseling, Adult and Higher Education
Northern Illinois University
DeKalb, Illinois

Kathryn S. Jaekel, PhD
Assistant Professor
Department of Counseling, Adult and Higher Education
Northern Illinois University
DeKalb, Illinois

Wendy K. Killam, PhD, LPC, CRC, NCC
Professor
Department of Human Services
Stephen F. Austin State University
Nacogdoches, Texas

Carrie A. Kortegast, PhD
Assistant Professor of Higher Education
Department of Counseling, Adult and Higher Education
Northern Illinois University
DeKalb, Illinois

Suzanne Maniss, PhD
Associate Professor
Department of Human Services
Stephen F. Austin State University
Nacogdoches, Texas

Lucy Parker, MA, NCC
Doctoral Student
Department of Counseling, Adult and Higher Education
Northern Illinois University
DeKalb, Illinois

Nathan C. D. Perron, PhD
Director of Online Training, Core Faculty
Counseling@Northwestern MA in Counseling Program
Northwestern University
Evanston, Illinois

Mandy Perryman, PhD
Assistant Professor
Department of Leadership and Counselor Education
The University of Mississippi
Oxford, Mississippi

Ricardo Phipps, PhD, NCC
Assistant Professor
Department of Psychology
LaSalle University
Philadelphia, Pennsylvania

Rebekah Reysen, PhD, NCC, LPC, DCC
Assistant Director of Academic Support Programs and Adjunct Assistant Professor
Center for Student Success and First-Year Experience
The University of Mississippi
Oxford, Mississippi

Waleed Sami, BA
Masters in Counseling Graduate Student
Department of Counseling
Wake Forest University
Winston-Salem, North Carolina

Kevin Stoltz, PhD
Associate Professor
Department of Individual, Family, and Community Education
University of New Mexico
Albuquerque, New Mexico

Ian S. Turnage-Butterbaugh, PhD
Adjunct Assistant Professor
Department of Counseling
Wake Forest University
Winston-Salem, North Carolina

Bill Weber, CRC, CVE, LPC
Professor
Department of Human Services
Stephen F. Austin University
Nacogdoches, Texas

Suzanna M. Wise, EdS, LPC, NCC
Doctoral Student
Department of Counseling, Adult and Higher Education
Northern Illinois University
DeKalb, Illinois

PREFACE

It is not uncommon for college students to struggle with the transition to college as they are confronted with new opportunities and new challenges. While dealing with the external world, they are also working their way through any number of personal, internal adjustments in terms of identity, cognitive processing, and so on. For instance, just determining a college major and potential career path can be a struggle that is influenced by a variety of factors. Some students make choices that lead to long-term complications in their academic, social, and professional realms. Some engage in experimental behaviors during the college years that become "history" around graduation time; other choices may have lasting consequences. The increasing cost of a college education leaves some students no choice but to work long hours while enrolled in classes. This can create challenges with time management and academic performance for many students. Nontraditional students may struggle to find balance among work, family, and college. Single mothers may feel torn between the many roles they must fill in their personal lives and the role of student. Veterans returning to college may struggle to adjust to civilian life and the need to work with traditional students who lack life experiences and may not take their academic coursework as seriously as former military men and women do. This panoply of challenging student circumstances presents student affairs professionals with the challenge to assist students with the numerous transitions and challenges they face. Through the application of relevant developmental theories, campus professionals will be able to engage in their work with additional insight and understanding of their student population.

THE SCOPE OF THE BOOK

This book was developed with both the student affairs professional and the student affairs graduate student in mind. For those already working in the field who are assisting students to reach their full potential, comprehension of the developmental issues and challenges faced by students throughout the framework of theory can be advantageous.

To further assist readers in the application of theory to practice, we have provided multiple case vignettes throughout the chapters of the book that address specific theories. Each vignette provides readers the chance to reflect on contemporary college student circumstances set amidst today's diverse campus. The vignettes encourage the considerations of developmental status and resolutions for those issues grounded in the theories presented. Chapters in the book address human development theories; racial identity development; theories of identity development; disability theories; lesbian, gay, bisexual, transgender, and queer (LGBTQ) identity development; and career development theories. When considering how best to help a student, however, it is necessary to develop an overarching understanding of student development on multiple levels and through intersecting theoretical constructs. Thus, understanding a student's ethnic identity process coupled with the student's sexual identity and psychosocial identity can provide a much more useful and informative portrait of his or her circumstances than merely knowing the student as a "19-year-old sophomore."

The book also provides information on the importance of understanding the issues current students face and the diverse nature of the college environment. While each student is unique and an individual, there are common concerns based on age and development faced by students. Being knowledgeable about these common issues can be beneficial in understanding how to implement best practices within the area of student affairs.

Theory-based chapters open with a vignette in which the reader is presented with specific details of a case study for consideration. These cases were chosen to highlight the diverse issues faced by students today as they deal with identity issues, personal issues, academic concerns, professional development, and family struggles. At the end of the chapter, the case is revisited and considered using a theoretical framework. Ideally, the reader will take away a deeper understanding of the student's worldview and perceptions based on theories. Each case vignette provides the reader with immersion into a diverse perspective, and the chapter authors provide a clear discussion of their conceptualization of the student. The reader also is provided with ideas on how to best assist the student with the challenges that he or she is currently facing. Additional case studies and related questions for reflection and consideration conclude these chapters as well.

WHO WILL BENEFIT FROM THE BOOK?

The intended audience for this book includes both students who are pursuing the education necessary to become student affairs professionals and current student affairs professionals who seek greater insight and comprehension of student development theories. Understanding and clearly assessing the unique needs and points of view of students can challenge individuals who are new to the field as well as those who are veterans in the student affairs profession. The ability to apply theories to student issues can facilitate greater understanding and clarity regarding the most effective method of assisting a student. By gaining conceptualization skills based on theory, student affairs professionals will be better positioned to have the most positive and effective influence they can. With a clear focus on the diverse student body on the contemporary college campus, readers will gain an in-depth understanding of the role of identity development in students' academic and social pursuits.

OVERALL VALUE OF THE BOOK

Although other books are available that focus on student development theory, this book provides a unique perspective in the application of case studies and the overall inclusion of specific career development theories, theories related to disability, and theories related to LGBTQ identity issues. Our goal was to ensure that the book would enable readers to feel prepared to meet the needs of an increasingly diverse college student population. By including diverse case studies representative of contemporary college students, we encourage readers to consider the practical application of theories. In summary, this book provides the opportunity for readers to develop the skills and gain the knowledge to view their professional role utilizing multiple theoretical lenses that will allow them to enhance their ability to meet the needs of the diverse students they serve. In support of the text, an Instructor's Manual, sample syllabus, and PowerPoints are available. **Qualified instructors can request these ancillaries by e-mail: textbook@springerpub.com.**

Wendy K. Killam
Suzanne Degges-White

ACKNOWLEDGMENTS

The editors would like to thank Nancy S. Hale for her support and guidance from the earliest stages of this project's development. We also would like to thank the insightful, knowledgeable, and creative contributors who shared their expertise through this book.

Wendy K. Killam and Suzanne Degges-White

Suzanne, you are amazing and wonderful. Thanks for your guidance and support on this project and willingness to work on it. This book would still be an idea without your gentle persistence to move forward on it. I am blessed to have the opportunity to work with a dedicated professional like you. I am also thankful to my husband Bil and son Michael for their continued support. While I have been working on this project, you have been encouraging and have allowed me the time and space I needed. Finally, to my dad, I appreciate your constant encouragement.

Wendy K. Killam

To my amazingly brilliant and committed coeditor, Wendy, I express my appreciation for all of the learning that I enjoyed through the development of this book! Collaborating with colleagues who care as much about "doing good and doing it right" as you do is deeply gratifying. Thanks, too, to all of those who have had a hand in growing me as a counselor, a counselor educator, and a person. This includes my amazing spouse, Ellen, and our three "emerging adult" children, each of whom is on a different path to career satisfaction and career success.

Suzanne Degges-White

PART I: INTRODUCTION AND FOUNDATIONS

CHAPTER 1

INTRODUCTION TO STUDENT AFFAIRS AND STUDENT DEVELOPMENT ISSUES

Wendy K. Killam and Suzanne Degges-White

It is essential that those who work in higher education institutions today possess a comprehensive understanding of the range of challenges that their students face. The college years provide students with numerous opportunities for growth and development as they face both normative and unexpected transitions that can influence an individual's future extensively. Although the roles that student affairs professionals play in assisting students are not new ones, they have expanded significantly in recent years. As with any profession, the application of relevant theories can facilitate the effectiveness of student affairs personnel. For this group, the use of a variety of developmental theories can aid their efforts to examine issues and gain insight into the ways in which students are handling challenges within a developmental framework. Student affairs professionals carry the responsibility of creating an atmosphere and environment that promotes student development both personally and professionally outside the classroom. In this chapter we briefly examine the history of the student affairs profession, specific issues students face when adjusting to college, and the role of student affairs professionals in providing support to students. We also discuss the importance of using theories to assist students.

HISTORY OF STUDENT AFFAIRS

In order to understand the current role of student affairs professionals, it is helpful to have an understanding of the history of the field, which goes back to colonial times here in the United States. When the Civil War ended, there were only a few universities and the main focus of these institutions was the education of ministers and doctors. Most of these colleges and universities were residential institutions and were staffed with tutors who resided with the students within the residence halls (Mann, 2010). During the early years of U.S. universities, the faculty was responsible for taking care of the students and actually took on a strongly *parental* role even caring for the moral development of students (Cook, 2009). Harvard University, in 1890, created the first dean position in higher education, the Dean of Men, and this is the most often cited origin of the field of student affairs (Mann, 2010). Coeducation and freshman orientation programs began in the 1800s as well (Cook, 2009). In 1877, student advising became a more formalized process as The Johns Hopkins University created a system for advising (Gordon, 2004). In the past, the cost of college tuition served as a barrier that excluded potential students from families of lesser economic means. Additional sociocultural barriers resulted in the majority of students tending to be White men. Few scholarships were available. However, a century later, the accountability movement began to open the doors for more people to be able to attend college, and there was a focus on fairness and advocacy for minority groups beginning in the 1970s (Arendale, 2004). Today, although more women than men attend college, contemporary institutions of higher education continue to serve mostly White students from higher socioeconomic status (SES) backgrounds than minority students (Arnett, 2016). Although there have been some minor changes in overall student demographic profiles, lower SES backgrounds are still underrepresented. Colleges have begun to provide an increasing number of services designed to assist less-prepared students to be successful and to be able to overcome barriers. These services include special programming in residence halls for residential universities as a means to ensure that students have an affordable and safe place to live where they can also learn and grow (Penven, Stephens, Shushok, & Keith, 2013).

STUDENT NEEDS

Helping students to develop intellectually, emotionally, and socially is the mission of colleges and universities. Contemporary students, however, often enter college with preexisting personal challenges or backgrounds that may have a profound impact on their developmental paths while on campus (Smyth, Ironside, Sims, Swenson, & Spence, 2008). The transition to college, for any student, brings with it additional challenges, such as leaving behind friends and family, experiencing feelings of loneliness, coping with difficulties related to interpersonal relationships, and, for some, being aware of a lack of adequate academic readiness (Conley, Travers, & Bryant, 2013). For many students, the difficulties faced in adjusting to and persisting in college can be overwhelming. This affects the dropout rate, which may be surprisingly high in many colleges as evidenced by statistics that show that less than half of the students who start at a college will graduate (Kneipp, Kelly, & Cyphers, 2009). This sobering fact is likely due in part to the numerous and unexpectedly disruptive transitions and milestones that may occur during the college years. The work of Arnett (2007) highlighted the transitions from adolescence to adulthood and he developed the construct to describe this period, which he labeled as *emerging adulthood*. This period occurs during the years in which many individuals attend college. The variety of transitions that an individual may face between the ages of 18 and 25 years is diverse and includes marriage, parenting, relationship issues, and occupational choices, among many others. For those who choose to attend college, there are additional choices and transitions that may be encountered along the way. In fact, emerging adults often experience a greater number of difficulties with relationships, unstable living conditions, limited financial resources, and a lack of meaning and purpose when compared with adults older than 25 years of age (Gutierrez & Park, 2015). How these challenges and developmental milestones are managed can influence whether or not a student is successful in earning an academic degree. We briefly examine some of those factors and challenges that can impact student success.

FAMILY SUPPORT

There have been numerous studies that have linked family support to college success. The transition to college is not always an easy path due to a host of factors, including the level of family support (Wodka & Barakat, 2007). Individuals with high levels of family support often exhibit higher aspirations for their educational plans. High levels of family support have also been linked to individuals' success in overcoming barriers to meet their high aspirations (Metheny & McWhirter, 2013). This finding highlights the need for student affairs professionals to consider the impact of family dynamics on their student populations.

Parental Divorce

Several studies have revealed that higher levels of adjustment issues and academic difficulties may be present for college students whose parents have divorced (Connel, Hayes, & Carlson, 2015). Given the prevalence of divorce today, it may be helpful to provide specific support opportunities to students who show signs of compromised functioning and reference parental divorce as a potential contributing factor to their concerns. In fact, the age at which the divorce occurs does not seem to make a difference in terms of adjustment difficulties (Connel et al., 2015). It is also important to consider that conflict *after* a divorce and related economic hardship due to a divorce can negatively affect the academic achievement of adolescents and young adults (Esmaeili, Yaacob, Juhari, & Mariani, 2011). Being sensitive to the needs of a student from a divorced family and understanding the impact that a divorce can have on the student can assist one in providing appropriate support services. Gaining an understanding of the unique family dynamics of an individual in terms of developmental theories can provide student affairs professionals with added insight as they seek to assist the student in achieving personal, social, and academic success. Although family dynamics and relationships are important, student affairs professionals should also consider the impact of overall wellness.

WELLNESS

Wellness can be defined as a multidimensional approach to examining and living life. Most models of wellness include multiple components, such as work, relationships, spirituality, and love. These areas are then often divided into subgroups depending on the model; overall wellness has also been linked to self-esteem and satisfaction with life (Degges-White & Myers, 2005). A person's level of wellness is determined by individual choices and these choices can serve as a source of empowerment (Myers, Willse, & Villalba, 2011). The college years present an unprecedented array of choices that range from choosing a major; deciding when, where, and what to eat and drink; exercise habits; and involvement in activities outside the classroom. However, during this period, students often try out novel activities and, in some cases, engage in risky behaviors, such as unprotected sex, binge drinking, and other forms of illicit and questionable behaviors. For most, it is an "experimental" phase of life, but it can lead to the development of ongoing issues and problems for others (Gates, Corbin, & Fromme, 2016). In fact, the use of alcohol by college students can often result in grave legal problems that may include sexual assault, vandalism, and driving under the influence (DUI) charges. For instance, college students are more likely to drive while drunk than their noncollege counterparts (Lewis & Myers, 2010). Although colleges and universities have taken steps to address the issues of risk-taking behaviors, they cannot eliminate them. From a developmental standpoint, student affairs professionals must bear in mind that traditional age college students are still in the midst of cognitive development. Thus, they may not focus on the impact of their choices or the need to develop a healthy lifestyle.

Physical health should also be considered by student affairs personnel as well. In a study by Wodka and Barakat (2007), it was revealed that students who suffered from chronic illness reported higher levels of anxiety and depression than other students. This certainly makes sense given the normative stressors already associated with the adjustment to college combined with the additional stress experienced when managing a chronic illness without the immediate support of family. Additionally, this added stress can negatively affect academic performance. In fact, a person's level of wellness can impact academic performance. Adams, Bezner, Garner, and Woodruff (1998) linked high levels of wellness to high levels of cognitive functioning and found that students who perform better academically were more likely to have higher levels of overall wellness. Although overall wellness and physical health are factors to consider in the adjustment of college students, mental health concerns also play a significant role in the way that transitions are managed.

In recent years, perhaps due in part to less stigma regarding mental illness and the Americans with Disabilities Act (ADA), college counseling centers have experienced an influx of students seeking mental health counseling as well as an increase in the number of students with several mental health issues needing psychotropic medication. Without support, these students may be unable to succeed in the college environment. Although few college counseling centers can provide long-term treatment and frequently make referrals to community-based clinicians or agencies, there is often external pressure placed on campus counseling centers to work with certain students throughout their college years (Meilman, 2016). Meeting the increased demands for counseling services has been an ongoing challenge for college counseling centers and, unfortunately, many centers are not accredited by relevant professional associations. Thus, it is especially important for college counseling center personnel to advocate for resources to meet the growing demands and needs of their students (Bishop, 2016). To meet the needs of as many students as possible, many centers limit the number of times a student can be seen during a semester. The limitations on sessions may create issues of entitlement for some students. Students who need help may not be able to afford to go elsewhere. Universities are caught in a dilemma of managing increasing student demand with limited resources (Stone & McMichael, 1996). In addition to meeting the needs of students, student affairs professionals are spending an increasing amount of time working with the parents of students who suffer from mental illness as well as providing consultation to other departments within the university (Brunner, Wallace, Reymann, Sellers, & McCabe, 2014). In many instances, college counseling centers are expected to provide increased services with decreased funding. Although working with students who present with severe mental health issues is important, focusing on providing short-term services for adjustment and relationship issues is also a priority.

Among the top reasons students seek counseling while in college are concerns related to relationships with parents and current relationship issues. It is important to note that the issues students faced growing up in terms of relationships with parents often transfer over into relationships with others in college years (Rhodes & Woods, 2014). When it comes to relating to others, individuals' core religious or spiritual beliefs may also influence their behavior and actions. During the college years, students often confirm their existing views or explore other viewpoints. Kneipp et al. (2009) found that spirituality was significantly linked to adjustment in college. Thus, having a spiritual foundation may serve as a source of support for students adjusting to and managing the numerous transitions they face during the college years. However, some students may be reluctant to discuss topics related to religion and spirituality with others if they are unsure how these discussions will be received. This highlights the need for student affairs professionals to be objective and accepting of differences in religious and spiritual beliefs. The impact of spiritual values on all areas of life, including views related to relationships and finances, is a consideration for many students and one that student affairs professionals need to address when working with students.

EDUCATION COST AND COLLEGE AFFORDABILITY

When considering the relationship between wellness and stress levels, the topic of finances often arises. For college students, financial issues are a major source of stress and many struggle to pay bills on time (Northern, O'Brien, & Goetz, 2010). This stress can negatively affect other areas of life and is definitely cause for concern given that more than 70% of college students in one study indicated that financial stress is a major problem (Trombitas, 2012). Stress generated by financial pressure can negatively affect the ability of students to focus on their academic work or to connect with others. Some may be so focused on and concerned about paying bills and affording college that these take a toll on mental health. During the college years, students become more financially independent from their parents and some may have difficulty with managing money or may even become involved in gambling (Shin & Montalto, 2015). All students do not arrive at college with the same level of financial literacy and many may be unprepared to handle financial responsibility independently. This may lead them to struggle with tasks related to managing their money and budgeting for expenses. In order to cover college costs, students may receive grants, scholarships, and loans; however, these sources may not be adequate for students to meet all of the financial demands of attending college.

The cost of a college education can be expensive even for students with seemingly generous financial aid packages; thus, working while in college is very common (Lang, 2012). Some students may attempt to pay for college by working, but this may not be realistic given the increase in tuition in recent years. Although many students *do* work, they may still rely on financial aid. Those who take out student loans may face an increased level of stress if they expect to owe a significant amount of money after graduation (Heckman, Lim, & Montalto, 2014). Failed courses or a major change may not only bring increased academic stress, but financial stress as well. Although there can be major benefits for students working during their college years, such as learning time management skills and gaining real-world work experience, there can also be drawbacks as well. Working can leave little time for social activities as well as limit study time (Lang, 2012). Additionally, Trombitas (2012) found that students who worked more than 20 hours a week often experienced high levels of financial pressure; further, stress related to the lack of adequate time to focus on academics due to work schedules can be compounded if an individual is not ready for the academic challenges and rigor of college.

ACADEMIC READINESS

Although the rate of high school students attending college has increased in the last several decades, more college students are needing to take remedial courses, which indicates a lack of academic preparedness for college (Porter & Polikoff, 2012). It is important, but unfortunate, to note that there are higher rates of minority and lower SES students among those needing remedial courses than White students and students from higher SES backgrounds (Attewell, Lavin, Domina, & Levey, 2006). This indicates that not all high schools embrace the same standards of excellence and academic rigor in their curricula. Because schools are under local control, and although common core standards have been adopted by many states, there are still differences in academic expectations and the content students learn across the nation. Although some factors can be controlled by the schools in terms of education other factors that impact learning, such as family support and environment, are not within the control of public schools (Venezia & Jaeger, 2013). There are often vast differences among students due to numerous factors including the availability of family resources to assist students who are struggling in high school. The lack of resources in high school can directly affect a student's readiness to attend college. Students may also lack study skills and a clear sense of direction. Many college students are often unsure of what college major to select and are expected to explore multiple potential career choices during their first year (Arnett, 2016). This uncertainty can impact the experience that college students have during the first year and in fact may account in part for the high dropout rates of freshmen.

NONTRADITIONAL COLLEGE STUDENTS

Much of the existing research has been focused on the needs of traditional college students; however, nontraditional college students often face additional distinct challenges. Nontraditional students often work full time, have dependents (spouses and children), and are older than 24 years. The number of nontraditional college students has increased significantly in the past decade. This has resulted in colleges attempting to meet the needs of this group of students by modifying policies and procedures (Forbus, Newbold, & Mehta, 2010). Such modifications include additional evening and nighttime course offerings as well as on-campus apartments for students and their families. These students often face multiple demands when it comes to their time and bring in unique and rich life experiences unlike those of traditional-aged students. The time demands can affect the students in terms of their ability to find sufficient time to study or to participate in campus events (Ross-Gordon, 2011). Additionally, spending extra money on campus events is often not a priority for students who are funding their own education independently while also supporting their families. Providing free events that allow family members to also attend can be beneficial in helping nontraditional students connect with the university and other students (Vale & Roat, 2015). Unfortunately, responding to the needs of nontraditional students can be challenging for colleges and universities that have programming models in place that were designed for traditional college students.

Veterans

Some institutions of higher education have responded to the needs of nontraditional college students by offering more courses and more degrees online (Ross-Gordon, 2011). Many universities have worked to better meet the needs of a unique subgroup of nontraditional college students—those who are veterans. The growing number of veterans' centers on college campuses reflects an increase in the number of veterans returning to college. These centers offer veterans the opportunity to connect with peers who can easily relate to the unique challenges associated with their integration back into civilian life and adjustment to the demands of college (Kirchner, 2015). Veterans on campus may feel uncomfortable in large classrooms as well as experience difficulty adjusting to the new need to create their own schedules and organize their own routines. They may also struggle in their attempts to connect socially with younger classmates. Additionally, they may believe that they are singled out at times when military issues are discussed in their classes or become upset with those who have viewpoints that are nonsupportive of the military (Gonzalez & Elliott, 2016). Faculty members may not be as well versed regarding military culture as they could be and may be ill prepared to provide an adequately safe environment for their student veterans to learn. This is an area that many institutions must continue to work on addressing (Kirchner, 2015). Student affairs professionals should gain as much insight and understanding into military culture as they can to better meet the needs of this population. Veterans, however, are not the only nontraditional student group that benefits from additional support.

Single Mothers

For single mothers, the return to school can be accompanied by frustration that arises from their efforts to find a balance among work, school, and caring for children. Research indicates that women who become mothers during high school encounter numerous barriers to attending and completing college (Lovell, 2014). One such barrier is the difficulty in locating affordable and reliable child care to allow them to attend class. Traditionally, institutions have focused on meeting the needs of traditionally aged college students rather than meeting the more diverse needs of nontraditional groups whose needs may differ significantly. However, the lack of child care can lead to a higher dropout rate for single mothers (Mahaffey, Hungerford, & Sill, 2015). The complex demands of caring for a child while earning a living can overwhelm single mothers who are also attempting to earn college degrees. Role conflict may occur and, due to the limited number of hours in a day, college work may be pushed to the side and this can lead to difficulty in completing the required coursework successfully. Finding time to engage satisfactorily in all roles does not always happen and internal conflicts can arise (Markle, 2015). For women who become pregnant during college, this development can diminish their motivation to complete their degrees (Lovell, 2014). This likely reflects a normal shift in priorities and focus as caring for a child can be extremely demanding especially without support and with limited resources.

IMPLICATIONS FOR STUDENT AFFAIRS PROFESSIONALS

For student affairs professionals, there is a need for collaboration and consultation across departments. Providing holistic care for students who need additional support requires cross-campus collaboration within student affairs and academic affairs (Kadison, 2006). As the needs of students change, institutions must adapt to meet those needs. For instance, residence life no longer focuses solely on housing students, but now encompasses a broader focus that includes the provision of learning activities and opportunities within residence halls. Some residence halls provide halls and floors that encourage students to reside with other students who are pursuing the same specific major; other residence halls focus on the needs of first-year students; and still others provide faculty-led experiences or foreign-language halls (Penven et al., 2013). University personnel should consider its target population when determining the programming and services that will be provided by residence life as not every "new thing" will work on every "old campus." Within universities that offer family housing, programming that allows the entire family to be involved can be beneficial. Beyond residence life, there are other areas that can be considered in terms of meeting student needs. Recreation and wellness are important aspects to consider.

When it comes to recreation, most campuses offer numerous activities that promote student engagement in wellness activities. Unfortunately, effective encouragement to participate may be lacking. In fact, there is limited research on the benefits or outcomes of implementation of a holistic wellness approach for college students. The research that is available, however, suggests that such programs could actually reduce stress and positively affect student self-efficacy and knowledge related to holistic wellness (Gieck & Olsen, 2007). Although colleges and universities offer opportunities for students to "work out," many do not have programs in place that encourage sedentary or nonathletic students to do so. For nontraditional students, programs should be tailored to support family involvement and be offered at no or low cost. The implementation of programs that offer support for overweight and nonathletic students could impact not just physical health, but mental health as well. Research shows that regular exercise can help combat stress, anxiety, and depression (Forsyth, Deane, & Williams, 2015). This is especially relevant due to the growing number of students who are entering college with severe mental health issues as previously noted. Thus, colleges need to be ready to handle not just the adjustment issues but deeper ones as well.

Counseling centers need to be prepared and staffed to assist students with the normative challenges faced during the transition to college along with other less normative issues. A significant challenge faced by counseling centers is the limited funding most receive as most are funded by student fees. However, using a collaboration model, programs can be designed that would address time management and stress management issues as they relate to mental health issues and delivered across campus through outlets other than solely the campus counseling center. Although many colleges offer orientation classes, they may not adequately address the unique needs of nontraditional college students. Ensuring that there are programs on campus to meet the needs of all students can be essential to ensuring that all students have the resources they need to successfully complete their degrees. In order to meet the needs of students it is important to understand the developmental context of students, which can vary depending on the unique needs of various student groups. To this end, the use of theories can be beneficial.

IMPORTANCE OF USING THEORIES

There are a number of different theories that are commonly used by student affairs professionals. Several of the most frequently used theories are addressed in this book. It is important to consider that theories provide a framework to guide and direct actions as well as to provide insight and understanding. For instance, through understanding the development level of a particular student or student population, student affairs professionals can better design and tailor programs to meet specific needs. When working with an individual student, the application of theory provides student affairs professionals with a framework through which to understand the needs of an individual student and the relevant issues and frames of reference that apply. Being able to understand where someone is "coming from," in terms of developmental issues, identity development, and cognitive and moral reasoning, will allow student affairs professionals to develop and implement more effective and appropriate interventions as well as to make appropriate referrals to other services on campus. When campus climates encourage the "silo-ing" of student affairs offices, there can be a lack of collaboration and effective and integrative programming. The use of theories as a framework can provide student affairs professionals a way to communicate across departments, and beyond the "silos," to ensure that programs are addressing the emotional, social, and cognitive needs of the diverse students who are pursuing their education on campus. Too often, the value of theory is overlooked; however, theoretical foundations and the implementation of theory are part and parcel of what defines student affairs as a profession, not just a job. As the profession continues to evolve and develop, and cross-campus collaboration grows in its prevalence and importance, there will no doubt be a greater emphasis on the theories that are used to help describe and explain student behaviors, which will then provide insight into the services needed.

CONCLUSION

Most professions develop a language of their own, whether it is considered jargon, idioms, or in-group vernacular. The student affairs profession, however, encompasses multiple campuses, disciplines, and student services, so there is not necessarily a single language that all professionals speak. This underscores the value of a shared foundational knowledge of the basic, relevant theories that can be used to describe the students the institution serves. Just as mathematics is the common language of the sciences, developmental theory can serve as the common language of those who work with individuals moving through their college years, whether they are emerging adults or older, single or coupled, or representing any other unique demographic or intersecting identity.

REFERENCES

Adams, T., Bezner, J., Garner, L., & Woodruff, S. (1998). Construct validation of the Perceived Wellness Survey. *American Journal of Health Studies, 14*, 212–219.

Arendale, D. R. (2004). Mainstreamed academic assistance and enrichment for all students: The historical origins of learning assistance centers. *Research for Education Reform, 9*(4), 3–21.

Arnett, J. J. (2007). Emerging adulthood: What is it, and what is it good for? *Child Development Perspectives, 1*, 68–73.

Arnett, J. J. (2016). College students as emerging adults: The developmental implications of the college context. *Emerging Adulthood, 43*, 219–222.

Attewell, P., Lavin, D., Domina, T., & Levey, T. (2006). New evidence on college remediation. *Journal of Higher Education, 77*, 886–924.

Bishop, J. B. (2016). A wish list for the advancement of university and college counseling centers. *Journal of College Student Psychotherapy, 30*(1), 15–22.

Brunner, J. L., Wallace, D. L., Reymann, L. S., Sellers, J. J., & McCabe, A. G. (2014). College counseling today: Contemporary students and how counseling centers meet their needs. *Journal of College Student Psychotherapy, 28*, 257–324.

Conley, C. S., Travers, L. V., & Bryant, F. B. (2013). Promotions psychosocial adjustment and stress management in first year college students: The benefits of engagement in a psychosocial wellness seminar. *Journal of American College Health, 61*, 75–86.

Connel, B., Hayes, D., & Carlson, M. (2015). Relation between parental divorce and adjustment in college students. *Journal of Divorce and Remarriage, 56*, 336–345.

Cook, S. (2009). Important events in the development of academic advising in the United States. *NACADA Journal, 29*, 18–40.

Degges-White, S., & Myers, J. E. (2005). Women at midlife: An exploration of chronological age, subjective age, wellness, and life satisfaction. *Adultspan: Theory, Research & Practice, 5*, 67–80.

Esmaeili, N., Yaacob, S., Juhari, R., & Mariani, M. (2011). Post-divorce parental conflict, economic hardship and academic achievement among adolescents of divorced families. *Asian Social Science, 7*(12), 119–124.

Forbus, P., Newbold, J. J., & Mehta, S. S. (2010). A study of non-traditional and traditional students in terms of their time management behaviors, stress factors and coping strategies. *Allied Academies International Conference: Proceedings of the Academy of Educational Leadership (AEL), 15*(2), 67–71.

Forsyth, A., Deane, F. P., & Williams, P. (2015). A lifestyle intervention for primary care patients with depression and anxiety: A randomised controlled trial. *Psychiatry Research, 230*, 537–544.

Gates, J. R., Corbin, W. R., & Fromme, K. (2016). Emerging adult identity development, alcohol use, and alcohol-related problems during the transition out of college. *Psychology of Addictive Behaviors, 30*, 345–355.

Gieck, D. J., & Olsen, S. (2007). Holistic wellness as a means to developing a lifestyle approach to health behavior among college students. *Journal of American College Health, 56*, 29–35.

Gonzalez, C. A., & Elliott, M. (2016). Faculty attitudes and behaviors towards student veterans. *Journal of Postsecondary Education and Disability, 29*(1), 35–46.

Gordon, V. N. (2004). The evolution of academic advising: One institution's historic path. *NACADA Journal, 24*(1 and 2), 17–23.

Gutierrez, I. A., & Park, C. P. (2015). Emerging adulthood, evolving worldviews: How life events impact college students' developing belief systems. *Emerging Adulthood, 3*, 85–97.

Heckman, S., Lim, H., & Montalto, C. (2014). Factors related to financial stress among college students. *Journal of Financial Therapy, 5*, 19–39.

Kadison, R. D. (2006). College psychiatry 2006: Challenges and opportunities. *Journal of American College Health, 54*(6), 338–340.

Kirchner, M. J. (2015). Supporting student veteran transition to college and academic success. *Adult Learning, 26*, 116–123.

Kneipp, L. B., Kelly, K. E., & Cyphers, B. (2009). Feeling at peace with college: Religiosity, spiritual well-being, and college adjustment. *Individuals Differences Research, 7*, 188–196.

Lang, B. K. (2012). The similarities and differences between working and non-working students at a mid-sized American public university. *College Student Journal, 46*, 243–255.

Lewis, T. F., & Myers, J. E. (2010). Wellness factors decrease the odds of drinking and driving among college students. *Journal of Addictions and Offender Counseling, 33*, 93–106.

Lovell, E. D. (2014). Female college students who are parents: Motivation clarified by the ages of their children. *Community College Journal of Research and Practice, 38*, 370–374.

Mahaffey, B. A., Hungerford, G., & Sill, S. (2015). College student mother needs at regional campuses: An exploratory study. *Association of University Regional Campuses of Ohio Journal, 21*, 105–115.

Mann, B. J. (2010). Preserving the history of a student affairs association. *College Student Affairs Journal, 28*, 164–183.

Markle, G. (2015). Factors influencing persistence among non-traditional university students. *Adult Education Quarterly, 65*, 267–285.

Meilman, P. W. (2016). Pressures we face in running counseling centers on college and university campuses. *Journal of College Student Psychotherapy, 30*(1), 7–11.

Metheny, J., & McWhirter, E. H. (2013). Contributions of social status and family support to college students' career decision self-efficacy and outcome. *Journal of Career Assessments, 21*(3), 378–394.

Myers, J. E., Willse, J. T., & Villalba, J. A. (2011). Promoting self-esteem in adolescents: The influence of wellness factors. *Journal of Counseling and Development, 89*, 28–36.

Northern, J. J., O'Brien, W. H., & Goetz, P. W. (2010). The development, evaluation, and validation of a financial stress scale for undergraduate students. *Journal of College Student Development, 51*(1), 79–92.

Penven, J., Stephens, R., Shushok, F., & Keith, C. (2013). The past, present and future of residential colleges: Looking back at S. Stewart Gordon's "living and learning in college." *The Journal of College and University Housing, 39*, 114–126.

Porter, A. C., & Polikoff, M. S. (2012). Measuring academic readiness for college. *Educational Policy, 26*(3), 394–417.

Rhodes, G. K., & Woods, L. F. (2014). Family conflict and college-student social adjustment: The mediating role of emotional distress about the family. *Couple and Family Psychology: Research and Practice, 3*, 156–164.

Ross-Gordon, J. M. (2011, Winter). Research on adult learners: Supporting the needs of a student population that is no longer nontraditional. *Association of American Colleges and Universities, Peer Review, 13*(1), 26–29.

Shin, S. H., & Montalto, C. P. (2015). The role of impulsivity, cognitive bias, and reasoned action in understanding college student gambling. *Journal of Youth Studies, 18*, 376–395.

Smythe, E. A., Ironside, P. M., Sims, S. L., Swenson, M. M., & Spence, D. G. (2008). Heideggerian hermeneutic research: As lived. *International Journal of Nursing Studies, 45*(9), 1389–1397.

Stone, G. L., & McMichael, J. (1996). Thinking about mental health policy in university and college counseling centers. *Journal of College Student Psychotherapy, 10*(3), 3–27.

Trombitas, K. S. (2012). Financial stress: An everyday reality for college students. Lincoln, NE: Inceptia. Retrieved from https://www.inceptia.org/PDF/Inceptia_FinancialStress_whitepaper.pdf

Vale, D., & Roat, A. E. (2015). Programming for the new majority: Non-traditional students. *Campus Activities Programming, 48*(4), 32–36.

Venezia, A., & Jaeger, L. (2013). Transitions from high school to college. *Future of Children, 23*(1), 117–136.

Wodka, E. L., & Barakat, L. P. (2007). An exploratory study of the relationship of family support and coping with adjustment: Implications for college students with a chronic illness. *Journal of Adolescence, 30*, 365–376.

CHAPTER 2

DIVERSITY AND SOCIOCULTURAL THEORIES OF LEARNING AND DEVELOPMENT

Carrie A. Kortegast

CASE VIGNETTE: HOPE AND JUAN

Hope and Juan are friends who decided to participate in the same 5-week study abroad program in Valencia, Spain. For Hope, this was the first time she had been on an airplane or away from her parents. Juan's parents immigrated to the United States from Mexico, and he had fond memories of spending summers in Mexico with his grandparents. In Valencia, Hope and Juan became friends with several other students in the program, and they all spent most of their free time exploring the city together. While hanging out at the beach after the first week of the program, Juan shared how great his host parents had been. Although he had been there only for a week, he felt he had already learned a lot about the Spanish culture from them. He shared that most of this learning happened during their nightly dinner conversations. Two other students, who were also fluent in Spanish, nodded along and said that they, too, had been having great interactions with their host families. Hope began to feel a bit left out. She liked her host family but struggled to communicate with them as she had only learned a few phrases so far. She also felt a bit lost and nervous when she had to do things on her own, such as taking the bus to school or having dinner with her host family, as she did not always understand the local customs. Going out with her friends was okay because several, like Juan, spoke Spanish and were able to translate for her. Hope was starting to think that she had made a mistake studying abroad and was feeling guilty about the sacrifices that her parents had made to financially support her study abroad experience.

OVERVIEW AND DESCRIPTION OF SOCIOCULTURAL THEORIES

Sociocultural theories situate learning and development as embedded within cultural, institutional, and historical contexts. Within these contexts, the focus is on how individual learning and development is mediated by social interactions and culturally organized activities. Scribner (1990) states, "human cognition is *culturally mediated*; it is founded on *purposive activity*; and it is *historically developing*" (emphasis in original; p. 109). The goal within a sociocultural approach is to understand the relationship among cultural, institutional, and historical situations and their influences on human cognition (Wertsch, del Río, & Alvarez, 1995).

The roots of sociocultural theories of learning and development are linked to the work of Lev Vygotsky. Vygotsky (1978) theorizes that humans do not interact directly with their environments; rather, individuals rely on tools, symbols, and labor activities as a means to interact in the world. For instance, the vignette indicated that Hope and Juan needed to know Spanish to communicate with their host families. Language is a tool that individuals use in order to interact with others. Thus, knowledge of the Spanish language was mediated through the interactions Juan and Hope had with their host families. These tools, symbols, and labor activities are culturally organized and maintained. Learning, then, occurs through mediated interactions with the world.

This chapter provides an overview of the history and development of sociocultural theories. Two specific sociocultural theories are discussed: Cultural-Historical Activity Theory (CHAT) and communities of practice. The chapter concludes with a discussion of the application of sociocultural theories and closing vignettes.

HISTORY AND DEVELOPMENT OF SOCIOCULTURAL THEORIES

Sociocultural theories developed out of the work of Lev Vygotsky (1896–1934), an early 20th-century Russian educational and child psychologist. Vygotsky's work did not receive much attention in North America until the posthumously translated release of *Mind in Society* in 1978. In his research, Vygotsky observed that children's cognitive development increased as they interacted with their social environment and participated in cultural activities. These observations led him to regard "education not only as central to cognitive development but as quintessential sociocultural activity" (Moll, 1990, p. 1).

Moreover, Vygotsky (1994) argued that, "cultural development consists in mastering methods of behavior which are based on the use of signs" (p. 58). For instance, a college diploma is a sign that carries particular cultural and symbolic meaning. To receive a college diploma, students must develop the skills necessary not only to complete coursework but also to understand the college-going process. Syllabi and course catalogs are artifacts that help students understand how to earn a college degree. Physical and symbolic artifacts are created over time by different cultures and serve as cultural mediators.

Vygotsky (1978) introduced the concept of the zone of proximal development (ZOPED) as the distance between what a student can accomplish on his or her own and what he or she can accomplish with the guidance of a more capable peer or adult. ZOPED focuses on the development that occurs rather than assessing the ability of students to perform particular tasks (Chaiklin, 2003). For instance, a simplistic example from the vignette is that Hope indicates being nervous about taking the bus to school. However, if she is shown how to use the bus system and which buses to take to school, this is a task that she could then accomplish on her own. Thus, the focus is on the capacity for development and learning with additional support. Within education, the concept of scaffolding learning is derived from the concept of ZOPED. Shifting understandings of education, from primarily an individual process to a process that occurs within a larger social context, affords new understandings of how students learn and develop through social participation during college.

Cultural Historical Activity Theory

Vygotky's work served as the groundwork for theories that focused on "activity" including CHAT. CHAT approaches understandings of learning and development as an interactive mediated activity system. CHAT evolved out of Vygotsky's concepts of mediation, which focused on the interplay among subject(s) (individuals, groups), object/motive (outcomes), and tools and artifacts (language, symbols; Vygotsky, 1987). Engeström (1999; Cole & Engeström, 1993) expanded Vygotsky's (1987) original concept of mediation in which cultural artifacts mediate humans in the development of CHAT. Activity systems (see Figure 2.1) consist of subject(s), object(s), mediating artifacts (tools and signs), rules, community, and division of labor (Cole & Engeström, 1993; Engeström, 1987; Engeström & Miettinen, 1999). These different elements shape individual learning in development through the interplay among subjects, their competing and/or complementary objects, mediating artifacts, social rules, communities, and division of labor.

Using the example from the vignette, Juan and Hope (subjects) are both participating in the activity system of studying abroad in Spain. They both indicate that learning about Spanish culture and increasing their Spanish-language skills (objects) are goals for studying abroad. Ultimately, the outcome for them is to be able to participate in the Spanish culture even if it is temporary. In order for them to do this, they need to learn the cultural rules that govern daily practices, such as meal times and that many businesses and stores were closed during siesta. For instance, communication with their host families was mediated by their Spanish-language (tools and signs) skills. Juan, who spoke fluent Spanish, was able to engage in different conversations than Hope could because of her limited knowledge of Spanish. Additionally, host families, peers, and faculty (community) helped mediate how

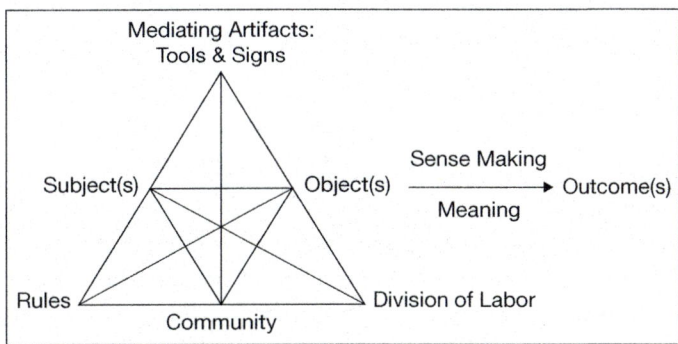

FIGURE 2.1 The structure of a human activity system.

students learned to participate in their study abroad experience and live in another culture. Moreover, the division of labor regarding how study abroad is mediated spread among different individuals. For instance, it was the responsibility of the faculty to design the course material that mediated what students learn about Spain, Spanish culture, and language in the classroom. Finally, Hope and Juan's study abroad experience was historically and culturally situated. In that, the institution of study abroad is linked to the historical practices of sending (wealthy) students to study European culture and art as well as contemporary efforts to increase international education and globalization.

Within CHAT, the unit of analysis is activity and the cultural practices that make up that activity (Engeström, 1987; Engeström et al., 1999; Scriber, 1997). Cultural practices are closely coupled with objects that are transformed into outcomes through sense-making activities. For instance, the object for a college student might be participating in a study abroad experience. The outcome and sense making of this activity is increased cultural awareness and knowledge. The object of activity focuses on how "people engaged in sociocultural endeavors with other people, working with the extending cultural tools and practices inherited from previous generations" (Rogoff & Chavajay, 1995, p. 871). As such, human behavior, learning, and development cannot be separated from historical contexts nor can these be attributed to individual sense making alone.

Essential to this framework is the understanding that "multivoicedness [coexists] within monism" (Engeström, 1999, p. 20). The concept of multivoicedness within an activity system refers to "multiple points of view, traditions, and interests" that "create different positions for the participants" (Engeström, 2001, p. 136). Put simply, although individuals might be participating in the same or similar activities systems, such as the example of Juan and Hope, how they participate in the activity system is mediated by different elements, which results in a multivoicedness of experiences within any given activity. For instance, Hope and Juan are participating in the seemingly same activity system—study abroad. Their participation is mediated differently based on their earlier educational and travel experiences, support systems, and ability to speak Spanish. Therefore, the students might create different understandings and meanings of the experience.

Ultimately, CHAT takes a systems approach to understanding learning and development as a mediated activity that is historically and culturally situational. Being able to deconstruct activity systems, as well as develop understandings for how individual learning is culturally and historically situated, allows educators to develop interventions that promote student learning and development.

Communities of Practice

Communities of practice, the central component of another sociocultural theory, developed out of the work of Jean Lave and Etienne Wenger on situated learning that focused on the role of participation in a community and social learning. Similar to other sociocultural theories, community of practice emphasizes learning as "an integral part of generative social practice in the lived-in world" (Lave & Wenger, 1991, p. 35). Learning is connected to, shaped by, and forms how individuals are able to engage in different environments. For instance, opportunities for learning and development for students might be different in various contexts, such as classes, student organizations, residence halls, and internships. Within each of these environments, there are different social practices that govern participation within these contexts.

Community of practice assumes that "learning is, in its essence, a fundamentally social phenomenon" (Wenger, 1998, p. 3). Community of practice is a way of understanding learning by studying the intersections of community, social practice, meaning making, and identity among individuals within communities. Embedded within communities of practice is the process in which newcomers to a community gain competencies in order to acquire membership within a particular community (Lave & Wenger, 1991; Wenger, 1998). These newcomers "interact with more experienced 'core' members in a range of tasks or activities" (Jackson, 2008, p. 43) in order to learn, participate, and establish membership within the community. For instance, using the example of Juan and Hope, study abroad students' membership in the host culture is temporary. However, the goal of study abroad is to gain and learn these sociocultural practices in order to participate in the local community.

Deriving from the ZOPED, Lave and Wenger (1991) put forth the concept of legitimate peripheral participation. Legitimate peripheral participation is when an individual gains membership within a community by "mastery of knowledge and skills" that moves him or her from being a newcomer to an individual with full participation in the sociocultural practices of a community. Within a community of practice, students gain assistance from more knowledgeable others in order to learn the skills needed to participate in the sociocultural practices of a community. For instance, Juan indicated learning more about Spanish culture through his interactions with his host family during nightly dinners.

Within communities of practice, participation is not a one-time activity; rather, it is an ongoing process of learning and knowing in which participation recurs and the accumulation of practices and interactions with others occurs that leads to knowing and membership within various communities (Wenger, 1998). In this sense, participation is both a process of doing as well as the interactions one has with others in a community. While "our engagement in practice may have patterns . . . it is the production of such patterns anew that gives rise to an experience of meaning" (Wenger, 1998, p. 52). Again, students become participants and agents in their learning process when they "begin to interact socially" (Stewart, 2007, p. 89). As learners participate in a community of practice, they begin to master knowledge and skills that moves them toward full participation within a community (Lave & Wenger, 1991). This social process includes becoming knowledgeable about the skills that lead toward membership within a community (Lave & Wenger, 1991, p. 29).

Wenger (1998) stated that in order for a group of individuals to be a community of practice, the group of people must include mutual engagement, joint enterprise, and shared repertoire. *Mutual engagement* is "engaged actions whose meanings [are] negotiated with one another" (p. 73). For example, using the study abroad example, Hope and Juan discussed becoming friends with other students from their study abroad program. As a group, they engaged in various activities together that allowed them to learn about living in Valencia and Spanish culture. It is not just about doing things, but that they did these activities purposefully in community with each other. This allowed for the sharing of different meanings of their study abroad experience, such as Juan and Hope talking about the different interactions with their host families.

Joint enterprise involves a fluid process of negotiating and renegotiating actions, behaviors, and participation that both "reifie[s] standards and competent engagement in practice" as "important aspects of becoming an experienced member" (Wenger, 1998, p. 82). That is, these joint enterprises are established and maintained by members but at the same time can be changed and adjusted by members within the community. Continuing with the study abroad illustration, the joint enterprise could be that the students shared the same desire to improve their Spanish and learn more about the culture by participating in daily activities. In order to do this, students often had to negotiate what they were going to do as well as what were the norms for the community. For instance, students who are more fluent Spanish speakers would translate for other students.

Shared repertoire is also a marker of community in which, over time, community members develop "coherence" in which "they belong to the practice of a community pursuing an enterprise" (Wenger, 1998, p. 82). Social practice becomes the source for coherent participation within communities. Again using the study abroad example, it is not just that students did things together; it is their participation that had purpose and meaning. Although this example focused on a friend-group community of practice, the other groups included the larger study abroad program, individual courses, as well as host families and roommates. Importantly, individuals can be a part of multiple communities of practice. However, proximity, in and of itself, does not make a community of practice. There needs to be mutual engagement, joint enterprise, and shared repertoire.

APPLICATION OF THE THEORY

Although sociocultural theories have gained traction in K–12 education and in workplace learning, there is still much potential for the use of these theories in postsecondary environments. Several higher education scholars have applied sociocultural theories to the college contexts. Examples include Gildersleeve's (2010) work on Mexican migrant students' college-going practices, Jackson's (2006, 2008) study exploring the relationship between language and cultural learning during study abroad, Rios-Aguilar and Kiyama's (2012) work advocating for the use of funds of knowledge to assist Latina(o) students' transition to college, and Kortegast and Boisfontaine's (2015) study looking at students' post–study abroad practices of negotiating meaning. However, there are other opportunities for student affairs educators to consider using sociocultural approaches. For instance, residential and nonresidential learning communities, student organizations, and service learning all have undertones of sociocultural approaches to learning and development given the emphasis on community, engagement, and social learning.

Beyond applications for students, there are examples of the use of sociocultural approaches in student affairs professional development. For instance, several student affairs professional associations have developed professional communities of practice, such as the Association of College Unions International (ACUI). The ACUI has several organized communities of practice based on different interests related to functional areas (e.g., late night programs), institutional type (e.g., Catholic colleges and universities), and social identity (e.g., women's leadership). In order to be an ACUI community of practice, there must be: (a) a community of people who have something in common; (b) a set of issues community members are interested in; and (c) a commitment to develop practices that help community members to be more effective with the set of issues (ACUI, n.d., para 2). These principles align with mutual engagement, joint enterprise, and shared repertoire (Wenger, 1998).

Finally, CHAT can provide a framework for program assessment in higher education. Withman and Bensimon's (2012) work provides an example of the use of CHAT to develop a culture of inquiry in order to promote equity in student outcomes. They described an evaluation process in which they mapped and evaluated how the university system was ensuring equitable student outcomes. They discussed using institutional data as mediating artifacts and outlined the different responsibilities that stockholders across the system had (division of labor). Moreover, they identified norms, policies, and institutional practices (rules) that mediated student outcomes. In assessing the university system and institutional practices, they were able to better understand how the university structured learning opportunities and also able to make recommendations to increase equitable outcomes.

CASE VIGNETTE WRAP-UP: HOPE AND JUAN

Two days before the end of the study abroad program in Valencia, Hope was feeling sad to be leaving her host family. Although she still struggled to communicate with them in Spanish, she learned enough words and phrases in her introductory Spanish class to hold short conversations with them. The previous day, while talking to her parents via Skype, she shared a story about playing a children's game, "Guess Who?" with her host family's young grandchildren. The game, which she remembered playing as a child, is a guessing game where you ask your opponent "yes or no" questions to guess what character is in front of the opponent. Hope shared her excitement about being able to ask simple questions in Spanish about hair and eye color as well as articles of clothing. Hope realized that although she was not fluent in Spanish, she had learned many of the country's customs and how to speak simple phrases. She had also grown more confident in her ability to navigate a new city. Much of what she learned happened out of the classroom and through friendships with her peers and host family.

CASE VIGNETTE 1 FOR READER REFLECTION: COURTNEY

Ever since Courtney received her first set of Legos as a child, she loved to build things. In particular, she loved to build things that would help people. When Courtney was in the ninth grade, she participated in an after-school program that encouraged girls to consider careers in engineering. Courtney had no idea what an engineer was, but loved the project she worked on—designing a car for people who use wheelchairs. During her first year of college, Courtney decided to pursue mechanical engineering, and with the help of her academic advisor, chose courses that aligned with that major.

(continued)

(continued)

Courtney quickly realized that she was one of three women in all of her classes. The men in the class would often avoid pairing up with her on group projects. And when she was in groups, the men would frequently assign her the role of secretary. Additionally, the men tended to want to design projects that made something faster or stronger, while she wanted to focus her designs on how they could improve people's lives. Courtney started to think that maybe being an engineer was not the right career path for her.

Despite doing well in her courses and having a higher grade point average (GPA) than many of the men in her groups, she was receiving messages from faculty and classmates that engineering was not for women. Her parents did not understand her change of heart as they have always believed she could be anything she wanted to be. When Courtney went to her advisor to discuss a new major, her advisor encouraged her to join U-WISE club—University Women in Science and Engineering. Courtney started attending meetings and found other women who were interested in engineering. Over the course of these meetings, the other women shared information with her about how to be successful in the classroom, which faculty members were supportive, and how to apply for internships as well as how to stand up for herself in group projects. Equipped with this new knowledge and support, Courtney continued her path toward being an engineer.

- What might have made Courtney's educational path less distressing?
- What are the institutional changes that could be considered across other fields of study?
- What types of resources should be in place to provide support to students in a predicament similar to Courtney's?

CASE VIGNETTE 2 FOR READER REFLECTION: SADE

Sade is a second-year Higher Education and Student Affairs (HESA) master's student and the graduate assistant for the lesbian, gay, bisexual, transgender, and queer (LGBTQ) student center at Oak University. Sade would often find LGBTQ students hanging out in the center's living room chatting or watching television in between classes. The center also hosted different educational programs as well as provided a meeting space to the LGBTQ student organization, Spectrum. As part of her graduate assistantship (GA), Sade was assigned to develop recommendations on how the center could better support first year LGBTQ students. Sade organized a series of focus groups with LGBTQ students to discuss their experience at Oak. One of the students, Avery, shared,

> When I first started at Oak, I attended the Welcome Week open house at the center. Afterward, a group of us went to dinner where the older students were like, "Listen, here are all the places on campus you need to avoid and here are the names of faculty that are cool." It was really helpful because I was new and didn't know anything.

Dan, another student, shared,

> I felt really lost in my first year. I had a roommate who would say homophobic things all the time like, "That's so gay." And it wasn't until I joined Spectrum that I finally felt like I made some good friends and got advice on how to deal with my roommate.

(continued)

(continued)

Lauren, another student, turned to Sade, stating,

> *The staff here have been really supportive. When I was having a roommate conflict, they helped me figure out who to talk to in housing. When I needed advice on how to come out to my parents, they talked to me about how I might talk to them.*

Avery followed up by sharing a story about a Spectrum meeting where they discussed going home for the holidays. Avery shared,

> *During the meeting, some students discussed how they can't be out at home and others discussed how supportive their parents are. We ended the meeting discussing ways to "survive" being home over the break. What I liked is that everyone was like 'Call me if you need to talk.' Everyone was so supportive.*

- What should Sade recommend the center do next year to support first-year LGBTQ students?

REFERENCES

Association of College Unions International. (n.d.). Communities of practice. Retrieved from https://www.acui.org/groups

Chaiklin, S. (2003). The zone of proximal development in Vygotsky's analysis of learning and instruction. In A. Koxulin, B. Gindis, V. S. Ageyev, & S. M. Miller (Eds.), *Vygotsky's educational theory in cultural context* (pp. 39–64). New York, NY: Cambridge University Press.

Cole, M., & Engeström, Y. (1993). A cultural-historical approach to distributed cognition. In G. Salomon (Ed.), *Distributed cognitions: Psychological and educational considerations*. Cambridge, UK: Cambridge University Press.

Engeström, Y. (1999). Innovative learning in work teams: Analysing cycles of knowledge creation in practice. In Y. Engeström, R. Miettinen, & R. Punamäki (Eds.), *Perspectives on activity theory* (pp. 377–406). Cambridge, UK: Cambridge University Press.

Engeström, Y. (2001). Expansive learning at work: Toward an activity theoretical reconceptualization. *Journal of Education and Work, 14*, 133–156. doi:10.1080/13639080020028747

Engeström, Y., & Miettinen, R. (1999). Introduction. In Y. Engeström, R. Miettinen, & R. L. Punamäki (Eds.), *Perspectives on activity theory* (pp. 1–16). Cambridge, UK: Cambridge University Press.

Engeström, Y., Miettinen, R., & Punamäki, R. (1999) *Perspectives on activity theory*. Cambridge, UK: Cambridge University Press.

Gildersleeve, R. E. (2010). *Fracturing opportunity: Mexican migrant students and college-going literacy*. New York, NY: Peter Lang.

Jackson, J. (2006). Ethnographic pedagogy and evaluation in short-term study abroad. *Languages for Intercultural Communication and Education, 12*, 134.

Jackson, J. (2008). Globalization, internationalization, and short-term stays abroad. *International Journal of Intercultural Relations, 32*(4), 349–358.

Kortegast, C. A., & Boisfontaine, M. T. (2015). Beyond "it was good": Students' post–study abroad practices for negotiating meaning. *Journal of College Student Development, 56*(8), 812–828.

Lave, J., & Wenger, E. (1991). *Situated learning: Legitimate peripheral participation.* New York, NY: Cambridge University Press.

Moll, L. C. (1990). *Vygotsky and education: Instructional implications and applications of sociohistorical psychology.* Cambridge, UK: Cambridge University Press.

Rios-Aguilar, C., & Kiyama, J. M. (2012). Funds of knowledge: An approach to studying Latina(o) students' transition to college. *Journal of Latinos and Education, 11*(1), 2–16.

Rogoff, B., & Chavajay, P. (1995). What's become of research on the cultural basis of cognitive development? *American Psychologist, 50,* 859–877.

Scribner, S. (1990). A sociocultural approach to the study of the mind. In G. Greenberg & E. Tobach (Eds.), *Theories of the evolution of knowing* (pp. 107–120). Hillsdale, NJ: Lawrence Erlbaum.

Stewart, S. (2007). Crossing borders/foreign identities: Echoes of symbiosis between classroom and community. In A. Wurr & J. Hellebrandt (Eds.), *Learning the language of global citizenship: Service-learning in applied linguistics* (pp. 82–114). Bolton, MA: Anker.

Vygotsky, L. S. (1978). *Mind in society: The development of higher psychological processes.* M. Cole, V. John-Steiner, S. Scribner, & E. Souberman (Trans.). Cambridge, MA: Harvard University Press.

Vygotsky, L. S. (1987). Thinking and speech (N. Minick, trans.). In R. W. Rieber & A. S. Carton (Eds.), *The collected works of L. S. Vygotsky: Vol. 1. problems of general psychology* (pp. 39–285). New York, NY: Plenum Press.

Vygotsky, L. S. (1994). The problem of the environment. In R. van der Veer & J. Vlasiner (Eds.), *The Vygotsky reader* (pp. 338–354). Cambridge, MA: Blackwell.

Wenger, E. (1998). *Communities of practice: Learning, meaning, and identity.* New York, NY: Cambridge University Press.

Wertsch, J. V., del Río, P., & Alvarez, A. (1995). *Sociocultural studies of mind.* Cambridge, UK: Cambridge University Press.

Withman, K. A., & Bensimon, E. M. (2012). Creating a culture of inquiry around equity and student success. In S. M. Museus & U. M. Jayakumar (Eds.), *Creating campus cultures: Fostering success among racially diverse student populations* (pp. 46–67). New York, NY: Routledge.

PART II: THEORIES OF DEVELOPMENT AS APPLIED TO COLLEGE STUDENTS

CHAPTER 3

SCHLOSSBERG'S TRANSITION THEORY

Susan R. Barclay

CASE VIGNETTE: REYNALDO

Reynaldo is in his final semester at Little Valley Tech, a local 2-year community college, where he is earning his associate's degree in accounting. Reynaldo has enjoyed his experience, and he knows he will qualify for an entry-level clerical accounting position on graduation. Recently, an admissions counselor from Grand Ridge University, a 4-year private institution, visited the campus to speak with students about furthering their education at Grand Ridge. Grand Ridge University and Little Valley Tech have an articulation agreement that allows students enrolled at Little Valley Tech to transfer college credits on comparable courses to Grand Ridge for application toward a 4-year degree. Reynaldo was unaware of this possibility until he happened to see a table Grand Ridge had erected in the student center. In looking through some of the available transfer brochures, Reynaldo learned that Grand Ridge offered not only a bachelor's degree in accounting, but also that by attending one extra year, he could earn a master's degree in accounting. The master's degree, combined with practical experience, would enable Reynaldo to sit for the certified public accountant exam—a goal he had never considered. Reynaldo decided to visit Grand Ridge University, and after learning more about the accounting program of study and career possibilities, Reynaldo knew he wanted to transfer to Grand Ridge in the fall on completion of his associate's degree.

OVERVIEW AND DESCRIPTION OF THE THEORY

Experiencing a transition can be disabling for many. In her book, *Overwhelmed*, Schlossberg (2008) described transitions as vicissitudes that disquiet us. Whether positive or negative, transitions disrupt our lives and create changes in the way we experience our existence. Schlossberg noted, also, that perception influences our transition. For example, transitioning to college might be exciting and anticipatory for one person, yet scary and dreaded for another.

Chickering and Schlossberg (2002) explained *transition* as an event that creates a disruption of roles, routine, and relationships for the individual experiencing the transition. In addition, transition prompts individuals to formulate new assumptions about themselves and their future. Furthermore, Schlossberg (2008) posited that those in transition experience a major life disturbance that necessitates a tremendous amount of adaptation "even when the benefits far outweigh the deficits" (p. 89). The goal, according to Anderson, Goodman, and Schlossberg (2012), is for the person in transition to experience a positive "emergent growth process" (p. 49) during the transition.

Transition is a process that takes place over time rather than at one point in time (Anderson et al., 2012), and every transition begins with an ending (Chickering & Schlossberg, 2002). For the student who is transitioning to college, there comes the end to living at home with parents and a disruption or potential ending to relationships with friends. The role of the student affairs professional is to help students take charge of their transitions and benefit from the challenges of the transition. To accomplish this, students need to learn how to evaluate their challenges, explore options, and increase their coping strategies. Schlossberg's (2008) *Transition Theory* provides the framework for practitioners to use in assisting students through their transitions.

The first piece of the framework includes understanding where students are in their transitions—whether they are *moving in, moving through,* or *moving out* in relation to their transition. Schlossberg (2008) explained that each phase of the transition allows for a way of viewing and navigating the transition. Moving in represents an assessment and planning period. For first-time college students, moving in prompts anxieties of moving to a new campus, having a potential stranger as a roommate, learning how to select and register for classes, and similar things that are new for the student. Moving through represents a time in transition for achieving as much learning about the new roles, relationships, and routines as possible. Moving through characterizes a time of balancing school, friends, and family, focusing on class content, and maintaining grades. Finally, moving out represents the process of completing a "smooth, solid transition to the next part of . . . life" (Chickering & Schlossberg, 2002, p. xv). Moving out might signify graduation, applying for jobs, or looking for a new place to live after graduation.

Mattering

After many years of research related to transition, Schlossberg (1989) became convinced that those in transition feel marginal, frequently, and as though they do not matter to others because of the changing roles they experience during transition. With a shift or overhaul of roles and identities comes a dissonance through which individuals must negotiate as they regain clarity in their roles and where they belong. The innate sense of belonging is common across all humans (Ansbacher & Ansbacher, 1956), and with the disruption in roles and relationships comes a disruption in the sense of belonging and the potential for feeling marginalized. Schlossberg described mattering in reference to the beliefs people hold, regardless of whether those beliefs were accurate, that they matter to someone significant. More so, Schlossberg described mattering as a reciprocal process—that not only do individuals matter to others, but there is an element of dependency of one on the other as well. As such, during times of transition, practitioners must help transitioners gain a sense of mattering to others. Helping those in transition identify the roles and relationships in which others depend on them, are interested in them, or are concerned with their experience provides transitioners with a more solid foundation on which to experience the transition.

Taking Stock—The Four Ss

In spite of the stress that ensues during times of transition, Schlossberg (2008) believed that individuals could navigate transitions more smoothly by going through a process she called *taking stock*. Taking stock is a process by which transitioners examine their situation and coping resources for the situation. Taking stock consists of analyzing four domains:

1. Situation—the situation at the time of the transition
2. Support—the people and assets that strengthen and encourage the student
3. Self—who the student is (identity), his or her optimism level, and dealing with ambiguity
4. Strategies—ways and functions of coping

Situation. Application of Schlossberg's theory begins with assessing the situation in which the student faces transition. Knowing whether the transition is anticipated, unanticipated, or a nonevent helps practitioners in knowing how to work with students through their transition. An *anticipated* event is an event the student could predict or knew was forthcoming (e.g., moving from home to attend college). An *unanticipated* event is one that the student did not know was forthcoming (e.g., being involved in an automobile accident that, in turn, delays college entrance). Often, unanticipated transitions occur suddenly. A *nonevent* is an event that the student desires, yet the event does not come to fruition (e.g., going to college; however, SAT/ACT scores are below minimum requirement for admission). Nonevents are idiosyncratic, and the amount of their affect on the student correlates to the amount of hope the student attaches to the nonevent (Schlossberg, Lissitz, Altman, & Steinberg, 1992).

Other considerations for assessing the situation include the timing of the transition, transition trigger(s), anticipated duration, previous experience with similar transitions, and whether the student is experiencing concurrent stress (Anderson et al., 2012). Because those in transition experience some level of stress, practitioners will want to process with students as to how the transition is affecting roles, relationships, and routines, as well as ascertain concurrent stressors. This can be an emotional time for the student transitioner; therefore, practitioners must be knowledgeable and skilled in working with students from both a student development and a mental health perspective. Critical to the process will be knowing when student needs surpass the expertise and skill level of the practitioner and when to refer for advanced assistance.

In her summary of taking stock of the situation, Schlossberg (2008, p. 54) offered the following questions to consider:

- From the student's point of view, is the situation good or bad?
- Did the student expect the situation, or was the situation unexpected?

- Has the situation come at the worst possible time or the best?
- Where is the student in the transition process—at the beginning, the middle, or the end?

Support. Support is critical to the everyday optimal functioning of human beings and, perhaps, even more so during times of transition. Men and women might experience support differently primarily because they experience stress differently (Schlossberg, 2008). However, regardless, a strong, positive support system can help individuals both physically and mentally.

Age is a factor in what a person's support system might look like because support systems can change over time. When students were younger, they might have relied on family members for support, whereas, as adolescents and emerging adults, they might rely more strongly on peers and other members of society. In addition, as individuals age, they tend to engage in social activities such as sport communities, extracurricular activities, and cultural organizations. All of these form the types of support for the individual involved in these things.In college, students can build support systems with peers, the campus community (e.g., sports, the campus gym), registered student organizations, and mentors (e.g., faculty advisor, professors). Kahn and Antonucci (1980) offered a method for assessing an individual's potential support system, which they labeled the *Convoy of Social Support*. The method consists of circles drawn on a page that resembles Bronfenbrenner's (1994) bioecological model in that assessment of support takes place across the individual's microsystem, mesosystem, and macrosystem. This is useful in the college setting and is a quick and relatively simple way of working with a student in identifying support systems.

In her summary of taking stock of supports, Schlossberg (2008, pp. 75–76) offered the following questions to consider:

- Is the student getting what he or she needs in terms of affection, affirmation, and aid?
- Does the student have a wide range of types of support (e.g., significant other, family or close friends, organizations)?
- Does the student know how to locate and connect with other forms of support (e.g., campus resources, faculty/staff)?
- How has the student's "convoy of social support" been interrupted by the transition?

Self. Anderson et al. (2012) indicated that humans attach meaning and purpose to their experiences; therefore, student development practitioners need to understand the transition experience from the perspective of the student. If students are to transition smoothly and with increased purpose, they need to be self-aware of their beliefs, self-perceived abilities, perceptions, and attitudes. Anderson et al. advocated two lenses through which to look when assessing the *self* domain.

Personal and demographic characteristics. Anderson et al. (2012) wrote, "An individual's personal and demographic characteristics . . . bear directly on how he or she perceives and assesses life" (p. 73), and this is especially true during times of transition. Personal and demographic characteristics include one's socioeconomic status, age, stage in life, state of health, ethnicity and culture, and gender. All of these characteristics influence the way in which students face and experience their transition. In their research, Pearlin and Lieberman (1979) found that socioeconomic status, gender, and age were the three prevailing influences as to how well individuals navigated transition. As applied to traditional-aged college students, students from diminished socioeconomic status might bring fewer internal and external resources to their transition. In one study, Zhang and Smith (2011) found that African American students experienced the transition into and through college more stressfully than White students did. Noting how both personal and demographic characteristics influence the perception students have of their transition event will be important.

Psychological resources. A second component to *self* is the psychological resources, or aids for coping with perceived threats, individuals bring to transitions they experience. These are nontangible, inner resources that every individual possesses. Such resources include state of ego development (e.g., maturity), outlook on life, and the level of commitment or resistance to the transition.

Those at a low level of ego development will be more prone to please others, in particular significant others, and will work harder for social acceptance. Anderson et al. (2012) called these individuals conformists. Those on a high level of ego development are more likely to be autonomous and tolerate ambiguity more easily. Anderson et al. called these individuals self-protective people. Conformists and self-protective students will experience transition unique to their individual ego development state (e.g., maturity level).

A person's outlook (i.e., positive or negative) influences the ways in which he or she perceives and assesses the transition. Students who believe they have some control over their transition (e.g., selecting the college to attend) fare better with the transition to college than students who do not have any control. Likewise, a person's levels of resilience and self-efficacy are contributing factors. Often, we distinguish resilient individuals as to how "strong" we perceive they are or are not. In her work, Schlossberg (2008) discussed resilience as a sense of hardiness. Related to transition, self-efficacy describes an individual's perceived ability to negotiate the transition successfully. Sometimes, individuals have a lowered self-esteem and doubt their ability to complete certain tasks, including moving through points of transition.

Because of the disquieting nature of transition, some individuals might be resistant to the transition or possess a lessened degree of commitment to the transition they face. Applying theoretical concepts from motivational interviewing (Miller & Rollnick, 2012) could be helpful to practitioners as they work with students before and during transitions. Applying these concepts can take place during casual conversations or in more formalized meetings such as during counseling sessions. Others purport the use of strengths-based techniques in assisting transitioners. For example, Schreiner, Louis, and Nelson (2012) purport the efficacy of strengths-based technique when working with students transitioning to college for the first time or with transfer students.

In her summary of taking stock of self, Schlossberg (2008, p. 62) offered the following questions to consider:

- Is the student challenged or overwhelmed by transition events or nonevents?
- What types of stress challenge the student? Overwhelm the student?
- Does the student face transition with a "fighting spirit," as a stoic, as a denier, as a helpless person, or as a believer in magic?
- Does the student feel a sense of control or mastery when facing transition?
- Does the student face life as an optimist or as a pessimist?

Strategies. Schlossberg (2008) described strategies as the coping resources individuals bring to transition—in other words, how well people negotiate transitions while, simultaneously, protecting themselves psychologically. Taking stock of coping resources is twofold. First, a person must identify his or her coping resources. For example, in the transition to college, a student might seek assistance from an advisor when formulating a schedule of classes, or the student might attempt to build the schedule independently. Which strategy is most effective for the student? Second, the person in transition must decide which of four strategies to use as a vehicle for transitioning. Options include modifying the situation, changing the meaning of the situation (before the emergence of stress), controlling and managing the situation (after the emergence of stress), or taking deliberate inaction (Schlossberg, 2008). Which option a person selects depends on the person (i.e., *self*) and the situation. For example, two students in a biology class might struggle with the course content, yet handle the situation very differently. One might choose to modify the situation by learning new approaches for learning and applying the content (*modifying the situation*), whereas the other student might become depressed and begin skipping class (*doing nothing/deliberate inaction*).

In her summary of taking stock of strategies, Schlossberg (2008, p. 103) offered the following questions to consider:

- Does the student in transition use a range of strategies?
- Is the student taking action to change the transition?
- Is the student attempting to change the meaning of the transition?
- How well does the student handle stress?
- How does the student decide that doing nothing is the best option?
- How does the student exercise flexibility in choosing various strategies depending on the challenge at hand?

HISTORY AND DEVELOPMENT OF THE THEORY

The earliest record of Schlossberg's model dates to 1965 when she presented a paper at the conference on The Training of Counselors of Adults (Schlossberg, 1965) in which she outlined her framework of transition. Her initial work involved trying to understand the experiences of adult men who wanted to change careers. Schlossberg asserted that those in transition experience a discontinuity in their lives, primarily through radical changes in both their internal and external reference frames and their environment. Furthermore, she posited that transition evoked "warring factions, uncertainties, [and] ambivalences" (p. 7) for transitioners and that this state of "becoming" (p. 14) represented a prime time for growth and development for the individual. The purpose of her presentation was to provide a framework for understanding the experiences of transition, and in doing so, Schlossberg articulated three elements to transition: exploration that leads to growth and development; the occurrence of transition within a social context; and opportunities for progress related to self-concepts and perceptions.

Later, Schlossberg (1981) extended her ideas regarding transition, which she defined as a time "of disequilibrium in which a person has to work out new ways of handling problems" (p. 6). In her research, Schlossberg noticed a "psychic growth" (p. 2) intrinsic to the transition process as transitioners negotiated new relationships, new behaviors, and new self-perceptions. Transition had either positive (e.g., development of new interests) or negative (e.g., boredom, feelings of worthlessness) effects on those in transition, and Schlossberg noted that the effects could be different for the same person experiencing different transitions. Several important elements of Schlossberg's model emerged at this time, including Schlossberg's articulation of what would eventually become the *Four S System*. Schlossberg believed that the transition itself was not of importance as much as how the transition fit with the transitioner's *stage, situation,* and *style* at the time of transition. Furthermore, Schlossberg outlined three key elements to her framework, which included the perceptions of the person in transition, the person's ability to adapt to the transition, and the degree of stress generated by the transition. Finally, Schlossberg discussed three groups of factors affecting adaptation to transition: the characteristics of the transition (e.g., role change, timing, duration), the characteristics of the pre- and posttransition environments (e.g., interpersonal and/or institutional support systems), and the characteristics of the individual (e.g., psychosocial competence, socioeconomic status, previous experience with a similar transition, state of health).

As researchers, including Schlossberg, tested the transition model, results of studies yielded information that assisted Schlossberg in fine-tuning her theory. One study (Schlossberg & Leibowitz, 1980) involving men laid off from National Aeronautics and Space Administration (NASA) provided data that indicated that those men experienced considerable stress because of multiple factors related to the transition. Those factors were the role loss the men experienced, the timing and suddenness of the transition, and duration uncertainty. One positive factor the men reported was institutional support in the form of workshops, counseling, and employment services, interventions that led to all of the men securing new jobs.

Schlossberg and Leibowitz (1980) explained that the aim of their, and other researchers', work (e.g., Lyons, 1980; Merikangas, 1980) was to formulate appropriate interventions and support for those experiencing transition. Later, Schlossberg (2008) described her framework as a "basic model that takes the mystery . . . out of change" (p. xv).

As Schlossberg continued to refine her model (Schlossberg, 1990), she realized that paying attention to additional transition elements was important for those who were trained and skilled to help transitioners. Elements that surfaced included the type of transition (i.e., anticipated, unanticipated, or nonevent); the degree to which someone in transition would experience alterations in his or her roles, relationships, routines, or assumptions; and a more formalized version of the Four S system (i.e., situation, self, support, and strategies) of *taking stock*.

Over the years, Schlossberg has continued to apply her theory to various populations and situations (e.g., higher education [Schlossberg, Lynch, & Chickering, 1989]; retirement [Schlossberg, 2004, 2009]; consultants and nonevents [Schlossberg, 2005]; adults [Anderson et al., 2012]), and her theory has become a staple in student development theory classes across the nation.

APPLICATION WITHIN STUDENT AFFAIRS

Perhaps one of the greatest strengths of Schlossberg's Transition Theory is the applicability across student affairs' functional areas and student profiles. College students experience transition constantly, beginning with transitioning into college up to, and including, graduation and transitioning to the world of work. As such, student affairs professionals have opportunities to apply Schlossberg's Transition Model often.

New Student Programming

Helping students transition to college is vital to their success in the university environment. Many institutions have created various initiatives to contribute to student success. All universities offer orientation, which assists incoming students in understanding the college environment better. In addition, many universities offer first-year experience courses, in which students learn about studying skills, time management strategies, campus resources, and support services.

Building student programming efforts around Schlossberg's Transition Model adds an important foundation to any transitional program. Incorporating the Four Ss as standard components ensures a holistic approach in bolstering student success and retention. For example, during orientation, the *situation* is implied. Obviously, the situation is that students are transitioning into the college environment. Practitioners could incorporate the *Transition Guide* (Kay & Schlossberg, 2014) as a transition assessment element that would assess across the Four Ss or integrate reflective pieces to the orientation that will prompt students' *self*-exploration into their personal characteristics and psychological resources that might help or hinder their transition.

Offices of Nontraditional Students/Veterans

The number of adults returning to college or initiating new educational experiences has increased significantly in recent years (American Council on Education [ACE], 2014; Soares, 2013). Stay-at-home parents might experience motivation to seek training or a degree after raising children. After completing their military service, veterans might choose to seek a college degree though benefits offered under the Post-9/11 GI Bill. Furthermore, adults who want to advance in their existing careers might pursue an advanced degree to assist them toward that goal. Whatever the reason, institutions have been responding by developing on-campus centers that provide support and resources targeted toward adults.

Adults who initiate academic endeavors are unique from traditional college students in that, typically, adults have been out of school for a number of years or even decades. Rather than transitioning straight from high school to college, adults transition from other life roles, and the transition to college could bring additional transition stressors that traditional students do not face. Whether college entrance is because of an anticipated or nonanticipated event, practitioners can offer *support* supplementary to the adult students' existing support system. For example, implementing social activities (e.g., family day on a weekend) could bring together these adults in activities that include the entire family. Adult learners would have the opportunity to connect with others who are experiencing the same types of stressors (e.g., balancing work, family, and school) and develop new relationships that could offer outside support and accountability. Likewise, these offices could be a resource of *strategy* ideas for success throughout this new phase in the lives of adult learners. In addition to brief student success strategy workshops, which might be well attended by adult learners because of multiple life-role fulfillments, practitioners might develop short (i.e., 2–3 minutes) online videos that offer strategies around specific topics such as note taking, studying, or incorporating family into the educational pursuit.

Schlossberg's Transition Theory applies to students across their educational experience, regardless of age or circumstances, as they are *moving in* (to college), *moving through*, and *moving out* (graduation) of their individual transitions. Schlossberg (1965, 1981, 2008) provided an excellent framework that can serve as the foundation to all functional areas of student affairs and offices of student services.

CASE VIGNETTE WRAP-UP: REYNALDO

Moving In: Reynaldo was excited about his decision to transfer to Grand Ridge University (anticipated situation). After completing all the requirements for admission, Reynaldo registered (strategy) with the Office of Transfer Services (support) on the advice of his admissions counselor (support). Reynaldo met with the transfer coordinator (support), who informed Reynaldo of the services designed specifically for transfer students. Included in these services were appointment-based meetings with Transfer Services staff (support) and a specialized one-credit-hour class for transfer students (support, strategy). In the class, transfer students perform reflective activities (strategy) to learn about their interests and values (self), which they can use to explore registered student organizations students might want to join (support, strategy). In addition, students enrolled in the course complete a scavenger hunt (strategy) in which they must locate a predetermined number of offices and resource centers on campus. This activity helps students, such as Reynaldo, familiarize themselves with the campus (strategy) and learn about the many resources available to all students (support). At the end of their meeting, the Transfer Coordinator referred Reynaldo to the Articulation Agreement coordinator (support), who collaborated with Reynaldo in developing a schedule with respect to Reynaldo's associate degree credits and a plan for the next 3 years of courses (strategy) to earn both his bachelor's and master's degrees.

Moving Through: During his 3 years at Grand Ridge University (situation), Reynaldo participated regularly (strategy) in the university's Accounting Club (support), first as a member and, later, as an executive board member. As a member and regular attendee to meetings, Reynaldo gained valuable knowledge about himself (self) and what to expect as he eventually graduated and transitioned to his professional life (strategy).

Moving Out: At the beginning of his last semester at Grand Ridge University, Reynaldo began contemplating graduation (anticipated situation). He made an appointment with the university career center (strategy, support). There, Reynaldo registered with Employ GRU

(continued)

(continued)

(strategy), an online system available to Grand Ridge students in which they can view current job opportunities, including job fairs available to students. In addition, Reynaldo met with a career development specialist (support) who assisted Reynaldo in developing a quality resume (strategy). Furthermore, Reynaldo participated in several mock interviews (strategy) to prepare him for upcoming employer interviews. At the career center, Reynaldo learned how to research job information and salary information (strategy), which prepared him better for the job negotiation process.

Graduation day for Reynaldo was exciting! Thanks to understanding his transition situations, learning more about himself during his years at Grand Ridge University, gaining support from various people and services across the campus, and employing several strategies to increase his opportunity for success, Reynaldo was looking forward to walking across the stage, securing his degree, and beginning his new work with his new employer.

CASE VIGNETTE 1 FOR READER REFLECTION: ALEX

Alex is a 17-year-old transgender teen who is leaving soon for college. From early childhood, Alex felt trapped in his male body, fantasized about life as a female, and expressed interest in stereotypical "girl" toys and hobbies. In the beginning, Alex's parents were confused, and on the advice of a well-intended physician, they tried to "teach" Alex how to be a boy by buying him only stereotypical boy toys, registering him for male-oriented sports, and—in all respects—treating him as a boy. Alex resisted this pressure and began exhibiting deepening signs of withdrawal and depression. By age 9, Alex's parents realized their son was not "just going through a phase" and began researching to understand more about parenting a gender nonconforming child. They joined a support group of peers who, like them, were parenting gender nonconforming children and decided to embrace Alex as a girl. Alex and his parents began counseling sessions with a gender identity specialist to learn how to assist Alex best with the gender identity transition. Alex began wearing feminine clothing and let her hair grow out. Under the care of a physician, Alex began cross-sex hormones at age 11.

Although exciting, the transition was challenging for Alex. She felt more genuine in her gender, and her teachers were supportive. Many of Alex's peers did not understand the change, and some continued to refer to Alex as a boy. Others teased and bullied Alex. To a few peers, the change did not matter, and one in particular even seemed supportive. Alex and Cheyenne became close friends quickly.

Now that Alex is graduating high school and leaving for college soon, she has concerns about being in a new environment that does not include her support system from home. Alex will be several states away from her parents, and Cheyenne will be attending a different university, which is also several states away. Alex wonders what her experience will be like and what others might say or do when they learn Alex is transgender.

- *What can colleges do to help staff and faculty be prepared to provide a supportive and nurturing environment for students like Alex?*
- *What stages of transition might be most challenging for Alex?*
- *In what ways might a transgender student, such as Alex, struggle with making connections to others on a college campus?*
- *What supports can be provided to help Alex successfully move through the transition stages in Schlossberg's theory?*

CASE VIGNETTE 2 FOR READER REFLECTION: HYUN

Hyun is an 18-year-old Korean boy whose family has chosen to send him to the United States to earn his bachelor's degree. Hyun comes from a traditional South Korean family, and although his family is excited for this impending educational opportunity for their son, they are anxious about the new experience. None from Hyun's family has ever travelled to the United States nor does Hyun know anyone at the university he is going to attend. Hyun plans to study engineering, and he communicated electronically with one of the professors before the family's decision. He wanted to learn more about the program, and the professor provided him with some basic program information and a website address.

As Hyun and his family prepare for Hyun's flight to the United States, they know Hyun is limited in the number of personal items he can take with him. This raises additional anxiety as they organize the best items to pack. They fear Hyun will not have what he needs and will not know how to navigate the community well enough to secure the provisions he needs on his arrival. Hyun tries to reassure his family that he will know how to take care of himself in his new environment.

Weeks after his arrival to the United States and the university, Hyun feels lost and alone. Although university staff assisted Hyun with locating his on-campus housing and included him in a mandatory orientation process when he first arrived, Hyun has not been able to make friends with other students. When in class, Hyun struggles to keep up with his note taking during lectures and presentations, and most students seem to leave quickly after class to get to their next class. Although Hyun has a roommate, the roommate is rarely in the room because he does much of his studying at the library and tends to stay out late with friends.

- *What are some of the unique challenges international students face with adjusting and transitioning to college?*
- *What specific programs and supports might assist Hyun in adjusting to college and making the transition easier?*
- *What training should be provided to resident assistance and other student affairs professionals, such as academic advisors, to recognize when a student is struggling with making the transition to college?*

REFERENCES

American Council on Education. (2014). Nontraditional students. Retrieved from http://www.acenet.edu/higher-education/topics/Pages/Nontraditional-Students.aspx

Anderson, M. L., Goodman, J., & Schlossberg, N. K. (2012). *Counseling adults in transition: Linking Schlossberg's theory with practice in a diverse world* (4th ed.). New York, NY: Springer Publishing Company.

Ansbacher, H. L., & Ansbacher, R. (Eds.). (1956). *The individual psychology of Alfred Adler: A systematic presentation of selections from his writings*. New York, NY: Basic Books.

Bronfenbrenner, U. (1994). Ecological models of human development. In *International encyclopedia of education* (Vol. 3, 2nd ed.). Oxford, England: Elsevier. Reprinted in M. Gauvain & M. Cole (Eds.), *Readings on the development of children* (1993, 2nd ed., pp. 37–43). New York, NY: Freeman.

Chickering, A. W., & Schlossberg, N. K. (2002). *Getting the most out of college* (2nd ed.). Upper Saddle River, NJ: Pearson.

Kahn, R. L., & Antonucci, T. C. (1980). Convoys over the life course: Attachment, roles, and social support. In P. B. Baltes & O. C. Brim, Jr. (Eds.), *Life-span development and behavior* (p. 273). New York, NY: Academic Press.

Kay, S., & Schlossberg, N. K. (2014). The transition guide: A counseling tool offering a new way to think about change. Retrieved from www.transitionguide.com

Lyons, J. (1980). *The effect of a structural group experience in the transition from the role of college student to the role of working professional.* Unpublished master's thesis, University of Maryland, College Park.

Merikangas, M. (1980). *The next step: A retirement planning seminar.* Unpublished master's thesis, University of Maryland, College Park.

Miller, W. R., & Rollnick, S. (2012). *Motivational interviewing: Helping people change* (3rd ed.). New York, NY: The Guilford Press.

Pearlin, L. I., & Lieberman, M. A. (1979). Social sources of emotional distress. In R. Simmons (Ed.), *Research in community and mental health* (Vol. 1, pp. 217–248). Greenwich, CT: JAI Press.

Schlossberg, N. K. (1965, May). *Adults in transition.* Paper presented at the Training of Counselors of Adults, Chatham, MA.

Schlossberg, N. K. (1981). A model for analyzing human adaptation to transition. *The Counseling Psychologist, 9*(2), 2–18.

Schlossberg, N. K. (1989, Winter). Marginality and mattering. Key issues in building community. *New Directions for Student Services, 48*, 5–15.

Schlossberg, N. K. (1990). Training counselors to work with older adults. *Generations, 14*, 7.

Schlossberg, N. K. (2004). *Retire smart, retire happy.* Washington, DC: American Psychological Association.

Schlossberg, N. K. (2005). Helping consultants to deal with transitions: The specific case of non-events. *The Educational and Vocational Guidance, 34*, 85–101.

Schlossberg, N. K. (2008). *Overwhelmed: Coping with life's ups and downs* (2nd ed.). Lanham, MD: M. Evans.

Schlossberg, N. K. (2009). *Revitalizing retirement: Reshaping your identity, relationships, and purpose.* Washington, DC: American Psychological Association.

Schlossberg, N. K., & Leibowitz, Z. (1980). Organizational support systems as buffers to job loss. *Journal of Vocational Behavior, 17*, 204–217.

Schlossberg, N. K., Lissitz, R., Altman, J., & Steinberg, L. (1992). *Non-event: Describing a new construct.* Unpublished manuscript.

Schlossberg, N. K., Lynch, A. Q., & Chickering, A. W. (1989). *Improving higher education environments for adults.* San Francisco, CA: Jossey-Bass.

Schreiner, L. A., Louis, M. C., & Nelson, D. D. (Eds.). (2012). *Thriving in transitions: A research-based approach to college student success.* Columbia: University of South Carolina Press.

Soares, L. (2013). *Post-traditional learners and the transformation of postsecondary education: A manifesto for college leaders.* Washington, DC: American Council on Education.

Zhang, P., & Smith, W. L. (2011). From high school to college: The transition experiences of Black and White students. *Journal of Black Studies, 42*, 828–845.

CHAPTER 4

ERIKSON'S THEORY OF PSYCHOSOCIAL DEVELOPMENT

Suzanne Degges-White

CASE VIGNETTE: NEHAL

Nehal was a 19-year-old college sophomore who lived at home with her mother and two sisters, one older and one younger. The family members were devout Muslims. Her father had died when Nehal was only 9 years old and her family has struggled financially since his death. Immediately after her father had initially been diagnosed with the disease that eventually took his life, he had asked Nehal and her sisters to pledge that they would always take care of their mother and to show her the respect she deserved. Nehal felt as if she and her mother were the closest of friends. She and her sisters and mother were typically able to talk about anything and the family was fortunate enough to live close to many extended family members, creating a web of support for the family.

Although Nehal had never questioned her faith growing up and had actively followed traditions and customs of the religion, she was experiencing new feelings and desires now that she was actively involved in college life. She felt that living at home was her duty, but she now found herself itching for independence as her involvement in college activities and organizations began to take up more of her time.

Around the midpoint of fall semester, Nehal realized that her calendar was crowded with multiple activities most days. She was working hard to maintain her high-B average, volunteering at the Muslim Student Center, working part time, and involved in service and social organizations, too. She also served as a volunteer Arabic translator on occasion at the university.

Nehal and her best friend, Marta, often carpooled to campus together from their small town 20 miles away. Their conversations had increasingly grown focused on their frustrations with the distance between their homes and "their lives," as Nehal described it to Mallory, the counselor she had come to see as a way to earn extra credit for one of her courses. Nehal initially had difficulty finding a topic to discuss with the counselor, but when

(continued)

(continued)

he asked her to tell him about her favorite and least favorite parts of the day, she was able to dive into the topic.
   As Nehal described it,

Actually my favorite and least favorite times of the day are like the sides of a coin ... I love being with my family. I love the feeling of being home and safe and warm and surrounded by my mom and my sisters. It feels so natural. But ... I also feel like this is the worst part of the day for me, too. It's like I'm going back in time to being a little girl again. I get so frustrated when my older sister starts bossing me around or my younger sister is constantly wanting to hang out with me and ask my opinion about everything. My mom is amazing. She's my hero. Yet when I'm home, it's like she treats me like a child, fixing our meals, doing our laundry, all that stuff. I don't guess it's a bad thing to be looked after, but I don't know that she should be doing this for her grown daughters. The whole situation is confusing.

OVERVIEW OF ERIKSON'S THEORY OF PSYCHOSOCIAL DEVELOPMENT

One of the more comprehensive and enduring theories of psychosocial development was created by Erik Erikson (Erikson, 1968). He developed a map of human psychosocial development that covered the crises and touch points humans experience from birth to death. Built on a framework that addressed the twin needs of connecting and relating to others, Erikson developed an eight-stage model in which relationships with others and oneself serve as the central focus. Erikson used opposing outcomes as the end points of a specific and unique vector for each chronological stage, such as *Trust Versus Mistrust*. Each new developmental stage is presumed to present a "crisis" that must be mastered successfully before subsequent movement through the developmental stages. Within each stage, he also included character virtues that were acquired through the successful transition through the developmental period. The following sections provide brief descriptions of each stage of Erikson's chronologically organized model.

Birth to 18 Months

Erikson (1968) postulated the first stage to be *Trust Versus Mistrust*. During this period, the initial relationship between an infant and his primary caregivers is first established and solidified. The development of a stable bond during this period is viewed as essential to the development of trust for a child. This trust is built over time as an infant's needs are met reliably and consistently by caregivers. This lets a child know that the world is a good place and that adults are in place to help him or her cope when he or she is in distress and needing comfort or when celebrating a victory and needing positive approval by others. The successful navigation of this crisis provides a child with the ability to feel *hope*, which is the basic virtue associated with this stage, according to Erikson. This is a period in which the first efforts to connect to a social and relational world begin.

Toddler Years (1.5–3)

The next developmental stage encountered addresses the *Autonomy Versus Shame and Doubt* crisis according to Erikson (1968). This is the stage through which all demanding toddlers must pass en route to the acquisition of independence, a trait that will carry them through later challenges. Research findings have suggested that a strong and secure parental attachment, a task that is typically worked out in that first year, results in less conflict in 3-year-olds (Panfile, Laible, & Eye, 2012). It is not surprising that Erikson associated the basic virtues of *willpower* and *self-control* with this conflict.

As young children begin to assert their individuality and their will, they will run up against authority figures (parents, caregivers, older children) who will block their efforts to get their way. When limits are put in place and enforced by caring and supportive adults, children learn that their desires cannot always be met, but that their identity as an autonomous individual warrants respect.

Preschool Years (3–5)

During the preschool years, children typically move into a wider social world in which they engage with a broader range of people. Encouraged to be more interactive and responsible, they now face the conflict of *Initiative Versus Guilt*. Aware of the need to be their own "little person," they also begin to understand that consequences exist for unacceptable behavior. Thus, *purpose* and *direction* in life are the basic virtues that children begin to develop during this period. Wanting to emulate and please their favored adults/parents at this stage, children are now cognizant of the impact of their actions. They are able to recognize when they have disappointed or disobeyed authority figures and they feel remorse or guilt for having done so.

If a child is raised in an environment in which he or she is not allowed the opportunity to make choices or try out new behaviors, or if these efforts are consistently met with negative caregiver responses or punishment, the child may be unable to successfully master this developmental stage. At the opposite end of the disciplinary spectrum, children who are given free rein to engage in any behaviors that they choose without the presence of adult guidance, however, may fail to develop a sense of purpose and may lack direction in later pursuits.

Primary School Years (5–12)

As children progress into the elementary school years, and if development has taken its normal, predicted course, they are ready to dive enthusiastically into learning in a manner that is seldom matched at any other point. The virtue associated with successful mastery of this stage is considered *competency*. Erikson (1968) labeled the crisis of this stage as *Industry Versus Inferiority*. This period represents the lull before the puberty-anchored emotional storm begins. Children enter this period hungry to increase their knowledge and understanding of the world, but they also meet up against the potential for public failure—grades grow in importance as teachers mete out approval or disapproval in the schools via evaluation and test scores. Friendship groups are often the center of "in-group" and "out-group" dynamics, with the risk of being "out" hinging on others' perceptions. Parents, too, have the power to mete out positive or negative responses to children's behavior.

The risks of feeling inferior to others in the classroom, social settings, and at home are daunting. It is unfortunate that a child's self-esteem is contingent on perceptions of how others perceive him or her; thus, this period can be instrumental in building and maintaining self-confidence. If a child is unable to develop a strong sense of competence during this stage, it may be difficult for him or her to participate in activities that are not easily mastered or to show persistence when faced with challenging tasks. Avoidance of opportunities may be the method of coping with the fear of failure for individuals who fail to master a sense of personal competence. In addition, feeling a sense of competence and self-worth is essential for successfully navigating the subsequent psychosocial crisis that revolves around identity and friendships.

Heading Toward Adulthood (12–18)

As puberty begins, not only are new hormones influencing young adolescents' behavior, but also the new developments in the socioemotional system of their brains (Steinberg, 2008). These developments are driving behavior as adolescents seek to manage the conflict of *Identity Versus Identity Confusion* (Erikson, 1968). This conflict can take the greatest toll on the parent–child relationship, as the goal is *individuation* and creating an identity separate and distinct from the family. There is a significantly charged allegiance to peers and this is the springboard to the solidification of the virtues of *fidelity* and *devotion*.

As an adolescent's peers grow in importance as the most highly valued reference group, parents typically feel a range of emotions, few of which are positive at the outset. However, adolescents are biologically driven to take risks and try on new behaviors as they prepare for the ultimate leap from child to partner to parent, themselves. Although not every adolescent will push with the same force against parental restraints, these years can generate intense battles that are reminiscent of the iconic toddler temper tantrum. Keeping a child too close will hinder development, but allowing too much freedom may provide peers with too much control over the teen's behavior and burgeoning identity.

Striking a balance between freedom and responsibility is the optimal goal. Mastering the ability to tell the difference between situations when it is advisable to take risks versus when it is better to play it safe is an important development that occurs during this period. Skills that require risk management and assessment, such as driving, have been shown to be more highly developed in adolescents who are more psychosocially mature (Bingham, Shope, Zakrajsek, & Raghunathan, 2008). This precollege period is the precursor to an individual's maturation into a productive and rational adult.

If an adolescent is unable to develop a sense of belonging to a peer group, the isolation that results may halt her psychosocial development. Being able to relate to others, offering and receiving support, and both experiencing a sense of understanding of others' perspectives as well as enjoying a sense of being understood are key milestones that allow adolescents to become independent young adults. If youths fail to push back against authority or are unable to connect with a social network, they may be challenged in later years to develop close personal relationships with others—within both platonic and romantic realms.

Finding a Partner and Settling Down (18–40)

This sixth stage is located in the early adulthood period in which individuals are struggling with *Intimacy Versus Isolation* (Erikson, 1968). The desire for a long-term romantic relationship coupled with a fear of being single and alone play out their drama during this period. *Love* and *affiliation* are the virtue rewards that arise from successfully establishing an authentic intimate relationship. Culturally and biologically, humans are programmed to find a life partner, settle down, and raise a family. Some women may become especially aware of the "social clock" ticking down and may experience both external and internal pressure to begin a family (Lois & Becker, 2014).

Although neuroscientific research findings have stretched the outer bounds of the adolescent developmental period into the mid-20s (Steinberg, 2008), the hurry to get on to the "next stage" of life can be intense. During this period, young adults may "try on" different romantic partners to see who might be the best fit. This period has the potential to be difficult or tumultuous as emotional investments in relationships may not provide the return that is sought. Some of the anticipated events of this time include leaving home for college or moving out as jobs bring financial independence and a new sense of maturity. Historically, the goal of this period has been assumed to be entry into a long-term, monogamous relationship; contemporary statistics, however, suggest that young adults are less likely to settle down with a partner as early as they once did (U.S. Bureau of the Census, 2015).

Much has been written about the construct of *emerging adulthood* (Arnett, 2000) in addition to extended adolescence. Research studies that have focused on the Millennial age group have also yielded evidence that priorities for young adults have shifted (Maguire & Austin, 2015), and they are happily allowing traditional age–related milestones to go unmet. This shift has resulted in a seemingly diminished interest in achieving financial or residential independence than in the past years. In fact, research suggests that this stage of psychosocial development may be prolonged in young adults (Cohen, 2003). Needing more time to learn how to function independently within a monogamous union may result in either a greater number of failed relationships on one hand or a fear of attempting to form a relationship at all, on the other.

Maturity and Giving Back (40–65)

As lives and relationships settle into place, with families underway or independence embraced, the decision to give back to the world or to retreat from it is faced through the conflict of *Generativity Versus Stagnation*, according to Erikson (1968). This is the period in which women often become part of the "sandwich generation," caring for their own immediate family or professional obligations, but now being needed to care for their aging parents. This may be the period in which men, and increasingly, women, focus most keenly on their career as these are often their most productive and highest earning years. The virtue that this period can build is related to *care* and *production*.

Recognizing the need to give back to others, either at work or within one's own family, can be a motivating force during this period. College students may actually benefit significantly through their relationships with campus faculty, staff, and volunteers within this age group. Examples of this include being part of an athletic team whose coach is highly invested in the players' personal development; receiving mentoring from individuals who are in the professions that students are actively pursuing; being taught by scholars who have spent their professional lives engaged in research in their field; and being the recipient of advising and guidance from campus personnel.

A Time of Review (65+)

The older adult years are truly a time in which we measure our days—not just those we have left to us, but the weight and quality of those that have made up our lives. We face the final crisis of *Integrity Versus Despair* as we work to own the values of wisdom and renunciation. This period, perhaps among them all, is the most essential to reaching a place where one can assert with confidence that he or she has lived a good life. It is during the process of assessing the self-assigned value of our days that will inform us if we have made the choices along the way that provide us with a sense of pride or peace or discontent. Deathbed confessions, long-awaited words of forgiveness, and honesty with oneself are all parts of the process of coming to terms with one's past.

Although there is some evidence that Erikson was developing a ninth stage to describe the transition from end-of-life to death, this chapter only focuses on the traditional eight stages. Each of these stages is expected to be experienced in a somewhat linear fashion. However, when circumstances occur that impede development, individuals may be "stuck" in a stage that is typically experienced at an earlier age. Following is a description of how traditional-aged college students may present on campus if their development has been blocked.

APPLICATION OF THE THEORY WITHIN STUDENT AFFAIRS

Erikson's model of sequential development implies that incomplete resolution of one developmental crisis may hinder future developmental progress regardless of an individual's chronological age. Thus, "arrested development" may lead to a variety of concerns, behavioral problems, or adverse events for students, regardless of their ages. Awareness of the role that psychosocial development can play in a student's maturity level or his or her adherence to rules and expectations can help student affairs professionals recognize and respond to student issues. Maturity, responsibility, and accountability are traits that are expected to be present in college-aged students, but this is not always the case. The following sections outline the ways in which obstructed development may create challenges for students on campus.

Trust Versus Mistrust: Hope

Trust is a requisite component of healthy adult relationships, including the student–instructor relationship as well as the peer-to-peer relationship. When college-aged students are still grappling with obstacles related to their ability to trust others, it may also be difficult for these individuals to trust in the educational process itself. They may ascribe poor grades to an instructor's personal feelings rather than being an accurate reflection of their academic work. Lacking trust in the academic process may lead these students to doubt themselves and to have little hope that they can master course material. They may skip classes and give up on the assignments rather than actively seek assistance.

Historically, college personnel were often considered to serve as *in loco parentis*, with students expected to be responsive to feedback and expectations (Lee, 2011). Even the term *alma mater* focuses on the parental role with which institutions were historically imbued. Student affairs professionals may still be needed as "para-parental authorities." Establishing rapport and healthy mutual relationships with students who are struggling with trust issues can help keep these students moving forward.

In summary, the failure of an individual to develop hope before arrival on campus may create troubling issues for the student both academically and socially. When students with little hope meet with difficult assignments, roommate squabbles, demanding instructors, or other significant challenges, efforts that are not met with the desired outcome may generate feelings of helplessness and hopelessness that are difficult for students to overcome. Thus, the feelings of hopelessness and mistrust can negatively affect multiple areas of a college student's life.

Autonomy Versus Shame and Doubt: Willpower

College students who are still wrestling with the conflict between autonomy and shame and doubt may find themselves feeling overwhelmed by the multitude of challenges that college life presents. This may be the first time that students have been away from home on their own for any significant length of time. If they have not been able to develop a sense of autonomy or adequate willpower to see challenges through to successful ends, they may be overwhelmed on campus as they are faced with the expansive range of activities and opportunities in academic and social sectors.

When a student lacks autonomy, he or she may be easily influenced by peers as he or she tries to fit in with others. Depending on the guidance or modeling done, a student may prioritize social events over academic pursuits. He or she may be encouraged to devalue coursework and overvalue partying or social activities. Willpower can be essential for long-term academic success; so if a student is not psychosocially mature, he or she may drop classes that are difficult, change majors if courses grow challenging, or possibly choose plagiarism or cheating in order to pass a class. In short, without a sense of autonomy and the willpower to stay on track, college students may face significant obstacles academically, socially, and, potentially, legally.

Initiative Versus Guilt: Purpose

Most of us think of the college years as the period in which a student's professional ambitions crystallize. Choosing a field of study and deciding on a major are two goals that students, parents, and college personnel often give high priority. It is unfortunate that when students have been unable to successfully resolve this stage of development, they may have a difficult time committing themselves to a major, to graduation, and to a professional goal.

When students are confronted with the wealth of choices, in terms of majors and career paths, on campus, they may be unable to select one and settle down.

They may try out a variety of majors along the way, which can add on additional semesters of study. Without having developed the necessary initiative and purpose to set a goal and work toward it, students may feel that they are drowning in options without a clear plan for graduation. Academic advisors and career services personnel can play a positive role in helping these students to identify suitable majors and to develop plans for success.

Finding a purpose in life not only provides a solution to an existential dilemma, but also is necessary for general success in life. If an individual reaches college without having effectively developed the virtue of purpose, this can create further obstacles to healthy development and maturation. Class attendance, diligence in following through with assignments, meeting with an advisor, and becoming involved in major/career-related organizations are behaviors that reflect age-appropriate psychosocial development. When students fail to exhibit these, the path to academic and career success is likely to be obstructed.

Industry Versus Inferiority: Competency

Just as a sense of purpose and initiative must be present for success in academic settings, so, too, must a commitment to industry and the virtue of competency. Self-efficacy, which is the belief that one is capable of completing a task (Bandura, 1977), is deeply connected to competency (Hughes, Galbraith, & White, 2011). When an individual fails to find reward through industry and fails to develop a sense of competency, college can present a myriad of seemingly insurmountable obstacles. In addition, social competence is necessary for students to develop a social support network and to build healthy relationships.

Students who do not possess academic or personal competence may have a difficult time on any campus. Students no longer have parents or other caregivers to remind them to complete homework, to wake them up for school each morning, or to hand in assignments on time. The stakes have been raised for students in direct relation to an increase in expectations of student accountability. If a student fails to prize industry or feels incompetent to complete his or her coursework, consequences may be significant, including the risk of academic probation for inadequate grades.

Identity Versus Role Confusion: Fidelity

Traditional-age college students typically first appear on campus on the cusp of young adulthood leaving the tumultuous period of adolescence behind. Although physical maturity may actually be occurring a little more quickly than in past generations, psychological and psychosocial maturity may now be slower to arrive (Steinberg, 2010). Therefore, the behavior of many students may reflect their continued efforts to take risks, push limits, and develop a sense of personal identity. Although campuses have long given birth to radical movements and alternative ideas, students who have yet to develop a sense of personal identity and boundaries may be overwhelmed by the diversity of activities and groups on campus.

Fidelity is not just an attribute shared by U.S. Marine Corps members; it is a sense of belonging and loyalty that is felt among friends and with romantic partners as well. Learning to be loyal, trusting, and trustworthy of others is an important element in being prepared to develop mature and lasting relationships of any sort. When freshmen arrive on campus, they may still be in the process of finding out who they are and where they would like to fit into the professional and social realms. Although many campuses may now have replaced the construct of the "Undecided Major" with terms related to "Exploring," the need to commit to a clear path toward graduation is inevitable.

Students dealing with more layered identity issues, such as questioning or closeting their true sexual identity or gender identity, may exhibit a lack of focus because of the inner struggles they are experiencing (Bennett & Douglass, 2013). Students who have trouble finding the social group to which they belong may lose interest in campus life or activities and lose drive to continue. For many students, Greek organizations or other interest-based groups provide the opportunity to commit to identities that reflect the ideals of the group. These organizations also foster a strong sense of connection with fidelity to other members in the penultimate expression of brotherhood or sisterhood.

Intimacy Versus Isolation: Love

During the traditional college-age years, the psychosocial trajectory is pushing young adults to seek a long-term partner and settle down. The college campus is the perfect setting for meeting potential partners and trying out new relationships. The goal is love and connection, either through intimate platonic relationships or romantic relationships. At this point in their lives, students are breaking free from parental supervision and parental rules and they may engage in sexual encounters that would never have occurred while they lived in their parents' homes as well as develop relationships with individuals of whom their parents would never approve. The freedom that college and young adulthood allow can create new distractions and potential crises for college students.

Safety concerns can arise during this stage specifically related to reproductive health and safety. Statistics indicate that 20% of women will be sexually assaulted on their college campuses (Krebs, Lindquist, Warner, Fisher, & Martin, 2007). Of these victims, about 90% know the person who committed the assault (Fisher, Cullen, & Turner, 2000), but only about 10% of all victims even report the crime (Fisher et al., 2000). Sexual assault prevention should be an essential goal for campus personnel and programming that addresses a variety of relevant topics from promoting healthy relationship behaviors to teaching self-defense tactics to use when threatened by a potential assault, physical or sexual. Other risks that may be triggered by the desire for intimacy may include sexual coercion or poor decision making in terms of sexual activities as well as unplanned pregnancies or sexually transmitted diseases.

During this stage of development, fear of not finding "the one," or fear of being the "40-year-old virgin," or the fear of rejection can create very real pressure to join organizations, try to meet potential sexual partners, and to appear "normal," however an individual self-defines this. Although the college campus provides the perfect setting to "try out" new relationships, there are potential risks involved that can be addressed and, hopefully, minimized by effective programming and awareness campaigns. It is also important to note that individuals who seem to be perennial loners or who spend all of their time alone in their residence hall or never seem to connect with classmates may need to be reached out to and connected with potential supportive offices, groups, or mentors. Although not every loner is likely to be suffering from significant psychological distress, the absence of connection can have devastating consequences in a variety of ways.

Nontraditional-Aged Students

Students aged 40 years and older have consistently comprised about one tenth of the student population enrolled in higher education over the past 6 or 7 years (U.S. Department of Education, 2014). When these older students arrive on campus, they may be at a strikingly different place in their lives than younger students. Their approach to their coursework, their priorities, and their overall expectations of their classes and their peers may be markedly different, as well.

Generativity Versus Stagnation: Care

The virtue that drives most midlife adults is care for others and for future generations. Their return to campus may be driven by the desire to enhance their own abilities to provide guidance to others and invest in the future. An increasing number of programs designed to meet the needs of adults are showing up across the country (Bergman, 2016). Although many of these programs are geared to help individuals move up the career ladder or stay current in their fields, the experience of returning to campus can be daunting to adults who are unfamiliar with contemporary campus settings. However, this population may also enthusiastically embrace the opportunity to engage with others in group projects or classroom discussions, which are in strong alignment with their expected psychosocial developmental stage. Student affairs professionals may want to address specific technology learning sessions or an orientation programming series for nontraditional students to ensure that they do not feel overwhelmed by the evolving campus learning environment. Developmentally, this group is balancing generativity, or giving back, against stagnation; thus, ensuring that the members feel prepared to be active learners is a key priority.

Integrity Versus Despair: Wisdom

During the older adult years, some individuals may feel that it is finally time for them to either return to college or to pursue higher education for the first time. Providing support services for older returning students, which parallel, in some ways, those that are provided to first-year students, can help them feel prepared for their coursework. Many campuses now offer specific programming for community members who are in this age group through continuing education or lifelong learning programming. The focus of these offerings may include a variety of subjects that reflect the expertise of campus faculty who enjoy the opportunity to share their knowledge with others. Some campus programs are "Lunch and Learn" events where community members bring their lunch or have lunch provided and listen to a faculty member or other expert give a mini-lesson during the lunch hour.

Research gives evidence of what most of us already believe—older adults are, indeed, vessels of significant wisdom when compared with traditional-aged students (Ardelt, 2010). Providing this group with opportunities to share its knowledge through community service pairings with traditional-aged students can be beneficial for both generations. Ensuring that older students feel welcome at campus events and campus activities can provide opportunities for these individuals to feel relevant and valued. As college campuses seek to grow their offerings and their appeal to diverse demographic groups, making space for older adult students can meet both institutional goals and objectives and personal needs of the students.

CONCLUSION

Erikson's model (1968) provides a clear and progressive path for emotional and social development. Each stage is predicated on the assumption that the prior stage has been successfully completed and there are clear hallmarks in behavior that are used as guides for assessing an individual's progress. Using Erikson's construct of crises and virtues, the development of students on campus can be framed within this model and attention provided to the psychosocial crisis of interest and the virtue that is in need of development. Following is a wrap-up of the case of Nehal as well as two additional cases for reflection.

CASE VIGNETTE WRAP-UP: NEHAL

As Mallory listened to Nehal describe her confusion and frustration, he used an Eriksonian lens to conceptualize her concerns. Mallory first normalized Nehal's feelings and confusion; he described to her that it was developmentally appropriate to feel torn between one stage of life and the next. Knowing that she was "normal" provided Nehal with significant relief and allowed her to further explore the concerns she was experiencing. Mallory described the psychosocial developments that were natural for an older adolescent and helped Nehal to reframe her perspective on her normal desire for growing up and creating her own identity beyond her family. Recognizing that this was to be expected in American culture helped her to understand that striving for independence was not the same as rejecting her family. The counselor and Nehal were able to help Nehal focus on ways in which she could change the circumstances that she felt were making her uncomfortable. She was able to focus on what she termed "culture clashes" in her counseling sessions and was able to gather the courage she needed to begin to visualize how she wanted the next few years to unfold. Mallory provided a safe environment that gave Nehal permission to explore potentially anxiety-producing topics in a calm and secure setting. Nehal's current goal was to begin working toward independence and possibly moving into an apartment near campus with her friend, Marta.

CASE VIGNETTE 1 FOR READER REFLECTION: MARIBEL

Maribel, an 18-year-old freshman, attended a midsize high school and was class valedictorian. Although exceptionally intelligent, Maribel had always felt that she somehow "didn't fit in" with her peers. Her interests seemed just different enough to set her apart from others. Her parents had enrolled her in after-school activities, yet Maribel had never developed the close friendships common to teenagers during high school. Her best friend is actually an adult neighbor who is a nurse-practitioner. Maribel is planning a career in medical research and enjoyed their engaging conversations about science. Her parents hoped that college would provide peers who shared Maribel's passion for learning and with whom she could forge friendships.

Maribel's grades and family resources allowed her to attend a selective private university a thousand miles from home. Although Maribel and her family were hopeful that this would be an optimal environment for academic and social opportunities, Maribel felt lost and alone several weeks into her first semester. The community advisor (CA) in her residence hall noticed Maribel's tendency to hang on the periphery of residence hall socials and she decided to check in with Maribel one-on-one in her room. Maribel confessed that she knew that she was being more reserved than she usually had been even in high school. Maribel shared that she felt reluctant to accept invitations from others, for fear of being seen as "boring" or "immature," as she described her fears to her CA. She also noted that she would rather Skype with her parents or her friend in her hometown than risk failing to make new friends on campus.

- *What Eriksonian crisis is Maribel likely facing?*
- *What virtue(s) might she need to develop?*
- *What might the CA do to assist Maribel?*
- *What are some campus resources that might be engaged?*

CASE VIGNETTE 2 FOR READER REFLECTION: MITCH

Mitch, a 22-year-old sophomore, has a history of dropping courses at the last minute and was still classified as a sophomore even though he had been on campus for seven semesters. He felt totally behind and doubted that there was any way that he would ever make it to the finish line and graduation. Mitch lived on his student loans and had no strong support system anywhere in his life. His mother had died of a drug overdose when he was only 2 months old and he had been taken in by his paternal grandparents. Unfortunately, both his grandparents suffered from health problems and were not as responsive to their grandson or as involved with his development as they would have liked to have been. Thus, Mitch learned early that the only person he could potentially trust to meet his needs was himself. Yet, now that he was in college, he didn't even trust himself to get him through to a college degree. Mitch's ability to succeed was being hindered by his lack of trust in himself and those who might help him cope with difficult classes or other challenging circumstances. Mitch knew that he needed to develop greater self-confidence, social connections, and study skills. He just wasn't sure where to turn.

- *What Eriksonian crisis/crises is Mitch likely facing?*
- *What virtue(s) might he benefit from developing?*

(continued)

(continued)
- *What are some activities that might help Mitch reach his goals of self-confidence and connection?*
- *What resources, programming, or individuals would best help Mitch?*

REFERENCES

Ardelt, M. (2010). Are older adults wiser than college students? A comparison of two age cohorts. *Journal of Adult Development, 17*, 193–207.

Arnett, J. J. (2000). Emerging adulthood: A theory of development from the late teens through the twenties. *American Psychologist, 55*, 469–480.

Bandura, A. (1977). Self-efficacy: Toward a unifying theory of behavioral change. *Psychological Review, 84*, 191–215.

Bennett, J. L., & Douglass, K. E. (2013). Growing pains: An Eriksonian view of the arc of presenting concerns in an LGBT community mental health center. *Clinical Social Work Journal, 41*, 277–287.

Bergman, M. (2016). From stopout to scholar: Pathways to graduation through adult degree completion programs. *International Journal of Information Communication Technologies and Human Development, 8*, 1–12.

Bingham, C. R., Shope, J. T., Zakrajsek, J., & Raghunathan, T. E. (2008). Problem driving behavior and psychosocial maturation in young adulthood. *Accident Analysis & Prevention, 40*, 1758–1764.

Cohen, J. (2003). Parasocial breakups: Measuring individual differences in responses to the dissolution of parasocial relationships. *Mass Communication & Society, 6*, 191–202.

Erikson, E. (1968). *Identity: Youth and crisis*. New York, NY: W. W. Norton.

Fisher, B. S., Cullen, F. T., & Turner, M. G. (2000). *The sexual victimization of college women*. Washington, DC: U.S. Department of Justice.

Hughes, A., Galbraith, D., & White, D. (2011). Perceived competence: A common core for self-efficacy and self-concept? *Journal of Personality Assessment, 93*, 278–289.

Krebs, C. P., Lindquist, C. H., Warner, T. D., Fisher, B. S., & Martin, S. L. (2007). *The Campus Sexual Assault (CSA) Study*. Prepared for National Institute of Justice, Washington, DC. Retrieved from https://www.ncjrs.gov/pdffiles1/nij/grants/221153.pdf

Lee, P. (2011). The curious life of *in loco parentis* in American universities. *Higher Education in Review, 8*, 65–90.

Lois, D., & Becker, O. A. (2014). Is fertility contagious? Using panel data to disentangle mechanisms of social network influences on fertility decisions. *Advances in Life Course Research, 21*, 123–134.

Maguire, J., & Austin, M. (2015, October). Millennials are creating unsafe conditions on the U.S. roads—But not in the way you might think. Standard & Poor's Financial Services, LLC. Retrieved from https://www.globalcreditportal.com/ratingsdirect/renderArticle.do?articleId=1466580&SctArtId=347989&from=CM&nsl_code=LIME&sourceObjectId=9373405&sourceRevId=1&fee_ind=N&exp_date=20251018-18:07:48

Panfile, T. M., Laible, D. J., & Eye, J. L. (2012). Conflict frequency within mother-child dyads across contexts: Links with attachment and security. *Early Childhood Research Quarterly, 27*, 78–106.

Steinberg, L. (2008). A social neuroscience perspective on adolescent risk-taking. *Developmental Review, 28*, 78–106.

Steinberg, L. (2010). A behavioral scientist looks at the science of adolescent brain development. *Brain and Cognition, 72*, 160–164.

U.S. Bureau of the Census. (2015). *Decennial censuses, 1890 to 1940, and current population survey, annual social and economic supplements, 1947 to 2015*. Washington, DC: Author.

U.S. Department of Education, National Center for Education Statistics. (2014, November). *Integrated Postsecondary Education Data System (IPEDS), Spring 2010, 2012, and 2014, Enrollment component.* Washington, DC: Author.

CHAPTER 5

PERRY'S THEORY OF MORAL DEVELOPMENT

Ian S. Turnage-Butterbaugh, Waleed Sami, and Ricardo Phipps

CASE VIGNETTE: FATIMA

Fatima Salahuddin is a 21-year-old double major in chemistry and international relations at a large midwestern American university. She was referred to student affairs by one of her professors due to a noticeable sense of depression and confusion. Fatima is a practicing Muslim woman who dons the headscarf, or hijab, as a symbol of piety in her religion, much like Christians who wear a cross around their neck. She says that she was raised in a happy family that instilled her with a strong religious background and upstanding morals. She was a scholarship student and head of several clubs in her high school, on her path to be a high-achieving student and community leader. Her parents are immigrants from Morocco and would like her to pursue a career in engineering or medical sciences, although her main interest lies in the liberal arts and policy making.

    Fatima describes that over the course of her college experience, she has dealt with an increasing sense of emptiness, and feels tempted to take off her hijab because she does not feel worthy of it anymore. She says that when she got to college, she spent a lot of time socializing with crowds that did not reflect her upbringing. She began to drink and party and her grades began to decline; however, she kept these issues hidden from her parents, who thought her academic difficulties were the result of stress and fatigue. Fatima explains that she does not think her parents can understand some of the struggles she has to face in college. Recently, she was at a party and an aggressive guy tried to pull her hijab off her head and yelled racial slurs at her. Fatima claims that this is an experience she has grown up with, but after discussing the event with friends at the university and reflecting on her college experience, she is beginning to struggle with the cultural traditions of her upbringing and maintaining her moral convictions. She feels obliged to her family and Muslim culture, but increasingly desires independence and the freedom to choose and express her own identity, values, and morals.

Attention to college student development has increased over the last two decades (Renn, Brazelton, & Holmes, 2014); however, the foundational research on intellectual and ethical development during the transitional college years stems from the 1950s and early 1960s when William G. Perry, Jr., explored how developmental shifts occur on the path from adolescence into adulthood (Love & Guthrie, 1999; W. G. Perry, 1968). Intrigued by qualitatively different styles of thinking among his students, Perry sought to better understand the developmental shifts that occur when confronted with a diverse, pluralistic college culture. Perry and his associates adopted an interactionist position (Zhang, 1999), in which development occurs in concordance with a changing social and cultural context. As such, they endeavored to map a path of development that transcended one's idiosyncratic experiences and reflected, on the other hand, his or her knowledge, values, and perceptions of the world. Perry presupposed that these forms of development, or the underlying structures that influence how one perceives and cares about his or her world, would endure the test of time and apply more generally across individuals and generations of individuals.

Although Perry and associates' "initial intention was purely descriptive, and not even systematically so" (W. G. Perry, 1968, p. 6), their research resulted in a developmental scheme involving a pervasive, iterative, and sequential process of self-examination, reexamination, ascription of responsibility, and personal commitment. Succinctly put, this process is one of personal affirmation, of commitment to maturation. Healthy development, Perry noted, however, could be thwarted by conditions of delay, deflection, and regression. At its best, those confronted with the novel diversity of experiences often encountered on the path to adulthood progressed through variegated levels of accommodation, assimilation, and commitment to new frames of reference; at its worst, development stagnated or reversed as individuals succumb to anxiety with or alienate themselves from the "course of maturation presumed in the scheme" (W. G. Perry, 1968, p. 9).

Perry's theory of development has had a significant impact on the field of psychology and is essential to understanding the cognitive development of college students. Despite having been scrutinized by modern researchers (Baxter Magolda, 1992; Belenky, Clinchy, Goldberger, & Tarule, 1986; King & Kitchener, 1994), Love and Guthrie (1999) refer to Perry's theory as the impetus from which other theories of cognitive development were generated, and affirm the salience it still has for educators and practitioners today. This chapter provides an overview of Perry's theory and describes the ways in which it still applies to college students on a diverse, pluralistic college campus.

HISTORY AND DEVELOPMENT OF THE THEORY

The 1950s and 1960s marked a fundamental shift in developmental psychology. Logical positivism, or behaviorism, dominated the field of psychology, which discounted the value of knowledge in cognitive processes (Kohlberg, 1971). Several psychologists, discouraged by the obscurities of behaviorism and in an attempt to remove the "blinders psychologists have worn [that] have hidden from them the fact that the concept of morality is itself a philosophical (ethical) rather than a behavior concept" (Kohlberg, 1971, p. 152), worked to integrate psychology and philosophy in their newfound interest in epistemological development (Hofer & Pintrich, 1997). As Peters (1963) asserted, psychological theories pertaining to ethics are inadequate if their philosophical implications are not identified and acknowledged. Similarly, Kohlberg suggested that an adequate psychological theory as to why an individual moves from one stage to the next and a philosophical explanation of why moving to a higher stage is more adaptive than remaining at a lower stage are equivalent theories extended in qualitatively different directions. The reorientation of psychology, and in particular developmental research, to include philosophical concepts, therefore, was central to the foundational theories of intellectual and moral development described by Piaget (1950/1952), W. G. Perry (1968), Kohlberg (1971), Gilligan (1982), and Welfel and Davidson (1986), among others.

The 1950s also marked an educational revolution in which liberal arts education utilized Socratic principles to go "beyond simple diversity into the disciplines of relativity of thought through which specific instances of diversity can be productively exploited" (W. G. Perry, 1968, p. 35). Perry's interest in epistemological beliefs at the intersection of psychology and philosophy was in response to noticeable differences in the ways in which students at Harvard University and Radcliffe University responded to the relativism they encountered in the pluralistic university setting. In the years following World War II and preceding the Civil Rights Movement, increasing numbers of students were entering college with a relativistic cultural understanding and awareness that liberated them to fully explore diverse ways of thinking and making sense of the world (W. G. Perry, 1968). In contrast, however, many students held rigid black-and-white thinking and one-dimensional belief systems, which prevented them from successfully resolving inner conflicts when faced with novel frames of reference. During a time of "activism, protest reform, involvement, and confrontation—both peaceful and violent" (W. G. Perry, 1968, p. ix), the exploration of these discrepancies in epistemological beliefs seemed relevant to the social milieu of the mid-1900s and vital to understanding students' paths of development during this time.

OVERVIEW AND DESCRIPTION OF THE THEORY

The earliest and best known framework for conceptualizing undergraduate student development was proposed by William G. Perry in the 1960s (Brand, 1988). During that time, he conducted a longitudinal study consisting of semi-structured interviews with male undergraduate students at Harvard University and Radcliffe University in order to gain an initial understanding of students' educational experiences. After the initial analyses of data collected from the first sample, however, Perry and his associates began to recognize the emergence of a developmental sequence that outlined the ways in which students made sense of an increasingly complex world. The emerging sequence extended the purpose of the study and necessitated additional interviews, which were conducted systematically and experimentally at the end of each academic year in an effort to increase the generalizability of the scheme, as if it were presented from the perspective of a "normative student" (W. G. Perry, 1968, p. 29). From a total of 464 interviews, the emergent pattern informed Perry's developmental scheme of moral development, which was validated through a series of judges' ratings that met acceptable estimates of reliability.

OVERVIEW OF PERRY'S DEVELOPMENT SCHEMA

According to Perry's theory, moral development involves progressing through nine phases, or positions, each corresponding to new ways of viewing the world, in light of increasingly complex or diverse experiences and knowledge. Development progresses along a continuum beginning with Position 1 (Basic Duality) at one extreme, the point at which individuals ascribe rightness and wrongness to some universal authority and blindly accept this authority-oriented right–wrong thinking (Felder & Brent, 2004; W. G. Perry, 1968). At the other extreme, development ends with Position 9 (Developing Commitments), indicated by individuals' ability to go beyond simply challenging authority to committing to values in the face of diversity and uncertainty and, in doing so, achieving ultimate self-expression (de l'Etoile, 2008; W. G. Perry, 1968). Interestingly, the positions are static, with development occurring not in the positions themselves, but during the transitions between them. W. G. Perry speculated, "perhaps development is all transition and 'stages only resting points along the way'" (1981, p. 78). Knefelkamp (1999) noted that Perry "emphasized our need to understand students in motion and not imprison them in stages" (p. xii).

The nine stages identified by Perry can be grouped into four discrete categories or levels of development:

1. **Dualism**, including Positions 1 and 2
2. **Multiplicity**, including Positions 3 and 4
3. **Contextual relativism**, including Positions 5 and beyond
4. **Commitment in relativism**, including Positions 6 through 9

Successfully progressing through Perry's developmental scheme requires the "restructuring of the way individuals interpret their perceptions of the world, allowing for an ever increasing ability to respond to changes or variations in the environment" (B. Perry et al., 1986). As such, each level of development represents an intrinsic change in the meaning-making process.

Dualism. Dualism, in its basic form, which marks the original position in Perry's scheme, is described as a worldview characterized by antithetical construals of truth and morality differentiated between one's in-group and out-group (W. G. Perry, 1968). Individuals making sense of the world from a dualistic position obey and adhere to an unexamined and taken-for-granted set of assumptions, beliefs, and values that prevent objectivity entirely and preserve the "homogeneity of family and community" (p. 72). A right, unquestionable answer exists for everything, and alternatives are unfathomable and intolerable.

Multiplicity. The waning of dualism and the transition to multiplicity begins when one is confronted with pluralism, diversity, ambiguity, and contingency. The result is cognitive dissonance (Festinger, 1957) as a "disequilibrium is introduced into the meaning-making process" (Evans et al., 2010, p. 86). W. G. Perry (1968) describes this transition as one of revolt as the individual acknowledges "the diversity of opinion in the larger world and [uses] it as a weapon against the orthodoxy from which he struggled to emerge" (p. 72). The taken-for-granted and unexamined "old morality" (W. G. Perry, 1968, p. 90) is questioned and uncertainty and frustration become unavoidable, as one begins to honor diversity without fully understanding what constitutes the right answers (Evans et al., 2010). All opinions seem relevant and valid, but evaluation and judgment prevail, without resolve. In essence, multiplicity manifests itself as a dual dualism in that right and wrong still exist, but they exist in an expanding universe consisting of a multiplicity of points of view. During multiplicity, the individual transitions from a holder of meaning to a maker of meaning, as meta-thought appears in the foreground, against the background of previously held assumptions and ways of thinking (W. G. Perry, 1981).

Contextual Relativism. Relativism is marked by a time of intellectual independence, based on a contextually defined thought. Relativistic thinkers recognize that problems can be approached from a variety of perspectives; yet, not all opinions are viewed as equally valid. Absolute answers remain unknown; however, they are unrequired because authoritative opinions are ignorant, to a certain extent (W. G. Perry, 1968). A developmental objective becomes finding one's own opinion, which is both painful and liberating. Apprehension builds as one understands that parsimonious answers often are illegitimate due to the contextual nature of knowledge and ideas. At the same time, however, accepting responsibility for one's personal truth can be exciting and freeing. Additionally, as Perry proffers, this new way of thinking can result in a greater sense of community among peers who share similar ideas and views of the world.

Relativism is differentiated from multiplicity in another important way. While multiplicity requires only assimilation of new information into the fundamental dualistic view one started with, relativism involves the addition of accommodation, in which individuals restructure their views of the world. That is, the dualistic framework from which individuals began is no longer sufficient nor adequate to assimilate the broadening generalizations of relativism, pluralism, and diversity (W. G. Perry, 1968). Relativism expands to all knowledge and all ways of thinking, requiring accommodation to previously held assumptions and knowledge. Therefore, absolutes and right–wrong thinking become anomalies in one's newly adopted relativistic context, which underscores the pervasiveness of relativism within this domain.

Commitment in Relativism. Commitment in relativism is differentiated from contextual relativism in that it involves a shift away from increasing cognitive complexity to identity development in an uncertain pluralistic environment (King, 1978; W. G. Perry, 1968). W. G. Perry (1981) described the process of commitment as one in which an individual "finds at last the elusive sense of 'identity' one has searched for elsewhere" (p. 97). In other words, individuals go beyond simply challenging authority to committing to values in the face of diversity and uncertainty and, in doing so, achieving ultimate self-expression (de l'Etoile, 2008; W. G. Perry, 1968).

DEFLECTIONS FROM GROWTH AND DEVELOPMENT

On the surface, Perry's developmental scheme offers a simplistically sequential, linear line of development, in which individuals progress from one position to the next in a predictable fashion. The reality, however, is that development rarely occurs without delay, deflection, or regression. Perry and his colleagues recognized, and even observed, this nonlinear pattern of development in their original research and integrated alternative paths of development, or a lack thereof, into their scheme. Depending on where an individual is in the main line of development, he or she can veer off the track of optimal development in one of three ways:

1. **Temporizing**—halting development at any position for a year or more due to the daunting task of accepting responsibility in additional personal growth.
2. **Retreat**—developmental regression to previously achieved positions due to the ambiguities presented by relativism.
3. **Escape**—abandoning responsibility entirely and avoiding commitment by exploiting the ambiguity offered in multiplicity and relativism.

APPLICATION OF THE THEORY WITHIN STUDENT AFFAIRS

Perry's theory of development is pervasive in the higher education literature (Gallagher, 1998; Lavis, Williams, & Thien, 2008; Marra, Palmer, & Litzinger, 2000). In this section, we discuss how Perry's theory continues to apply to the diversified college student population common in modern American institutions of higher education (Love & Guthrie, 1999). In particular, we apply the theory to Fatima's experience outlined in the aforementioned Case Vignette. Although Fatima appears to view the world and make meaning from Position 6 in Perry's scheme of development, an understanding of the experiential and developmental contexts that led to her current level of growth and maturation is important to determine how to work with Fatima currently and in the future. Table 5.1 outlines the ways in which Perry's scheme applies to Fatima, the contextual and pluralistic challenges faced at each position, and future development, should Fatima continue to courageously accept responsibility for her moral development and overcome the ambiguities of relativism. This section describes utilizing Perry's scheme as a lens through which to view Fatima's development, anticipate deflections from growth, and identify strategies and campus and community resources to foster inclusivity, personal exploration, and continued development.

TABLE 5.1 Applying Perry's Scheme of Moral Development to Case Vignette: Fatima

DUALISM	
Position 1	*Position 2*
Fatima, like many people who grow up, is indebted to the value and moral systems of her family. She believed that wearing the headscarf was a must, in order to express her Islamic identity, one taught to her by her parents, and clergy who agree with that interpretation. When she was young, she looked up to her parents, and saw them as moral exemplars and teachers on how to live a good life. Furthermore, she was convinced that this was the only way to express her identity, and religiosity.	When confronted by other Muslims who did not practice like she did, when she got into high school, she often dismissed them as not understanding the religion deeply enough. Furthermore, she was judgmental and viewed them as lax in this regard. She felt they were misguided, and only hung out with Muslim friends who practiced the same type of religiosity as her.
MULTIPLICITY	
Position 3	*Position 4*
Naturally, growing up will challenge anyone's values. Fatima knows that her parents struggle generationally and culturally, to understand her life as she lives it. Sometimes, they provide confusing answers to her questions, and sometimes, no answers at all. For example, is she allowed to ask the teacher for 5 minutes during the afternoon to pray?	Fatima has increasingly been exposed to different ideas, values, and beliefs. As a result, she now knows that there are many ways to express one's Muslim identity and religiosity, and many different lifestyles one can live as a Muslim, let alone a human being. This causes her to clash a bit with her parents, who feel she is changing. Fatima now wonders which is the correct way to live as a human being.
RELATIVISM	
Position 5	*Position 6*
Now that Fatima has entered college, and has lived long enough to have a wide variety of friends from all sorts of backgrounds, she now feels that every person and every community have their own way of living, which they view as correct. Furthermore, she believes that they are all correct, when applied to each person's and community's own unique history. Hadji Murád (as cited in Tolstoy, 1911/2003) provides an old proverb that reflects Fatima's development in Position 5: "The dog gave meat to the ass and the ass gave hay to the dog, and both went hungry ... its own customs seemed good to each nation" (p. 83).	This is the point Fatima is at in our vignette. Fatima understands that she must have a set of values to call her own, and her own way of looking at the world. Although she realizes this is just one of the many paths available to her, she feels she must make a commitment to personal truths, valuable relationships, worthwhile activities, and unique values, despite the ambiguity of relativism.

(continued)

TABLE 5.1 Applying Perry's Scheme of Moral Development to Case Vignette: Fatima *(continued)*

COMMITMENT TO RELATIVISM		
Position 7	*Position 8*	*Position 9*
Quite simply, Fatima decides to either uphold the Muslim identity she was raised with or take the first step in adopting a new set of values.	Fatima now realizes that she must take a nuanced version of her understanding of religiosity and carry that with her in all interactions, including those with her parents who raised her with a certain understanding as well as with those who are ignorant of her beliefs, and seek to put her in a preconceived box.	Fatima now realizes that her understanding of her identity, morals, and religion will be complicated and ongoing. It is a lifelong process from which she must learn and adjust too. She will constantly examine her own beliefs and renegotiate understanding the way she was raised with the way she sees the world.

Source: Adapted from W. G. Perry (1968).

Exploring Fatima's Positioning Within Perry's Scheme

As you continue to work with Fatima, she describes increasingly acute anxiety stemming from the novel frames of reference she has been faced with since leaving home and attending the university. No longer are the values and morals she wholeheartedly accepted as a child and young adolescent congruent with her new way of making sense of herself and the world. Fatima recognizes that in order to affirm her own worldview and morals, she must decide to what degree she will continue with the values of her past and to what degree she will break with them (W. G. Perry, 1968). At the same time, however, Fatima recognizes that reason, in and of itself, cannot justify her newfound views of the world, which have created doubt, anxiety, and contention.

Fatima feels hopeless, and feels no one can understand her. She is oscillating between the comfort of old values and the ambiguity of the new. She has begun withdrawing emotionally, has grown somewhat cynical, and is very hesitant to make a decision about her identity. You explore this with her, and Fatima mentions that one of her best friends, who is also a young Muslim woman, recently dropped out of the university and moved back in with her parents due to insurmountable confusion about what to do with her life and fear of alienating herself from her family if she deviated from their values and vision for her future. Similarly, Fatima fears breaking with the tradition of her upbringing, despite the desire to freely express her adapting identity and moral resolve. Fatima's development and optimism about the future begins to stagnate, as she recognizes that committing to her own unique values would require her to detach from her cultural upbringing and family of origin.

Potential for Deflections From Development

Using Perry's scheme as a vantage point from which Fatima's plight could be viewed, you recognize that she is beginning to deflect from the main line of development. Currently, Fatima is temporizing, evident by her confusion about how to proceed, unwillingness to accept responsibility for her continued growth, and lack of fortitude in overcoming the ambiguities and anxieties of relativism. Her development is suspended, and she mentions that she just wishes that something would happen to point her in the right direction. At the same time, you realize the potential for a more dramatic deflection from development. It seems reasonable to anticipate Fatima to follow in footsteps similar to those of her friend who dropped out of college, in an attempt to escape her responsibility in expressing her newfound identity, her responsibility in taking a stand, and the painful consequences of doing so.

IMPLICATIONS FOR STUDENT AFFAIRS PROFESSIONALS

Several researchers have proposed guides and models for implementing Perry's theory, which provides guides for student affairs professionals and educators working with students like Fatima. For example, Knefelkamp (1999) identified a developmental instruction model that aids in operationalizing Perry's model by introducing four challenge and support variables based on student characteristics.

1. **Structure**—Structure exists along a continuum from a low degree of structure to a high degree of structure. Students in the earlier positions of Perry's framework will benefit from more structure and view it as supportive, whereas students who have reached more advanced positions of development require more autonomy.
2. **Diversity**—A diversity of alternative perspectives, belief systems, and values is encouraged. When incorporating diversity into learning activities, quantity and complexity should be considered. Diversity has applications for instructional strategies as well as learning experiences outside of the classroom.
3. **Experiential Learning**—Experiential learning exists on a continuum ranging from vicarious learning to direct learning. In considering Fatima's needs, and those of students like her, student affairs professionals should endeavor to include role-plays and facilitate self-reflection in learning activities. Evans et al. (2010) suggest that students in earlier positions of Perry's model are most in need of this type of support.
4. **Personalism**—Creating a safe environment that encourages risk taking is highly encouraged and valuable. Personalism involves creating enthusiasm for, a personal investment in, and direct feedback about new material. Again, this type of support is particularly important for students in early developmental positions.

As the name suggests, Knefelkamp's model can be used for instructional design; however, it also applies to other instructional settings across campus.

Lochrie (1989) summarized literature identifying additional sources of support for students progressing through Perry's developmental positions. Most notably, he pointed out that development through the positions is often painful and threatening. W. G. Perry (1981) acknowledged the need to "allow for grief"

(p. 108) in the process of development. Educators and student affairs professionals should assume the role of a sympathetic enabler, or adopt imaginative empathy for their students. By understanding the needs of our students; recognizing the pain associated with their development; and providing them with the support, time, and space to experience and overcome their grief, we can enable them to continue to develop.

Implications for Practice

A widely accepted point of view is that the college experience should have a role in the moral development of students (Mayhew, Seifert, & Pascarella, 2012). Various organizations and other entities have articulated statements that reflect this belief. The Association of American Colleges and Universities (AACU) published five Core Commitments about how institutions of higher learning can support the development of personal and social responsibility on college campuses. Of those five Core Commitments, the third reads, "Contributing to a larger community: recognizing and acting on one's responsibility to the educational community and the wider society, locally, nationally, and globally" (McTighe Musil, 2011, Core Commitments: A Clarion Call section, para. 3). Higher education is the setting from which students are pushed into ever-expanding circles of influence and transformation of the world around them.

Various peer-reviewed journals have emerged that treat the topic of moral development in college students. The *Journal of College and Character* was first published in 2000 by the National Association of Student Personnel Administrators with a focus on how colleges and universities can support moral and civic learning of students. The *Journal of Moral Education*, published by the Association for Moral Education, is another forum for the exchange of ideas about moral education and development, including but extending beyond higher education. Student affairs personnel can stay abreast of current trends and thoughts in the area of moral development of students by accessing these and similar resources.

Student affairs personnel have a unique opportunity to create intentional spaces for students to actively work on their own moral development across disciplines and academic majors. Mayhew, Vanderlinden, and Kim (2010) cite campus-wide programs, such as leadership summits, workshops in conflict mediation, and community volunteering projects, as key ways to engender moral consciousness in students. Leadership summits that involve civic leaders from the community can introduce students to skills in community organizing and social justice that they may not otherwise encounter and provide them with practical opportunities to utilize the skills in the community. Conflict mediation equips students with the skills to diffuse tension around different points of view and to rechannel the tension to positive directions, eliciting exchange of differing ideas and common ground building. Volunteerism creates a setting for students to better understand needs and dynamics that are perpetuated by systematic injustice and to think creatively about alternative systems to mitigate inequalities (Pascarella & Terenzini, 2005).

Mayhew et al. (2010) assert that opportunities for students to learn from their peers and to support each other in making sense of learning moments in terms of justice and fairness are critical. Peer effects are very powerful for student learning and moral development (Pascarella & Terenzini, 2005), and student affairs offices have a unique position in campus life to be able to foster such interaction. Healthy debate among students fosters greater understanding of their own points of view and provides challenges that broaden perspectives. Students also find strength and support in numbers in terms of mobilization efforts for social justice projects. Student affairs personnel can provide the resources and encouragement students need to mobilize and initiate action.

Finally, because moral development for college students places value on increasing the circle of influence and transformation for students, college personnel cannot seek to stimulate this type of growth in a vacuum. Other community stakeholders, such as churches and other places of worship, faith-based organizations, and civic groups should be invited into this process. The intense growth that can take place during the college years, including concerning spiritual and religious connections, can be liberating for some students and disconcerting for others, particularly depending on where they are positioned on Perry's Scheme (Hindman, 2002). Student affairs is the appropriate division of campus administration to make possible connections between faith-based groups or civic organizations if students desire those interactions. Organizations, such as a Muslim Student Association or Campus Crusaders for Christ, may form or continue on campus through the efforts of students, the support of campus leadership, as well as through the sponsorship of community institutions. Philanthropic and social service–oriented organizations, like the United Way, have divisions for college students, such as Student United Way, where students can find a platform for engaging in community development and transformation projects. Again, these connections can be stimulated by student affairs personnel, simply by exposing students to the work and mission of such groups.

In their examination of the religious needs of college students, Paragament et al. (1984) identified the importance of a feeling of belonging and sense of community. A supportive group is essential to combat the isolating effects often inherent in personal development and the college campus. Therefore, instructional methods and experiential activities should be designed to include opportunities of interpersonal involvement with others who provide a balance of support and challenge. Sometimes the university setting can seem too large and impersonal to provide these needs, so seeking opportunities to connect with others in the community may be particularly beneficial.

CASE VIGNETTE WRAP-UP: FATIMA

You have been working with Fatima for a few months and have applied research related to Muslim identity and Perry's developmental scheme as a guide for working with her. Additionally, you are engaged in a process of imaginative empathy, drawing on your own experience of identity development and consulting with others to better understand the unique struggle Fatima is experiencing. You recognized Fatima's deflection from continued growth

(continued)

(continued)

and identified that her needs were a sense of community and a supportive group with which she can explore her identity development. At the same time, she needed to feel included in the social milieu on campus and afforded safe places to continue to express her Muslim identity.

Acting as an advocate and an enabler, you connected Fatima with several groups, created opportunities for interpersonal interactions with meaningful others, and worked with administration to promote inclusivity. In particular, the Muslim Student Association on campus provided the sense of community she was looking for and connected her with others struggling with the same issues of identity development. You helped Fatima find an off-campus community that engages in service activities, which allows them to engage in the religious, charity, and cultural facets of her Muslim identity. The university also has several interfaith learning campaigns, which have allowed Fatima to further explore her identity while experiencing other religious and cultural traditions. Finally, you connected Fatima with the university counseling center, where she is working to further explore her identity along with the emotional pain she is experiencing, which affects other domains of functioning. Fatima now acknowledges that she has been temporizing, but due to the additional support she has received, she is interested in moving to the next level, where she will have to learn to incorporate different viewpoints and ideas into her worldview. She appears more optimistic now about her future, and realizes that there is no shame in her struggles, as it is very developmentally appropriate for individuals her age. Fatima is pleased with the change she is starting to see in her personal life, and reports feeling much more enthusiastic about her education and social experience at the university.

As a helping professional on a college campus, how would you encourage Fatima and enable her to continue along Perry's moral development scale? You now know that Fatima must make a commitment in relativism in order to progress to positions 7 through 9. What interventions would you use, while being culturally sensitive and empathic? What personal or external resources do you have that would help you develop imaginative empathy? From a student affairs perspective, what resources can you link her to? Which of the challenge and support variables in Knefelkamp's (1999) model seem most important for Fatima? What sources of support can you identify on your campus or in your community that would provide Fatima with those variables and help ensure she is enabled to take the next steps toward continued development?

CASE VIGNETTE 1 FOR READER REFLECTION: TINA

Tina is an Asian female from a small, single-parent family in New England. She has been the primary caretaker of her elderly grandmother as well as a "second mother" to her younger teenaged sisters. Now that she is on campus and living independently, she is dealing with a great deal of guilt about leaving her family to struggle without her while she is struggling with finding her identity in the wider world. She is recruited as a leader in the campus Asian Student organization, which not only gives her the opportunity to

(continued)

(continued)

feel less out-of-place on the campus, but also makes her wonder if separating herself from other students based on her ethnic identity is the best path for her at this stage in her life.

- *If Tina was one of the student advisees assigned to you, and she revealed her feelings of conflicted loyalty and identity, how would you encourage exploration of the issues?*

CASE VIGNETTE 2 FOR READER REFLECTION: BRENDAN

Brendan is a White man from a large, southern city, where he was raised by a very conservative Christian family. He is in his first year at a small liberal arts college in New England and has settled in well—he is fitting in socially, maintaining decent grades, engaging in several extracurricular and social activities, and participating in service activities, which reflect and adhere to his upbringing and values. He is, however, beginning to question the staunch beliefs he has embraced since he was a child. Several of his friends in the Christian Campus Ministry have what he considers to be very liberal views; his professors have challenged his belief system regarding social and cultural policies; and because this is an election year, he has begun to identify with more moderate candidates who hold views that oppose his upbringing. Overall, he is beginning to feel very narrow minded, is unsure of what is truly "right" anymore, and is uncomfortable with his seeming lack of moral resolve as he begins to "play with fire" by considering those views he so recently thought to be "wrong." He wants to fit in with his peers but is afraid of losing himself in the process, and fears that doing so will distance himself from his loved ones and his cultural upbringing.

- *What is your responsibility, as an educator, in helping Brendan transcend his simpler ways of knowing?*
- *In what ways can you help Brendan identify the certainties that exist for him, but also continue to grapple with unresolved dilemmas?*
- *W. G. Perry (1981) describes a process of "allowing for grief" (p. 108) in the process of personal growth and development. Brendan fears losing a comfortable part of himself or the connection he has with loved ones. What resources are available on your campus that may help him come to terms with the losses associated with his current developmental position, which might enable him to move to higher levels of development?*
- *What ways can you incorporate each challenge and support variable in Knefelkamp's (1999) developmental instruction model into the work you do with students like Brendan?*
- *Lochrie (1989) discussed the importance of being an enabler for students progressing through Perry's developmental positions. What does being an enabler mean to you and how can you put that definition to practice?*
- *What other sources of support are you aware of that might aid Brendan in his identity development?*

REFERENCES

Baxter Magolda, M. B. (1992). *Knowing and reasoning in college: Gender-related patterns in students' intellectual development.* San Francisco, CA: Jossey-Bass.

Belenky, M. F., Clinchy, B. M., Goldberger, N. R., & Tarule, J. M. (1986). *Women's ways of knowing: The development of self, voice, and mind.* New York, NY: Basic Books.

Brand, M. (1988). Toward a better understanding of undergraduate music education majors: Perry's perspective. *Bulletin of the Council for Research in Music Education, 98,* 22–31.

de l'Etoile, S. K. (2008). Applying Perry's scheme of intellectual and ethical development in the college years to undergraduate music therapy education. *Music Therapy Perspectives, 26*(2), 110–116.

Evans, N. J., Forney, D. S., Guido, F. M., Patton, L. D., & Renn, K. A. (2010). *Student development in college: Theory, research, and practice* (2nd ed.). San Francisco, CA: Jossey-Bass.

Felder, R. M., & Brent, R. (2004). The intellectual development of science and engineering students. Part 1: Models and challenges. *Journal of Engineering Education, 93*(4), 269–277.

Festinger, L. (1957). *A theory of cognitive dissonance.* Stanford, CA: Stanford University Press.

Gallagher, S. A. (1998). The road to critical thinking: The Perry scheme and meaningful differentiation. *National Association of Secondary School Principals, 82*(595), 12–20.

Gilligan, C. (1982). *In a different voice: Psychological theory and women's development.* Cambridge, MA: Harvard University Press.

Hindman, D. M. (2002). From splintered lives to whole persons: Facilitating spiritual development in college students. *Religious Education, 97*(2), 165–182.

Hofer, B. K., & Pintrich, P. R. (1997). The development of epistemological theories: Beliefs about knowledge and knowing and their relation to learning. *Review of Educational Research, 67*(1), 88–140.

King, P. M. (1978). William Perry's theory of intellectual and ethical development. In L. L. Knefelkamp, C. Widick, & C. A. Parker (Eds.), *Applying new developmental findings: New directions for student services* (No. 4, pp. 35–51). San Francisco, CA: Jossey-Bass.

King, P. M., & Kitchener, K. S. (1994). *Developing reflective judgment: Understanding and promoting intellectual growth and critical thinking in adolescents and adults.* San Francisco, CA: Jossey-Bass.

Knefelkamp, L. L. (1999). Introduction. In W. G. Perry, Jr. (Ed.), *Forms of intellectual and ethical development in the college years: A scheme* (pp. xi–xxxviii). San Francisco, CA: Jossey-Bass.

Kohlberg, L. (1971). From is to ought: How to commit the naturalistic fallacy and get away with it in the study of moral development. In T. Mischel (Ed.), *Cognitive development and epistemology* (pp. 151–235). New York, NY: Academic Press.

Lavis, C. C., Williams, K. A., & Thien, S. J. (2008). Assessing intellectual development of horticulture undergraduates using the Perry scheme and Learning Environment Preferences Instrument. *NACTA Journal, 52*(4), 25–31.

Lochrie, J. S. (1989). Perry revisited—A fresh look at Forms of Intellectual and Ethical Development in the College Years. *Studies in Higher Education, 14*(3), 347–350.

Love, P. G., & Guthrie, V. L. (1999). Perry's intellectual scheme. *New Directions for Student Services, 88,* 5–15.

Marra, R. M., Palmer, B., & Litzinger, T. A. (2000). The effects of a first-year engineering design course on student intellectual development as measured by the Perry scheme. *Journal of Engineering Education, 89*(1), 39–45.

Mayhew, M. J., Seifert, T. A., & Pascarella, E. T. (2012). How the first year of college influences the moral reasoning development for students in moral consolidation and moral transition. *Journal of College Student Development, 53*(1), 19–40.

Mayhew, M. J., Vanderlinden, K., & Kim, E. (2010). A multi-level assessment of the impact of orientation programs on student learning. *Research in Higher Education, 51*(4), 320–345.

McTighe Musil, C. (2011). Education for personal and social responsibility: Applying the life of the mind to the work of the world. *Diversity and Democracy, 14*(1). Retrieved from https://www.aacu.org/publications-research/periodicals/education-personal-and-social-responsibility-applying-life-mind-0

Paragament, K. I., Echemendia, R. J., Johnson, S. M., McGath, C. A., Maatman, V., & Baxter, W. (1984). Assessing the religious needs of college students: Action-oriented research in the religious context. *Review of Religious Research, 25*(3), 265–285.

Pascarella, E. T., & Terenzini, P. T. (2005). *How college affects students - Volume 2: A third decade of research*. San Francisco, CA: Jossey-Bass.

Perry, B., Donovan, M. P., Kelsey, L. J., Paterson, J., Statkiewicz, W., & Allen, R. D. (1986). Two schemes of intellectual development: A comparison of development as defined by William Perry and Jean Piaget. *Journal of Research in Science Teaching, 23*(1), 73–83.

Perry, W. G., Jr. (1968). *Forms of intellectual and ethical development in the college years: A scheme*. New York, NY: Holt, Rinehart and Winston.

Perry, W. G., Jr. (1981). Cognitive and ethical growth: The making of meaning. In A. W. Chickering (Ed.), *The modern American college* (pp. 76–116). San Francisco, CA: Jossey-Bass.

Peters, R. S. (1963). Reason and habit: The paradox of moral education. In W. R. Niblett (Ed.), *Moral education in a changing society*. London, UK: Faber & Faber.

Piaget, J. (1952). *The origins of intelligence in children* (M. Cook, Trans.). New York, NY: International Universities Press, Inc. (Original work published 1950)

Renn, K. A., Brazelton, G. B., & Holmes, J. M. (2014). At the margins of internationalization: An analysis of journal articles on college student development, learning, and experiences, 1998–2011. *Journal of College Student Development, 55*(3), 278–294.

Tolstoy, L. (2003). *Hadji Murád* (A. Maude, Trans.). New York, NY: The Modern Library. (Original work published 1911)

Welfel, E., & Davidson, M. L. (1986). The development of reflective judgment during the college years: A 4-year longitudinal study. *Journal of College Student Personnel, 27*(3), 209–216.

Zhang, L. F. (1999). A comparison of U.S. and Chinese university students' cognitive development: The cross-cultural applicability of Perry's theory. *The Journal of Psychology, 133*(4), 425–439.

CHAPTER 6

THEORIES OF MORAL DEVELOPMENT

Rebekah Reysen, Mandy Perryman, and Ricardo Phipps

> *Conformity is doing what everybody else is doing, regardless of what is right. Morality is doing what is right, regardless of what everybody else is doing.*
> —Evette Carter

Morality: The beliefs about what is right behavior and what is wrong behavior
—By permission. From *Merriam-Webster's Collegiate® Dictionary*,
11th Edition © 2016 by Merriam-Webster, Inc. (www.Merriam-Webster.com)

CASE VIGNETTE: MADISON

Madison is an 18-year-old, White, female college student from an upper-middle-class family. She is attending her parents' alma mater about 500 miles from home. Madison is thrilled to be accepted into the sorority that her mother, aunt, and older sister had previously pledged at her large Southern university. With her status as a legacy member, her above-average grade point average, and her easy ability to make friends, she believes she will be able to navigate the process successfully and become a full-fledged sister of Zeta Alpha Zeta. Over the course of her time as a sorority sister, Madison struggles with fitting into the Greek life system and also experiences weight-based shaming. A discussion of how Madison's moral development unfolds is couched within two models of moral development, in order to serve as a comparison between these two models.

Every society has a list of social rules or mores, either spoken or unspoken, that its citizens must follow in order to be accepted by the group as a whole. Guiding these principles are moral standards and ethics—what is considered to be appropriate or inappropriate behaviors. How individuals develop moral standards has been a topic of psychological research for decades. Several of the most well-known moral development researchers included Jean Piaget, Lawrence Kohlberg, and Carol Gilligan (Nairne, 2009).

Colleges and universities are governed by their own subset of society's larger set of ethical rules and standards. These standards are dictated by government legislation and upheld by higher educational professionals. Students who enroll in colleges and in universities must also follow specific rules of conduct, which focus on any number of issues, including academic honesty/dishonesty, treating peers according to a university creed, classroom behavior, Greek life, alcohol consumption, and campus safety, to name a few (e.g., University of Mississippi, 2015a). Whether or not students remain at the university depends on if they decide to follow these moral principles. And, as college students are considered to be the next generation of leaders for society, being able to operate according to ethical principles is crucial.

MORAL DEVELOPMENT ON CAMPUS

Integral to theories of moral development is the matter of not only what individuals think but also how they think. Across the life span, moral development is shaped by challenging events that prompt individuals to question the frameworks they have created for finding ways to determine what is good and what is bad. For college students, moral development is largely influenced by the family community value systems with which students first arrived on campus and even the attachment styles they adopted from family life (Samuolis, Layburn, & Schiaffino, 2001). College provides an opportunity for students to learn higher order thinking. College students encounter new ideas and values that differ from those of their families, in the classroom, in the residence hall, in the dining facility, in the student union, and sometimes on the athletic field or court.

In order to illustrate how moral development unfolds within a college student population, we are introducing a fictitious character who displays each stage of moral development for two theories—Lawrence Kohlberg's (1963, 1984) and Carol Gilligan's (1982) models of moral development. Although there are numerous student affairs topics to choose from, we have opted to include issues pertaining to Greek life, as well as body image disturbance, which can lead to eating disorders. The prevalence of Greek involvement on college campuses varies by school and region, with 42% of undergraduates currently participating in a sorority or fraternity at our Southern university (University of Mississippi, 2015b). The percentage of women who participate in sorority life varies depending on the university, but has been shown to be as high as 81% at some institutions (*U.S. News and World Report*, 2016). Additionally, research indicates that the greatest risk factor for an eating disorder is being a woman (Striegel-Moore & Bulik, 2007), with approximately 90% of those who seek treatment for an eating disorder being women (Garfinkel, Kennedy, & Kaplan, 1995). Thus, creating a case study based on a sorority sister who experiences weight-based bullying seemed to be a good blend of these two areas.

Before launching into the case study, we first discuss the underpinnings of two specific moral development theories, that of Lawrence Kohlberg (1984) and that of Carol Gilligan (1982). Although the focus of this chapter is the theories of Kohlberg and Gilligan, it is relevant to mention the work of Noddings (1984). In 1984, Nel Noddings constructed a similar moral development model based on the premise that care is a primal need and a viable framework for human attitudes, decisions, and choices.

Noddings stressed that care has to be taught and cultivated in individuals. She labels care as a professional skill in which formation should begin in the home, but be nurtured by all educational experiences, including college and university life. Following are deeper explorations into the broadly applicable theories of Kohlberg and Gilligan.

The Concept of Moral Development According to Kohlberg

Dr. Lawrence Kohlberg developed one of the most influential theories of moral development (Nairne, 2009). A psychology professor at Harvard University, he developed his theory based on the stages of cognitive development identified by Dr. Jean Piaget. These included the sensorimotor, preoperational, concrete operational, and formal operational stages. Piaget categorized specific tasks as representative of specific developmental levels. The sensorimotor stage, experienced from birth to age 2 years, is the stage in which children typically accomplish object permanence (realizing that just because an object is hidden does not mean that it does not exist), as well as become more adept at body control and speech patterns. From ages 2 to 7 years, in the preoperational period, a child is able to become immersed in playtime using his or her imagination, as well as increasing the number of words in his or her vocabulary. The concrete operational phase, from ages 7 through 11 years, is when children begin to think more abstractly as well as order and categorize information. The last period, known as the formal operational period, is where the most cognitively sophisticated individuals arrive, from age 11 years onward. This stage involves more advanced abstract reasoning capabilities (Nairne, 2009).

Like Piaget's stages of cognitive development, Kohlberg's Theory of Moral Development described the ways in which individuals mature over the course of several stages. Individuals are expected to fully achieve a stage before moving into the next sequential stage (Kohlberg, 1963, 1984). His theory is comprised of six stages, with two stages at each of three levels: the Pre-Conventional Level (Stages 1 and 2), Conventional Level (Stages 3 and 4), and Post-Conventional Level (Stages 5 and 6), with the most maturely developed individuals arriving at the Post-Conventional Level. With each stage of development, individuals grow in their ability to make moral and ethical judgments (Kohlberg & Hersh, 1977).

During the Pre-Conventional Level, individuals make decisions that they perceive as being either right or wrong based on the types of consequences they expect to receive from their environment. For example, a young girl may choose *not* to steal her sister's candy because she knows that her mother would punish her if she did. This first level involves the most simplistic decision making, because little abstract thinking is involved (Nairne, 2009). This is Stage 1, *punishment-and-obedience orientation*. Stage 2, known as the *instrument-relativist orientation*, involves a self-centric view of wanting primarily to fulfill the needs of one's self, yet at times will also focus on fulfilling those of others. Although reciprocity occurs, it happens in a business-like fashion, not based on values such as justice (Kohlberg & Hersh, 1977). The majority of children younger than 9 years, along with some adolescents, as well as adult criminals, may fall into this stage (Kohlberg, 1986).

Individuals whose moral decision-making patterns rest in the Conventional Level look at situations from a social perspective. Using more abstract reasoning than in the previous stage, conventional stagers may look at laws or societal norms in order to make decisions, simply because society says these are the norms and standards that need to be followed. For example, a teenager may opt *not* to steal cigarettes from the gas station because the law prohibits such behavior, and breaking this law is considered wrong (Nairne, 2009). During Stage 3, the *interpersonal concordance,* or "good boy–nice girl" stage, individuals conform to society based on how well intended a person was with his or her actions. During Stage 4, the *law and order phase,* individuals look toward respecting authority figures and keeping the peace for the sake of being dutiful (Kohlberg & Hersh, 1977). According to Kohlberg (1986), the majority of adults and adolescents develop no further than this stage.

Using principles based on intellect and the ability to think abstractly is what distinguishes the Post-Conventional Level from its predecessors (Nairne, 2009). Individuals in this stage accept the principles and morals of society, but only because they understand that these rules might be helpful for any number of reasons. Furthermore, there may be times when these individuals disagree with the rules in specific cases. They realize that although rules have merit, rules cannot be applicable to absolutely every situation in the same way and that rules necessitate deviation in some case (Kohlberg, 1986). During Stage 5, the *social-contract, legalistic phase,* "right action tends to be defined in terms of general individual rights and standards which have been critically examined and agreed upon by the whole society" (p. 55). During Stage 6, the *universal–ethical–principle orientation,* one's conscience prescribes decision making in which rules are not hard and fast and set in stone, but rather, based on ethics and moral judgments (Kohlberg & Hersh, 1977).

In short, during the Pre-Conventional Level, individuals look to societal norms as being outside of himself or herself. The Conventional Level is about taking societal norms as one's own. Finally, the Post-Conventional Level is about understanding the rules of society, and then deciding which ones to follow or agree with (Kohlberg, 1986).

According to Kuhn, Langer, Kohlberg, and Haan (1977), very few adolescents or adults stay at the concrete operational level. This is because most individuals begin to think abstractly, at the formal operational level, as they move through adolescence. Kohlberg (1986) argued that being able to think at a higher level of moral reasoning was because of being able to think logically; morals, he purported, cannot be exercised without logic.

In order to assess an individual's level of moral development, Kohlberg would ask participants to evaluate a case study. Depending on the participants' responses regarding what they believed the protagonist should do, Kohlberg would rate the stage at which he thought the participants had developed moral reasoning. An example of a case study used by Kohlberg (1963) titled, "Heinz Steals the Drug," is summarized as follows:

> In Europe, a woman was near death from a special kind of cancer. There was one drug that the doctors thought might save her. It was a form of radium that a druggist in the same town had recently discovered. The drug was expensive to make, but the druggist was charging ten times what the drug cost him to make. He paid $200 for the radium and charged $2,000 for a small dose of the drug.
> The sick woman's husband, Heinz, went to everyone he knew to borrow the money, but he could only get together about $1,000

which is half of what it cost. He told the druggist that his wife was dying and asked him to sell it cheaper or let him pay later. But the druggist said: "No, I discovered the drug and I'm going to make money from it." So Heinz got desperate and broke into the man's store to steal the drug for his wife. Should the husband have done that?

Whether or not a participant could argue for stealing the drug depended on the level of moral development he or she had achieved.

History of Gilligan's Theory of Moral Development

Dr. Carol Gilligan is another well-known moral development theorist, who began working with Lawrence Kohlberg in 1968, when she began teaching at Harvard University. Gilligan believed that Kohlberg's stages were outdated and gender biased toward men. In Kohlberg's model, men were reported to reach more advanced stages than women, suggesting that men have a greater ability to reach higher levels of cognitive functioning than women. Gilligan viewed this finding as not reflective of women's levels of moral maturity, but a reflection of the values they placed on decision making that takes into account others' emotions as a priority, not necessarily simply the societal norms (Medea, 2009). After questioning the validity of Kohlberg's theory, Gilligan constructed her own model, known as Gilligan's Stages of the Ethics of Care (Gilligan, 1982). Her theory included three levels, the *pre-conventional*, *conventional*, and *post-conventional* levels. Unlike Kohlberg, she viewed maturity from one stage to the next as a process of ego development, not cognitive capacity.

Looking deeper at Gilligan's model, the *pre-conventional level* is about survival; individuals will base their decisions on their own self-interest and preservation. Moving from the *pre-conventional* to the *conventional level* involves progressing from a self-centered view to a view that takes into account others' needs and ways to assist them. Individuals at the *conventional level* are considered to be more self-sacrificing than in the previous stage. The *post-conventional level* is exemplified by an individual's ability to treat self and others with respect. As with the other models of moral development, Gilligan's model reflects the expectation that individuals move sequentially through the stages (Gilligan, 1982).

In order to illustrate how one could conceptualize a case study from the framework of Kohlberg's and Gilligan's models of moral development, we have conceptualized the case study, discussed in the following section.

EXPLORING MADISON'S POSITIONING WITHIN KOHLBERG'S SCHEMA

Level 1: Pre-Conventional Morality

Madison has always been impressed by the values-based, social Greek organization that declares "Loyalty above all else!" During Rush, Madison attends several social functions at the sorority and fraternity houses on campus. Although it violates campus policy, there is alcohol at one of the fraternity parties and Madison, along with several of her friends, drinks to excess and poses for some racy pictures. Several shots of the group are taken and posted to various social media sites, causing a flood of sharing, reposts, and comments about the girls, especially Madison. One remark read, "Look at Madison! What a whore! Zetas don't stand for that! She needs her a** kicked!" In the days following the party, Madison is devastated and fearful that she will not be given a bid to Zeta Alpha Zeta (ZAZ), which has been her dream since she was a young girl. She remembers when her older sister was put on academic probation in college and had her sports car taken away for a semester. That experience had always motivated Madison to be a "good girl" and not be like her sister, who, in Madison's estimation, deserved what she got (Stage 1: Obedience and Punishment Orientation).

Madison's only hope is that ZAZ will understand that her behavior at the party was not the norm and that she is still worthy of membership (Stage 2: Individualism and Exchange).

Level 2: Conventional Morality

The next weekend, Madison is invited to another fraternity Rush event, a Phi Mu Iota (PMI) pool party, where all of the ZAZ sisters will be attending; so she perceives this as a positive sign that perhaps ZAZ has forgiven her. After the festivities are well underway, some of the ZAZ pledges are escorted to a room in the back of the house by the social chair of the fraternity and their newly initiated members. The women are asked to strip to their bathing suits, which they do, though several of them appear apprehensive and unsure. Some of the younger PMI members are surprised by these instructions and feel uneasy as the women disrobe, but they do not question the actions of their older brothers, who will soon vote to determine if the new initiates are allowed to become active brothers. Once the ZAZ pledges are all standing in their swimsuits, the PMIs are told to use the provided permanent markers to circle the physical flaws on the ZAZs. The PMI social chair explains that it is their "duty to help the girls with their flaws so they will be acceptable candidates for the sorority." He goes on to clarify that this type of assistance is provided by the fraternity each year to the sorority and that though it may be difficult now, it will be appreciated later (Stage 3: Good Interpersonal Relationships).

Even though some of the women begin to cry quietly, feeling ashamed, and many of the men seem reluctant to participate, everyone does as told and no one attempts to stop the process or leave the room (Stage 4: Maintaining the Social Order).

Level 3: Post-Conventional Morality

At 8 a.m. the following Monday, a female student meets with the Dean of Students to report what took place at the pool party. She is fully aware that her actions will result in her being dropped from the sorority, jeopardize her social relationships at college, and may even produce a level of fallout that could make it impossible to continue her education at the university. However, she believes what is at stake outweighs her own potential challenges and that she is working for the greater good.

In the future, she goes on to become a human rights advocate and travels the world to bring attention to women's issues and promote equality, especially in regions where it is unpopular or even dangerous to do so (Stage 5: Social Contract and Individual Rights).

She is not Madison (Stage 6: Universal Principles).

EXPLORING MADISON'S POSITIONING WITHIN GILLIGAN'S SCHEMA

Pre-Conventional Stage

Returning to the beginning of Madison's story, readers are invited to view her experiences and development through the lens of Carol Gilligan's theory. In order to survive this incident unscathed, Madison terminates her Facebook account and has decided to lie and say she was not in the photos, it was another girl pledging ZAZ, who has the same hair color, and so forth (Stage 1: Goal Is Individual Survival). After a few conversations with her sister and best friends and being reminded that ZAZ stands for "Loyalty above all else," Madison feels guilty about lying and putting another girl's ZAZ membership in jeopardy to save herself, and so she decides to come clean to the pledge officers and hopes they understand that her behavior at the party and in the days following was not the norm and would not happen in the future (transition from selfishness to a sense of responsibility to others).

Conventional Stage

Madison's pledge officers are pleased with her honesty and acknowledge that she took a big risk by admitting her mistakes about the party and her lying. They have decided to reward her by allowing her to continue with the ZAZ pledging process. Madison is ecstatic by the news and feels her sacrifice paid off and now others see her as a good person and hopefully a good Zeta (Stage 2: Self-Sacrifice Is Goodness).

Soon, Madison is invited to another fraternity Rush event, a Phi Mu Iota pool party, where all of the ZAZ sisters will be attending. After the festivities are well underway, some of the ZAZ pledges are escorted to a room in the back of the house by the social chair of the fraternity and their newly initiated members. The women are asked to strip to their bathing suits, which they do, though several of them appear apprehensive and unsure. Madison desperately wants to be a "good" pledge and to do as she is told, but she simultaneously feels her dignity is being robbed from her! Returning to the narrative that described the pledge event in which the young women were instructed to allow other sorority members to use permanent markers on their bodies, Madison became outraged by the PMI's behavior and began putting her clothes back on over her swimsuit. She realized that although the men may feel they have a job to do, she does, too. Her job is to stand up for herself because she is as important as anyone else (transition from goodness to the truth that she is a person, too).

Post-Conventional Stage

As Madison is about to leave the back room of the fraternity house, she observes another girl crying. The PMI is not only drawing and marking all over her, but is also pinching her and making degrading comments. Madison defiantly demands that the boy "Stop right now!" She grabs the girl's clothes and tells her to put them on while the room is completely silent and everyone is frozen. The girl quickly dresses and she and Madison leave (Stage 3: Do Not Hurt Others or Self). On the way back to the dorm, the two girls discuss how glad they are that they did not put up with that treatment any longer and how thankful they are to each other for caring enough to help. Madison smiles as they walk knowing that whether she gets into ZAZ or not, she will always have a friend she can count on who is also smiling and walking right next to her.

CASE VIGNETTE WRAP-UP: MADISON

In Kohlberg's Stages of Moral Development, Madison moves through the various stages of development through thinking more and more abstractly about how to follow the rules of both campus and her sorority. Most simplistically, she makes the choice to not be like her sister (Stage 1: Obedience and Punishment Orientation), decides that even though she violated rules at the fraternity party that she was still good enough to be a sorority member (Stage 2: Individualism and Exchange). She goes along with the body-shaming exercise of circles being drawn around the flaws of her body so that she does not disappoint the fraternity brothers (Stage 3: Good Interpersonal Relationships), as well as to avoid causing a fuss (Stage 4: Maintaining Order). She learns from this process and grows significantly to become a human rights advocate (Stage 5: Social Contract and Individualism), but because women do not typically rise to the highest stage in Kohlberg's theory, Madison stays at Stage 5.

In comparison to Kohlberg's model, Gilligan's model involves Madison making choices based not so much on rules, but on the ways that decisions affect relationships. At first, Madison lies about violating rules by saying that her sorority sister was the one posing in racy photos, and not Madison (Stage 1: Goal Is Individual Survival), but then shows maturity when she confesses to lying, so that her sorority sister does not get in trouble (Stage 2: Self-Sacrifice Is Goodness). Madison also courageously stands up to a fraternity brother who makes her sorority sister cry (Stage 3: Do Not Hurt Others or Self). In Gilligan's model, Madison matures to the highest level, but in Kohlberg's model, Madison reaches only the second highest rung. Hence, analyzing a college student case study, and arriving at certain conclusions, depends on the specific model of moral development that is used.

CASE VIGNETTE 1 FOR READER REFLECTION: SELECTIVE COMMUNITY INTERESTS

A group of Greek fraternity students at a large state-supported university on the West Coast decided to go to a local homeless shelter to serve lunch for their annual service project. The students helped to prepare the meals, served them, and cleaned the kitchen and serving area afterward. They had even collected toiletries and distributed them to those who requested the items. Some of the students were quite proud of their work and concluded that they should attempt to do this same project each semester rather than annually. One student felt that there was much more that the group could do to empower persons served by the shelter. He went back to talk with the director about the possibility of linking the shelter with the university to offer a GED program at the shelter and subsequent employment search support. When the student shared this information with

(continued)

(continued)

his fraternity members at a house meeting, he was told that the idea was useless because everyone knows homeless people do not want to study and learn or look for stable jobs. The student went to an advisor for Greek life in the student affairs office to seek guidance on the issue.

- *How can a greater sense of empathy and compassion be cultivated in students about the dynamics of economic disempowerment?*

CASE VIGNETTE 2 FOR READER REFLECTION: TOWN VERSUS GOWN

A large private university located in a large city on the East Coast has announced plans to construct a new football stadium on the edge of campus. The university is located adjacent to a lower socioeconomic neighborhood that is affected by abandoned housing, unemployment, and other social problems. Neighborhood activists have expressed the concern that the construction of a new stadium will mean the demolition of homes in the area and the displacement of people who have lived in the area for many years. The university has committed that it will also partner with developers to construct new homes, condominiums, around the stadium. Neighborhood residents would likely not be able to afford to live in the new housing. Athletes at the university see this as an opportunity to galvanize more support for the football team and to boost morale. Some students who grew up in the neighborhood join the activists in expressing concerns. At a protest planned by the activists, students on opposing sides of the issue become very aggressive with each other.

- *What can be done on campus to help all students reframe the way they view this development project and the impact it will have on the neighborhood?*
- *How can students then be a part of engaging the neighborhood residents in an honest conversation about their needs as well as the needs of the university?*

REFERENCES

Garfinkel, P. E., Kennedy, S. H., & Kaplan, A. S. (1995). Views on classification and diagnosis of eating disorders. *Canadian Journal of Psychiatry. Revue Canadienne de Psychiatrie, 40*(8), 445–456.

Gilligan, C. (1982). *In a different voice: Psychological theory and women's development*. Cambridge, MA: Harvard University Press.

Kohlberg, L. (1963). The development of children's orientations toward a moral order: I. Sequence in the development of moral thought. *Vita Humana, 6,* 11–33.

Kohlberg. L. (1984). *The psychology of moral development*. New York, NY: Harper & Row.

Kohlberg, L. (1986). A current statement on some theoretical issues. In S. Mogdil & C. Mogdil (Eds.), *Lawrence Kohlberg: Consensus and controversy* (pp. 485–545). Philadelphia, PA: The Falmer Press.

Kohlberg, L., & Hersh, R. H. (1977). Moral development: A review of the theory. *Theory Into Practice, 16*(2), 53–59.

Kuhn, D., Langer, J., Kohlberg, L., & Haan, N. S. (1977). The development of formal operations in logical and moral judgment. *Genetic Psychology Monographs, 95,* 97–188.

Medea, A. (2009). Carol Gilligan. In *Jewish women: A comprehensive historical encyclopedia.* Jewish Women's Archive. Retrieved from http://jwa.org/encyclopedia/article/gilligan-carol

Morality, n. (2016). *Merriam-Webster's Collegiate® dictionary* (11th ed.). Springfield, MA: Merriam-Webster, Inc.

Nairne, J. (2009). *Psychology* (5th ed.). Belmont, CA: Thomson Learning.

Noddings, N. (1984). *Caring: A feminine approach to ethics and moral education.* Berkeley: University of California Press.

Samuolis, J., Layburn, K., & Schiaffino, K. M. (2001). Identity development and attachment to parents in college students. *Journal of Youth and Adolescence, 30*(3), 373–384.

Striegel-Moore, R. H., & Bulik, C. M. (2007). Risk factors for eating disorders. *The American Psychologist, 62*(3), 181–198.

University of Mississippi. (2015a). University of Mississippi M book (2015–2016 ed.). Retrieved from http://conflictresolution.olemiss.edu/wp-content/uploads/sites/2/2014/09/MBOOK20153.pdf

University of Mississippi. (2015b). *Fraternity & sorority community academic report.* University, MS: Author.

U.S. News and World Report. (2016). Most students in sororities. Retrieved from http://colleges.usnews.rankingsandreviews.com/best-colleges/rankings/most-sororities

CHAPTER 7

KOLB'S THEORY OF EXPERIENTIAL LEARNING

Kathryn S. Jaekel

CASE VIGNETTE: MARIA

Maria has been training new residence assistants (RAs) in her residence hall for the past 3 years. Each year, she is excited to meet her new staff and share with them tools and strategies they can use to help students living in their residence halls feel welcomed and included. She is concerned, however, because each year, some of the new RAs disengage when she begins to discuss different forms of diversity.

When the new RAs come for their weeklong training, she notes that just as in previous years, each new RA is engaged in the team-building exercises she arranges. She also notes that all of the RAs take notes and are actively engaged in sessions that outline how to handle specific situations that are likely to arise. Frieda and Jason, both brand new RAs this year, are very active during these sessions in particular, asking specific questions about how to handle roommate conflicts, instances of theft, and details about when they are on-call. Maria notes, though, that when she moves to her presentation about inclusion and diversity, Frieda and Jason disengage. They sit together, whispering and laughing. When Maria asks them why they are not listening, Frieda sighs and says that she is sick of hearing the same things over and over about diversity. As Frieda says this, Jason nods and adds that he does not see how any of this matters, and shares, "We have heard this all before. We get it. Why do we have to listen to all of this again?"

OVERVIEW AND DESCRIPTION OF EXPERIENTIAL LEARNING THEORY

At its core, Kolb's construct of experiential learning is more than simply a theory. Rather, it is a philosophy of education that proposes a radical notion: Learning is not a passive event whereby students merely absorb information. Experiential Learning Theory (ELT) holds that learning is "the process whereby knowledge is created through the transformation of experience" (D. A. Kolb, 1984, p. 41). Knowledge results from the combination of grasping and transforming experience. Central to ELT is the commitment to learning as a student-centered and active process in which students engage in a hands-on experience (A. Y. Kolb & Kolb, 2005). In this way, ELT provides a "push back" on traditional forms of education and, instead, proposes that learners experience and reflect in order to transform experiences into knowledge. How an individual learns, according to Kolb (A. Y. Kolb & Kolb, 2005), actually shapes their personal development.

Furthermore, according to Kolb, individuals learn differently. Although on the surface this may not seem too radical a notion, in many ways, it is in direct opposition to traditional ideas of learning. Traditional models of learning are built on the notion that all learners will sit passively, absorb information, and engage in learning in the same exact manner. Instead, for Kolb, learning is a process that occurs differently for individuals and one that centers upon "doing" (D. A. Kolb & Fry, 1975).

HISTORY AND DEVELOPMENT OF ELT

David Kolb recognized early in his career that educational institutions were not taking into consideration the diversity of learners, career paths, or different styles of learning and development. Instead, according to D. A. Kolb (1981), universities "emphasized the unitary linear trend of human growth and development at the expense of acknowledging and managing the diverse developmental pathways that exist within different disciplines and professions" (p. 233). According to Kolb, institutions and educators often failed to take into consideration different learning styles and the different disciplines that asked for varying types of skills. For Kolb, this was seen as a detriment; students should be recognized as learning differently from one another. Furthermore, they should be actively engaged through a variety of methods so that their learning styles would be met.

In an effort to find a better way of facilitating and understanding learning, Kolb turned to the literature on education and learning. Drawing on the work of several 20th-century scholars and philosophers, such as Dewey, Lewin, and Piaget, Kolb noted that each stressed the central role experience plays in learning (D. A. Kolb, 1984). Unlike traditional ways of learning, Kolb noted these individuals expressed that learning is more than cognition. Additionally, unlike behaviorists who touted that learning is independent of individuals' experiences and learning styles, these scholars detailed the importance of active engagement and reflection on those experiences. Moreover, he noted that others, such as Friere, discussed the centrality of active learning avoiding the "banking concept" of education, where students are understood as passive entities that are empty vessels, to be filled with knowledge by an expert. In concert with these scholars, Kolb created a holistic, multilinear model (D. A. Kolb, 1984), which summarized six common elements that underscore learning.

The first element that Kolb identified is that learning should be understood as a *process*, not as something that is outcomes based. Learning should be recursive and not simply end once an outcome has been reached. The second element is that all learning is in fact, *relearning*. That is, learners already have ideas or beliefs about the world around them. Thus, real learning must bring in those ideas and beliefs to the learning process. The third element holds that *conflict* in learning, that is, two opposing ideas, is what actually drives learning. Here, in order to learn, students must be able to go from one conflicting idea to another, reflecting on each in order to ultimately solve the conflict. The fourth element is that learning must be a process that engages in more than mere cognition; it must engage the senses and *whole person*. The fifth element is that learning results from *interactions* between environment as well as the social world. The final element of learning posits that, "social knowledge is created and recreated in the personal knowledge of the learner" (A. Y. Kolb & Kolb, 2005, p. 194). In other words, knowledge is created because of the transactions between the learner and the social world.

Using each of these underlying characteristics of learning, Kolb constructed a four-stage cycle of learning. It is important to note that the stages used in the model are not stages of development; rather, they are stages of a learning process whereby students may enter at any point. Each stage offers a way of experiencing, reflecting, thinking, and acting—or "touching all the bases" (A. Y. Kolb & Kolb, 2005, p. 194).

The four stages outlined in this model include: *concrete experience*, or experiencing an event; *reflective observation*, or observing during the experience; *abstract conceptualization*, that is, generating or coming up with theories and ideas to explain or make sense of the observations; and *active experimentation*, or using those theories to make a decision or take action. Kolb further explains that concrete experience and abstract conceptualization are opposites in that there is a cyclical process between concrete experience and abstract conceptualization. Learners move between the two stages in order for learning to occur. This learning is facilitated through active experimentation and reflective observation in which learners move back and forth between an activity and then observations about that activity. This cycle is ideally a recursive one in which a learner continuously cycles through this process.

In addition to these four stages in the cycle of learning, Kolb also noted that students approach learning differently based on where they enter the model and how they experience education. Specifically, in his Learning Style Inventory (LSI), a tool created to assess different styles of learning, Kolb noted four different learner types: Diverger, Assimilator, Converger, and Accommodator.

Within the LSI, the *diverging* group, or the learners who enter the model between concrete experience and reflective observation, approach learning in a manner that is highly social. These learners excel in group work, brainstorming, information gathering, and engaging in various viewpoints to better understand a situation. Those with the diverging learning style, according to Kolb, are reported to be emotional, imaginative, and getting feedback (D. A. Kolb, 1984; A. Y. Kolb & Kolb, 2005).

Those who have an *assimilating* learning style, whose dominant learning styles are reflective observation and abstract conceptualization, tend to approach learning through a more abstract conceptualization and then through reflective observation. Unlike those who are divergers, assimilators focus on the abstract versus the social. That said, although these learners prefer the abstract, they still find it important that theories and ideas be logical versus practical. Assimilators, who are often said to excel in science fields, prefer logical, concise information and prefer lectures and analytical models and, importantly, need time to reflect on these (D. A. Kolb, 1984).

Those whose learning styles are *converging* have the dominant learning styles of abstract conceptualization and active experimentation. These learners are problem solvers who prefer active experimentations to better understand the abstract.

They excel at using ideas and theories for practice purposes. Convergers prefer technical tasks and problems and often have careers in technology. These learners excel at practical application and decision making and prefer classrooms that use simulations and laboratory environments (D. A. Kolb, 1984).

Finally, those learners with the *accommodating* learning style have the dominant styles of active experimentation and concrete experience. This group prefers the hands-on approach to learning. Often relying on their "gut" versus the logical, these learners prefer to participate in group work, engage in various approaches to complete tasks, and complete fieldwork. This group of learners enjoys working with others and setting goals for themselves (D. A. Kolb, 1984).

APPLICATION OF THE THEORY WITHIN STUDENT AFFAIRS

Although ELT is often used in formal classroom settings, there are many out-of-classroom environments in student affairs that use and benefit from it as well. One way in which colleges and universities use experiential learning is through service-learning courses and projects. Service learning, broadly defined, is an organized, service-oriented activity that meets the needs of a particular community (Bringle & Hatcher, 1995). Although this method of learning may seem similar to internships and volunteering, service learning is different because of its "intention to equally benefit the provider and the recipient of the service as well as to ensure equal focus on both the service being provided and the learning that is occurring" (Furco, 1996, p. 7). ELT plays a large role in service learning as students are often asked to make sense of their service through reflective processes. In reflecting on their experiences, students can come to know more about not only the activity, but also the community and other learning goals.

Several scholars have reported that using service learning in conjunction with ELT provides students with meaningful ways to engage not only with the community, but also to come to know more about diversity and social justice. Studies have shown that students who participate in service-learning projects reported that they became more aware of stereotypes and their negative effects (Jones & Abes, 2004), had an increased awareness of their own privilege (Einfeld & Collins, 2008), and became more aware of systems inequalities (Mitchell, 2007). In using Kolb's ELT in service-learning courses or projects, learners are given impactful experiences and then given opportunities to reflect on those experiences. In asking students to reflect on their service learning, students were able to come to know more about others' experiences.

Another sector of higher education in which ELT is embedded is within study abroad programs. As participation in study abroad increases, institutions are exploring ways to ensure that these programs provide clear opportunities for student learning to avoid them becoming little more than a vacation (Passarelli & Kolb, 2012). That is, mechanisms must be constructed to facilitate meaning making of these experiences by students (Kortegast & Boisfontaine, 2015). As such, so that students participate on more than a surface level, well-defined opportunities must be built into the overall study abroad programming to allow the experience to be transformational and knowledge building. ELT is a method that can allow for deeper understanding as its principles encourage students to engage in reflections over their experiences, see experiences from different points of view, and make sense of what they see.

Not all study abroad programs use experiential learning; however, study abroad as a field "shares experiential education's goals regarding the empowerment of students to work for personal and social transformation but also provides study abroad with a pedagogical paradigm that can help it to fully achieve its objective of education for global citizenship" (Lutterman-Aguilar & Gingerich, 2002, p. 48). Thus, ELT can easily be integrated into study abroad experiences, which will, in turn, create more meaningful learning experiences. Student affairs educators can aid in these learning experiences by leading facilitation, provide opportunities for reflection, and create opportunities for students to discuss their experiences.

Finally, another area of student affairs that often uses ELT is in leadership development. Although student engagement in leadership activities offers opportunities to further develop and grow, simply engaging in leadership activities does not necessarily constitute learning (Guthrie & Bertrand Jones, 2012). Rather, students must participate in experiential learning, taking time to move between experience and reflection in order to learn from their experiences. To help the students with this process, student affairs professionals can provide opportunities for different forms of reflection for students.

According to Guthrie and Bertrand Jones (2012), it is valuable to provide structured opportunities for reflection. These may consist of asking students to write reflections, keep journals, create concept maps, do role-playing activities, and participate in self-assessment. Each of these activities offers students space to engage in critical reflection about everything from their experience to asking questions such as, "What kind of leader am I? What have I learned about leadership? How did I learn it?" (Guthrie & Bertrand Jones, 2012, p. 58).

Although these are only three examples of how ELT may be integrated into student affairs practice, note that there are many other spaces in which it can assist in creating opportunities for students to engage in "deep learning." Because out-of-classroom learning is such a key component in higher education and in the holistic development of students, using Kolb's experiential learning model can aid students in meaning making as it facilitates personal growth.

CASE VIGNETTE WRAP-UP: MARIA

Although resistance to diversity and inclusion is not a new idea to Maria, she is still taken aback when Frieda and Jason share their opinions. Maria realizes that both of these RAs may have heard this information before, but possibly have never seen it. She notes that this information is too important to just give a presentation to her new staff. Instead, they need to be engaged and active in order to really learn. She decides to section up the new RAs into groups. In their groups, they are asked to walk around residence halls and campus buildings, examining the spaces with the guiding question, "Who would feel comfortable in these spaces? Who may not?" The groups are asked to document and photograph evidence of what they find.

When the groups return, the RAs gather and share what each group found. Some shared that they went to the music building and saw posters that represented musicians. This group shared that they thought students who played instruments would feel included because of these visuals. Another group shared that the posters in another campus building showed only White individuals and documented that people of color were

(continued)

(continued)

excluded. Maria took this opportunity to discuss with her new staff how that affects and how students encounter that space. When it is Frieda's group's turn, they shared that they found homophobic slurs on the bathroom wall in the library. Each RA looked at the picture of the wall Frieda's group took. Frieda shared, "I was so socked. I can't believe this stuff is still around." As the session progressed, Maria had the group process how they felt about what they encountered and how they could use this to make their own floors more inclusive and accepting. Maria ended the session by saying that today was a good start in learning more about inclusion but their work was not over. Although they had this one experience today, the new RAs needed to continue to engage and reflect upon experiences like this.

CASE VIGNETTE 1 FOR READER REFLECTION: STEVE

Steve is the assistant director of his university's service-learning program and is coordinating a new service-learning course. Students in the course are asked to collect information from the different dining halls on campus in order to increase awareness about food waste as well as food insecurity in the university community and surrounding areas. Steve is passionate about this course and believes that not only will it give students hands-on experience, but it will also lead to less food waste and help end food insecurity.

Before the project begins, Jamie and Travis, two undergraduate students, ask Steve more about the project and specifically enquiring about the course assignment requirements. Steve explains that much of the class will be spent in the dining hall interviewing students about how much food they take and throw away. Students enrolled in the class will also be out in the community researching levels of food insecurity. Although some parts of the class will be spent sharing the information they gather and putting it into posters and brochures, students' final grades will come from reflections and reflective conversations they have with one another processing what they found through their research.

Immediately after Steve shares this, Jamie and Travis smile. Travis turns to Jamie and says, "See, I told you this would be an easy 'A.' We just have to write stupid made-up reflections." Jamie nods her head and the two decide to sign up for the class. On seeing their reaction, Steve is concerned. It never occurred to him that students would think reflections were "easy," or that they would be "made-up." He wonders if he should avoid using reflection in the course or have more of a formal classroom environment so that students take it seriously.

- *How can Steve ensure his learning outcomes are met when he has students' complete reflections?*

CASE VIGNETTE 2 FOR READER REFLECTION: CORA

Cora, who is the director of her institution's Lesbian, Gay, Bisexual, Transgender, and Queer (LGBTQ) student center, has recently begun tracking the academic persistence

(continued)

(continued)

of students who frequent her office. Over the past 2 years, she has tracked that almost half of the students her office has worked with either have dropped out or are in poor academic standing. In the hopes of creating more community, increasing persistence, and providing a more supportive space for the students, Cora develops a plan for a living learning community where LGBTQ students can live together on a floor of the residence halls.

A draft of her proposal is due to her supervisor soon in which she has to outline not only the logistics of the living learning community, but also the curriculum and learning activities that will go along with it. Although she knows that living in this learning community will help students feel more comfortable and that it will create a community, she is not sure what types of experiences she should include in order to make the learning community a transformational experience for the students. Moreover, she knows that students will be having different types of learning styles, but she is not sure how to accommodate those styles or how to capitalize on the diversity of learning types to further students' understandings.

- *Given the situation, what could Cora do to engage students in experiential learning and reflection?*
- *How could she create experiences or spaces that will allow for different learning styles?*

REFERENCES

Bringle, R. G., & Hatcher, J. A. (1995). A service-learning curriculum for faculty. *Michigan Journal of Community Service Learning, 2,* 112–122.

Einfeld, A., & Collins, D. (2008). The relationships between service-learning, social justice, multicultural competence, and civic engagement. *Journal of College Student Development, 49,* 95–109.

Furco, A. (1996). Service-learning: A balanced approach to experiential education. In Corporation for National Service (Ed.), *Expanding boundaries: Serving and learning* (pp. 2–6). Columbia, MD: The Cooperative Education Association.

Guthrie, K. L., & Bertrand Jones, T. (2012). Teaching and learning: Using experiential learning and reflection for leadership education. *New Directions for Student Services, 140,* 53–63.

Jones, S. R., & Abes, E. S. (2004). Enduring influences of service-learning on college students' identity development. *Journal of College Student Development, 45,* 149–166.

Kolb, A. Y., & Kolb, D. A. (2005). Learning styles and learning spaces: Enhancing experiential learning in higher education. *Academy of Management Learning & Education, 4*(2), 193–212.

Kolb, D. A. (1981). Learning styles and disciplinary differences. *The Modern American College, 1,* 232–255.

Kolb, D. A. (1984). *Experiential learning: Experience as the source of learning and development.* Upper Saddle River, NJ: Prentice-Hall.

Kolb, D. A., & Fry, R. (1975). Toward an applied theory of experiential learning. In C. Cooper (Ed.), *Theories of group processes.* New York, NY: Wiley.

Kortegast, C. A., & Boisfontaine, M. T. (2015). Beyond "it was good": Students' post–study abroad practices for negotiating meaning. *Journal of College Student Development, 56*(8), 812–828.

Lutterman-Aguilar, A., & Gingerich, O. (2002). Experiential pedagogy for study abroad: Educating for global citizenship. *Frontiers: The Interdisciplinary Journal of Study Abroad, 8*(2), 41–82.

Mitchell, T. D. (2007). Critical service-learning as social justice education: A case study of the Citizens Scholars program. *Equity & Excellence in Education, 40,* 101–112.

Passarelli, M. A., & Kolb, D. A. (2012). Using experiential learning theory to promote student learning and development in programs of education abroad. In M. V. Berg, M. Page, & K. Lou (Eds.), *Student learning abroad*. Sterling, VA: Stylus.

CHAPTER 8

PERSONALITY TYPES BASED ON THE MYERS–BRIGGS TYPE INDICATOR

Christine Borzumato-Gainey

CASE VIGNETTE: REBECCA, AN INTROVERT SENSING THINKING JUDGING (ISTJ)

Rebecca, a tall, red-haired, first-year student, entered the counseling office calmly stating that she was uncomfortably sad and anxious. Her dilemma was twofold. She had met a young man she really liked and their relationship was getting serious—serious enough that the life plans she had made when she was in grade school were in jeopardy. Rebecca's boyfriend was in the military and if Rebecca was going to be with him after graduation, it would require her to travel around the world and their home would likely not be in the grand metropolis of her dreams. Along with this alteration in her postgraduation plans, she was reconsidering her major also. Rebecca had taken classes throughout high school in order to prepare to be a broadcast journalist. She had applied the early acceptance route to the Communications School. She knew that she wanted to work in a television studio based in Manhattan reporting the nightly news—until she took several general education classes. These classes offered her a new way of looking at the world that she found highly intriguing. In addition, a profound teacher had sparked her interest in public health policy. She began to envision herself making a difference in people's lives as a hospital administrator. Though this opening of her mind was precisely what one may hope for from higher education, Rebecca was painfully unsettled. A normally decisive and determined person, perseverance had always been one of her strengths. To change her dream in midstream shook her sense of herself. And, typical of someone with an ISTJ personality who is in crisis mode, she believed her conflicts about her career to mean complete disaster and feared that she would be a failure.

OVERVIEW AND DESCRIPTION OF THE THEORY BEHIND THE MYERS–BRIGGS TYPE INDICATOR

The Myers–Briggs type indicator (MBTI) was designed to help people understand themselves and others by helping them appreciate the diverse strengths of different personality types. It is widely used in the corporate arena, life coaching, counseling, and education. In academic institutions, student development professionals use the MBTI for program planning, leadership training, relationship building, personal growth, conflict resolution, and advising (Bayne, 2003; Shaffer & Zalewski, 2011). Specific examples of the instrument's use would include helping roommates resolve their cleanliness differences, programming to nurture student leaders' strengths, and guiding a student's investigation of potential majors. In the opening vignette, a professional counselor drew on his knowledge of the MBTI to assess, discuss, and provide guidance to the student.

Katharine Cook Briggs and her daughter, Isabel Briggs Myers, developed the MBTI using Jung's psychological type theory (1971; originally published in 1921). Since its publication, the MBTI has been used by millions of people around the world (Martin, 1997). It has been widely used in counseling as well as business to work on team building and relationships. There is, therefore, room for using this assessment within the field of student affairs to help build teams and groups both for professionals in the field and for students. In this chapter, we discuss the basic information about the MBTI and implications for student affairs. The instrument is considered as a personality assessment for normal individuals designed to assess personality type.

Assessing Personality Type

The MBTI presents the participant with a series of self-report forced-choice questions to define opposing preferences on four scales. The scales measure individual preference for the following personality dichotomies: Introversion versus Extroversion or one's source of personal energy; Sensing versus Intuition as a means of acquiring information; Thinking versus Feeling as the dominant factor in drawing conclusions; and Judging versus Perceiving for organizing one's world.

Extrovert or Introvert?

Most people have a good idea of their tendencies toward extroversion or introversion by the time they reach college. Extroverts often have an easier time adjusting to the new social environment and new class settings, as they tend to draw energy from being around other people. They also have a tendency to speak up in class in both small groups and large groups. Introverts, on the other hand, tend to become drained in new social settings and when required to engage in socializing with new people. The need for "down time" may be exceptionally strong for those who strongly identify as introverts and they may feel that their voices get lost in a crowd.

Sensing or Intuitive?

Individuals who are strong sensing types tend to rely on "hard information" or physical facts as they gather information from their environments. They need data that can be assessed by their senses. Intuitive individuals, however, pick up on the things that are not necessarily verbalized or tangible as they gather data about the world.

Thinking or Feeling?

You can usually determine if someone is a "thinker" or a "feeler" by the words used to describe beliefs. If they start off a sentence with "I think . . . ," they are likely to be people who prefer to make decisions based on rational assessments. Those who open with "I feel . . . ," tend to use data that is not as logically or rationally grounded when making decisions.

Judging or Perceiving?

Although the term *judging* sounds as if a person is judgmental, what this term refers to in this setting is a person's tendency to prefer to make decisions in an orderly manner. Individuals with this preference may come across as more regimented or rigid than their opposites, the perceivers. Those who have the tendency to be more flexible and spontaneous in their planning are considered perceivers who respond to the environment as it presents itself. This vector of preferences is often most clearly visible when two opposing individuals are trying to work together to achieve a goal.

Combining the Types

There are 16 possible combinations of the eight preferences from the four scales resulting in 16 personality MBTI types. Each of these types is a unique configuration of the four scales. Although the four preference scales are integral to each type, the overall MBTI personality type is more complex because of the interaction between each scale (Myers & McCaulley, 1985).

Descriptions of the 16 Personality Types

- **ISTJ** (introvert/sensing/thinking/judging) types are responsible and serious, and work diligently toward their goals. They are detail-oriented pragmatists who make decisions based on their personal experiences.
- **ISFJ** (introvert/sensing/feeling/judging) types are quiet, warm, and caring. They often put the needs of others above their own. They are practical and tradition oriented.
- **ISTP** (introvert/sensing/thinking/perceiving) types are logical and practical. They are good problem solvers. They often enjoy sports and may have strong mechanical skills.

- **ISFP** (introvert/sensing/feeling/perceiving) types are caring, playful, and realistic. They tend to enjoy living in the present and are often creative.
- **ESTP** (extrovert/sensing/thinking/perceiving) types are energetic, fun-loving people who relish variety and hands-on experiences. As they are not particularly interested in theory, the traditional classroom does not hold a great deal of appeal for them.
- **ESFP** (extrovert/sensing/feeling/perceiving) types are pragmatic, fun-loving people. They excel at living in the moment and providing enjoyment to the people who are willing to go along for the ride.
- **ESTJ** (extrovert/sensing/thinking/judging) types are excellent organizers. Thanks to a strong sense of direction, they complete their work efficiently. They often have forceful personalities and enjoy holding leadership positions.
- **ESFJ** (extrovert/sensing/feeling/judging) types are warm-hearted and conscientious people. Often putting others' needs first, they may place themselves in caretaking roles. They thrive on positive relationships.
- **INFJ** (introvert/intuitive/feeling/judging) types are quietly forceful, conscientious, and concerned for others. They tend to hold firm to their principles.
- **INTJ** (introvert/intuitive/thinking/judging) types are skeptical, critical thinkers, and determined. Thanks to a sense of single-mindedness, they are often able to overcome obstacles in order to achieve their goals.
- **INFP** (introvert/intuitive/feeling/perceiving) types are quiet and caring idealists. They tend to become invested in projects and people. They also tend to have highly developed language skills and good writing skills.
- **ENFP** (extrovert/intuitive/feeling/perceiving) types are enthusiastic and tend to see opportunities in every situation. They are strongly drawn to new experiences and care deeply about others. Frequently they rely on improvisation instead of preparation.
- **INTP** (introvert/intuitive/thinking/perceiving) types tend to be highly individualistic, critical thinkers who highly value knowledge and competence. They gravitate toward theoretical or scientific pursuits.
- **ENTP** (extrovert/intuitive/thinking/perceiving) types are intellectually quick, outspoken, and logical. Known to be good at many things, they relish a good debate.
- **ENFJ** (extrovert/intuitive/feeling/judging) types express a great deal of empathy and warmth toward others. Both sensitive and sociable, they are responsible, capable, and charismatic leaders.
- **ENTJ** (extrovert/intuitive/thinking/judging) types are logical and articulate. They are often eloquent public speakers. Because of their vision and strong organization skills, they often rise to leadership positions.

APPLICATION OF THE THEORY WITHIN STUDENT AFFAIRS

Thanks to a great deal of research using the instrument, there are significant findings detailing the role of the 16 psychological types pertaining to many aspects of life. The range of available literature is extensive and spans the personal and professional spheres. There are guides available for parents that address effective parenting strategies based on the personality types of children and parents, the role of personality type on study habits and academic performance, and many resources related to career choice and people management based on type. In addition, there is an extensive list of settings within higher education in which the use of the MBTI typing would be appropriate. For instance, it is quite common for a career counselor to reference a list of careers in which each personality type tends to find job satisfaction in order to help guide students' career searches. When program planning, residence life staff can develop a workshop to appeal to all types. They can include activities that appeal to extroverts who prefer to talk as well as introverts who prefer to think through a problem quietly. They can present information that inspires the feeling types, depicts the big picture for the intuitive types, and offers facts for the sensing types. Leadership professionals can encourage students to build on the strengths of their psychological type while building skills in areas of need. Even for an ESTJ who is a natural leader, it is helpful to know that he or she must accommodate his or her communication style to express appreciation for the contributions of the feeling types.

Ideally, colleges and universities would offer all students the opportunity to take the MBTI as part of its college transition program. When students and staff are familiar with the MBTI and know their MBTI type, the campus community benefits from having a common language to discuss individual preferences and differences. Some of the ways in which the MBTI has been integrated into campus settings include the use of the assessment with students from a variety of majors from hospitality (Weber, Lee, & Dennison, 2015) to nursing (Kim & Han, 2014) to teacher education (Rushton, Mariano, & Wallace, 2012). It has also been explored as a tool for the development of effective resident hall assistants (Konyak & Kelly, 2013).

When trained to use the MBTI, a student affairs professional can identify preferences by listening to client strengths and observing client behavior. Sometimes a person's preference is not clear and one must ask appropriate questions to assess type. It may be tricky to determine if a talkative person gains energy from spending time with others or becomes drained after a few hours of socializing. The level of a client's flexibility in his or her approach to life is sometimes quite apparent; however, under stress or in a certain environment, clients may seem more rigid and goal-oriented than they prefer to be. Moreover, a person may have skills that would seem to indicate a type that is not his or her preferred mode. For instance, just because a teenage girl with a perceiving preference is highly organized does not mean it is her preferred mode.

CONCLUSION

The college years are a time of transition, and exposure to new ideas along with a firming of individual identity. Having traversed the challenges of basic questions of identity, emerging adults continue to wrestle with major life questions particularly in the areas of school, career, and relationships. The MBTI offers strength-based guidance in every realm of living concerning individual growth to interpersonal relationships, in academic matters to spiritual terrains. From the office of the president to the chaplain, the MBTI is a useful and effective tool on a college campus.

CASE VIGNETTE WRAP-UP: REBECCA

The vignette is an example of the typical use of the MBTI in personal counseling. The counselor used Rebecca's MBTI type to conceptualize Rebecca's presenting concerns. Although she enjoyed occasional social engagements, Rebecca was feeling exhausted from life at the university, her academic demands, as well as the stress from all the changes she has been experiencing transitioning as a first-year student. She desperately needed "down time" to reenergize, and sharing her dorm with extroverted roommates was impeding Rebecca's normal means of recovery. The counselor discussed places on and off campus Rebecca could go to be alone. Likewise, the counselor connected Rebecca's type, ISTJ, to her strong reaction to change in her life. As a responsible and goal-oriented ISTJ who is yet to be exposed to a breadth of ideas or people, Rebecca had prematurely decided on her career aspirations. Her current shift toward a career in hospital administration with its consistency and structure may be a step toward a better fit for Rebecca's personality type than a high-profile journalist would have been.

Moreover, the counselor framed Rebecca's dilemma using the strength-oriented language of the MBTI. As Rebecca had taken the MBTI, this provided a shared, easy-to-understand language and helped normalize the problem for Rebecca. The counselor acknowledged Rebecca's gifts for goal setting, hard work, and persistence. Over the course of their relationship, the counselor encouraged Rebecca to consider some career possibilities and to evaluate how different courses of action might work for her. Rebecca came to understand herself better along with the importance of making decisions that uniquely fit her, not just plans that "sounded great" and made "objective sense." They were able to develop a new, personalized, but more flexible, plan than Rebecca had ever had in the past. And Rebecca was pleased that her new career plans allowed for her marriage plans to her boyfriend.

CASE VIGNETTE 1 FOR READER REFLECTION: MAKAYLA

Makayla, a particularly enthusiastic ENFP, is a junior in a small liberal arts college. She is an honors fellow, a research assistant to her faculty advisor, a photographer for the student newspaper, a member of the women's rugby team, a resident assistant, and the philanthropy chair of her sorority. Over the course of this semester, her grades have been gradually slipping and recently she failed to complete an assignment given by her faculty advisor. Her faculty advisor became concerned when Makayla did not have the assignment. Also during this conversation, the faculty advisor recognized that Makayla seemed scattered and anxious. When the advisor asked Makayla if they could talk about how she was doing in general, Makayla shared that she was in the midst of planning her sorority's major fundraiser for the year and was overwhelmed by the fundraiser and her schoolwork.

The advisor, hoping to help, investigated Makayla's circumstances a little further and uncovered Makayla's numerous extracurricular activities. Using Makayla's strengths as an ENFP to frame the conversation, the advisor complimented Makayla's interest and dedication to this array of exciting activities. Then gently shifting the conversation,

(continued)

(continued)
the advisor asked Makayla some open-ended questions intended to make her use the undeveloped introversion to prioritize her interests. Makayla agreed that she had to reduce her commitments and, like most extroverts, found it extremely helpful to verbalize the pros and cons of her involvement in each. In addition, the advisor offered some efficiency and scheduling tips for Makayla because organization was not a natural strength as a perceiving type.

- *What are Makayla's greatest needs?*
- *What campus-based services might be most beneficial to her?*
- *What are some goals you would like to see Makayla reach?*

CASE VIGNETTE 2 FOR READER REFLECTION: MICHAEL

Michael, an ENTJ, is a senior business management major. He feels optimistic about graduation; however, he has had several interpersonal problems lately. He was not elected president last spring and he believes it is because of a handful of fraternity brothers who have been talking about him behind his back. This term the brothers went to the beach for the weekend without inviting him. When he expressed his anger about this situation to his fraternity "little brother," he was told that the other brothers felt like Michael had walked all over them during the Greek Week events. In addition, his girlfriend of 2 years has been argumentative and pouty, preferring to spend time with her sorority sisters than with him. He is not certain why she has been acting this way except that she got angry when he accepted a postgraduation job across the country. He had told her she was welcome to move there as long as she found an apartment of her own. Now he is feeling uncharacteristically isolated from everyone.

Michael is about to make a major life transition. Introverted feeling is his least-favored function and he is not inclined toward reflecting on the meaning inherent in this change. As an ambitious, career-minded, MBTI type, he has equated college success with leadership positions and career success. Slightly unsettled by the impending changes and recent "failures," he is not feeling as confident as he had been. It seems almost as if everything he does or says is wrong. As an extrovert, Michael is accustomed to high levels of social interaction; so not having his cronies bothers him. His strong preference for thinking has been valuable in the development of objectivity and analytical performance; however, he has not learned to refrain from using these skills in his close personal relationships. When busy or stressed, he quickly forgets to consider others' feelings because this sensitivity to feelings does not come naturally to ENTJs and Michael is suffering the repercussions. In an attempt to return to his normal healthier and happier self, Michael goes to the gym to blow off steam where the Director of Campus Recreation notices that Michael is not his usual gregarious self.

- *What are Michael's greatest needs?*
- *What campus-based services might be most beneficial to him?*
- *What are some goals you would like to see Michael reach?*

REFERENCES

Bayne, R. (2003). Love, money, and studying. *The Psychologist, 16,* 529–531.

Jung, C. (1971). *Psychological types.* Princeton, NJ: Princeton University Press.

Kim, M., & Han, S. (2014). Relationships between the Myers-Briggs Type Indicator personality profiling, academic performance and student satisfaction in nursing students. *International Journal of Bio-Science and Bio-Technology, 6*(6), 1–12.

Konyak, J. C., & Kelly, D. L. (2013). Exploring MBTI as a training and development tool for undergraduate resident assistants. *Leadership & Organizational Management Journal, 2013,* 114–136.

Martin, C. (1997). *Looking at type: The fundamentals.* Gainesville, FL: The Center for Psychological Type.

Myers, I. B., & McCaulley, M. H. (1985). *Manual: A guide to the development and use of the Myers–Briggs Type Indicator* (2nd ed.). Palo Alto, CA: Consulting Psychologists Press.

Rushton, S., Mariano, J. M., & Wallace, T. L. (2012). Program selection among pre-service teachers: MBTI profiles within a college of education. *Creative Education, 13,* 16–23.

Shaffer, L. S., & Zalweski, M. (2011). "It's what I've always wanted to do!" Advising the foreclosure student. *NACADA Journal, 31,* 62–77.

Weber, M. R., Lee, J. H., & Dennison, D. (2015). Using personality profiles to help educators understand ever-changing hospitality students. *Journal of Teaching in Travel & Tourism, 15*(4), 325–344.

PART III: IDENTITY DEVELOPMENT IN COLLEGE STUDENTS

CHAPTER 9

OVERVIEW OF IDENTITY DEVELOPMENT IN YOUNG ADULTHOOD

Suzanne Maniss

CASE VIGNETTE: SOFIA

Sofia is a first-generation college student from a low-income family. She is the youngest child in her family and the only child who was born in the United States. Her family, although proud of her, has not been overly encouraging of her attending college. Sofia's family is from Mexico and they expect her to marry young, be a housewife, and have children like her two older sisters. Many people in her family work at low-paying jobs or for cash, only because they are not U.S. citizens. Sofia wants more from her life and was encouraged by her school counselor to consider going to college. Her school counselor encouraged her to apply to colleges and to apply for scholarships. She was accepted to Marymond University, which is 3 hours away from her hometown. She is receiving financial aid, including a scholarship that covers room and board, and works part-time on campus.

Sofia is struggling to address her desire to pursue a scientific or medical field, which would require advanced degrees, and her family wishes that she select a more traditional occupation for a woman such as a teacher. She has considered becoming a research chemist or a doctor. As a sophomore, she will soon have to make a firm decision on her major. She enjoys classes and is doing well, but has struggled to make friends in her residence hall. Most of the students are from upper class families and go home when they want on the weekends. Sofia seldom goes home on weekends as she does not have a car and her parents are not always able to afford the gas money for her to come home for the weekends. The other students have cars and money to eat out frequently and hire tutors. Sofia does not have the money for such luxuries. At times, she feels like she does not fit and is struggling to figure what she wants out of life. On the one hand, she appreciates that her sisters are enjoying life, raising children, and do not have the stress of going to college. On the other hand, Sofia wants to be independent and not have to depend on someone else financially. She has seen her aunts stay with abusive husbands, both because it was expected and because they had no job skills. Despite having limited support and finances,

(continued)

> *(continued)*
>
> *Sofia is doing well in her classes. She has joined a few campus organizations, but still does not feel well connected to others.*
>
> *Although Sofia has few close friends, she has been invited to parties off campus. The parties were a bit wild, with underage drinking, and at one party, some people were smoking marijuana. Sofia felt accepted at the parties, but was a bit nervous about "breaking rules." She knows that if her parents ever found out they would be upset with her. She is expected to be a "good girl" and was raised with very traditional Hispanic values. However, Sofia is now questioning those values as she becomes more exposed to mainstream values at college. She is also exploring different religious viewpoints and learning more about other cultures as well. Yet, when she is able to visit her family, it is expected that she adhere to the rules that were in place while she was in high school. She is upset that her parents do not understand that she is now an adult and instead continue to treat her as a child. This has created some tension on her rare visits home.*

CHALLENGES TO IDENTITY DEVELOPMENT

As the case of Sofia illustrates, college is a time for changes and challenges when it comes to identity development. Perhaps no other period in the life span of a human being is more fraught with challenges, opportunities, and possibilities than young adulthood. Likewise, no other period of human development is more replete with complex growth, changes, and transformation in so many areas of functioning than young adulthood. The study of human development, broad in scope and diverse in nature, has been the focus of research by psychologists, sociologists, educators, human ecologists, and many others since the early to mid-20th century. This chapter provides an overview of identity development in young adults and discusses how these issues can impact college success based on various theories.

FACTORS THAT INFLUENCE IDENTITY DEVELOPMENT

During the college years, individuals gain insight into different perspectives and have the opportunity to examine their own values and learn more about diversity as they are exposed to diverse opinions and various ways of living (Azmitia, Syed, & Radmacher, 2008). College students may engage in risk-taking behaviors, such as binge drinking, and although for most it may be just a phase, for some it can lead to ongoing issues and contribute to problems in the future (Gates, Corbin, & Fromme, 2016). Many students feel caught between two worlds, not quite an adolescent but not quite an adult. Arnett (2000) described this period as emerging adulthood. During this period, people struggle to establish their own identities, understand their values and examine them, as well as try to establish a career path and build long-term relationships. The degree to which the person's family impacts this transition may be based on culture. This is a time of challenges and personal examination. Many theories have been proposed to explain the stages and steps through which a person goes. We begin with an overview of some of these theories as they relate to identity development.

OVERVIEW OF RELEVANT THEORIES

Initial theories across multiple domains of development (e.g., cognitive, psychological) have focused primarily on child and adolescent changes based on the assumption that most development slowed considerably or crystallized and stopped completely after late adolescence. Notable examples include the theories of Freud and Piaget. Subsequent research, acknowledging that the average life expectancy increased significantly in the 20th century, began to emphasize a life-span perspective influenced by complex biological, psychological, and social factors. As a result, developmental issues in young adulthood (approximately ages 18–24 years) received greater scrutiny, and theoretical frameworks for understanding these aspects emerged. Next, we examine some of the issues and theories that impact identity development during this period in life.

PSYCHOSOCIAL DEVELOPMENT THEORIES

When studying stages or periods of human development, it is useful to ask two questions: What changes generally occur during a specific age range, and what milestones or accomplishments should be achieved during this time (Knefelkamp, Widick, & Parker, 1978)? Most young adults are exploring possibilities in terms of intimate relationships, education or training, work or career choices, and social identity, all of which have profound significance pertaining to their long-term adult roles. Psychosocial developmental theories offer frameworks for conceptualizing the issues individuals encounter at various points across the life span and have provided structure for more recent research as well. Psychosocial theorists, such as Erik Erikson, James Marcia, Ruthellen Josselson, and Arthur Chickering and Linda Reisser, are often referenced in discussion of age-related milestones and developmental tasks. We now briefly examine a few of them that are not addressed more fully in other chapters.

Marcia's Model of Identity Development

Several theories and theoretical frameworks have been based on Erik Erikson's (1959/1980) model of psychosocial development, which was presented in Chapter 4. For instance, Marcia (1966) focused on identity development in young adults, specifically *identity versus role confusion/identity diffusion*, as described in Erikson's linear model of development. Examining ways in which individuals resolved identity-related crises, Marcia proposed four identity statuses or ways in which individuals explored these crises and made their subsequent commitment to a resolution: *foreclosure, moratorium, identity achievement,* and *diffusion.*

According to Marcia (1966), *foreclosed* individuals have not experienced crises of identity, generally committing to traditional norms held by family members or other authorities in their lives without question or exploration. Young adults or college students in this state may have difficulty dealing with challenges and handling problems on their own in the absence of authority figures. The *moratorium* status is characteristic of individuals who have begun an exploration process, but may not have considered all possible alternatives, and who have not made a commitment or personal choice in terms of an identity. Lack of a commitment may produce vacillation and anxiety or instability of identity until a determination is made. Individuals in the *identity achievement* status have endured a period of crisis (exploration), examined options, and made choices resulting in commitments to varied aspects of identity: relationships, occupations, worldviews, and so on. The final status, *diffusion*, occurs when individuals have not experienced a crisis or explored options related to identity development and have not made commitments to life choices.

It is expected that individuals will experience identity crises, explore options, and begin moving toward commitments by the completion of college, but individuals who do not may experience poor or insufficient identity development in addition to difficulty navigating young adulthood. Rather than a time of opportunity, joy, and learning, college may be experienced as frustrating, confusing, or overwhelming. The model was adapted with the need for consideration of specific issues faced by women (Josselson, 1978/1991).

Josselson's Work With Women's Identity Development

Adapting Marcia's model (1966), Ruthellen Josselson studied women's identity development and observed similar statuses (1978/1991): *foreclosures: purveyors of heritage; moratoriums: daughters of crisis; identity achievements: pavers of the way;* and *identity diffusions: lost and sometimes found.*

Female college students in the *purveyors of heritage* status have experienced little identity conflict, but are highly committed to traditional or familial roles and identity. They make relational, occupational, and other choices in young adulthood and during college based on the expectations of others. Frequently, these young women experience crises later in life and are able to explore at that time. *Daughters of crisis*, however, find themselves in ongoing and often unstable searching, exploration, and experimentation. Many graduate from college while still in moratorium and require additional years to complete exploration leading to commitment or clarity of identity. As with individuals in Marcia's identity achievement status, young women in Josselson's *pavers of the way* state have successfully moved from childhood to young adulthood, making choices and constructing their identity as they matured. Finally, characterized by an absence of defining crises and exploration and a lack of commitment, female college students in the *lost and sometimes found* category, remained confused, conflicted and without a well-defined identity or purpose (Josselson, 1996). This construct relates back to identity versus role confusion in Erikson's model (Erikson, 1959/1980).

"Emerging Adulthood" as a New Life Stage

Based on his own research in recent years, psychologist Jeffrey Arnett has proposed a change to the psychosocial models discussed earlier (Arnett, 2001, 2003, 2007). After interviewing a group of 18- to 25-year-old Americans and asking if they felt that they had reached adulthood, Arnett identified a new transitional period between adolescence and adulthood: *emerging adulthood*. Most of the young adults questioned for his study indicated that they had moved beyond adolescence, but had not completely moved into a full adult identity. Similar to Erikson's (1968) recognition that industrialized societies provide for a prolonged adolescence and identity exploration, Arnett (2000) attributed the development of this *emerging adulthood* transitional period to significant demographic changes that have occurred since the mid-20th century in industrialized societies. He points to a rise in the median age of marriage and of first childbirth and to the number of young adults pursuing higher education after high school. Describing this transitional period, Arnett (2000) stated the following:

> [T]he goals of identity explorations in emerging adulthood are not limited to direct preparation for adult roles. On the contrary, the explorations of emerging adulthood are in part explorations for their own sake, part of obtaining a broad range of life experiences before taking on enduring—and limiting—adult responsibilities. (p. 474)

In addition, Arnett maintained emerging adulthood is not the same as young adulthood as young adults have already reached adulthood; individuals in the liminal or transitional period of emerging adulthood are neither adolescents nor adults. He suggests that the age range for young adulthood be reconsidered and possibly applied to the 30s. Ramifications of Arnett's transitional developmental period are significant for college students. In many instances, the time allowed for identity exploration and development will increase and the expectations for commitments regarding intimate partners, occupations, and other areas will lessen. Many individuals will complete a degree and graduate before resolving conflicting identities or making commitments to life choices.

SOCIAL IDENTITY DEVELOPMENT THEORIES

In the second half of the 20th century, greater emphasis has been placed on understanding identity development in terms of the self in relation to society (Patton, Renn, Guido, & Quaye, 2016). Social identity theory (Tajfel, 1982) proposes that an individual's identity or sense of self is connected to the groups that he or she belongs to. Recent social movements and their corresponding identity development models based on varying aspects of individual identity and experience have provided new perspectives for considering social identity development. Research has focused on the many facets and dimensions of identity such as race, ethnicity, class, ability, sexual orientation, gender identity, and faith/spirituality. The number of identity domains is extensive and only a few are described here; please also note that specific related theories are discussed in subsequent chapters. Vignoles, Schwartz, and Luyckx (2011) provided a model for organizing and integrating the diverse social identity domains: *individual* or *personal* based on personal goals and values; *relational* defined by the self in relation to others; *collective* developed from an individual's sense of belonging to various groups or categorizations; and *material* often defined by geographic or material possessions.

Race, a collective domain, is one of the most widely studied aspects of identity. Racial identity development theories identify the role of race as it impacts the self-concept and the perception of common experiences with other members of the racial group. In 1979, Atkinson, Morten, and Sue developed one of the first minority identity development models. Subsequently, Sue and Sue (2003) continued research on the model and renamed it the racial and cultural identity development model. Since then, the model has served as an example for other identity development theories based on race. Models or theories based on race include but are not limited to those for Black (Helms, 1990), Latino/a (Ferdman & Gallegos, 2001), and American Indian (Horse, 2012) identity development. As college students examine and define their personal racial identity, they need campus experiences that are inclusive, supportive, and that facilitate exploration. University personnel must work to ensure that the campus environment includes interactions across differences and encourages growth.

Another collective domain emphasized by social identity theories is sexual identity. Given that one of the primary developmental tasks for college students and young adults is the ability to form and maintain intimate relationships, a well-developed sexual identity is important. Without a clear sexual identity, dating and relationships may be chaotic, unfulfilling, and unsatisfying. College campuses must be welcoming, inclusive, and supportive in this area of development as well. Examples of theories focused on this aspect include a more general and unifying model developed by Dillon, Worthington, and Moradi (2011) applicable to individuals of any sexual identity, as well as those specifically addressing homosexuality and bisexuality (Cass, 1979; Fassinger, 1998) and heterosexuality (Worthington, Savoy, Dillon, & Vernaglia, 2002). In addition, working from a model of lesbian, gay, and bisexual development, Bilodeau (2005) developed a model for gender identity development for transgender individuals.

As young adults, college students are constantly involved in the individual or personal identity domain process of making meaning and constructing a worldview—a personal set of values and beliefs crucial to informing identity development. Religious and spiritual affiliation are two significant aspects of social identity based on values and worldview as well as collective identity; however, other purpose- or value-based characteristics, such as political affiliation and community involvement, may provide meaning that contributes to the identity development of young adults (Huddy, 2001; Yates & Youniss, 1998). Examples of social identity theories informing religious and spiritual development include those related to faith (Fowler, 1981) or religious development (Peek, 2005). The process of identity development involves young adults questioning family and societal traditions and beliefs, involvement in communities of shared values, and a commitment to a personal set of mores. This process is facilitated through a campus climate of psychological safety where differences can be examined and where diverse groups can coexist.

Recognizing and integrating the various components of their multiple, complex identities are a daunting challenge for college students. Although it may be tempting to consider aspects in isolation, many factors are interrelated or form multidimensional components (e.g., influence of religion on sexual identity, class on political philosophy). Social identity development is a complex, multifaceted process and young adults who struggle to recognize, accept, and integrate the diverse domains of their identity face subsequent frustration as they move on to subsequent life-span development periods.

Whether viewed from a psychosocial or social identity perspective, young adulthood is a period of life characterized by constant change, continual exploration, a myriad of possibilities, and countless choices. Not all individuals experience the same level of opportunity for identity development because of differences in background, personality, cultural factors, resources, and experiences. Yet all must live through a life-span period that has incredible ramifications for future development. As college students, young adults need intellectually challenging, psychologically safe, and supportive environments that facilitate and enhance this time of identity exploration and formation. If, as Arnett (2000) argued, college students are actually in a period of emerging adulthood with less pressure than historically present to make decisions and commitment to life roles and more extensive time allowed for exploration, then it is vitally important for college personnel to be knowledgeable about the issues facing students and to develop the skills, opportunities, activities, and organizations to enhance and facilitate this distinct and incredibly significant time of growth.

CASE VIGNETTE WRAP-UP: SOFIA

Sofia has to make a decision about a college major and it scares her to go against her family's wishes. She is struggling with what she wants to do and the expectations others have for her. This is not uncommon in many cultures. Sofia meets with her academic advisor and is upset and crying because she really is unsure about what to do. The advisor patiently listens to her and discusses different options including perhaps becoming a science teacher. Sofia had not considered that option, but is still not sure if she wants to be a teacher. The advisor refers her to the Career Center and also provides her with information on various campus activities. It is evident, however, that despite Sofia's earlier attempts to get involved in campus activities, she has few friends. By using one of the theories related to identity development discussed in this chapter, one can gain a clearer picture of the unique challenges faced by students like Sofia. One can also then begin to consider what additional campus resources might be beneficial for her to utilize, as well as what colleges and universities can do to meet the needs of a growing and diverse student body.

CASE VIGNETTE 1 FOR READER REFLECTION: JEFF

Jeff is a 28-year-old army veteran who had served in a combat zone. He was injured when an improvised explosive device exploded incurring severe injuries that continue to cause pain despite surgery and rehabilitation therapy. These injuries led to his medical discharge from the army. Jeff went straight from high school into the military, and it is the only life he has known as an adult. Since his discharge, he has struggled to adjust to civilian life.

(continued)

(continued)

Shortly after enlisting, Jeff married his high school sweetheart and they have two children. The couple has marital problems and has been separated twice. They are currently trying to work things out, but it has been a difficult process.

Jeff could not find work and decided to use his Veterans Affairs benefits to earn a college degree. He hates college for a number of reasons. First, he was upset that the students seemed immature. He also became angry when a political science professor shared her views on why the military needs to be limited and why the United States should never have been involved in the Gulf Wars. When working on group projects, Jeff becomes highly agitated when people are late, and he often tries to take charge. He yelled at a fellow student who did not complete her part of a group project and did not care that her mother was in critical condition in the hospital. It got so tense in the group meeting that another group member asked him to step outside for a few minutes to try to get him to calm down. He left the room and slammed the door, screaming about how irresponsible she was and how she let the team down. When confronted by his professor about the incident he stated that he was correct and that she had failed to complete the "mission."

In addition, Jeff is often quiet in class yet feels quite angry that people do not understand the sacrifices of the military. He has a hard time relating to other students. When students on campus protested the recent presidential election results, he told a group in the student union to "grow up." The college he is attending does not have a Veteran's Center and although he has tried to get involved with organizations, he becomes upset when meetings start late or when the leadership seems disorganized.

- *How might the use of identity development theories be beneficial in understanding Jeff's development?*
- *What can student affairs professionals do to assist Jeff in adjusting to college?*
- *How might Jeff's military experience impact his view of himself and others?*

CASE VIGNETTE 2 FOR READER REFLECTION: LEON

Leon is a biracial male. His mother is White and his father was African American. He is 18 years old and a freshman in college. He was raised by his mother. His father died when he was 2 years old. Leon has always struggled with finding his place and often feels caught between two worlds. His mother's family did not fully accept him and sometimes seemed distant, and his maternal grandparents showed favoritism toward his cousins when he was growing up. He has had limited contact with his father's family since his mother moved to a different state after his father's death. His mother remarried a White man 3 years ago and Leon has a 1-year-old half-sister. His relationship with his stepfather has been stressful and difficult. The stepfather often makes insulting comments about African Americans and encouraged Leon to distance himself from his African American heritage. Although Leon was once close to his mother, they grew apart after his mother remarried. He believes that his mother changed and perhaps even regrets having a biracial son. Thus, in selecting a college, Leon chose one far from home. He thought this would allow him to explore his African American heritage. Leon has made friends at college but struggles sometimes in understanding African Americans. His cultural norms

(continued)

(continued)

tend to be more aligned with his Caucasian roots. Leon has been fortunate to meet a few other biracial students, and there is even a biracial club on campus. However, he has yet to attend a meeting. He is getting As and Bs, but his stepfather has threatened to cut off any support unless he makes all As. Leon does not feel adequately prepared for college and has struggled with study skills and time management.

- *What theories might be used to help Leon understand his racial identity?*
- *Are there resources on college campuses that might assist Leon in learning time management and study skills?*
- *Based on development theories, how might Leon's relationship with his mother and stepfather change as he progresses through college?*

REFERENCES

Arnett, J. J. (2000). Emerging adulthood: A theory of development from the late teens through the twenties. *American Psychologist, 55*(5), 469–480.

Arnett, J. J. (2001). Conceptions of the transition to adulthood: Perspectives from adolescence to midlife. *Journal of Adult Development, 8*, 133–143.

Arnett, J. J. (2003). Conceptions of the transition to adulthood among emerging adults in American ethnic groups. In J. J. Arnett & N. I. Galambos (Eds.), *New directions for child and adolescent development* (No. 100, pp. 63–75). San Francisco, CA: Jossey-Bass.

Arnett, J. J. (2007). Emerging adulthood: What is it and what is it good for? *Child Development Perspectives, 1*, 68–73.

Atkinson, D. R., Morten, G., & Sue, D. W. (1979). *Counseling American minorities* (1st ed.). Dubuque, IA: William C. Brown.

Azmitia, M., Syed, M., & Radmacher, K. (2008). On the intersection of personal and social identities: Introduction and evidence from a longitudinal study of emerging adults. In M. Azmitia, M. Syed, & K. Radmacher (Eds.), *The intersections of personal and social identities: New directions for child and adolescent development* (Issue 120, pp. 1–16). San Francisco, CA: Jossey-Bass.

Bilodeau, B. L. (2005). Beyond the gender binary: A case study of two transgender students at a Midwestern university. *Journal of Gay and Lesbian Issues in Education, 3*(1), 29–46.

Cass, V. (1979). Homosexuality identity formation: A theoretical model. *Journal of Homosexuality, 4*(3), 219–235.

Dillon, F. R., Worthington, R. L., & Moradi, B. (2011). Sexual identity as a universal process. In S. J. Schwartz, K. Luyckx, & V. L. Vignoles (Eds.), *Handbook of identity theory and research* (pp. 649–670). New York, NY: Springer.

Erikson, E. H. (1980). *Identity and the life cycle.* New York, NY: Norton. (Original work published 1959)

Fassinger, R. E. (1998). Lesbian, gay, and bisexual identity and student development theory. In R. L. Sanlo (Ed.), *Working with lesbian, gay, bisexual, and transgender college students: A handbook for faculty and administrators* (pp. 13–22). Westport, CT: Greenwood.

Ferdman, B. M., & Gallegos, P. I. (2001). Racial identity development and Latinos in the United States. In C. I. Wijeyesinghe & B. W. Jackson, III (Eds.), *New perspectives on racial identity development: A theoretical and practical anthology* (pp. 32–66). New York, NY: New York University Press.

Fowler, J. W. (1981). *Stages of faith: The psychology of human development and the quest for meaning.* New York, NY: Harper & Row.

Gates, J. R., Corbin, W. R., & Fromme, K. (2016). Emerging adult identity development, alcohol use, and alcohol-related problems during the transition out of college. *Psychology of Addictive Behaviors, 30,* 345–355.

Helms, J. E. (1990). *Black and white racial identity: Theory, research and practice.* Westport, CT: Greenwood Press.

Horse, P. G. (2012). Twenty first century Native American consciousness: A thematic model of Indian identity. In C. I. Wijeyeslinghe & B. W. Jackson III (Eds.), *New perspectives on racial identity development: A theoretical and practical anthology* (pp. 91–107). New York, NY: New York University Press.

Huddy, L. (2001). From social to political identity: A critical examination of social identity theory. *Political Psychology, 22*(1), 127–156.

Josselson, R. E. (1991). *Finding herself: Pathways to identity development in women.* San Francisco, CA: Jossey-Bass. (Original work published 1978)

Josselson, R. E. (1996). *Revising herself: The story of women's identity from college to midlife.* New York, NY: Oxford University Press.

Knefelkamp, L. L., Widick, C., & Parker, C. A. (1978). Editors' notes: Why bother with theory? In L. L. Kefelkamp, C. Widick, & C. A. Parker (Eds.), *Applying new developmental findings.* New Directions for Student Services (No. 4, pp. vii–xvi). San Francisco, CA: Jossey-Bass.

Marcia, J. E. (1966). Development and validation of ego-identity status. *Journal of Personality and Social Psychology, 3,* 551–558.

Patton, L. D., Renn, K. A., Guido, F. M., & Quaye, S. J. (2016). *Student development in college: Theory, research, and practice* (3rd ed.). San Francisco, CA: Jossey-Bass.

Peek, L. (2005). Becoming Muslim: The development of a religious identity. *Sociology of Religion, 66*(3), 215–242.

Rest, J. R. (1986). *Moral development: Advances in research and theory.* New York, NY: Praeger.

Sue, D. W., & Sue, D. (2003). *Counseling the culturally diverse: Theory and practice* (4th ed.). New York, NY: Wiley.

Tajfel, H. (1982). Social psychology of intergroup relations. *Annual Review of Psychology, 33,* 1–39.

Vignoles, V. L., Schwartz, S. J., & Luyckx, K. (2011). Introduction: Toward an integrative view of identity. In S. J. Schwartz, K. Luyckx, & V. L. Vignoles (Eds.), *Handbook of identity theory and research* (pp. 1–30). New York, NY: Springer.

Worthington, R. L., Savoy, H. B., Dillon, F. R., & Vernaglia, E. R. (2002). Heterosexual identity development: A multidimensional model of individuals and social identity. *Counseling Psychologist, 30,* 496–531.

Yates, M., & Youniss, J. (1998). Community service and political identity development in adolescence. *Journal of Social Issues, 54,* 495–512.

CHAPTER 10

CHICKERING'S THEORY AND THE SEVEN VECTORS OF DEVELOPMENT

Suzanna M. Wise

CASE VIGNETTE: JONAH

Jonah is a 19-year-old college sophomore at a public 4-year university in the Midwest. Jonah identifies as male, gay, and biracial. His mother is of Scottish, Irish, and Welsh ancestry, and his father is Native American. They met during college while on an intervarsity service trip. Jonah is currently majoring in biology and wants to become a doctor. His grades vary with the difficulty of course material, and he currently has a 2.8 grade point average (GPA). He will need at least a grade of 3.5 to apply for the premed program, and he is worried that he will not be able to achieve that. Both his parents graduated from college, but are working in jobs they do not like. They support his being in college and are financially responsible for his education, but they worry about his ability to be successful in his program. When Jonah is at home on weekends, they often suggest that he take time off to choose another major and work while he decides. He turns to his parents most often for advice and guidance. Even though Jonah's school friends challenge him to do well, they intimidate him with their success, and he sometimes shields them from his true performance. Jonah's childhood friends are always there for him, but are relatively low achieving—none of them attended college and they seem content to just work and hang out. Several are in relationships and starting families.

With grades teetering, and concerns about his future career choice, Jonah is wondering if he has chosen the right path. He has the desire to be a doctor and there is great mentorship in his program, but he is not sure if he can be successful and gets very discouraged. He wonders daily if another career path might be a better choice. The advisors in his department are very approachable and knowledgeable, but he worries that they may be too myopic and will only point him toward medical-affiliated careers, so he makes an appointment to see a liberal arts and sciences advisor for broad-based guidance.

(continued)

> *(continued)*
>
> *With every successive generation, college students increasingly experience struggles and difficulties on and off campus; many are surmountable with environmental support, but some challenges require professional intervention. As the progressive demands of society require students to adapt and change at a rapid pace, student affairs professionals are in a prime position to provide the resources necessary for student success (Chickering & Reisser, 1993; Faye & Sharpe, 2008; Hinkelman & Luzzo, 2007). This chapter specifically addresses Jonah's case through the lens of Chickering's framework of college student development. The chapter also briefly outlines Chickering's life work, and ways in which practitioners can apply his theory to their daily interactions with college students.*

OVERVIEW AND DESCRIPTION OF CHICKERING'S THEORY

Concurrent with the release of *Education and Identity* in 1969, the United States was at the nexus of social unrest and expanding funding and support for educational initiatives. The decades of the 1950s and 1960s saw a great increase in research and practice focused on developmental theorists working in the area of higher education. At the forefront of this work was theorist Arthur Chickering. The primary construct of Chickering's (1969) work is the *Seven Vectors of Development*. The discussion that follows is based on the second edition of *Education and Identity* (1993). The vectors are: (a) developing competence, (b) managing emotions, (c) moving through autonomy toward interdependence, (d) developing mature interpersonal relationships, (e) establishing identity, (f) developing purpose, and (g) developing integrity. Of special note is that progressing through the vectors is not a linear or rigid process, but each vector layers onto another and the lines are not distinct. A student will cycle through these vectors as needed in new areas of development, retaining previous learning, and accommodating the fresh learning and experiences.

Developing Competence

This vector addresses competence across three domains: intellectual, physical and manual, and interpersonal. Intellectual competence refers to the knowledge one gains in new experiences, from the transition of what it means to be a student in high school versus college, to learning complex course material, and developing critical thinking skills. Physical and manual competence reflects generally more involvement in athletic pursuits and experiential activities, such as alternative spring breaks and service-learning projects to build and develop resources in communities affected by natural disasters. Finally, interpersonal competence describes learning how to listen and communicate effectively with individuals and groups, balancing one's needs with the needs of those involved, and responding appropriately to social cues and invitations to engage with others. It is in this developmental area that students who are not accustomed to diverse populations will meet new friends and acquaintances with differing identities and life experiences. This will require that students begin to accommodate the complexities of human nature.

Managing Emotions

Emotion regulation is a developmental milestone for adolescents and early adults, often occurring in educational or occupational spaces in relation to others. College can be a tumultuous emotional experience, especially for those students living away from home for the first time. The proximal separation from childhood friends, the formation of new friendships, and the confronting nature of the responsibilities of adulthood has a sometimes disorienting effect on new college students. Additionally, students from historically marginalized groups may form supportive communities in college, where they previously could not, but the overall welcoming and acceptance may not be what they hope for, resulting in feelings of depression, sadness, loneliness, and anger.

A college student's initial feelings of freedom, joy, excitement, and wonderment, tempered by fear, anxiety, confusion, abandonment, and loss can be overwhelming, and they may want to return home within the first few weeks. On the other side, frightening initial feelings can grow into happiness and contentment for the new experience as students find support and settle in. Learning how to manage fluctuating feelings is a continual task for students, both how to express them in healthy ways, and how to restrain them in healthy ways.

Moving Through Autonomy Toward Interdependence

Although a simplification of this vector, developing autonomy certainly does involve learning to do one's own laundry; this process involves not only becoming accustomed to being on one's own, but also learning to develop healthy relationships of give-and-take where one's emotions and actions are not dependent on another's. This vector builds on the vectors before it and bridges the following, as development involves learning to take responsibility for one's own actions, to be self-directed and self-sufficient in the activities and needs of daily living, and developing problem-solving skills. Fostering interdependence helps one rely on others in times of need and stand on one's own two feet in all other times. Difficulties arise when decisions are outsourced, or when one hands his or her personal power to others for fear of making the wrong choices, abdicating responsibility for the outcome.

Developing Mature Interpersonal Relationships

Developing mature and healthy relationships means seeing people for who they are, and not simply for what they represent through stereotypes or labels. It means having your needs met by others and helping others to meet their needs without recrimination, resentment, or scorekeeping. Intimacy becomes more than just physical closeness, but emotional depth of understanding as well. Tolerance becomes acceptance, whether for unique personality characteristics, cultural belongingness, or social affiliation. This vector reflects the previous one in interdependence, a growing understanding of the connectedness among people and recognizing that we are all human with personal strivings and narratives.

Establishing Identity

Likely one of the most important vectors for individuation and differentiation of self, establishing one's own identity separate from others involves developing a strong sense of agency, self-determination, personal drive, and motivation to succeed independent of others' expectations or successes. This process also involves a lot of experimentation as students "try on" many behaviors, personality traits, and appearance styles in the effort to find a good fit. Chickering and Reisser (1993) provide the following list of the elements that characterize a strong sense of identity:

1. Comfort with body and appearance
2. Comfort with gender and sexual orientation
3. Sense of self in a social, historical, and cultural context
4. Clarification of self-concept through roles and lifestyle
5. Sense of self in response to feedback from valued others
6. Self-acceptance and self-esteem
7. Personal stability and integration (p. 49)

As graduation approaches, and with a stable developmental trajectory, this identity discovery and experimentation process usually wanes, and students have settled into a personal style that works for them. However, when it concerns deeper identity issues, such as sexual orientation, gender identity/expression, cultural membership, and the intersectionality of these, the process of solidifying authenticity may take much longer.

Developing Purpose

This vector is crucial for maintaining the drive and motivation one develops in life, for it sustains meaningful activities, commitments, and intentionality. Many students start on the college track and persist due to family desires or established patterns of behavior, but do not decide for themselves why they are studying what they are studying, or investigate whether they are satisfied with the choices they are making. Students who become aware of their individual aspirations earlier to or in this phase will be able to engage in long-term planning with regard to career and life goals.

Developing Integrity

Finally, achieving this vector of developing integrity means that one has created a strong sense of self, takes responsibility and accountability for one's words, beliefs, values, and actions, and can accommodate differing points of view and the perspectives of others without feeling threatened.

The Seven Factors of Environmental Influences

Chickering (1969, 1993) meaningfully situated his vectors within the *Seven Factors of Environmental Influences* to describe the critical importance of the institutional setting and the impact the environment has on student success. These factors include: (a) institutional objectives, (b) institutional size, (c) student–faculty relationships, (d) curriculum, (e) teaching, (f) friendships and student communities, and (g) student development programs and services (Chickering & Reisser, 1993). Taken together, these factors provide the foundation for the developmental process of the seven vectors. Without clear and representative institutional objectives, a manageable size, accessible student–faculty relationships with a small enough ratio, learner-centered curriculum, student-centered teaching, the availability and diversity of student organizations, and supportive programs and services, students will not have the tools to be successful on campus.

HISTORY AND DEVELOPMENT OF CHICKERING'S THEORY

Personal experience drove Arthur Chickering's professional motivation to immerse himself deeply in the work of higher education student affairs, and college student development, because he later understood what his own needs and challenges were while growing up in the educational system (Garfield & David, 1986). He began his career in high schools and moved into colleges and universities as his career evolved and his desire to effect specific change grew. In an interview with Garfield and David (1986), Chickering described a sort of *planned happenstance* (Krumboltz, 2009) career path, "I've never had any design for a career. All my professional moves have been quite serendipitous. Opportunities have presented themselves and I have gone toward them" (p. 488). Chickering's own path through several schooling experiences taught him that he required quite an individualized approach, and sought to provide that to students with whom he worked.

After 10 years of practice in the field as a student affairs professional in positions of varying roles and progressive responsibilities, Chickering wrote his seminal text *Education and Identity*. The book arose from his belief in the possibility of an intentional design for student experiences in college (Garfield & David, 1986), which resulted in the seven vectors framework approach described in the previous section.

Professionals in the field of higher education student affairs and those connected to it are right to regard Chickering as deeply rooted in the profession. His work possesses a relevant and engaging look at college student development that timelessly connects interdisciplinary theory to practice in an accessible way (Garfield & David, 1986; Hinkelman & Luzzo, 2007), with an eye toward changing trends in the status of the modern college student (MacKinnon-Slaney, 1994). Specifically, Chickering highlighted the trend of moving away from the "traditional" full-time college student in residence definition of the typical college student, and shone a light on the needs of the adult learner returning to college, or arriving for the first time (MacKinnon-Slaney, 1994). No matter the age of the student, Chickering believed that the college or university environment was the ideal setting to support student development due to the concentrated resources ready and available to help students succeed at the level that they needed guidance and direction (Chickering & Reisser, 1993).

APPLICATION OF CHICKERING'S THEORY

Widely accepted as one of the prevailing and highly relevant theorists in college student development, Chickering recognized that development is a dynamic phenomenon, difficult to nail down, and only able to focus on a moment in time of a student's college career (Evans, Forney, Guido, Patton, & Renn, 2010). Experiences differ between students, certainly depending on their readiness for college, their previous life experiences, and the available amount of environmental support that help propel students toward success (Zubernis, Snyder, & McCoy, 2011). Chickering used a progressive view of changing social dynamics in his work and demonstrably respected individual worldviews and perspectives. To this end, students benefitting from Chickering's framework have access to supportive services and interventions that are cognizant of their current developmental vectors and the environmental influences that surround them.

College and university campuses routinely employ Chickering's theory of development and his work is quite familiar to the profession of student affairs. In particular, three areas of application are explored as follows to aid in the clarification of services helpful to students.

Programming

First- and second-year programs for students can be especially helpful in the transition process from high school, especially for non–college-ready students (Hinkelman & Luzzo, 2007). These programs can support students in several ways:

- Encourage their academic success by organizing study groups
- Host weekly or monthly workshops with faculty who talk about their research interests and provide opportunities for students to join their research projects
- Organize weekend social outings
- Facilitate mass shopping trips for students who do not have transportation
- Check in on students in residence halls
- Training residence hall staff to recognize issues typical of a first-year college student
- Provide incentives for class attendance or other game-style contests
- Collaborate with offices across campus to highlight available services for students
- Maintain current campus and community referral list for students who need additional or targeted support

Advising

Support services related to the function of academic and other advising increasingly focus on retention in today's universities, due to waning enrollment in higher education nationwide. Students who struggle with academic coursework, relating to their peers, or effectively communicating with their instructors all play a role in whether a student stays in school or adds to the attrition rate. Rather than just encourage students to stay in school and figure things out for themselves, advisors, faculty, staff, and other university personnel can intentionally build relationships with students to create a community of support and connection. Students who feel as if they are a part of a larger whole will be more likely to seek help and mentorship when experiencing struggles (Drake, 2011).

Interventions

As mentioned in the beginning of this chapter, some struggles that students experience require intervention that is more extensive. With a background in school psychology and a developmental focus that is rooted in psychosocial health, Chickering's work lends itself nicely to crossover with mental health services (Garfield & David, 1986).

College students' mental health involves a unique blend of concerns, often difficult for the student to tease out clearly, ranging from stress spurred on by roommate disagreements to mounting pressures to perform well in order to meet the required benchmarks of their program (Gerdes & Mallinckrodt, 1994). Often, concerns are overlapping and complex, and can be scary. To address these issues, most college campuses have a university-wide counseling center, while others have complementary student supports, such as spiritual or religious centers, or peer mentoring/counseling services. Many universities with graduate level programs in psychology, marriage and family therapy, social work, or clinical mental health counseling will have a supervised graduate training clinic available to the campus and surrounding community with free or reduced cost services. Any of these services are available to students for a predetermined or unlimited amount of time, and if a student is in crisis while in the presence of faculty, staff, or other university personnel, those individuals can walk the student to the appropriate offices to receive support. Additionally, trained personnel in career services offices and psychological services offices on campus are available to conduct formal assessments to assist students in understanding themselves better and charting a course for success (Hinkelman & Luzzo, 2007). Career counselors are especially helpful in assisting students to explore career barriers, which often include family dynamics and social concerns. Although most career services representatives are not trained mental health counselors, many are, and can attend in part to these issues (Hinkelman & Luzzo, 2007).

CASE VIGNETTE WRAP-UP: JONAH

Jonah chose to attend general academic advising to explore alternative career paths in case he cannot pull up his GPA and achieve acceptance into the premed program. His academic work to date focused on science-heavy coursework and some general

(continued)

(continued)

education requirements, thus allowing no room for electives. Before discussing what other majors he might be interested in, the advisor told him that if he were to switch majors at this point, he might have to spend more time in school filling in the gaps. Jonah knows that this is a serious consideration for his parents because they are paying for his education right now, and for him, if he should need to arrange for financial aid. The advisor proceeds to explore Jonah's interests, attitudes, and college experiences with informal assessments and discussion. Together they investigate each major that the college offers and narrow down a list. The advisor recommends that Jonah also make an appointment with the career services office to take formal career-related assessments in an effort to hone in on Jonah's specific career interests. In addition, his advisor recommended that he join a student academic support group to bring up his grades. After a few weeks fully immersed in self-reflection, Jonah felt ready to make a change in major.

CASE VIGNETTE 1 FOR READER REFLECTION: MICHELLE

Michelle is a 27-year-old college junior studying economics and political science. She came back to college after a long absence while she served in the armed forces. On separation from the military, Michelle worked as a security guard for a community college while she completed her associate's degree. She has always enjoyed her classes and is looking forward to a career in politics, though she is uncertain what her focus will be. Michelle's husband Paul is in his first year of graduate school and neither of them has a job. Michelle's GI bill will carry her through the rest of her undergraduate education and her husband is using student loans. Michelle and Paul's relationship is essentially a happy one, but they are under a considerable amount of financial and academic stress. They live with her parents because they do not have to pay for rent, utilities, or food. Despite the benefits of living at home, they have a 1-hour commute each way in a shared car. It is challenging to respect her parents' stringent rules, as well as to accommodate the amount of time her parents want to spend with them, not to mention their desire for grandchildren. Paul has a bit of a loner personality and is content to spend as much time alone as he can get, but Michelle is trying to make friends at school so that she feels she has a semblance of a social life. She is not quite sure where to start, as she is new at this university and is older than most of the students with whom she takes classes, with a unique background and life experiences.

- *What are Michelle's greatest needs?*
- *What campus-based services might be most beneficial to Michelle?*
- *What are some goals you would like to see Michelle reach?*

CASE VIGNETTE 2 FOR READER REFLECTION: TAYLOR

Taylor is a 22-year-old African American female, a current junior in college who is considering applying for graduate school. She is a first-generation college student who struggled through high school, but found eventual academic success in college despite personal barriers. Taylor's high school was located in a low-income urban area known for its violence and lack of opportunity. The teachers and administrators in her school were well meaning, but overstretched, and unable to provide the individualized support many students needed to be successful. A local Upward Bound program helped students persist through high school and apply to college. During her sophomore year, one of Taylor's teachers recognized that she had the potential to succeed and recommended her to the program. At first, her mother was reluctant because close parental involvement was required and she worked double shifts, but the program advisors agreed to create a flexible arrangement. When Taylor received her college acceptance letters, she was both excited and nervous, because although she was proud of her success, she knew that she would be paying for school on her own. College proved to be more academically rigorous than Taylor was prepared to handle and she nearly failed out her first semester. Overwhelmed and confused by the college environment, she considers dropping out and getting a job. Taylor returns home for winter break and finds it difficult to interact with the friends she went to high school with because she is the only one going to college. One of her friends jokes that Taylor "sounds White" now, and she must think she is better than everyone else is. Her family wants to support her, but is not sure how. They agree that it would be easier to come home and get a job, make some money, and maybe try again later.

- *What are Taylor's greatest needs?*
- *What campus-based services might be most beneficial to Taylor?*
- *What are some goals you would like to see Taylor reach?*

REFERENCES

Chickering, A. W. (1969). *Education and identity*. San Francisco, CA: Jossey-Bass.

Chickering, A. W., & Reisser, L. (1993). *Education and identity* (2nd ed.). San Francisco, CA: Jossey-Bass.

Drake, J. (2011). The role of academic advising in student retention and persistence. *About Campus, 16*, 8–12. doi:10.1002/abc.20062

Evans, N. J., Forney, D. S., Guido, F. M., Patton, L. D., & Renn, K. A. (2010). *Student development in college: Theory, research, and practice* (2nd ed.). San Francisco, CA: Jossey-Bass.

Faye, C., & Sharpe, D. (2008). Academic motivation in university: The role of basic psychological needs and identity formation. *Canadian Journal of Behavioural Science, 40*(4), 189–199.

Garfield, N. J., & David, L. B. (1986). Arthur Chickering: Bridging theory and practice in student development. *Journal of Counseling & Development, 64*(8), 483–491.

Gerdes, H., & Mallinckrodt, B. (1994). Emotional, social and academic adjustment of college students: A longitudinal study of retention. *Journal of Counseling & Development, 72*(3), 281–288.

Hinkelman, J. M., & Luzzo, D. A. (2007). Mental health and career development of college students. *Journal of Counseling & Development, 85*(2), 143–147.

Krumboltz, J. (2009). The happenstance learning theory. *Journal of Career Assessment, 17*(2), 135–154.

MacKinnon-Slaney, F. (1994). The adult persistence in learning model: A road map to counseling services for adult learners. *Journal of Counseling & Development, 72*(3), 268–275.

Zubernis, L., Snyder, M., & McCoy, V. A. (2011). Counseling lesbian and gay college students through the lens of Cass's and Chickering's developmental models. *Journal of LGBT Issues in Counseling, 5*(2), 122–150. doi:10.1080/15538605.2011.578506

CHAPTER 11

BLACK AND BIRACIAL IDENTITY DEVELOPMENT THEORIES

Ricardo Phipps

CASE VIGNETTE: JAMAAL

Jamaal is an African American freshman from Harlem (NYC), attending a small, Catholic liberal arts college in the Northeast. College leadership has recently decided to observe February as Black History month and encourage students across the campus community to participate in research presentations throughout the month. Jamaal goes to the library for his normal study time and finds several students, mostly of European descent, making poster presentations about various topics pertaining to Black and African American history. One of Jamaal's professors sees him and asks him why he did not do a poster presentation. Jamaal responds that he did not know about the activity. However, Jamaal had read a campus-wide e-mail inviting students to participate. He quickly deleted the e-mail thinking that the activity was a waste of time and felt that the Black History month programs were superficial and patronizing, giving campus administrators an outlet for pretending to care about the needs of Black students on campus. He was afraid that, if he told his professor how he really felt, there would be repercussions that could affect his academic standing.

Racial identity development, like gender identity or national identity development, is a defining process in the life of any individual, which significantly affects all levels of psychological well-being and interpersonal relationships. Helms (1990) defined racial identity as "a sense of group or collective identity based on one's perception that he or she shares a common racial heritage with a particular racial group" (p. 3). Although general identity development begins at birth, as individuals struggle to make sense of their place in the world around them, identity can remain quite amorphous into the years of college life and emerging adulthood, and in some circumstances, far beyond those phases of life. The traditional college experience can be a time of identity searching for young people as they find themselves living in environments with limited parental influence.

Given the racial dynamics of the United States, with the history of the enslavement of people of African descent and subsequent segregation and institutional discrimination and racism, Black identity development cannot be adequately understood without including the context of oppression and marginalization. As college students transition from home environments, which may have provided insulation from the effects of discrimination or that may have been marked by the racial identities of their families of origin, they often confront the challenge and the opportunity of forging their own racial identities. For this reason, student affairs professionals should seek to understand the various dynamics of Black identity development and how these dynamics are manifest on college campuses with students of African descent. Harper and Quaye (2007) postulate that identity conflict is linked to a large number of premature terminations of students' college careers. According to the Pew Research Center, 1.7 million Blacks aged 18 to 24 years were enrolled in college in 2012 (Krogstad & Fry, 2014). Over two thirds of African American men who begin undergraduate studies never graduate (National Center for Education Statistics [NCES], 2005), which Cuyjet (2006) and Harper (2004) attribute to racial identity issues.

Biracial and multiracial identity development has layers of complexity that include the dynamics of oppression connected to Black identity development. In many cases, society has assigned biracial individuals the racial identity of the parent of color. The historical "One Drop Rule" promoted the rule that any person born with any African ancestry should be identified as Black (Root, 1990). Biracial and multiracial individuals in the United States have found themselves in an ongoing struggle between external identification and self-identification. Not until the 2000 U.S. census did designations for individuals who do not identify as monoracial appear among census demographic categories (Pew Research Center, 2015). President Barak Obama (1995), often acclaimed as the first Black or African American president of the United States, described his identity development as a biracial student at the Yale University in his memoir *Dreams From My Father*.

A critical part of understanding how racial identity development affects the collegiate experience of students is linked to having an appreciation for how racial identity development takes places for students who identify as Black American or African American. It is important to note that college students of African descent who were born on the continent of Africa or who are the second generation of immigrant families may not identify as Black American or African American, and the dynamics of racial identity development may unfold very differently for them (Awokoya, 2012). This chapter focuses on the racial identity development of Black or African American college students and of students who identity as biracial or multiracial. Although racial identity development theories do not support biological distinction between racial groups in the United States, they recognize how different conditions of domination or oppression of various groups have influenced their construction of self (Helms, 1995). In this chapter Black is used to refer to the racial identity of U.S.-born persons of African descent who may categorize themselves as Black, Black American, African American, or Afro Caribbean. The term biracial will be used to describe persons with two parents of differing monoracial or multiracial descents (Renn, 2004). It is worth noting that some individuals may claim Black racial identity although neither of their parents identify as Black, such as the case of civil rights activist Rachel

Dolezal (Caldera, 2015). This chapter goes in depth into such alternative experiences of Black identity development.

HISTORY AND DEVELOPMENT OF BLACK IDENTITY DEVELOPMENT THEORIES

Racial identity development theories do not provide universal models that apply perfectly to every individual in a particular racial category, for within-group differences drive a great deal of variation. Racial identity development theories for people of color do attempt to provide a picture of how differing racial groups navigate through a culture that seeks to preserve Whiteness (Evans, Forney, Guido, Patton, & Renn, 2010; Salazar & Abrams, 2005). Several models of Black Identity Development have been created to explain how individuals come to understand their "Blackness" in a traditionally Eurocentric society. The Cross Nigrescence model is possibly the most influential and most widely known. Educated as a psychologist and active in the Civil Rights Movement, William Cross outlined a five-stage process model that explains how Blacks in the United States shift from a White frame of reference to a positive Black frame of reference. The word *nigrescence* is from the French language, meaning "turning black." The five stages were identified as preencounter, encounter, immersion–emersion, internalization, and internalization–commitment (Cross, 1995, 1978; Cross, Parham, & Helms, 1991).

The preencounter stage involves a conscious or unconscious identification of Black values, culture, and traditions as less valuable than Eurocentric values, culture, and traditions. Individuals in this stage may intentionally strive to assimilate into White systems. Vandiver (2001) describes this stage as one that is marred by self-hate, low self-esteem, and poor mental health. College students in late adolescence may find themselves in this preencounter stage for various reasons. Individuals who have grown up in racially homogeneous communities and find themselves in the numerical minority for the first time as they begin college may demonstrate preencounter stage qualities if their precollege training did not include formation in Black history and heritage, rather from the family, school, church, or larger community. Fries-Britt and Griffin (2007) report that high-achieving Black students at predominantly White universities purposely distance themselves from certain racialized activities and groups to avoid being associated with negative stereotypes about Blackness.

Second, the encounter stage is characterized by some significant, critical event creating a disturbance in the tendency to view Black identity in a negative light, which characterizes the preencounter stage. This disturbance leads individuals in the encounter stage to reassess how they view themselves and their cultural backgrounds in larger society. Individuals at the encounter stage may feel that the White society has betrayed them and purposefully perpetuated a social order that seeks to keep people of color in a disempowered position. College students, like Jamaal in the case vignette, may grow increasingly frustrated that interest in African American culture and history is consistently relegated to limited times of the academic year.

The immersion–emersion stage of the Nigrescence model is an exploratory time during which individuals intentionally distance themselves from the dominant, Eurocentric culture and seek greater exposure to African American culture.

This stage is a time for questioning the negative stereotypes that are linked with being Black and adopting a more positive lens (Ritchey, 2015). The feelings of anger and guilt associated with the encounter stage may dissipate, being supplanted by a growing sense of pride. Students in the immersion–emersion stage may organize a demonstration on campus to raise awareness about the alarming number of young Black men who have died in police-related violence in the United States.

The internalization stage is a time for integration of the newly found pride from the previous stage into the personal experiences of individuals. Individuals in the internalization stage tend to become more open to and appreciative of multicultural perspectives, seeing the richness of their own cultural and ethnic identities while also seeing the value in other identities. Black college students in this phase may explore campus activities that promote awareness of other cultural heritages, such as lesbian, gay, bisexual, transgender, and queer (LGBTQ) or Asian American culture, and also engage in activities focused on education and activism around Black culture and history.

Lastly, the internalization–commitment stage is characterized by a shift from exploration to activism. Individuals in this stage are confident about their own cultural and racial identities and also have a strong sense of the universality of humanity. They are actively committed to social justice and transformation and see their Black identity as a call to promote equity across cultures and groups. College students in this stage may involve themselves in a number of campus initiatives geared toward change, ranging from raising awareness about refugee crises throughout the world to spearheading health education about HIV/AIDS. In the internalization–commitment stage, engaging in advocacy that supports the interests of non-Black communities is in no way seen as a rejection of Black identity.

Cross has conducted several quantitative surveys to assess how accurately the model depicts how Blacks experienced identity development, which has led to various revisions. Cross (1991, 1995) eventually combined the fourth and fifth stages into one stage, namely internalization, noting that there were only minute differences between internalization and internalization commitment. In this revised version of the model, Cross identified individuals in this fourth and last stage as falling into one of three categories: Black nationalism (high importance attributed to Black identity), biculturalism (high importance attributed to both Black identity and to American identity), or multiculturalism (strong sense of identity formation across multiple identities, including gender, sexual orientation, as well as race).

One criticism of the original and revised versions of the Cross Nigrescence model is that they limit individuals to stagewise progressions through a hierarchy of stages, each representing higher levels of Black identity development than the previous. The ambiguity of how these linear stages operate in the lives of individuals has also led critics to cite the need for qualitative research to strengthen the model (Bridges, 2015).

Other models have emerged to compensate for the limitations of the Cross model. Helms (1995) created the People of Color Racial Identity using the Cross model as a foundation. Helm attempted to address the identity development experiences of all marginalized groups, proposing a model identity development for African Americans, Asian Americans, Pacific Islanders, Native Americans, and Latino Americans.

HISTORY AND DEVELOPMENT OF BIRACIAL/MULTIRACIAL IDENTITY DEVELOPMENT THEORIES

Changing attitudes in the United States toward the concept of biracial identity have driven the evolution of theories of multiracial identity development. Anti-miscegenation laws extend back to the 17th century in the United States, making interracial marriage illegal (Cruz & Berson, 2001). The practice of hypodescent, also known as the "One Drop Rule," consequently emerged in the United States, dictating that persons born with "one drop" of blood of a non-White race should be automatically assigned to the non-White race (Root, 1990). This was institutionalized through the 1896 U.S. Supreme Court decision *Plessy v. Ferguson* (1986), which upheld the classification as Black of a person documented as seven eighths White and one eighth Black with predominant White physical features (Cruz & Berson, 2001). The predominant view of biracial identity until the 1960s and 1970s was that of biracial identity as inferior status associated with rejection, isolation, and stigmatization. Shih and Sanchez (2005) cite that research routinely was conducted within clinical populations with persons with behavioral and psychological problems, further contributing to the bias that biracial individuals endure lifelong negative psychological consequences due to their racial identity.

In 1967, the U.S. Supreme Court case *Loving v. Virginia* (1967), which invalidated the prohibition of interracial marriages in the United States, brought about the mitigation of legal pressure against the very existence of biracial individuals. *Loving v. Virginia*, along with the energy of the Civil Rights Movement, prompted various biracial researchers to undertake studies that led to viewing biracial identity through a much more positive lens. The prevailing view was that biracial individuals would identify with their non-White heritage, not unlike hypodescent, but with a positive approach (Shih & Sanchez, 2005). Monoracial identity development models, like the Cross model, were applied to the biracial identity development experience. Critics, like Renn (2004), see the reliance on monoracial identity development models to describe biracial identity development as greatly limiting. Cross's model involves a rejection of White culture as an essential middle stage, which may not accurately depict the experiences of many biracial individuals.

The 1990s and 2000s brought about a new approach to biracial identity that was a reaction against confining biracial individuals to monoracial identity development models, allowing for varieties of identity development pathways. Stephan (1992) and Brown (1995) concluded in two separate quantitative studies that the majority of biracial individuals do not self-identify as being members of a singular racial heritage. The 2000 U.S. census was the first to provide the option of endorsing more than a singular racial category (Pew Research Center, 2015). More recent models of biracial identity development recognize the agency of individuals to self-identify racially and to adjust this according to context (Miville, Constantine, Baysden, & So-Lloyd, 2005).

An early, well-known model authored by Poston (1990) has a similar alignment to the original Nigrescence model, also having five stages: personal identity, choice of group categorization, enmeshment/denial, appreciation, and integration. A contemporary of Poston, Root (1990) offered a different model largely based on the assumption that biracial and multiracial individuals begin life as "marginal" because of the unequal statuses that society associates with their different racial compositions and the ambiguity of their racial identities. For Root, biracial identity development is largely about resolving this marginality.

Unlike the stage models, Root identifies four possible means of resolution of marginality. The biracial individual may accept the identity assigned by society, which can be a positive choice if the individual experiences family and community support and is personally satisfied with the identification choice. Society may largely make assumptions about racial identity based on phenotypical characteristics. Assumptions about identity may also vary according to social or geographic context, for example, a college student with one Black parent and one White parent may be viewed in one way at historically Black colleges and universities and identified in a very different way at predominantly White colleges and universities. Biracial individuals may choose to identify with more than one group in their backgrounds, shifting identification according to setting and preference. A biracial college student with both Latino American and Asian American parentage may choose to actively celebrate both identities. Some biracial individuals may opt to self-identify as a single racial identity. This can be a psychologically healthy choice provided persons do not deny their other racial identities. Finally, biracial individuals may self-identify as biracial or multiracial, choosing to view themselves with a blended identity outside traditional racial categories. Using Root's model as a base, Renn (2003) has added a fifth possible means of resolution of marginality, citing that some biracial individuals choose to opt out of racial categories all together.

Renn (2003) suggests that biracial identity development be viewed through an ecological lens, using Bronfenbrenner's Ecology Model as a conceptual framework. An ecological biracial identity development model focuses both on development outcomes and development processes. Concerning college students, environment, context, and time influence how biracial individuals respond to biracial marginality. Using Bronfenbrenner's terminology, Renn reports that biracial college students may self-identify differently according to how they interact with others at the microsystem (face-to-face interactions involving the individual), mesosystem (interaction of two or more microsystems), exosystem (interactions that affect but do not include the individual), and macrosystem (interactions among the microsystem, mesosystem, and exosystem) levels.

Other contextual theories exist to describe the process of identity development in biracial individuals. Seeing biracial identity development as unique for each individual, Wijeyesinghe (2001) proposes the Factor Model of Multiracial Identity (FMMI), which rejects the notion that universal outcomes for racial identity development exist. Rather, the FMMI theorizes that there are certain factors that have varying levels of impact on racial identity. The factors are racial ancestry, early experiences and socialization, cultural attachment, physical appearance, social and historical context, political awareness and orientation, other social identities (e.g., gender, class), and spirituality. These eight categories constitute a constellation of characteristics that influence how and when racial identity crystallizes or shifts for biracial individuals.

APPLICATION OF THEORIES WITHIN STUDENT AFFAIRS

In conclusion of a quantitative study with African American and White undergraduates, Chavous (2005) reported that diversity related issues are still substantial sources of conflict on campuses nationwide, suggesting that predominantly White institutions should be intentional about creating environments more welcoming to diversity. It is imperative that college/university student affairs personnel understand Black identity development in students and its affect on early termination and graduation rates if higher education professionals are to make significant progress in reducing the attrition rates of African American students in college environments. Enhanced understanding of Black identity development in traditional college age students can also potentially aid recruitment efforts with those considering college.

Racial identity development affects both the in-the-classroom and out-of-the-classroom experiences of Black and biracial college students. Courses and seminars that deal with diversity can be effective starting places for helping all students grow in awareness of the importance of university communities being environments respectful of racial diversity. It is critical that student affairs personnel facilitate the establishment and growth of student organizations that support the development of positive self-images in terms of racial identity (Harper & Quaye, 2007). Some may view Black student centers/organizations as divisive and separatist, but they function as resource centers that can serve the whole university community in growing in appreciation of the history and current state of African American thought and culture (Patton, 2006). The student organizations that biracial students seek out as they navigate their identity development can be as diverse as the students themselves, including monoracial student communities as well as multicultural/multiracial organizations.

It is important for student affairs personnel to be aware of both explicit and implicit ways in which university cultures may convey messages of unwelcome to Black and biracial students. In a qualitative study exploring racial microaggressions in residence halls at predominantly White institutions, Harwood, Browne-Huntt, Mendenhall, and Lewis (2012) express alarm about inadequately addressed use of racial slurs and racialized jokes in residence halls and about racial segregation in residence halls. These researchers suggest that universities be more intentional in fostering residence halls serving as "living-learning communities," where students learn socialization in diverse and inclusive environments. This can be accomplished by providing training to staff and students on how to address microaggressions and how to lead meaningful conversations and discussions about race and racial microaggressions (Sue & Constantine, 2007). Nadal et al. (2011) further highlight that the biracial individuals experience racial microaggressions at the hands of Whites as well as monoracial people of color. The phenomenon of colorism, by which lighter complexioned Blacks are seen as superior to darker complexioned Blacks, may have a parallel for biracial individuals.

Student affairs offices should work closely with campus counseling center staff to make sure that clinicians are culturally sensitive and that adequate outreach is done that reaches across all campus groups. College counselors should be aware of the stigmatization that may be an obstacle to certain cultural groups seeking counseling services and employ evidence-based interventions that are effective with people of color (Kearney, Draper, & Baron, 2005; Masuda et al., 2009).

Student affairs personnel can also aid in healthy racial identity development of Black and biracial students by engaging off-campus community partners who can reinforce positive self-image, such as churches. Black Greek fraternities and sororities have long been sources of support and mentorship for Black college students, helping them connect with professionals who can shape their career paths, political and service involvement, and cultural identity (Hevel, Martin, Weeden, & Pascarella, 2015).

At the institutional level, student affairs professionals may need to serve as the conscience of the college or university. Forms on which students are required to provide racial classification should be made as broad and inclusive as possible in order to help students feel as though their identity is welcome. Of even greater importance, Bridges (2011) asserts that faculties need to reflect the diversity of student bodies, which can be a challenge at some predominantly White colleges and universities. The recruitment of Black tenure-track professors as well as biracial and multiracial professors should be a goal that student affairs professionals continuously reiterate.

Political activism can be a very influential aspect of racial identity development, providing healthy and productive outlets for students seeking ways to expose themselves more to unique cultural community needs or to foster change and transformation. College students were integral parts of the Civil Rights Movement, organizing sit-ins to protest discriminatory store and restaurant policies and participating in the Freedom Rides to challenge systematic segregation in Southern states (Morris, 1981). Organizers, like Congressman John Lewis and Julian Bond, as college students, spearheaded voting rights activism through the Student Nonviolent Coordinating Committee, which was comprised primarily of African American college students and young adults in the 1960s (Stoper, 1977). Student affairs personnel are in a unique position to support African American student activism in the current climate. Hope, Keels, and Durkee (2016) hold up the Black Lives Matter movement, which has arisen as a vehicle of protest against violence against young African Americans by law enforcement personnel, particularly by White law enforcement personnel, as a means for college students to combat institutional discrimination. Student affairs professionals often have relationships with students and student organizations that allow them to encourage peaceful protest while also promoting more honest, amiable relationships between students and campus police or between students and city law enforcement.

Finally, student affairs professionals should stay abreast of the current research on Black and biracial students and identity development, continuously preparing for growth in this demographic among college student bodies. The college experience for Black and African American students and biracial students can be the backdrop for discerning and formulating personal values and also reviewing racial self-identification. How this unfolds for students depends on a number of factors, such as demographics of the institution, the degree to which students engage in campus life, and the baseline racial identity with which students begin their college careers. Biracial students may face the added challenge of being marginalized by other monoracial students of color, including Black students. Student affairs professionals, along with other campus administrators, faculty, and staff, have a tremendous responsibility and opportunity to create environments where students can positively own their cultural identities, respect and celebrate the cultural backgrounds of others, and develop an appreciation for solidarity among cultural groups, especially concerning those affected by social injustice.

CASE VIGNETTE WRAP-UP: JAMAAL

Jamaal is experiencing unexpressed resentment toward his college community due to a lack of consistent efforts to celebrate Black history and culture. Using the Cross Nigrescence model of Black identity development, Jamaal seems to be in the encounter stage. The student affairs staff could help Jamaal and other students transition into the immersion–emersion stage or into the internalization stage by inviting them to participate in the planning of forums to expose the college community to Black issues and thought throughout the academic year. Forming a student and faculty diversity committee that audits various campus processes for inclusion and cultural sensitivity could help students like Jamaal move into the internalization–commitment stage, where they become more vigilant and advocate for inclusion of all underrepresented groups. A joint student–faculty committee would also offer Jamaal and other students opportunities to establish mentorship relationships with culturally diverse faculty members, helping students move from frustration to creative activism on issues of identity.

CASE VIGNETTE 1 FOR READER REFLECTION: LALITA

Lalita is a 22-year-old college senior at a university in Southern California. Her mother is the daughter of Mexican immigrants, and her father is African American. She was raised mostly by her mother and her maternal grandfather. Her father and mother never married and grew apart shortly after Lalita was born due to the disapproval of her maternal grandparents of the relationship of Lalita's parents. Lalita has self-identified as Latina all of her life. As a political science major, Lalita has accepted an invitation to work on the campaign of a local candidate for political office, who is Latino.

One of Lalita's campaign responsibilities is to reach out to the local National Association for the Advancement of Colored People (NAACP) to garner support and an endorsement for her candidate. Before this experience, Lalita only had surface knowledge of the work of the NAACP. She was initially resistant to her assignment, having grown up hearing her grandparents question the validity of claims of racism and discrimination by African Americans given the challenges that Latino Americans face. Lalita was surprised to learn of the parallels and similarities between the history of African Americans and the history of Latino Americans in the United States. For the first time in her life, Lalita began to feel disconnected from a significant part of her heritage. Her roommate, a Latina student, does not know that Lalita is biracial and chides her for becoming excessively involved in building bridges between the political campaign and the NAACP. Lalita goes to the university counseling center and reports the reason for her visit as anxiety about her postgraduation plans. When the counselor asks about how her family values shape the career path she is trying to shape, Lalita bursts into tears.

- *How does the clinician identify the role of racial identity development in Lalita's anxiety?*
- *What resources might help Lalita as she addresses this personal challenge?*

CASE VIGNETTE 2 FOR READER REFLECTION: TIFFANY AND FUMALAYA

Tiffany and Fumalaya are first-year students at a predominantly White university in the Southern United States and are roommates at one of the residence halls. Tiffany grew up in a community near the university. Fumalaya was born in Ghana and moved to the United States when she was 10 years old. Her parents are both physicians at a local hospital. The two students are having difficulties adjusting to living together. Tiffany has lots of friends who like to visit her often in the room to study together and to socialize. Fumalaya is often perturbed by what she feels as disrespect for her need for quiet to study and to rest. One night before midterm examinations began, Tiffany and Fumalaya have a heated disagreement in their room, which draws the attention of their residence hall advisor, a White female graduate student. The residence hall advisor asks them about the argument and comments that the two of them should get along because they have so much in common as young Black women.

- *What sensitivities might the residence hall staff need in order to address this tension effectively?*
- *How could the residence hall staff help reframe this situation as a positive opportunity?*

REFERENCES

Awokoya, J. (2012). Identity constructions and negotiations among 1.5- and second-generation Nigerians: The impact of family, school, and peer contexts. *Harvard Educational Review, 82*(2), 255–281.

Bridges, E. M. (2011). Racial identity development and psychological coping strategies of undergraduate and graduate African American males. *Journal of African American Males in Education, 2*(2), 150–167.

Brown, U. M. (1995). Black/white interracial young adults: Quest for racial identity. *American Journal of Orthopsychiatry, 65*, 125–130.

Caldera, A. G. (2015). How Rachel Dolezal forced us to examine who gets to be Black. *Proud Flesh: New Afrikan Journal of Culture, Politics and Consciousness, 11*. Retrieved from http://africaknowledgeproject.org

Chavous, T. M. (2005). An intergroup contact-theory framework for evaluating racial climate on predominantly white college campuses. *American Journal of Community Psychology, 36*(3/4), 239–257.

Cross, W. E., Jr. (1978). The Thomas and Cross models of psychological nigrescence: A review. *The Journal of Black Psychology, 5*(1), 13–31.

Cross, W. E., Jr. (1991). *Shades of black: Diversity in African-American identity*. Philadelphia, PA: Temple University Press.

Cross, W. E., Jr. (1995). The psychology of nigrescence: Revising the Cross model. In J. Ponterotto, M. J. Casas, L. A. Suzuki, & C. M. Alexander (Eds.), *Handbook of multicultural counseling* (pp. 93–122). Thousand Oaks, CA: Sage.

Cross, W. E., Jr., Parham, T. A., & Helms, J. E. (1991). The stages of Black identity development: Nigrescence models. In R. Jones (Ed.), *Black psychology* (3rd ed., pp. 319–338). San Francisco, CA: Cobb & Henry.

Cruz, B. C., & Berson, M. J. (2001). The American melting pot? Miscegenation laws in the United States. *OAH Magazine of History, 15*(4), 80–84.

Cuyjet, M. J. (2006). African American college men: Twenty-first-century issues and concerns. In M. J. Cuyjet (Ed.), *African American men in college* (p. 323). San Francisco, CA: Jossey-Bass.

Evans, N. J., Forney, D. S., Guido, F. M., Patton, L. D., & Renn, P. A. (2010). *Student development in college: Theory, research, and practice* (2nd ed.). San Francisco, CA: Jossey-Bass.

Fries-Britt, S., & Griffin, K. (2007). The Black box: How high-achieving Blacks resist stereotypes about Black Americans. *Journal of College Student Development, 48*(5), 509–524.

Harper, S. R. (2004). The measure of a man: Conceptualizations of masculinity among high achieving African American male college students. *Berkeley Journal of Sociology, 48,* 89–107.

Harper, S. R., & Quaye, S. J. (2007). Student organizations as venues for Black identity expression and development among African American male student leaders. *Journal of College Student Development, 48*(2), 127–144.

Harwood, S. A., Browne-Huntt, M., Mendenhall, R., & Lewis, J. A. (2012). Racial microaggressions in the residence halls: Experiences of students of color at a predominantly White university. *Journal of Diversity in Higher Education, 5*(3), 159–173.

Helms, J. E. (Ed.). (1990). *Black and White racial identity: Theory, research, and practice*. Westport, CT: Greenwood Press.

Helms, J. E. (1995). An update of Helms's White and people of color racial identity models. In J. G. Ponterotto, J. M. Casas, L. A. Suzuki, & C. M. Alexander (Eds.), *Handbook of multicultural counseling* (pp. 181–198). Thousand Oaks, CA: Sage.

Hevel, M. S., Martin, G. L., Weeden, D. D., & Pascarella, E. T. (2015). The effects of fraternity and sorority membership in the fourth year of college: A detrimental or value-added component of undergraduate education? *Journal of College Student Development, 56*(5), 456–470.

Hope, E. C., Keels, M., & Durkee, M. I. (2016). Participation in Black Lives Matter and deferred action for childhood arrivals: Modern activism among Black and Latino college students. *Journal of Diversity in Higher Education, 9*(3), 203–215.

Kearney, L. K., Draper, M., & Baron, A. (2005). Counseling utilization by ethnic minority college students. *Cultural Diversity and Ethnic Minority Psychology, 11*(3), 272–285.

Krogstad, J. M., & Fry, R. (2014). More Hispanics, Blacks enrolling in college, but lag in bachelor's degrees. Pew Research Center. Retrieved from http://www.pewresearch.org/fact-tank/2014/04/24/more-hispanics-blacks-enrolling-in-college-but-lag-in-bachelors-degrees

Loving v. Virginia, 388 U.S. 1 (1967).

Masuda, A., Anderson, P. L., Twohig, M. P., Feinstein, A. B., Chou, Y. Y., Wendell, J. W., & Stormo, A. R. (2009). Help-seeking experiences and attitudes among African American, Asian American, and European American college students. *International Journal for the Advancement of Counselling, 31*(3), 168–180.

Miville, M. L., Constantine, M. G., Baysden, M. F., & So-Lloyd, G. (2005). Chameleon changes: An exploration of racial identity themes of multiracial people. *Journal of Counseling Psychology, 52*(4), 507–516.

Morris, A. (1981). Black southern student sit-in movement: An analysis of internal organization. *American Sociological Review, 46*(6), 744–767.

Nadal, K. L., Wong, Y., Griffin, K., Sriken, J., Vargas, V., Wideman, M., & Kolawole, A. (2011). Microaggressions and the multiracial experience. *International Journal of Humanities and Social Sciences, 1*(7), 36–44.

National Center for Education Statistics. (2005). *Integrated postsecondary education data system*. Washington, DC: U.S. Department of Education, Institute of Education Sciences.

Obama, B. (1995). *Dreams from my father: A story of race and inheritance*. New York, NY: Times Books.

Patton, L. D. (2006). The voice of reason: A qualitative examination of Black student perceptions of Black culture centers. *Journal of College Student Development, 47*(6), 628–646.

Pew Research Center. (2015). Race and multiracial Americans in the U.S. census. Retrieved from http://www.pewsocialtrends.org/2015/06/11/chapter-1-race-and-multiracial-americans-in-the-u-s-census

Plessy v. Ferguson, 163 U.S. 537 (1896).

Poston, W. S. (1990). The biracial identity development model: A needed addition. *Journal of Counseling and Development, 69,* 152–155.

Renn, K. A. (2003). Understanding the identities of mixed-race college students through a developmental ecology lens. *Journal of College Student Development, 44,* 383–403.

Renn, K. A. (2004). *Mixed race students in college: The ecology of race, identity, and community.* Albany, NY: SUNY Press.

Ritchey, K. (2015). Black identity development. *The Vermont Connection, 35*(1), 12.

Root, M. P. (1990). Resolving "other" status: Identity development of biracial individuals. In L. S. Brown & M. P. Root (Eds.), *Diversity and complexity in feminist therapy* (pp. 185–205). New York, NY: Haworth Press.

Salazar, C. F., & Abrams, L. P. (2005). Conceptualizing identity development in members of marginalized groups. *Journal of Professional Counseling: Practice, Theory & Research, 33*(1), 47–59.

Shih, M., & Sanchez, D. T. (2005). Perspectives and research on the positive and negative implications of having multiple racial identities. *Psychological Bulletin, 131,* 569–591.

Stephan, C. W. (1992). Mixed-heritage individuals: Ethnic identity and trait characteristics. In M. P. Root (Ed.), *The multiracial experience: Racial borders as the new frontier* (pp. 50–63). Thousand Oaks, CA: Sage.

Stoper, E. (1977). The Student Nonviolent Coordinating Committee: Rise and fall of a redemptive organization. *Journal of Black Studies, 8*(1), 13–34.

Sue, D. W., & Constantine, M. G. (2007). Racial microaggressions as instigators of difficult dialogues on race: Implications for student affairs educators and students. *College Student Affairs Journal, 26*(2), 136.

Vandiver, B. J. (2001). Psychological nigrescence revisited: Introduction and overview. *Journal of Multicultural Counseling and Development, 29*(3), 165–173.

Wijeyesinghe, C. L. (2001). Racial identity in multiracial people: An alternative paradigm. In C. L. Wijeyesinghe & B. W. Jackson III (Eds.), *New perspectives on racial identity development: A theoretical and practical anthology.* New York, NY: New York University Press.

CHAPTER 12

OTHER THEORIES OF MINORITY IDENTITY DEVELOPMENT

Jesus Cisneros

CASE VIGNETTE: WILLIAM

William, a residence hall director at Southwestern University, will be supervising a staff of six resident assistants (RAs) during the upcoming academic school year. Following a successful leadership retreat, his RAs are expressing a sense of connectedness and cohesion as a staff. Because William is interested in helping his staff members feel as connected on campus as they do on staff, he invites his RAs to share the way they feel following the leadership retreat, in comparison to how they feel on campus day to day.

Robert, a sophomore, is the first to share his perspective. He discusses the difficulty in feeling connected to campus.

> It's hard to feel connected on campus when you are constantly being told that you don't belong here. This is the first space on campus I genuinely feel accepted and welcomed for who I am. I'm proud to be Mexican. Knowing where I come from is really important to me. My parents came to the U.S. to build a better future for my siblings and me. They are the reason why I am taking 18 credits, balancing two jobs, and driving home on the weekends to help around the house. Not even within the on-campus Latinx student organizations do I feel supported. They don't understand what it means to be Mexican, much less what it means to be an immigrant.

Anna, a junior, shares her experience as a highly involved student leader on campus, and a first-generation student:

> I feel really comfortable in this space, and on campus. I feel affirmed by staff and faculty for my leadership and involvement within different student organizations. I think it's because I am not your stereotypical quiet, "don't rock the boat" Filipina. I'm just a normal person like everybody else. It's my parents who don't understand. They

(continued)

(continued)

want me to focus on academics, get married, and start a family. My parents just don't understand that this is not the Philippines. We live in America.

Jerssay, a sophomore, points out that while he feels really comfortable in the group, he feels largely isolated on campus and at home:

Well, I grew up in the reservation and I identify with my Native heritage. I'm the first one from my family to go to college, and sometimes I feel like I am the only Indian on campus. There is no one like me here. Did I mention my family distrusts the educational system? They don't understand why I chose to come here. They would have preferred that I never left the reservation. I'm kind of an outsider both here in college and at home.

William is left wondering how to maintain the connectedness that the students have developed as a staff, while also addressing the concerns they have raised about feeling disconnected elsewhere. Aware that each student is exploring various aspects of their social identities, William wonders how he can best support them using minority identity development theories.

OVERVIEW AND DESCRIPTION OF MINORITY IDENTITY DEVELOPMENT THEORIES

Latinx

The panethnic term *Latinx* is used to refer to individuals whose ethnic origins are found in Central American, Caribbean, and South American countries. The larger category of Latinx is comprised of many subgroups, typically identified in terms of national origin. Given the complexity and heterogeneity of Latinx experience, social processes differ systematically across subgroups, and their reduction to the single category of Latinx or Hispanic poses challenges, given the depoliticization of each group's distinct history with the United States (e.g., immigration, colonization, exploitation). Despite these limitations, there are a few models of identity development that primarily describe patterns of Latinxs' awareness of an association with Latinx or Hispanic culture and heritage (Ferdman & Gallegos, 2001; Keefe & Padilla, 1987; Torres, 2003). These models appear to be more open to the nuances in Latinx or Hispanic heritage, calling out the ways that students might define their heritage or culture and then how they dissociate with it in the college environment.

Latinx Racial Identity Orientations

Ferdman and Gallegos (2001) created a model of Latinx identity that considers the racial system in the United States. It offers a descriptive approach to capturing some of the richness and variety inherent in the Latinx experience, and is intended for practitioners seeking to understand or work with Latinxs in a way that more broadly recognizes and accepts the breadth of their experience. Based on patterns observed,

Ferdman and Gallegos (2001) provide six different orientations that serve as lenses through which Latinxs view themselves, and that can help in cross-cultural collaboration among subgroups of Latinxs and between Latinxs and other groups.

Latinx-integrated individuals understand and are able to deal with the full complexity of Latinx identity. They are aware of their own subgroup background and culture, as well as how these relate to those of other Latinx subgroups (Ferdman & Gallegos, 2001). Their identification with Latinxs as a group encompasses both positive and negative attributions. Thus, they are able to fully identify with their culture and appreciate many aspects of it, while still being able to criticize other features. Whites and members of other groups are also viewed broadly, and the complexity of their cultural and individual orientations is recognized and accepted.

Latinx-identified individuals maintain a pan-Latinx identity that places culture, history, and other ethnic markers in a prominent place. Their notion of race is uniquely constructed, whereby Latinx is regarded as a distinct racial category across subgroups, and more fluid, inclusive, and dynamic than the either/or nature of U.S. racial constructs. They view other groups in categorical and relatively rigid, unshifting terms, and Whites as potential barriers or allies, depending on their behavior.

Subgroup-identified individuals think of themselves primarily in terms of their own ethnic or national-origin subgroup, which is the focus of their identification. They view themselves as distinct from Whites, but do not necessarily identify or easily connect with other Latinxs or people of color. Subgroup-identified individuals do not have a broad pan-Latinx perspective, and employ a more narrow and exclusive view of their groupness. Furthermore, Whites are not central to their thinking, though they are conscious that Whites can be barriers to their full inclusion. Because they do not view race as a central or clear organizing concept, they view nationality, ethnicity, and culture as preeminent.

Individuals with the orientation of *Latinx as "Other"* are not very aware of their specific Latinx background, history, and culture. They see themselves as "not White" and do not have a clear view or much knowledge of their own group. Because of mixed background, phenotype, prevailing racial constructions as well as other factors, they see themselves as people of color, without distinguishing themselves from other subgroups. They may also describe themselves as a minority. Individuals in this orientation see their color as a major unifying factor that connects them to other people of color rather than to the dominant group.

Individuals with an *Undifferentiated* orientation prefer to identify themselves and others as "just people," often claiming to be color blind. They do not share the focus of racial categorization, and accept the dominant norms of our society without question. When they encounter barriers to their inclusion, they attribute these setbacks to individual behavior rather than intergroup dynamics. Generally, they do not seek any particular association with other Latinxs, because they view each person as being distinct from their racial or ethnic identity.

Individuals with a *White-identified* orientation are likely to see themselves racially as White, and as distinct from and superior to people of color. Although people in this orientation may be bicultural, they value Whiteness as an essential and primary element of their identity, preferring Whites and White culture over

Latinxs and Latinx culture. This orientation is also reflected in people who recognize, either consciously or unconsciously, that they are different from Whites, but they continue to prefer all that is connected to Whiteness.

Model of Hispanic Identity Development

Torres (2003) focuses on the formation of ethnic identity among Hispanics, and how an individual comes to understand his or her ethnicity. The model examines the ways students changed in their association with being Hispanic based on conflicts with their culture and changes in their environment. The model can be categorized into two brackets: *Situating Identity,* or the starting point of identity development in college, and *Influences on Change* in identity development.

According to Torres (2003), three conditions help explain the *Situating Identity* category: (a) the environment where they grew up, (b) family influences and generation in the United States, and (c) self-perception of status in society. These conditions identify the influences that distinguish the different starting points of the participants.

The composition of the environment where students grew up influences their cultural orientation and how they self-identify ethnically. Hispanics who are exposed to a lot of diversity growing up will have a stronger sense of ethnicity and be more open to people from other backgrounds. Similarly, students who grow up surrounded by the majority White culture will relate more with the dominant culture. Family influences and generational status influence the way students identify themselves. Students in their first year of college are likely to use the same terms and language their parents use, and share similar views on ethnicity and its role in their life. Regarding generational status, second- and third-generation students will be more acculturated to majority culture and experience less conflict with parents than first-generation students, who are often caught among the expectations, traditions, and knowledge from the majority culture and their culture of origin. The self-perception of their status in society regards the sense of privilege students felt growing up, as compared with others. Students who perceive a sense of privilege are more likely to believe in the negative stereotypes about Hispanics and not see the stereotypes as applying to them. Students who do not perceive any sense of privilege are more likely to open up to others and recognize racism in society. This condition focuses more on how individuals react to others and their ability to recognize racism when it is occurring to them or around them (Torres, 2003, p. 539).

Regarding *Influences on Change* in identity development, Torres (2003) found that students' identities could change when they experience conflict with culture, and when they experience a change in relationships within the environment. Investigating one's culture might resolve a cultural conflict in one student, whereas parental pressures and cultural expectations can create conflict in another student. Similarly, the peer group that an individual seeks out while in college can influence change on identity development. Changes in personal relationships and involvement in Latinx student groups can influence personal growth and identity development.

Asian American and Pacific Islander

Some models homogenize the identity development of Asian Americans into a single model (e.g., Maekawa Kodama, McEwen, Liang, & Lee, 2002). Although this serves a positive purpose in terms of coalition building, it also means some important cultural and historic facts get lost in the search for a common story. With more than 30 different national origins included in the Asian American category in the United States, some Asian American identity development models have been more geared toward particular ethnic groups within this large, diverse population (Perry, Vance, & Helms, 2009). Because Asian American identity is multidimensional, the following highlights a couple of models that consider individual subgroups and their unique histories.

Filipino American Identity Development Model

Because of a distinct history and culture that differentiates them from other Asian groups, Nadal (2004) concentrated his theoretical efforts on Filipino identity development. Influenced by Kim's (1981) Asian American identity development model, Nadal (2004) offered a six-stage model of development that describes the process of ethnic identity formation for native-born/second-generation Filipino Americans in the United States. The model is nonlinear, and participants may advance through the stages in a progressive manner, but may occasionally jump back and forth between stages. Depending on their environments, surroundings, and influences, some people may remain in certain stages for their entire lives or not progress through all of the stages.

The *Ethnic Awareness* stage begins at the Filipino Americans' earliest memories (generally 2–5 years of age), where children have a positive/impartial view of Filipino culture because it is the only living culture of which they are aware. Filipino Americans are somewhat indifferent to other Asian and minority groups at this stage because, as children, they have a minimal concept of race or ethnicity. However, they may develop a positive view of the White/dominant group because they may be accustomed to seeing them on television or viewing pictures of them in books.

Filipino Americans in the *Assimilation to Dominant Culture* stage are distinguishable by their preference for dominant cultural values over their own. They strive for Whiteness and assimilation. This stage can begin as early as 5 years old and can possibly continue for a person's entire adult life. The continual realization of a White-dominated American society will entice Filipino Americans to view themselves and other Filipino Americans in negative and depreciating ways. Similarly, Filipino Americans will hold the same beliefs about Asian Americans as they do about their own ethnic group, and will not want to be affiliated with any minority group at all in order to push themselves away from a minority status.

In the *Social Political Awakening* stage, Filipino Americans begin to realize the social injustice and racial inequality in the world around them, and their inability to rise to the standards of Whiteness. This can be triggered by a racial prejudiced experience, or simply by education or enlightenment (Nadal, 2004). In this stage, Filipino Americans feel a sense of community involvement and a need to encourage others of their same group to become more socially or politically aware. Similarly, they will seek out and form allegiances with other Asian Americans and minority groups who have been oppressed. At this stage, Filipino Americans are very angry with the superiority of White culture in society, and are automatically prejudiced against every White person they encounter.

In the *Panethnic Asian American Consciousness* stage, Filipino Americans are socialized to accept their role in the Asian American paradigm and see themselves as members of a greater panethnic group. They join the Asian American social and community groups in an attempt to find similarity and power in numbers, feel more accepted, have a greater sense of belonging, and feel part of a community. In this stage, Filipino Americans understand their role in a centralized "Asian" sense (Nadal, 2004), and advocate for the issues and needs of Asian Americans as a whole, while retaining a positive and accepting outlook on other minorities and negative views of the White society.

Filipino Americans in the *Ethnocentric Realization* stage are triggered by an event that helps them understand that they are unjustly classified in the Asian American paradigm. They gain self-empowerment to advocate for their needs as Filipino Americans, and think of themselves as Filipinos, not Asian Americans. Similarly, Filipinos may begin to pledge allegiance to other Pacific Islander cultures (e.g., Samoans, Native Hawaiians) that have also been marginalized in the Asian American racial category. In an effort to advance the separation of Filipinos from the Asian American paradigm, they may feel the need to become more tolerant and educate their White counterparts regarding the uniqueness of Filipinos.

Finally, the *Incorporation* stage encompasses a positive and comfortable Filipino American identity with consequent respect for other cultural or racial heritages, including the White majority. Filipino Americans no longer feel a need to identify either with or against White people. This stage is focused more on Filipino American pride, gratification, and appreciation. Filipino Americans do not necessarily see their placement in the Asian American category as a completely negative factor, but will continue to advocate for themselves and their Filipino community, and social justice in general (Nadal, 2004).

South Asian American Identity Development

The model proposed by Ibrahim, Ohnishi, and Sandhu (1997) similarly subscribes to the panethnic Asian American identity development models proposed by previous scholars (e.g., Kim, 1981), but argues that the stages of minority identity development are mediated by generation in the United States. This model specifically addresses the issues of immigration and colonization that affect the ethnic identity development of South Asian American immigrant populations, primarily Indian and Pakistan Americans.

Because South Asian immigrants are from countries with histories of colonization, Ibrahim et al. (1997) asserted that South Asian Americans could clearly see and accept the cultural differences between them and the host culture. As such, there is no *Preencounter* or *Conformity* stage, as postulated by the models of minority ethnic identity (e.g., Kim, 1981; Uba, 1994). "The acceptance of cultural differences is a reality of life for this group" (Ibrahim et al., 1997, p. 42). Additionally, because South Asian Americans may hold a belief that the "American dream [means] that hard work will overcome all differences" (p. 42), the *Dissonance* stage for members of this generation occurs when they realize that hard work is not enough, that cultural differences cannot be overcome, and acceptance by White Americans or other U.S.-born ethnic minorities will not occur based on the perceived differences.

In line with other minority identity development models, in the *Resistance* and *Immersion* stage, South Asian immigrants revert to their own heritage, rejecting all mainstream and other ethnic minority assumptions and values. Furthermore, there is a commitment and identification with South Asian culture and an interest in reaffirming their ethnic identity. In this stage, South Asian immigrants may seek out ways to align with other minority groups that have been oppressed in a like manner.

Then in the *Introspection* stage, South Asian Americans are sufficiently secure about their identity to begin to question previously held dogmatic beliefs. They also begin to seek their individuality as members of a minority group, but also recognize some positive elements in the dominant culture. Finally, in the *Synergistic Articulation* and *Awareness* stage, South Asian Americans develop a strong sense of self-worth and individuality. They are able to accept or reject the cultural values of the dominant and the minority groups on an objective basis. Furthermore, they recognize that accepting and valuing their own ethnic group does not mean that other groups do not also have positive attributes (Ibrahim et al., 1997).

American Indian

Three labels commonly used to refer to aboriginal people of America include Indian, American Indian, and Native American, and the terms are often used interchangeably. However, tribal or national affiliation has greater importance than broad terminology. Pan-Indian perspectives that transcend the specificity of each individual tribe can efface the geographical, linguistic, cultural, and historical differences among the more than 500 recognized Native nations of North America. "Indianness" becomes even more complicated when considered within the context of tribal diversity. Despite these limitations, a few models attempt to address the nuances of American Indian identity development.

Five Categories of Indianness

Building on the work of several researchers, LaFromboise, Trimble, and Mohatt (1990) classified Indians according to residential patterns, level of tribal affiliation, and extent of commitment to maintaining their tribal heritage. In these categories, the level of acculturation to U.S. mainstream culture is contrasted with the maintenance of the ethnic identity exhibited by the individual. The five categories of Indianness are described as follows:

- *Traditional*: These individuals generally speak and think in their native language and know little English. They observe "old-time" traditions and values.
- *Transitional*: These individuals generally speak both English and the Native language in the home. They question basic traditionalism and religion, yet cannot fully accept dominant culture and values.

- *Marginal*: These people may be defensively Indian, but are unable either to live the cultural heritage of their tribal group or to identify with the dominant problems (e.g., socioeconomic status, religion, politics) due to their ethnicity.
- *Assimilated*: Within this group are the people who, for the most part, have been accepted by the dominant society. They generally have embraced dominant culture and values.
- *Bicultural*: Within this group are those who are, for the most part, accepted by the dominant society. Yet, they also know and accept their tribal traditions and culture. They can thus move in either direction, from traditional society to dominant society with ease (LaFromboise et al., 1990, p. 638).

These categories focus on the level of acculturation and maintenance of ethnic identity that an individual exhibits. Though it is unclear what developmental process, if any, occurs within these categories, these categories can serve as a tool to help describe the diversity among American Indian students.

Native American Identity Model

Horse (2001) developed a framework to provide understanding of Native American racial identity based primarily on what he termed as individual and group "consciousness." This consciousness captures the unique and collective experiences of American Indians within a psychosocial context (Horse, 2012). There are five cross-generational psychological influences that effect American Indian consciousness.

- Knowledge of native language and culture
- The validity of one's genealogical heritage as Indian
- Adoption of a worldview that respects Native traditions and philosophies
- The degree to which a person identifies as Indian
- One's status as a member of an officially recognized tribe

Horse (2012) offered additional considerations for thinking about American Indian consciousness across generations and time. American Indians of the future will define Indianness in their own time and as circumstances may dictate. "Contemporary influences of racial awareness, the legal status of Indians, and potential loss of native languages and culture will all figure into the Indian identity equation" (p. 110). Several areas of consciousness expected to influence American Indian identity in the 21st century are described as follows:

- *Eras of change in Indian consciousness:* American Indian consciousness is shaped by tribal histories and cultures, and the tension between past and current situations. The first era refers to when Indians were totally independent, before the establishment of European or American colonies. The second era began with the U.S. Declaration of Independence and the subsequent westward expansion of the new nation. The third era covered the latter part of the 19th century, when Indians were adjudicated by the Supreme Court as being domestic dependent nations (Horse, 2012, p. 110). Today's era encompasses the 21st century, where Americans strive for more independence from the U.S. government.
- *Orientation to race consciousness:* Many American Indians view themselves as "the people" (Horse, 2012, p. 111), rather than as a race. Indian sensibilities about

race will evolve as each succeeding generation comes to know themselves in relation to their tribal affiliations and in relation to the larger modern society.
- *Orientation toward political consciousness:* The legal status of Indian tribes as sovereign nations is critical to how Indians see themselves. Being aware of the political struggles, Indian tribes' experience is important to understanding current political events.
- *Orientation toward linguistic consciousness:* Language is the most potent aspect of one's tribal identity (Horse, 2012, p. 114). One of the most salient issues for Indian tribes is the dwindling number of fluent speakers. Hence, the struggle for new generations of American Indians is to maintain their native language amid the social complexities and economic imperatives of the modern world.
- *Orientation toward cultural consciousness:* The cultural consciousness of Indians depends on the extent to which individuals take responsibility for learning and maintaining cultural elements, whether old, renewed, or new. Culture, which is intertwined with language, shapes American Indian identity in ways that Western culture cannot. Maintaining cultural traditions in an ever-changing world will be the challenge for new generations of American Indians.

HISTORY AND DEVELOPMENT OF THE THEORIES

Historically, there has been a lack of attention toward underrepresented students within the foundational theories of college student development. Several development theories cannot be fully applied to minority students due to the fact that their cultures differ greatly from that of mainstream culture. Hence, with the diversification of higher education, researchers became concerned that race and ethnicity were not yet given in-depth consideration in students' development in college. Because racial identity is an important element of both individual and group identity, minority identity development models were developed to help explain the integration of race into an individual's sense of self (Sue & Sue, 2013; Wijeyesinghe & Jackson, 2012). Minority identity development models are anchored in the belief that all minority groups experience the common force of oppression, and as a result, will generate attitudes and behaviors consistent with a natural internal struggle to develop a strong sense of self and group identity, in spite of the oppressive conditions.

IMPLICATIONS FOR STUDENT AFFAIRS PRACTITIONERS

The general racial/ethnic identity theories offer some insight into possible ways to approach diversity education within all aspects of student affairs. Students should be provided opportunities to explore their backgrounds and identities in a space conducive to learning and development. Student affairs professionals and faculty could facilitate educational programs, seminars, and workshops that challenge students to confront issues of prejudice and racism as well as to cultivate racial or ethnic pride. These programs should address the external conditions in which students explore their identity and how to make meaning of shifting thoughts as they progress in their racial or ethnic identity development. By looking at diversity through the lens of racial or ethnic orientation, professionals can meet students where they are and help them not only understand other cultures, but also how they fit into their own race/ethnicity.

Practitioners might also use these models as a way to gain insight as to where students might be in their racial/ethnic identity development. Having such understanding would enable practitioners or faculty to better advise, supervise, or support students in their learning and development during college. Although these theories are useful for understanding potential issues that subgroups of students may experience, all students should still be seen and treated as individuals who may not necessarily fit into essentialized models.

CASE VIGNETTE WRAP-UP: WILLIAM

William recognizes that in order for his students to feel as connected on campus as they do on staff, he will have to work with them individually throughout the upcoming school year. He schedules regular one-on-one meetings with each staff member to revisit some of the concerns they expressed during the leadership retreat.

With Robert, for example, they focus on the ways that his Mexican identity affects how he regards the environment, as well as other Latinxs on campus. Because he thinks of himself primarily in terms of his national origin, Robert might fall within the Subgroup-identified orientation of Ferdman and Gallegos's (2001) model, where students view themselves as distinct from Whites, but do not necessarily identify or easily connect with other Latinxs or people of color. Hence, their one-on-one meetings focus on increasing Robert's awareness of Mexican background and history, and how these relate to the struggles of other Latinx subgroups.

Given Anna's preference for dominant cultural values over her own, she may be situated in the Assimilation to Dominant Culture stage of Nadal's (2004) model. Hence, with Anna, William focuses on sociopolitical awareness. Through conversation regarding social injustice and racial inequality, William seeks to increase Anna's understanding of her cultural heritage in order to enrich her perspective of her ethnic community and expose her to the struggles of other Asian American students on campus.

Jerssay's inability to move in either direction from traditional society to dominant society with ease suggests that he may be situated in the Transitional category of LaFromboise et al.'s (1990) model of Indianness. With Jerssay, William seeks to identify some of the challenges impeding his mobility within both cultures. They discuss the history associated with Jerssay's culture, recognizing the role of colonization and its effect on Native Americans' views of the educational system. Similarly, William helps Jerssay identify resources focused on Native American culture, including student organizations and cultural centers.

In addition to the regular one-on-one meetings, William also relies on intercultural programming opportunities. For example, one week he invites all members of his staff to bring a cultural artifact to their staff meeting and share aspects of their culture that they are most proud of. Another week, students explore their family tree and discuss the differences and similarities they observe across cultures. Other weeks, he invites speakers from the Office of Diversity and Inclusion to present on topics regarding privilege and oppression as it pertains to ethnic minority and majority groups in the United States. The objective of these efforts is to provide his RAs opportunities for personal/professional development, challenge his staff to think about race and ethnicity more complexly, and lead his RAs to seek out/create visible support structures on campus for similarly identified students.

CASE VIGNETTE 1 FOR READER REFLECTION: JULIA

Julia is a freshman student living in Bear Hall at Southwest University, a Hispanic Serving Institution. As the Residence Life Coordinator for Bear Hall, you are working late in your office one day when Julia walks in and asks to speak with you. Julia states that she feels rejected by other Latinx students in the residence hall for being more American than Latinx. She says,

"Every moment I am in this place I struggle with who I am and where I fit in. Why does everyone feel the need to label me? Can't I just be a student? I don't understand why people segregate themselves by race when we are all just people."

As her residence life coordinator, you are concerned that Julia is not connecting well with other residents. After talking further with Julia, you learn that she comes from a predominately White high school, and this is the first time she has been challenged to think about her ethnic identity for the purpose of making friends.

- *Using student development theory as a guide, how can you help Julia acknowledge and develop her Latinx identity?*

CASE VIGNETTE 2 FOR READER REFLECTION: MARK

Mark is a sophomore in college, and a social work major applying for a summer position within a local nonprofit organization. Part of his application requires a statement of interest that describes how his identity has shaped his approach toward working with underrepresented students. Though he identifies as American Indian, Mark feels guilty writing about his indigenous roots, given how he does not speak his native language and knows very little about his tribe's culture. He did not take previous interest in learning about the traditions and philosophies of his tribe because he did not see it as relevant to his life outside of the reservation. Not really knowing how to respond to his essay prompt, Mark comes to you for advice.

- *As his mentor and adviser, how can you use student development theory to support Mark as he explores his American Indian identity?*

REFERENCES

Ferdman, B. M., & Gallegos, P. I. (2001). Racial identity development and Latinos in the United States. In C. L. Wjeyesinghe & B. W. Jackson III (Eds.), *New perspectives on racial identity development* (pp. 32–66). New York, NY: New York University Press.

Horse, P. G. (2001). Reflections on American Indian identity development. In C. L. Wijeyesinghe & B. W. Jackson III (Eds.), *New perspectives on racial identity: A theoretical and practical anthology* (pp. 91–107). New York, NY: New York University Press.

Horse, P. G. (2012) Twenty-first century Native American consciousness. In C. Wijeyesinghe & B. W. Jackson (Eds.), *New perspectives on racial identity: Integrating emerging frameworks* (2nd ed., pp. 108–120). New York, NY: New York University Press.

Ibrahim, F., Ohnishi, H., & Sandhu, D. S. (1997). Asian American identity development: A culture-specific model for South Asian Americans. *Journal of Multicultural Counseling and Development, 25*, 34–50.

Keefe, S. E., & Padilla, A. M. (1987). *Chicano ethnicity.* Albuquerque: University of New Mexico Press.

Kim, J. (1981). *Processes of Asian American identity development: A study of Japanese American women's perceptions of their struggle to achieve positive identities as Americans of Asian ancestry.* Unpublished doctoral dissertation, University of Massachusetts, Amherst.

LaFromboise, T. D., Trimble, J. E., & Mohatt, G. V. (1990). Counseling intervention and American Indian tradition: An integrative approach. *The Counseling Psychologist, 18*(4), 628–654.

Maekawa Kodoma, C., McEwen, M. K., Liang, C. T., & Lee, S. (2002). An Asian American perspective on psychosocial student development theory. In M. K. McEwen, C. Maekawa Kodoma, A. N. Alvarez, S. Lee, & C. T. H. Liang (Eds.), *Working with Asian American college students* (pp. 45–59). San Francisco, CA: Jossey-Bass.

Nadal, K. L. (2004). Pilipino American Identity development model. *Journal of Multicultural Counseling and Development, 32*(1), 45–62.

Perry, J. C., Vance, K. S., & Helms, J. E. (2009). Using the People of Color Racial Identity Attitude Scale among Asian American college students: An exploratory factor analysis. *American Journal of Orthopsychiatry, 79*(2), 252–260.

Sue, D. W., & Sue, D. (2013). *Counseling the culturally diverse: Theory and practice* (6th ed.). New York, NY: Wiley.

Torres, V. (2003). Validation of a bicultural orientation model for Hispanic college students. *Journal of College Student Development, 40*(3), 285–298.

Wijeyesinghe, C., & Jackson, B. (Eds.). (2012). *New perspectives on racial identity development: Integrating emerging frameworks* (2nd ed., pp. 81–120). New York, NY: New York University Press.

CHAPTER 13

WHITE IDENTITY DEVELOPMENT

Ian S. Turnage-Butterbaugh

CASE VIGNETTE: CRAIG

Craig is a lower-middle-class White male student from a small Southern town with very little racial or cultural diversity. He is in his first year at a public state university where he is pursuing a bachelor's degree in general studies, unsure of what he wants to be or do with his life. The transition to university life has been tumultuous. He is doing relatively well academically, but is having difficulty successfully integrating into the college social scene and is conflicted about the sociopolitical environment at the university. Recently, African American students at the university engaged in nonviolent protests across campus, calling for the reform of policies that perpetuate academic inequalities based on students' racial heritage. During a discussion about diversity, inclusion, oppression, and racism in Craig's social problems course, he and a couple of his White friends voiced their views that the African American community on campus was generally oversensitive and whiny. In particular, he said that he came from a relatively poor family of Italian descent, had to work hard to get into college on scholarship, and faced his own barriers to success, but never complained about it. Furthermore, he and his friends stated that they did not understand why the problems of African Americans on campus seemed more important than those he and his friends face. When he faces challenges, he buckles down, works hard, and overcomes them; anyone who cannot overcome the challenges they face must be lazy and their struggles are well deserved.

It may be surprising to learn that investigations into White identity development began to emerge in the mid-1980s, after the exploration, development, testing, and refinement of racial identity models for minority groups in America (Rowe, Bennett, & Atkinson, 1994). Additionally, since the mid-1980s, the amount of research and literature pertaining to White identity development pales in comparison to that of the racial identity models pertaining to minority groups in general. The relatively new interest in White identity development and the sparse literature delineating the developmental path toward a healthy White identity may, in some ways, serve as a metaphor for the racial identity development process often engaged in by White Americans. That is, as Todd and Abrams (2011) pointed out, White racial identity is often developed passively partly due to defensive mechanisms preventing White Americans from identifying as White (Katz & Ivey, 1977), as well as their unawareness of racial issues, institutional discrimination, and racial privilege (Neville, Lilly, Duran, Lee, & Browne, 2000). The result is that many White Americans "have no consistent conception of a positive White identity or consciousness" (Helms, 1990a, p. 50). Just as White Americans have the choice whether or not to attend to their Whiteness and typically only do so after coming into contact with other racial or ethnic groups, research examining White identity was not attended to until the emergence of racial identity development theories pertaining to non-White racial groups (Kim, 1981).

HISTORY AND DEVELOPMENT OF WHITE IDENTITY DEVELOPMENT THEORIES

On the heels of the 1954 Supreme Court decision in *Brown v. Board of Education*, the Civil Rights Act of 1964, the Voting Rights Act of 1965, and the repealing of anti-miscegenation laws in 1967, interracial interactions increased in many professional and educational settings (Baum, 2006), creating new questions regarding issues of race and racism. One area of uncertainty regarding the influences and effects of interracial interactions was that of counseling and psychotherapy, which led to the proliferation of interracial models of mental health services (Banks, 1975; Gardner, 1971; Harrison, 1975; Jones & Seagull, 1978) and served as the impetus for racial identity development models. Initially, racial identity development models were limited to racial/ethnic minority groups such as African Americans (Butler, 1975; Cross, 1971; Milliones, 1980) and Asian Americans (Kim, 1981); however, Hardiman (1982) and Helms (1984) extrapolated and applied those early models to the racial identity development of White Americans. The Hardiman (1982) and Helms (1984) models were a function of the sociopolitical environment following the Civil Rights and Black power movements of the 1960s and 1970s (Hardiman & Keehn, 2012). Believing that members of all socio-racial groups traverse a similar racial identity development process, these new models modified previous typologies to include and reflect the unique power, privileges, and socialization processes experienced by White Americans, as well as variegated reactions to that socialization (Helms, 1995).

OVERVIEW AND DESCRIPTION OF WHITE IDENTITY DEVELOPMENT THEORY

No single White identity development theory exists; however, dominant theories have emerged, resulting from continued research, modification, verification, and scrutiny. Table 13.1 summarizes informal and formal White identity development theories, their respective developmental distinctions, and the growing complexity involved in achieving healthy identity formation. At their core, all White identity development theories share that common goal: the development of a healthy White

TABLE 13.1 White Racial Identity Development Models

AUTHOR	STAGE 1	STAGE 2	STAGE 3	STAGE 4	STAGE 5	STAGE 6	STAGE 7
Ganter (1977)	Denial and protest	Guilt and despair	Integration of awareness and freedom from racism				
Terry (1977)	Color blind	White Blacks	New Whites				
Hardiman (1982)	Naiveté	Acceptance	Resistance	Redefinition	Internalization		
	Abandonment of racism (Phase 1)			Defining a nonracist White identity (Phase 2)			
Helms (1984)	Contact	Disintegration	Reintegration	Pseudo-independence	Immersion/emersion	Autonomy	
Sabnani, Ponterotto, and Borodovsky (1991)	Preexposure/precontact	Conflict	Prominority/antiracism	Retreat into White culture	Redefinition and integration		
	Underachieved White racial consciousness				Achieved White racial consciousness		
Rowe, Bennett, and Atkinson (1994)	Avoidant	Dependent	Dissonant	Dominative	Conflictive	Reactive	Integrative
Sue and Sue (2003, 2013)	Naiveté	Conformity	Dissonance	Resistance and immersion	Introspection	Integrative awareness	Commitment to antiracist action

Note: Although the term stage is used to distinguish levels of development in this table, not all White racial identity models are stage models. For example, in 1995, Helms relabeled stages as statuses; Rowe, Bennett, and Atkinson (1994) describe developmental attitudes; and Sue and Sue (2003) outline distinct *phases*.

identity. This goal is not profound, as developmental theories in general identify stages, statuses, positions, or phases that, if successfully completed, result in healthy development. Healthy racial identity development for White Americans, however, describes a process of overcoming individual, institutional, and cultural racism in order to redefine a view of self as "a racial being that does not depend on the perceived superiority of one racial group over another" (Helms, 1990a, p. 49). Succinctly put, healthy White identity development is achieved if three outcomes are realized: (a) abandoning racism, (b) acceptance of Whiteness, and (c) adopting a nonracist and nondefensive White identity.

Informal and loosely generated models of White identity development began to emerge in the late 1970s and early 1980s (Ganter, 1977; Hardiman, 1982; Terry, 1977); however, the first formal White identity development model, or typology, was proposed by Helms in 1984. Subsequently, White racial identity development models gained the attention of additional scholars and researchers and several dominant, and largely comparative theories emerged. The most widely cited, implemented, and accepted model of White identity development is that of Helms (1984). The next section of this chapter describes her model, followed by an application of the model to the opening vignette.

Helms's Contributions

Although formal in its intent and purpose, the development of Helms's model used neither scientifically nor experimentally sound methodology. In attempting to understand how White Americans developed a racial identity, Helms, with the help of a graduate student, interviewed "a few White friends and colleagues to determine how they viewed the development of their racial consciousness" (Helms, 1984, p. 155). The initial result was a five-stage developmental model; however, the stages were renamed ego statuses to more accurately reflect the complex cognitive and affective processes of racial identity development, as opposed to nominal categories into which individuals could be assigned (Helms, 1992, 1994; Helms & Piper, 1994). Additionally, an Immersion/Emersion status was added (Helms, 1990a), resulting in a total of six statuses: (a) Contact, (b) Disintegration, (c) Reintegration, (d) Pseudoindependence, (e) Immersion/Emersion, and (f) Autonomy. Helms further categorized the statuses into two phases, depicted in Table 13.2. The first three statuses represent a process of abandoning one's racist attitudes, whereas the last three statuses involve redefining one's Whiteness as nonracist, transcending cultural and institutional racism. Successfully progressing through the developmental statuses results in positive growth from racial naiveté and a simple awareness that people of color exist to a sophisticated identity status of understanding, accepting, appreciating, and respecting one's own and others' racial diversity and cultural norms (Helms, 1990a). It is important to note, however, that Helms (1984) cautioned that there is the potential for either a positive or negative resolution of each developmental status and Utsey and Gernat (2002) suggest that development is contingent on the individual's societal context.

Contact. The first White racial identity status begins when one becomes aware of the presence of people of color, either vicariously through the experiences and reports of others, or directly through interactions with members of racial minorities (Helms, 1990a). During Contact, one automatically views members of diverse

TABLE 13.2 Summary of Helms's (1984, 1995) White Racial Identity Development Model

PHASE/STATUS	DEVELOPMENTAL MILESTONES	OBLIVIOUSNESS AND NAIVETÉ
1. Abandonment of racism		
a. Contact	Awareness of persons of color, but evaluations of others are based on societal stereotypes, unaware of their racism and prejudices	
b. Disintegration	Ambivalent White racial identity due to conflict related to racial inequalities	Disorientation, confusion, and suppression of information
c. Reintegration	Reaffirmation of White superiority over persons of color and entrenchment in racist beliefs	Selective distortion of information
2. Defining a nonracist White identity		
d. Pseudo-independence	Acceptance of responsibility in racism and attempts to alter racist attitudes, beliefs, and behaviors	Reshaping race-related stimuli to fit their own liberal societal framework
e. Immersion/emersion	Exploration of what it means to be White resulting in changed race-related beliefs and emotional catharsis	
f. Autonomy	Enhanced multicultural competence and internalization of White racial identity devoid of superiority to others	Flexible interpretations and responses to racial material and stimuli

racial backgrounds through the lens of their socialized racial beliefs and evaluates persons of color based on societal stereotypes, unaware of their racism and prejudices. The duration of the contact status depends on the type of experiences one has with persons of color and the reactions to those experiences. The White individual who has few interracial interactions likely will experience stagnated racial identity development. Conversely, the White individual who engages in continuous interactions with members of diverse racial groups likely will move to the next identity status due to the dissonance between their racial biases and the reality of racism in America. Similarly, the White individual who approaches and responds to interracial interactions with fear may remain in the contact status longer than the individual who adopts a curious stance toward racial differences (Helms, 1990a).

Disintegration. One's Whiteness, as a conscious racial identity, is a hallmark of the Disintegration status and emerges due to the conflicted awareness of one's moral virtues against the fractured racial equity in America. The result often is an ambivalent racial identity in which one is trapped between his or her own racial group and that of others, which may lead to feelings of guilt, depression, helplessness, or anxiety (Helms, 1990a; Sue & Sue, 2013). Progression beyond Disintegration in Helm's developmental sequence is contingent on one's response to and resolution of these feelings, and responses to these feelings are largely dependent on the degree to which interracial interactions are avoidable. Helms suggests three possible reactions: (a) avoiding further contact with persons of color, (b) combating racial beliefs, and (c) adopting new beliefs about racism, its existence, and its cause. If interracial interactions are unavoidable and one adopts new beliefs, he or she moves to the reintegration status.

Reintegration. Sue and Sue (2013) describe the Reintegration status as a regression in racial identity development in which "the pendulum swings back to the most basic beliefs of White superiority and minority inferiority" (p. 653). During this time, White people reaffirm the belief that unequal positions in society are earned, deserved, and justifiable due to strengths of White culture and society and the shortcomings of persons of color (Helms, 1990b; Siegel & Carter, 2014). The result typically is the entrenchment of rigid racial attitudes and beliefs that can only be overcome if one experiences a new event that challenges his or her racial identity to a degree that it has not been challenged previously.

Pseudoindependence. This status marks the transition from Phase 1 to Phase 2 of Helms's model, during which one moves from abandoning racism to redefining a positive White identity. As such, individuals engaging in Pseudoindependence begin to become acutely aware of racial inequities, accept their responsibility in perpetuating racism, and identify with persons of color. Although individuals have the best of intentions at this developmental status, the irony is that they may unknowingly preserve racial dynamics through superficial and misguided attempts to help individuals of racial minority groups to adopt White standards and values. Only when individuals begin to expand their understanding of White identity beyond racial factors, do they move to the next developmental status.

Immersion/Emersion. During this status, the individual engages in an exploration of what it means to be White. This question, answered only by an awareness, understanding, and acceptance of historical aspects of Whiteness in America, often compels individuals to consume literature in an attempt to identify a developmental template from the experiences of White leaders and heroes from the past. The developmental tasks are twofold: First, rather than attempting to force persons of color to adapt to White norms, individuals aspire to change their own beliefs and attitudes; second, individuals attempt to enhance their cognitive, emotional, and experiential understanding of multiracial interactions that were overlooked or misunderstood in previous statuses (Lipsky, 1978; Sue & Sue, 2013). The result often is an emotional catharsis that not only reinforces one's redefined White identity but also serves as a catalyst for future developmental tasks involving transcending racism and oppression (Helms, 1990a).

Autonomy. Internalizing and actualizing one's newfound racial self-identity, developing multicultural sensitivity and awareness, accepting one's responsibility in perpetuating racism, and eliminating oppression and abandoning racism are the major goals of the Autonomy status (Helms, 1990a). As Sue and Sue (2013) put it, an individual maintaining the status of Autonomy "walk the talk" (p. 657) in that they seek out interracial experiences that are not distorted by fear, intimidation, or defensiveness. Although the autonomous person is not perfect, he or she engages in an ongoing process of developing multicultural competencies and sensitivity with a curious, respectful, and egalitarian attitude.

APPLICATION OF THE THEORY WITHIN STUDENT AFFAIRS

By turning our attention back to the opening vignette and applying Helms's (1995) model to conceptualize Craig's White racial identity development, we can arrive at a clearer understanding of the cognitive–emotional processes sustaining his racist attitudes and guiding his view of self and others. For Craig, the dominant ego status governing his racial reaction likely is Reintegration, as he is interpreting and distorting social information in a way that conforms to racial stereotypes and minimizes differences between himself and others. Additionally, he is angry with and intolerant of people from other racial backgrounds and lacks an understanding of or empathy for others' histories. Because there is no history of violence, and because of his intolerance, it is very likely that he has adopted a passive expression of interaction with people of color, attempting to avoid environments in which encounters with people of color are possible (Daniels, 2001).

Craig's White racial identity development has stagnated and moving beyond this developmental status will be a challenge. Helms (1990a) suggested that individuals may very well remain in the Reintegration status for the duration of their lives. This developmental stagnation is more probable if an individual chooses a passive expression of White superiority. Because Craig comes from a small, predominately White Southern town, it is likely that he has been socialized to believe White people have earned their superiority and the benefits of privilege and preference. In the absence of contradictory experiences, which Craig is avoiding, his socialized view of race-related issues and differences will endure. While Craig has acknowledged his White racial identity, although conflicted and precursory, it is rigidly defined as racist and fuels the negative interracial interactions he has with others on campus.

Developmental Tasks and Conditions for Change

Helms (1990a) suggested that in order for persons functioning from the Reintegration ego status to move toward healthier development, they must experience a jarring or traumatic event that challenges them to the degree that they are compelled to engage in self-reflection and reevaluate their beliefs systems. Again, because Craig likely is avoiding contact and engagement with persons of color, it is unlikely that he will experience a situation that adequately confronts the discrepancies between his racist attitudes and beliefs and the realities of the racial inequalities on campus and the myth of White superiority in general. The following section identifies strategies for educators and student affairs practitioners to work with students like Craig to begin to more fully understand his Whiteness, the sociopolitical realities of race on campus and, in general, increase his multicultural competence, and engage in healthy interracial interactions. Implications are drawn for educators first, followed by strategies for working with and promoting racial identity development among students.

IMPLICATIONS FOR HELPING PROFESSIONALS ON A COLLEGE CAMPUS

Much research has been conducted on the conditions needed to reduce racism and prejudice, stemming from the work of Allport (1954; Dovidio, Glick, & Rudman, 2005). In their summary of the research, Sue and Sue (2003) identified seven basic principles of prejudice reduction, including the importance of efforts taken and supported by authorities and leaders. Because the focus of this book is on identifying ways in which helping professionals, educators, and student affairs practitioners can work with students on a diverse college campus, this principle will serve as a guide for the remainder of this chapter. The next section is a summary of the literature examining the steps educators and student affairs practitioners can take to promote their own cross-cultural interactions and multicultural knowledge in order to more effectively work with students struggling with their own racial identity, followed by the strategies to promote healthy interracial interactions among students.

Enhancing One's Own Racial Identity Development and Multicultural Competences

Rieger (2015) applied Helms's (1992) model to teacher education and, in doing so, proposed several activities educators should engage in to promote their own White racial identity development and increase their understanding of the needs of culturally and racially diverse students. Rieger's model is adapted for this chapter in Table 13.3.

Sue and Constantine (2007) suggested that activities such as those listed in Table 13.3 are essential for educators to (a) understand themselves as racial–cultural beings, (b) understand the worldviews of other racial groups, and (c) develop the expertise needed to facilitate difficult dialogues on race.

Promoting White Racial Identity Development and Healthy Interracial Interactions Among Students

A number of obstacles prevent White individuals from exploring their own racial identity and difficult race-related issues including negative emotions, such as anxiety, guilt, and fear (Helms, 1984; Sue & Constantine, 2007). Although resistance is rooted in anxiety, it is possible to recognize and overcome anxiety-provoking racial dialogues and interactions. Some strategies for helping students such as Craig acknowledge their anxiety, overcome their defenses, explore their White racial identity, and have healthier interactions with others from diverse racial and cultural backgrounds are listed as follows.

Deconstructing Whiteness. Poignant interrogations of what it means to be White, with the power to expose the hegemonic invisibility Whiteness, are needed to indefinitely overcome racial ignorance and increase multicultural competencies. Ortiz and Rhoads (2000) proposed an educational framework specifically designed to deconstruct Whiteness among college students. Although a detailed description of their framework is beyond the scope of this chapter, they identify activities to

TABLE 13.3 Activities Designed to Enhance One's Own Racial Identity Development and Multicultural Competence

DIVERSE SETTINGS	SELF-REFLECTION	UNCOVER BIASES
Educators should be placed in or seek out settings with a diverse body of students. As research indicates, and as Helms's model suggests, homogeneous classroom settings lead to decreased awareness of racial issues, whereas culturally diverse classroom settings lead to an increased awareness of such issues and increase teacher effectiveness (Groff & Peters, 2012)	Multiracial fieldwork is even more meaningful when educators engage in critical self-reflection on issues related to privilege and power. Educators can use Helms's model as a guide for self-reflective journaling in order to critically examine their own Whiteness, which Austin and Hickey (2007) describe as a "process of critical autoethnographic interrogations of Self" (p. 82)	Educators should seek to uncover their implicit racial biases and how they impact the ways in which they work with their students. Rieger suggests that using the Implicit Association Test (IAT) will help prepare educators to engage in dialogues about their biases as well as antibiased behaviors in the college classroom
SERVICE-LEARNING PROJECTS	**CREATING A POSITIVE CLIMATE FOR MULTIRACIAL DIALOGUE**	**EXPLORING THEORIES OF RACIAL IDENTITY DEVELOPMENT**
In order to become allies and agents of change, educators should engage in service-learning projects at their college or in the community so they can become "co-creators of meaningful, wanted change" (Ullucci, 2010, p. 152) and serve as models or mentors for others	Educators should engage in conversations with colleagues and peers about race-related issues that often are overlooked in order to gain a deeper understanding of their own racial identity. Mueller and Pope (2001) found that those who openly explore the meaning of being White often have increased multicultural competence	Exploring racial identity should extend beyond Helms's model and include other theories of racial identity development. An integrative approach of exploration may lead to more advanced levels of multicultural and multiracial awareness

help students develop an understanding of culture, learn about other cultures, recognize and deconstruct White culture, recognize the legitimacy of other cultures, and develop a multicultural outlook.

Recognizing and Reducing Microaggressions. Craig's language about persons of color on campus takes the form of microaggressions, or what Sue et al. (2007) describe as brief, everyday exchanges that direct denigrating messages and negative racial slights toward people of color because of their membership in a racial minority group. Educators should endeavor to create safe and supportive, yet structured environments, in which Craig and others can be challenged to self-examine. Goals of self-examination include increasing students' ability to identify racial microaggressions in themselves and others, understanding how microaggressions negatively impact persons of color, and recognizing and accepting their responsibility in taking positive steps in overcoming racial biases.

Engaging in Difficult Dialogues. Watt (2007) highlights the importance of engaging students in difficult discussions pertaining to stereotypes, diversity, social justice, and their privileged identities, as well as the appropriateness of student affairs practitioners and educators for leading these discussions. Although dialogue is essential for critical consciousness, defensive reactions to difficult or sensitive topics create challenges for effectively facilitating such discussions. Power Carter et al. (2007) have identified five strategies that help facilitators avoid silencing or shutting down difficult dialogues: (a) interrogate the various ways that privilege functions within their own lives and experiences, (b) facilitate an environment of respect in which students can reflect on their own experiences, (c) facilitate an environment where students hold each other accountable by questioning and challenging each other's comments and ideas, (d) be willing to find comfort in discomfort as difficult dialogues often breed tension and intense emotions, and (e) listen and pay attention. In particular, listen to the silences. Nonverbal communication, such as body language and eye movements, are often the initial entry points of difficult conversations.

Enhancing Experiential Reality. Sue and Sue (2013) suggest that it simply is not enough to increase understanding through reading and discussing differences. Rather, factual information must be supplemented with experiential reality of the groups one hopes to better understand. Increasing and repeating intergroup contact is well documented as an effective way to reduce prejudice (Allport, 1954; Dovidio et al., 2005; Mallett & Wilson, 2010; Pettigrew & Tropp, 2000); however, these interactions must be carefully planned and implemented under favorable conditions. Implementation of the strategies given previously helps create favorable conditions for intergroup interaction, such as increasing out-group knowledge (Aydogan & Gronsalkorale, 2015); remaining aware of one's language, thoughts, and emotions (Sue & Sue, 2013); and reducing participants' anxiety through thoughtful dialogue and self-reflection (West, Shelton, & Trail, 2009).

CASE VIGNETTE WRAP-UP: CRAIG

Engaging in the activities and implementing the suggestions mentioned earlier will help ensure that educators and administrators have a better understanding of their own racial identity development, are able to understand Craig's needs, have the personal tools to effectively work with him, and are able to provide him with the corrective experiences needed in order to begin redefining his White racial identity as nonracist. Encouraging Craig to adopt a multicultural perspective through the process of deconstructing his Whiteness and challenging the universalization of White superiority will help him take the first steps toward redefining a positive White identity. Similarly, facilitating difficult race-related dialogues may create contradictory experiences needed for Craig to begin to abandon his essentially racist identity. If, on the other hand, discussions are not adequately challenging, having Craig engage in structured, nonthreatening interracial interactions may lead Craig to adopt new standards against which to evaluate self and others. As a result,

(continued)

(continued)

Craig may begin to accept and become curious about racial minority groups, leading to further willingness to engage in difficult discussion, self-examine, and redefine his White racial identity.

Reflect on the suggestions and conditions that enhance racial identity development in this case and ask yourself these questions:

- *What about your own racial identity development could help you better understand and work with a student like Craig?*
- *Who can you turn to in order to engage in discussion about the complex issues of race that impact you and the students you work with?*
- *What outreach opportunities are available that would help you become an ally and agent of change on campus or in the community?*
- *What opportunities exist, or can be created, to increase interracial experiences among your students?*
- *What conditions and/or resources can you identify within the college administration that might help a student like Craig to continue to develop a healthy White racial identity?*
- *What challenges might you face in facilitating and engaging students in difficult dialogues about stereotypes, diversity, social justice, and their privileged identities?*
- *How would you overcome those challenges and students' defenses against such dialogues?*

CASE VIGNETTE 1 FOR READER REFLECTION: STUDENTS WRESTLING WITH GUILT

Recently, a hate crime was committed against several members of a racial minority group on the campus where you work as a student affairs practitioner. Your office has been working with students in response to the crime and the impact it has had on the students, campus, and community. Several White students come to you because of increased feelings of guilt and shame for belonging to the same racial group of those that committed the hate crime. Although they were not the perpetrators, they have become aware of the discrimination and racial inequalities on campus and feel simultaneously disconnected from their White peers and those of racial minorities. Additionally, they are beginning to understand how their upbringing socialized them to overlook these race-related issues in the past and recognize that their obliviousness to racism has inadvertently contributed to it. In the wake of the hate crime, they want to actively engage in the discussions and responses across campus, but feel marginalized themselves, and are unsure of where to make a difference.

- *What are some suggestions you might have for providing direction to the students?*
- *What are some of the concerns you have about their potential activities?*
- *What should they be aware of?*

CASE VIGNETTE 2 FOR READER REFLECTION: WHITE STUDENTS RESPONDING TO A HATE CRIME

Based on your understanding of Perry's developmental framework, what position are the students in Case Vignette 1 functioning from? Which of the strategies to promote White racial identity development and healthy interracial interactions seem most appropriate to focus on when working with these students? Because these students are beginning to question their socialized privileged position, what interventions can you identify that might help them develop a greater understanding of how White culture has been universalized as the norm? These students want to engage in meaningful action in response to the hate crimes. Ortiz and Rhoads (2000) suggested that developing a multicultural outlook is a prerequisite for action.

- *What campus or community opportunities exist that may help these students gain more multicultural competence, which may empower them to engage in the desired meaningful actions?*
- *How has the university responded to the hate crime and how might those responses influence these students' own responses and continued White racial identity development?*

REFERENCES

Allport, G. W. (1954). *The nature of prejudice.* Cambridge, MA: Perseus Books.

Austin, J., & Hickey, A. (2007). Writing race: Making meaning of White racial identity in initial teacher education. *International Journal of Pedagogies and Learning, 3*(1), 82–91.

Aydogan, A. F., & Gronsalkorale, K. (2015). Breaking down a barrier: Increasing perceived out-group knowledge reduces negative expectancies about intergroup interaction. *European Journal of Social Psychology, 45*(4), 401–408.

Banks, H. C. (1975). The Black person as client and as therapist. *Professional Psychology, 8*(4), 470–475.

Baum, B. (2006). *The rise and fall of the Caucasian race: A political history of racial identity.* New York, NY: New York University Press.

Brown v. Board of Education, 347 U.S. 483 (1954).

Butler, R. O. (1975). Psychotherapy: Implications of a Black-consciousness process model. *Psychotherapy: Theory, Research, and Practice, 12*(4), 407–411.

Cross, W. E., Jr. (1971). The Negro-to-Black conversion experience. *Black World, 20*(9), 13–27.

Daniels, J. A. (2001). Conceptualizing a case of indirect racism using the White Racial Identity Development model. *Journal of Mental Health Counseling, 23*(3), 256–268.

Dovidio, J. F., Glick, P., & Rudman, L. A. (2005). Introduction: Reflecting on *The Nature of Prejudice: Fifty years after Allport.* In J. F. Dovidio, P. Glick, & L. A. Rudman (Eds.), *On the nature of prejudice: Fifty years after Allport* (pp. 1–15). Malden, MA: Blackwell.

Ganter, G. (1977). The socio-conditions of the White practitioner: New perspectives. *Journal of Contemporary Psychotherapy, 9*(1), 26–32.

Gardner, L. H. (1971). The therapeutic relationship under varying conditions of race. *Psychotherapy: Theory, Research, and Practice, 8*(1), 78–87.

Groff, C. A., & Peters, T. (2012). "I don't see color": The impact of field placements on preservice teachers' white racial identity development. *Journal of Educational and Developmental Psychology, 2*(2), 1–15.

Hardiman, R. (1982). White identity development: A process-oriented model for describing the racial consciousness of White Americans. *Dissertation Abstracts International, 43,* 104A.

Hardiman, R., & Keehn, M. (2012). White identity development revisited: Listening to White students. In C. L. Wijeyesinghe & B. W. Jackson, III (Eds.), *New perspectives on racial identity development: Integrating emerging frameworks* (2nd ed., pp. 121–137). New York, NY: New York University Press.

Harrison, D. K. (1975). Race as a counselor/client variable in counseling and psychotherapy: A review of the research. *The Counseling Psychologist, 5*(1), 124–133.

Helms, J. E. (1984). Toward a theoretical explanation of the effects of race on counseling: A Black and White model. *The Counseling Psychologist, 12*(4), 153–165.

Helms, J. E. (1990a). Toward a model of White racial identity development. In J. E. Helms (Ed.), *Black and White racial identity: Theory, research, and practice* (pp. 49–66). Westport, CT: Praeger.

Helms, J. E. (1990b). *Training manual for diagnosing racial identity in social interactions*. Topeka, KS: Content Communications.

Helms, J. E. (1992). *A race is a nice thing to have*. Topeka, KS: Content Communications.

Helms, J. E. (1994). Racial identity and other "racial" constructs. In E. J. Trickett, R. Watts, & D. Birman (Eds.), *Human diversity* (pp. 285–311). San Francisco, CA: Jossey-Bass.

Helms, J. E. (1995). An update of Helms's White and people of color racial identity models. In J. G. Ponterotto, J. M, Casa, L. A. Suzuki, & C. M. Alexander (Eds.), *Handbook of multicultural counseling* (pp. 181–198). Thousand Oaks, CA: Sage.

Helms, J. E., & Piper, R. E. (1994). Implications of racial identity theory for vocational psychology. *Journal of Counseling Psychology, 44*(2), 124–138.

Jones, A., & Seagull, A. A. (1978). Dimensions of the relationship between the Black client and the White therapist. *American Psychologist, 32*(10), 850–855.

Katz, J. H., & Ivey, A. E. (1977). White awareness: The frontier of racism awareness training. *Personnel and Guidance Journal, 55*(8), 485–488.

Kim, J. (1981). The process of Asian-American identity development: A study of Japanese-American women's perceptions of their struggle to achieve positive identities as Americans of Asian ancestry. *Dissertation Abstracts International, 42*, 1551A. (University of Massachusetts Microfilms No. 8118010)

Lipsky, S. (1978). Internalized oppression. In J. Duncan (Ed.), *Black reemergence* (Vol. 2). Seattle, WA: Rational Island.

Mallett, R. K., & Wilson, T. D. (2010). Increasing positive intergroup contact. *Journal of Experimental Social Psychology, 46*(2), 382–387.

Milliones, J. (1980). Construction of a Black consciousness measure: Psychotherapeutic implications. *Psychotherapy: Theory, Research and Practice, 17*(2), 175–182.

Mueller, J. A., & Pope, R. L. (2001). The relationship between multicultural competence and White racial consciousness among student affairs practitioners. *Journal of College Student Development, 42*, 133–144.

Neville, H. A., Lilly, R. L., Duran, G., Lee, R. M., & Browne, L. (2000). Construction and initial validation of the Color-Blind Racial Attitudes Scale (CoBRAS). *Journal of Counseling Psychology, 47*(1), 59–70.

Ortiz, A. M., & Rhoads, R. A. (2000). Deconstructing Whiteness as part of a multicultural educational framework: From theory to practice. *Journal of College Student Development, 41*(1), 81–93.

Pettigrew, T. F., & Tropp, L. R. (2000). Does intergroup contact reduce prejudice? Recent meta-analytic findings. In S. Oskamp (Ed.), *Reducing prejudice and discrimination: Social psychological perspectives* (pp. 93–114). Mahwah, NJ: Lawrence Erlbaum.

Power Carter, S., Honeyford, M., McKaskle, D. Guthrie, F., Mahoney, S., & Carter, G. D. (2007). "What do you mean by Whiteness?": A professor, four doctoral students, and a student affairs administrator explore Whiteness. *College Student Affairs Journal, 26*(2), 152–159.

Rieger, A. (2015). Making sense of White identity development: The implications for teacher education. *Multicultural Learning and Teaching, 10*(2), 211–230.

Rowe, W., Bennett, S. K., & Atkinson, D. R. (1994). White racial identity models: A critique and alternative proposal. *The Counseling Psychologist, 22*(1), 129–146.

Sabnani, H. B., Ponterotto, J. G., & Borodovsky, L. G. (1991). White racial identity development and cross-cultural counselor training: A stage model. *The Counseling Psychologist, 19*(1), 76–102.

Siegel, M. P., & Carter, R. T. (2014). Emotions and White racial identity status attitudes. *Journal of Multicultural Counseling and Development, 42*(4), 218–231.

Sue, D., & Constantine, M. (2007). Racial microaggressions as instigators of difficult dialogues on race: Implications for student affairs educators and students. *College Student Affairs Journal, 26*(2), 136–143.

Sue, D. W., Capodilupo, C. M., Torino, G. C., Bucceri, J. M., Holder, A. M. B., Nadal, K. L., & Esquilin, M. (2007). Racial microaggressions in everyday life: Implications for clinical practice. *American Psychologist, 62*(4), 271–286.

Sue, D. W., & Sue, D. (2003). *Counseling the culturally diverse* (4th ed.). New York, NY: Wiley.

Sue, D. W., & Sue, D. (2013) *Counseling the culturally diverse* (6th ed.). New York, NY: Wiley.

Terry, R. W. (1977). *For Whites only.* Grand Rapids, MI: William B. Eerdmans.

Todd, N. R., & Abrams, E. M. (2011). White dialectics: A new framework for theory, research, and practice with White students. *The Counseling Psychologist, 39*(3), 353–395.

Ullucci, K. (2010). What works in race-conscious teacher education? Reflections from educators in the field. *Teacher Education Quarterly, 37*(2), 137–156.

Utsey, S. O., & Gernat, C. A. (2002). White racial identity attitudes and the ego defense mechanisms used by White counselor trainees in racially provocative counseling situations. *Journal of Counseling and Development, 80*(4), 475–483.

Watt, S. K. (2007). Difficult dialogues, privilege and social justice: Uses of the Privileged Identity Exploration (PIE) model in student affairs practice. *College Student Affairs Journal, 26*(2), 114–126.

West, T. V., Shelton, J. N., & Trail, T. E. (2009). Relational anxiety in interracial interactions. *Psychological Science, 20*(3), 289–292.

CHAPTER 14

LESBIAN, GAY, BISEXUAL, TRANS, AND QUEER IDENTITY DEVELOPMENT

Christian D. Chan, Adrienne N. Erby, Laura Boyd Farmer, and Amanda R. Friday

CASE VIGNETTE: MARCUS

Marcus is a 21-year-old Asian American cisgender male (i.e., identifying as male and assigned male at birth) student who carries heritages from the Vietnamese and Chinese ethnic identities. Until the beginning of his senior year, Marcus had been in a long-term 3-year relationship with a cisgender woman (i.e., identifying as female and assigned female at birth) he had met in his senior year of high school. They were "high school sweethearts" and had carried an inspirational and seemingly romantic relationship. Although he experienced strong feelings of love for his previous partner, he felt there was a missing part of their relationship. He wished deeply that he could continue this relationship, but he also foresaw that he would not be able to marry her, despite her wishes and the wishes of both their families. A specific fear that he had been experiencing on a repeated basis was his confusion over the love he experienced with his previous partner and a new attraction Marcus was experiencing with his best friend—a male friend he had met during his first year in college who also identifies as a gay male.

After matriculating to colleges approximately 3 hours apart by car, Marcus's long-term relationship with his high school sweetheart also became a long-distance relationship. Despite the time spent apart, Marcus noticeably spent much of his time in college with his best friend. They would have meals, hang out, watch television shows, watch movies, and play video games together. During the 3 years they knew each other, Marcus noticed his relationship with his girlfriend increasingly dissolving, whereas he felt the closest person to share his struggles and celebrations was with his best friend. He felt that his time with his girlfriend was becoming far less, and he had more difficulty sharing deep, personal reflections about life, the future, and his family with her. One specific issue was that Marcus did not share the sudden, unexpected death of his uncle. Immediately, he approached his best friend with this well-hidden secret, but

(continued)

(continued)

unconsciously, he did not approach his girlfriend during that time. Another dark secret that he held for much of his time growing up was a deep affection for the male friends in his life. Specifically, he could not consistently identify that the attraction was purely physical, as he occasionally noted a deep, emotional attraction to his male friends. Marcus feared sharing this information with anyone else, especially with his girlfriend, but he managed to share some of the information with his best friend. His girlfriend broke up with him because of the distance, which caused Marcus to seek even more support from his best friend. On this realization, Marcus felt deeply connected to his best friend.

Marcus questioned if he might actually be gay. Marcus also grew up in a small town in upstate New York, where he never felt comfortable asking questions about sexuality or sharing his experiences with anyone else in his life. He also never had friends who identified as gay, lesbian, bisexual, or transgender while growing up, but he noted a deep emotional and physical attraction to men in his life. Marcus had initially struggled with this perspective because he did not know any other family members in his life that identified as gay. Marcus also questioned if he was gay because he often argued that he was masculine, but he continued to feel a deep attraction to his best friend.

As a result of Marcus's questioning, he found himself visiting the multicultural student services office at his college as he had previously heard that there might be additional resources there. He also kept a friendly relationship with many staff at the office because of his involvement with the Asian American Organization. In addition, he hoped to speak more with one of the directors in the office, specifically the director who handled the LGBTQ Resource and Issues Center. Marcus hoped to confide this information in the director and initiate a conversation about how he is wrestling with his sexuality.

THEORETICAL FOUNDATIONS OF IDENTITY DEVELOPMENT

Identity development refers to the ongoing process of exploring, forming, committing to, and expressing an identity. Identity development includes establishment of both a congruent sense of self and an expression consistent with that identity (Erikson, 1968; Konik & Stewart, 2004). Identity development operates on two simultaneous continuums, level of exploration and level of commitment (Marcia, 1966). High levels of exploration and high levels of commitment suggest identity achievement, denoting the active process of developing an identity. Identity foreclosure (i.e., low exploration and high commitment), identity moratorium (low exploration and low commitment), and identity diffusion (i.e., high exploration and low commitment) suggest incomplete processes of identity development. Despite the emphasis on identity commitment, Erikson (1968) also understood identity as continually developing across the life span. There is a fundamental paradox that must be understood in recognizing identity as both a constant entity and an ever-changing process. Although identity includes acceptance of and commitment to an identity (e.g., identifying as a lesbian), one's experience of an identity can change over time (e.g., lesbian newly coming out, lesbian parent, lesbian queer community advocate).

Identity development is often a focal point when discussing gender and sexual minorities, largely because of the heteronormative and gender conforming assumptions that pervade society. Although Erikson (1968) describes identity development as an essential psychosocial task for healthy functioning for all individuals, it is vital to understand the importance of identity within social identity (e.g., race, gender identity, sexual orientation). With social identity groups, identity encompasses several unique facets because of the influence of the sociopolitical context (i.e., privilege and oppression) associated with social identity (Allport, 1954). Understanding oneself as a gay person is not simply understanding one's attractions and sexual/affectional orientation, but also understanding that identity within a context, in which one might face marginalization from the larger community, institutional discrimination, and internalized homonegativity. In the same way, lesbian, bisexual, transgender, gender nonconforming, and queer identities also experience stigmatization. This is in stark contrast to heterosexual identity, which is often more aligned with identity foreclosure, expressing high commitment with little exploration (Konik & Stewart, 2004). Understanding one's identity both individually and in the social context is a central task, particularly for gender and sexual minorities.

Heteronormative and gender-restrictive assumptions further complicate identity development as most gender and sexual minorities are assumed to be in the majority and are raised with the norms and familiarity of being within the dominant group. Unlike racial minorities, many gender and sexual minorities do not grow up with many role models who share their identities, and are often alone in developing identity. For lesbian, gay, bisexual, transgender, and queer (LGBTQ) individuals, emergence of identity development begins with an initial questioning of one's heterosexuality or gender conformity (Cass, 1979; McCarn & Fassinger, 1996; Weinberg, Williams, & Pryor, 1994; Wilchins et al., 2004). This questioning begins the developmental process of exploring, forming, and adopting a sexual or gender minority identity. Sexual orientation identity development is the process by which individuals come to understand, adopt, and express their sexual/affectional orientation. Similarly, transgender identity emergence is the process by which an individual comes to recognize one's gender nonconformity or incongruence, develop an understanding of gender identity, and express gender in a way that is congruent. To self-identify as LGBTQ, one must actively relinquish the heterosexual and/or gender conforming identity and privilege therein to adopt a congruent, but stigmatized identity (Paul & Frieden, 2008).

Given this, gender and sexual minorities face the challenging task of incorporating a healthy sense of identity in a largely heteronormative and gender restrictive social context. Because individuals are socialized in a heterosexist and transphobic environment, they are raised with the values, norms, and biases of the heterosexual and gender conforming mainstream. Identity development for both gender and sexual minorities includes awareness of a lack of congruence with the preferred identity; thus, the assumption of heterosexuality or gender conformity is replaced by the recognition of and adoption of a socially stigmatized identity. The assumptions regarding heterosexuality and gender conforming as the normal, desired, and correct way of being have negative implications for healthy minority identity.

Cass's (1979, 1984) research on identity development formed the foundation of sexual orientation identity research. The model takes a linear stage model approach and emphasizes the process of finding congruence with one's same-gender loving identity. The stages of this model include (a) identity confusion, characterized by feeling different from others; (b) identity comparison, in which the individual experiences dissonance with attractions, often involving rationalizing or justifying one's attractions; (c) identity tolerance, characterized by the realization that the individual likely has a same-sex orientation; (d) identity acceptance, which includes increased recognition of the identity and increased contact with the sexual minority community; (e) identity pride, characterized by immersion in the gay community and a dualistic view of heterosexuals; and (f) identity synthesis, characterized by integration of gay identity as a part of overall identity.

There has been both support and criticism of the model in the literature, with a focus on the need to expand understanding of sexual orientation identity development (Bilodeau & Renn, 2005; Degges-White, Rice, & Myers, 2000; McCarn & Fassinger, 1996). Strengths of the model include its intuitiveness and general applicability. Critiques include questions of methodology in participant self-categorizing stages, exclusion of gender variation in terms of sexual orientation identity, and cultural generalizability. With its strengths and limitations, Cass's (1979) model remains widely cited and serves as a foundational framework in conceptualizing sexual minority identity development. Further scholarship (Degges-White et al., 2000; McCarn & Fassinger, 1996; Weinberg, Williams, & Pryor, 2004) has expanded on Cass's framework, addressing lesbian and bisexual identity, seeking to address some of the gaps identified in Cass's work. The literature (Brown, 2002; McCarn & Fassinger, 1996) suggests that women's experiences, both lesbian and bisexual, are more relational oriented than solely individual. Furthermore, Degges-White et al.'s (2000) research with lesbian women suggest that identity synthesis may be achieved even without passing through all stages sequentially.

Similarly, transgender identity follows a path of identity exploration and commitment. As with sexual/affectional orientation identity, similarities along exploration and commitment can also be found in transgender identity emergence theory and research (Rankin & Beemyn, 2012). Transgender identity emergence typically begins with early awareness of gender incongruence, although the transgender or gender nonconforming label of transgender may not occur until later in adolescence or adulthood (Rankin & Beemyn, 2012). Although there is no single experience or process in which gender identity emerges, there are some commonly expressed themes and experiences (Beemyn & Rankin, 2011; Wilchins et al., 2004). Wilchins et al. describe six main processes, typically following a sequential order, including (a) awareness, characterized by early recognition of difference or incongruence related to gender identity and sex; (b) seeking information and reaching out, which includes one's process of searching for information for self-understanding; (c) disclosure to significant others, characterized by sharing one's dissonance with others; (d) exploration of identity and self-labeling, characterized by initial understanding of oneself as a transgender or gender nonconforming person; (e) exploration of transition issues/possible body modifications, which can encompass physical transitions and changes including dress, manner, hormone therapy, and/or gender confirmation surgery; and (f) integration, characterized by internalization of one's identity and living congruently with one's identity. Levitt and Ippolito's (2014) research found that transgender individuals described identity development as an ongoing balancing act between the need for authenticity and having the resources to cope within a trans-prejudiced society. Although there is a smaller body of literature on transgender emergence, increasing transgender and gender nonconforming visibility has resulted in growing awareness of transgender experiences.

Although identity development is a normative task of life, developing identity as an LGBTQ person includes not only understanding oneself inwardly, but also understanding oneself within a social context that is often discriminatory and even hostile. As gender and sexual minorities form a sense of self, they also face the formidable task of adopting a stigmatized identity. Although models of identity development are rarely complete in addressing all components of identity development, they provide an overarching framework to conceptualize these experiences.

APPLICATIONS OF THE THEORIES WITHIN STUDENT AFFAIRS

The presence of LGBTQ identity development theories grounded in conceptual and empirical literature represents a significant avenue to develop student affairs practices to meet the changing needs of college students. In fact, Ortiz, Filimon, and Cole-Jackson (2015) observed the trends in content within higher education and student affairs training programs with a significant emphasis on student development and social justice. Their review of trends within student affairs primarily targets the needs of diverse students, especially when considering additional domains of student life (e.g., mental health; classroom learning; physical health, emotional health, policy; Kinzie, 2015; Munsch & Cortez, 2014; Protivnak, Paylo, & Mercer, 2013). Weaving LGBTQ identity development theories into enacting new practices and policies with student affairs, new trends of social justice efforts are deeply embedded to create environments that welcome, affirm, and celebrate individuals within the LGBTQ community. We address two examples that student affairs practices can adopt in LGBTQ-inclusive spaces to offer avenues for student development.

MULTICULTURAL STUDENT SERVICES AND AFFAIRS

There is extensive scholarship detailing the evidence for increasing multicultural competence among student affairs practitioners in addition to adopting equitable and inclusive practices within college and university environments (Charles, Longerbeam, & Miller, 2013; Gayles & Kelly, 2007; Goodman & Bowman, 2014; Kimball & Ryder, 2014; Kinzie, 2015; Petryk, Thompson, & Boynton, 2013). Holding to inclusive practices and policies, multicultural student affairs gains extensive traction in student development by creating learning environments and spaces that affirm diversity and welcome individuals from diverse social identities and cultural groups (Ahmed, 2007a, 2007b, 2012). Offices and staff within multicultural affairs often negotiate policies and practices grounded in privilege in order to meet the needs and disrupt the invisibility experienced by diverse students. In addition, the professional organization Student Affairs Administrators in Higher Education (NASPA) has also heavily emphasized "equity and inclusion" as a significant area within student affairs practitioners' scope of practice, which recognizes a largely contextualized need within professional competencies for student affairs (Munsch & Cortez, 2014). Furthering this call to meet standards and values of social justice is the publication of the 2010 American College Personnel Association/NASPA Professional Competency Areas for student affairs practitioners.

Referring specifically to students within the LGBTQ community, multicultural affairs offices and staff offer a wide array of opportunities to engage individuals from a marginalized group. In taking the lead on diversity and multiculturalism within a college or university environment, it is a common assumption for student affairs practitioners to hold significant training among LGBTQ culture and the growing list of constructs within the community culture. Multicultural affairs can take these unique opportunities to bolster their training within their contexts and within the larger context of the college or the university to ensure that there is an open and welcoming learning environment for students. Consequently, multicultural affairs can address the needs of residential life, academic affairs, faculty training, career services, Greek life, study abroad programs, and international services offices. It is also incumbent on multicultural affairs offices to develop a working and growing knowledge of lived intersections and representations to feature a variety of social and cultural identities (e.g., race, ethnicity, sexual identity, gender identity, and ability status).

On a microsystemic level, the validation and celebration of lived experiences within the LGBTQ community will offer a significant developmental space for students to seek additional understanding about personal identity, sexual identity, and gender identity. Considering a grounding in developmental theory, it is imperative to note that student affairs practitioners observe the possibilities of students potentially wrestling with gender identity and sexual identity throughout their college and university careers. It would be an important practice to ask students about the use of gender pronouns and the identification with specific gender pronouns (e.g., he, she, they, zie, sie, ve, per, e/ey). They also offer an open and supportive space for LGBTQ students, which leads to significant avenues of building relationships between students and student affairs practitioners or counseling professionals. While directors and staff in multicultural affairs might not necessarily offer direct advising for academics, sports, or residential life, they can often hold a LGBTQ resource center or section within the overarching domain of their office practices and environment. This resource center can expand knowledge on LGBTQ identity, communities, and resources, specifically to expand awareness and prevent isolation for students working through their identity development as LGBTQ individuals. More importantly, these resource centers can offer supports (systemic or individual) to indicate different domains where students need guidance in order to navigate community building, residential life, and personal development.

On a macrosystemic level, multicultural affairs offices hold a responsibility to identify needs for diversity within the overarching college or university environment. As a result, they assume the role as a prime communicator for diversity initiatives within the college and university contexts. One avenue within their scope of practice is to create training initiatives for other departments and divisions of the university. Although multicultural affairs has the potential to give voice to LGBTQ concerns, they can hold an active responsibility to identify concerns about LGBTQ identity development and issues within other departments to extend their scope and practice within diversity. For example, faculty can learn extensively about LGBTQ identity development and issues to ensure their classroom practices critically engage marginalized students and increase awareness about diversity issues. Another specific viewpoint integrated into classroom pedagogy and curriculum development is an awareness of terminology and constructs within LGBTQ. Classrooms might also represent a diverse space of represented identities, but the misuse of inaccurate terminology or gender pronouns could result in microaggressions, which are insidious and everyday slights ostracizing and discriminating marginalized communities (Nadal, Wong, Griffin, Davidoff, & Sriken, 2014).

COLLEGE COUNSELING AND MENTAL HEALTH

Another specific avenue to address LGBTQ identity development is within college counseling centers—a significant resource to largely address mental health issues within college and university contexts. Research has pointed to the health disparities of LGBTQ individuals within college and university contexts, often resulting in suicidal ideation, mental health issues, lower rates of mental health service utilization, and death (Borders, Guillen, & Meyer, 2014; Johnson, Oxendine, Taub, & Robertson, 2013). Even far more challenging are the mental health disparities among LGBTQ individuals, minority stress, and LGBTQ persons of color (Bockting et al., 2016; Frost, Meyer, & Hammack, 2015; Goldberg & Meyer, 2013; Meyer, 2003, 2010).

As college counselors also operate with a variety of mental health professionals (e.g., licensed clinical social workers, licensed professional counselors, licensed psychologists), it is important to integrate several domains of student development into college counseling and mental health practices within these environments. More specifically, the counseling profession adopts an approach heavily emphasized in wellness, strengths-based perspectives, development, holistic practices into counseling practices, and training (Kaplan, Tarvydas, & Gladding, 2014). Within these specific practices, individual development operates within the contextual domains of family, career, and culture. Considering this unique identification overseeing the wellness, development, and ultimately, success, of each student, college counseling centers can benefit extensively from adopting constructs based in a particular LGBTQ identity development theory or model. For example, a mental health professional working with a client identifying as a gay man could gain further context by assessing where this client might surface within an identity development model. The specific perspective of sexual identity development and gender identity development can lead to detailed discussions about the context and socialization situating this individual. In addition, the discussion can also identify specific resources used or unused within the community. Professionals in college counseling centers could assist clients with recognizing their own marginalization and discrimination, which elicits information about issues with contexts, systems, and social structures in the college and university environment. Consequently, practitioners could use identity development to reinforce growth-oriented resources and internal resources developed by the client about navigating sexual identity and gender identity development.

College counseling centers could also expand on outreach initiatives to other departments and divisions within the university. Major critiques on college counseling centers has identified the lack of information offered on resources and websites for LGBTQ individuals (McKinley, Luo, Wright, & Kraus, 2015; Wright & McKinley,

2010), which speaks to a larger overarching issue on mental health discrepancies and services for LGBTQ individuals seeking help. For instance, mental health professionals and staff within college counseling centers can collaborate with college student personnel for referrals and dissemination of resources on mental health services within the university. When discussing sexual identity and gender identity development, it would be important for college student personnel and college counseling centers to provide resources and work collaboratively with victims of heterosexism (Meyer, 2010), homophobia, and genderism. A significant note is that individuals within the LGBTQ community are also subject to the experience of genderism (Farmer & Byrd, 2015).

CONNECTING THE VIGNETTE AND STUDENT AFFAIRS

The considerations of student development are instrumental to the coalescing nature of personal development and identity development. Student development and identity development can emerge through polymorphous forms to represent needs and changes within a diversity of systems within college and university contexts (e.g., multicultural affairs, student services, admissions, academic affairs, registrar, college counseling centers, academic advising). Student affairs practitioners build a variety of resources into their policies, contexts, and most importantly, their relationships with students. Similar to counseling paradigms, collaborative relationships of service can offer a sense of empowerment and growth.

CASE VIGNETTE WRAP-UP: MARCUS

Returning to the story of Marcus, it is clear that he had been searching for resources and supports regarding his sexual identity development. He had been wrestling specifically with his understanding of the possibility of identifying as a gay male. As an integrated component in his story, Marcus wrestled with the differentiated notion of affectional orientation and sexual orientation. His life narrative garnered a discussion on the socialization of masculinity and the diverse representation of gay men. In addition, he became subject to internalized homophobia and stereotypes about the LGBTQ community, specifically with gay men. Initially, he operated with a lens that gay men must be effeminate in order to fully integrate with the sexual identity. Within his identity development, he also recognized the variability of intimate relationships and dating, where dating an individual of another gender restricts or holds the sexual identity as a static construct.

Connecting with student affairs practices and contexts, Marcus's initial search with multicultural student services represents the major resource of multicultural affairs and diversity initiatives within college and university campuses. Specifically, multicultural affairs hold a strength in identifying a community for individuals often situated as minorities or marginalized populations. In addition, it offers a context for garnering resources in order to navigate sexual and gender identity development such as career services and mental health services. Individuals with a working knowledge of LGBTQ identity development can offer collaborative relationships to celebrate the lived experiences and resilience of individuals within these identities.

CASE VIGNETTE 1 FOR READER REFLECTION: VADA

Vada, who is 19 years old, was assigned female at birth and has spent the last 3 years dating only women. Since childhood, she had always felt different from her peers. As a teenager, she assumed she must be lesbian because she was attracted to girls; yet she was grossed out by "girly" stuff. She adamantly told friends and family that she would never be "caught dead" in a dress or a skirt. She only wanted to wear baggy shirts and jeans in an effort to hide her breasts and figure.

As a sophomore in college, Vada did not feel she fit in with the lesbian crowd either. She still felt like she was different from everyone else, and this made her feel oddly alone. She wanted to present herself in as masculine a way as possible; she cut her hair very short, wore boxer shorts, grew out her body hair, and got several tattoos. It was not enough. She hated her body and her curves, and she was feeling more depressed and isolated as time went on. She wondered, "Is it possible I was born in the wrong body?"

Toward the end of her sophomore year, Vada began to realize that her true identity was that of a boy. While in some ways this realization made life more complicated, for the first time in her life, it all made sense. Still, it all felt so overwhelming and she did not know of anyone else who could relate to what she was experiencing. Vada felt desperate, misunderstood, full of self-hatred, and was contemplating suicide. She decided that she had to do something to make life bearable, or she would surely take her own life to end the misery she felt.

- What are Vada's greatest needs?
- What campus-based services might be most beneficial to Vada?
- What are some goals you would like to see Vada reach?

CASE VIGNETTE 2 FOR READER REFLECTION: TY

Ty is a 19-year-old, Latino/European American junior in college who began to self-identify as female-to-male (FTM) transgender during the last year. Leading up to Ty's freshman year, he had identified as "Summer" and used the pronouns "she" and "her." However, during his freshman year he became very confused about who he was, including his sexual attractions and feelings about his body, and began to experience anxiety related to that confusion. Ty had previously rejected the label of FTM transgender until he entered a romantic relationship with a close friend, Sarah, 7 months ago. Since the start of that relationship Ty has expressed feeling "more free," "like myself for the first time," and "truly happy for the first time." Although many of Ty's friends are supportive of him, two formerly close friends recently distanced themselves from him, and others in their group have followed suit. Ty still gets angry over the loss of his friends, but he joined many LGBTQ on-campus groups on his return to school after the summer break. There he has found new friends who have welcomed him into their community. Ty and his family have had

(continued)

(continued)

difficulties since he came out. His father had not spoken to him from the beginning of sophomore year until the summer before his junior year. Since that summer, Ty's mother and father have been more open, and while he is hopeful, they have not fully accepted his new name.

Ty's experience over the past 2 years has not been without stigma or discrimination directed toward him. His apartment has been burglarized four times last year and both friends and acquaintances have shunned him. At times, Ty is angry with himself and society, but recognizes that the discrimination he experiences will be present for much of the rest of his life.

- *What are Ty's greatest needs?*
- *What campus-based services might be most beneficial to him?*
- *What are some goals you would like to see Ty reach?*

REFERENCES

Ahmed, S. (2007a). "You end up doing the document rather than doing the doing": Diversity, race equality and the politics of documentation. *Ethnic and Racial Studies, 30*(4), 590–609. doi:10.1080/01419870701356015

Ahmed, S. (2007b). The language of diversity. *Ethnic and Racial Studies, 30*(2), 235–256. doi:10.1080/01419870601143927

Ahmed, S. (2012). *On being included: Racism and diversity in institutional life*. Durham, NC: Duke University Press. Retrieved from http://www.ebrary.com

Allport, G. W. (1954). *The nature of prejudice*. Reading, MA: Addison-Wesley.

Beemyn, G., & Rankin, S. (2011). *The lives of transgender people*. New York, NY: Columbia University Press.

Bilodeau, B. L., & Renn, K. A. (2005). Analysis of LGBT identity development models and implications for practice. *New Directions for Student Services, 111*, 25–39. doi:10.1002/ss.171

Bockting, W., Coleman, E., Deutsch, M. B., Guillamon, A., Meyer, I., Meyer, W . . . Ettner, R. (2016). Adult development and quality of life of transgender and gender nonconforming people. *Current Opinion in Endocrinology, Diabetes, and Obesity, 23*(2), 188–197.

Borders, A., Guillén, L. A., & Meyer, I. H. (2014). Rumination, sexual orientation uncertainty, and psychological distress in sexual minority university students. *The Counseling Psychologist, 42*(4), 497–523. doi:10.1177/0011000014527002

Brown, T. (2002). A proposed model of bisexual identity development that elaborates on experiential differences of women and men. *Journal of Bisexuality, 2*, 67–91. doi:10.1300/J159v02n04_05

Cass, V. C. (1979). Homosexual identity formation: A theoretical model. *Journal of Homosexuality, 4*(3), 219–235. doi:10.1300/J082v04n03_01

Cass, V. C. (1984). Homosexual identity formation: Testing a theoretical model. *The Journal of Sex Research, 20*(2), 143–167. doi:10.1080/00224498409551214

Charles, H., Longerbeam, S. D., & Miller, A. E. (2013). Putting old tensions to rest: Integrating multicultural education and global learning to advance student development. *Journal of College and Character, 14*(1), 47–58. doi:10.1515/jcc-2013-0007

Degges-White, S., Rice, B., & Myers, J. E. (2000). Revisiting Cass' theory of sexual identity formation: A study of lesbian development. *Journal of Mental Health Counseling, 22*(4), 318–333.

Erikson, E. H. (1968). *Identity: Youth and crisis*. New York, NY: W. W. Norton.

Farmer, L. B., & Byrd, R. (2015). Genderism in the LGBTQQIA community: An interpretative phenomenological analysis. *Journal of LGBT Issues in Counseling, 9*(4), 288–310. doi:10.1080/15538605.2015.1103679

Frost, D. M., Meyer, I. H., & Hammack, P. L. (2015). Health and well-being in emerging adults' same-sex relationships: Critical questions and directions for research in developmental science. *Emerging Adulthood, 3*(1), 3–13. doi:10.1177/2167696814535915

Gayles, J. G., & Kelly, B. T. (2007). Experiences with diversity in the curriculum: Implications for graduate programs and student affairs practice. *NASPA Journal, 44*(1), 193–208.

Goldberg, N. G., & Meyer, I. H. (2013). Sexual orientation disparities in history of intimate partner violence: Results from the California Health Interview Survey. *Journal of Interpersonal Violence, 28*(5), 1109–1118. doi:10.1177/0886260512459384

Goodman, K. M., & Bowman, N. A. (2014). Making diversity work to improve college student learning. *New Directions for Student Services, 2014*(147), 37–48. doi:10.1002/ss.20099

Johnson, R. B., Oxendine, S., Taub, D. J., & Robertson, J. (2013). Suicide prevention for LGBT students. *New Directions for Student Services, 2013*(141), 55–69. doi:10.1002/ss.20040

Kaplan, D. M., Tarvydas, V. M., & Gladding, S. T. (2014). 20/20: A vision for the future of counseling: The new consensus definition of counseling. *Journal of Counseling & Development, 92*(3), 366–372. doi:10.1002/j.1556-6676.2014.00164.x

Kimball, E. W., & Ryder, A. J. (2014). Using history to promote reflection: A model for reframing student affairs practice. *Journal of Student Affairs Research and Practice, 51*(3), 298–310. doi:10.1515/jsarp-2014-0030

Kinzie, J. (2015). Characterizations of students and effective student affairs practice. *New Directions for Student Services, 2015*(151), 27–37. doi:10.1002/ss.20135

Konik, J., & Stewart, A. (2004). Sexual identity development in the context of compulsory heterosexuality. *Journal of Personality, 72*, 815–844. doi:10.1111/j.0022-3506.2004.00281.x

Levitt, H. M., & Ippolito, M. R. (2014). Being transgender: The experience of transgender identity development. *Journal of Homosexuality, 61*, 727–758. doi:10.1080/00918369.2014.951262

Marcia, J. E. (1966). Development and validation of ego-identity status. *Journal of Personality and Social Psychology, 3*, 551–558.

McCarn, S. R., & Fassinger, R. E. (1996). Revisioning sexual minority identity formation: A new model of lesbian identity and its implications for counseling and research. *The Counseling Psychologist, 24*, 508–534. doi:10.1177/0011000096243011

McKinley, C. J., Luo, Y., Wright, P. J., & Kraus, A. (2015). Reexamining LGBT resources on college counseling center websites: An over-time and cross-country analysis. *Journal of Applied Communication Research, 43*(1), 112–129. doi:10.1080/00909882.2014.982681

Meyer, I. H. (2003). Prejudice, social stress, and mental health in lesbian, gay, and bisexual populations: Conceptual issues and research evidence. *Psychological Bulletin, 129*(5), 674–697. doi:10.1037/0033-2909.129.5.674

Meyer, I. H. (2010). Identity, stress, and resilience in lesbians, gay men, and bisexuals of color. *The Counseling Psychologist, 38*(3), 442–454. doi:10.1177/0011000009351601

Munsch, P., & Cortez, L. (2014). Professional competencies for student affairs practice. *New Directions for Community Colleges, 2014*(166), 47–53. doi:10.1002/cc.20101

Nadal, K. L., Wong, Y., Griffin, K. E., Davidoff, K., & Sriken, J. (2014). The adverse impact of racial microaggressions on college students' self-esteem. *Journal of College Student Development, 55*(5), 461–474. doi:10.1353/csd.2014.0051

Ortiz, A. M., Filimon, I., & Cole-Jackson, M. (2015). Preparing student affairs educators. *New Directions for Student Services, 2015*(151), 79–88. doi:10.1002/ss.20139

Paul, P. L., & Frieden, G. (2008). The lived experience of gay identity development: A phenomenological study. *Journal of LGBT Issues in Counseling, 2*, 26–52. doi:10.1080/15538600802077509

Petryk, T., Thompson, M. C., & Boynton, T. (2013). Building multicultural residential communities: A model for training student staff. *New Directions for Student Services, 2013*(144), 69–78. doi:10.1002/ss.20070

Protivnak, J. J., Paylo, M. J., & Mercer, J. C. (2013). The perceived value of counselor preparation for student affairs professionals. *Journal of Counselor Preparation and Supervision, 5*(1), 49–65. doi:10.7729/51.00128

Rankin, S., & Beemyn, G. (2012). Beyond the binary: The lives of gender-nonconforming youth. *About Campus, 17*(4), 2–10. doi:10.1002/abc.21086

Weinberg, M. S., Williams, C. J., & Pryor, D. W. (1994). *Dual attraction: Understanding bisexuality.* New York, NY: Oxford University Press.

Wilchins, R., Hall, R., Lorde, A., Israel, G., Tarver, D. E., Sullivan, L., . . . Eckhardt, M. (2004). Transgender emergence: A developmental process. In A. I. Lev (Ed.), *Transgender emergence: Therapeutic guidelines for working with gender-variant people and their families* (pp. 229–269). New York, NY: Routledge.

Wright, P. J., & McKinley, C. J. (2010). Mental health resources for LGBT collegians: A content analysis of college counseling center web sites. *Journal of Homosexuality, 58*(1), 138–147. doi:10.1080/00918369.2011.533632

CHAPTER 15

DISABILITY AND IDENTITY DEVELOPMENT

Yuleinys A. Castillo

CASE VIGNETTE: MELANIE

After graduating from high school, Melanie, a White working-class student, enrolled at a local community college to start working on her goal of becoming a math teacher. She has been in college for almost 2 years taking core and developmental courses. She actively participates in the college community and benefits from the disability services available on campus. In fact, she attends support groups for future teachers, acts as a treasurer in the Rehab Club on campus, and promotes early intervention services for children with disabilities. At 20, she is getting ready to transfer to a 4-year institution.

Melanie has cerebral palsy (considered in this discussion as a physical disability). She lacks muscle coordination, experiences exaggerated reflexes sometimes, and drags a leg when walking. As a child, she had seizures, but they stopped when she was in middle school. She has received proper medical and rehabilitation services growing up while attending local K–12 schools. She has also participated in early intervention services, supportive therapy treatments, and complementary medicine. On campus, she sometimes uses a rolling walker to travel long distances, but she knows that other students tend to "notice" her more when using it.

On graduation, she wants to teach high school math because she lacked caring and passionate teachers in her school. Of course, she had to show people over and over that she can do math. Others often assume that she cannot comprehend math because she has a disability and needs accommodations. However, Melanie understands the lack of knowledge and understanding about cerebral palsy.

OVERVIEW

As diverse student populations gain visibility in colleges and universities across the United States, higher education counselors and student affairs professionals aim to effectively serve and meet the needs of these students. Individuals with disabilities (IWDs) represent one of these previously segregated diverse voices and perspectives that have recently experienced positive developments from inclusive college experiences. College students with disabilities (CSDs) represent an important segment of the growing student population. In 2014, the National Center for Education Statistics reported that approximately 11.1% of all undergraduate students and 5.3% of post baccalaureate students enrolled in college had a disability in the 2011 to 2012 school year in the United States.

As CSDs are less likely to pursue a college degree, successfully transition to college services, and obtain employment, student affairs practitioners are called on to facilitate the educational path of these students. Specific tasks that contribute to a positive collegial experience include identification and removal of potential barriers; educating themselves about disabilities and related symptoms and implications; and participating in disability awareness trainings (Burgstahler & Moore, 2009). In addition, CSDs do not receive adequate guidance addressing the connection between vocational rehabilitation and financial aid applications nor do they receive reliable information about financial resources, continued support, and accommodations available in college (National Council on Disability [NCD], 2015). Therefore, the different sectors within student affairs services may need to take on new roles to coordinate efforts to retain and graduate CSDs while improving disability services available on campus and reducing the stigma of disabilities.

Students with disabilities have actively pursued higher education for many decades; however, social demands for equal rights have resulted in a variety of legislative changes that guarantee access to education for this group (Rubin & Roessler, 2008). Section 504 of the Rehabilitation Act of 1973 is a disability rights legislation action that mandates any organization receiving federal funding, such as academic institutions, to provide students with disabilities equal services and opportunities (U.S. Department of Education, 2012). These students are also entitled to equal access to classrooms and the receipt of adequate accommodations. In addition, the Americans with Disabilities Act (ADA) also protects individuals against disability discrimination in public academic institutions (Title II) and private and for-profit colleges (Title III). The Individuals with Disabilities Education Act (IDEA) is another document that addresses the education of IWDs, but mainly that of primary and secondary students. Even though higher education has no obligations under IDEA, high schools provide transition services for high school students to facilitate the movement from school to post–high school activities, including college education.

CSDs may be referred to student support departments where information and documentation related to accessibility services, academic modifications, and assistive technology services are provided. Disability services coordinators and student service affairs professionals may also work together to prevent discrimination as well as to create a pleasing college environment that promotes equal access to education and advocacy (Hadley, 2011). These disability services and programs are a result of governmental mandates that aim to provide quality education to students with disabilities. Accordingly, each student must disclose his or her disability in order to receive academic accommodations.

Brief Background on Disability Models

There a number of models about the perspective, experience, and definition of disability; however, few models address the development of a disability identity. Disability, as a social construct, is considered as *other* in comparison to the majority culture (McEwen, 2003). Usually, this *other* is devalued and considered abnormal (Smart, 2015) while being powerless in society as a result of ableism or able-bodied individuals having social and power privileges (Hutcheon & Wolbring, 2012). This view of disability leads to discrimination and social, political, and environmental disadvantages for IWDs, including students.

Medical advances, the Civil Rights Movement, and changing views of minority groups combined with legislative mandates (Rubin & Roessler, 2008) have resulted in different models to explain the experience of IWDs. The medical model of disability is a model that emphasizes the need to fix the individual and locates the disability in the person (Gibson, 2006), whereas the newer social model of disability places the disability within the larger context of society and considers physical environments and attitudes (Smart, 2015). These are some of the existing models that have influenced social and political programs as well as explained the views and experiences of disabilities (Kaplan, 2000). A minority model proposes that people with disabilities, who experience similar experiences of other marginalized and oppressed groups, need to have primary voices in decisions that directly affect them (Gill, 1997). The Affirmative Model of Disability proposes that disability is a nontragic part of the individual's identity, which possesses positive social identities based on the benefits of having a disability (Swain & French, 2000). This model is an opposing model to the stance of a personal tragedy model that results from disabilities.

A disability continuum, which offers a new way to define and conceptualize disability, comes from the National Institute on Disability and Rehabilitation Research (NIDRR, 1998). This definition moves away from older definitions that attribute the cause of limitations in daily activities or social roles to an individual's characteristics. A similar disability spectrum originated from the Disability Rights Movement offering an interpretation for disability identity. From this perspective, disability leads to a fluid identity because any person may have a disability at any time (Scotch, 1989). For example, an individual can have a temporary disability after an injury and return to being temporarily able-bodied after healing. The disability paradigm locates the construct of disability on a continuum from enablement to disablement (NIDRR). This view of disability identity emphasizes vulnerability and interaction between characteristics of the individual and natural, cultural, and social environments.

Even though college students with disabilities have had a place at higher education institutions for some time, research in student affairs has recently begun to focus on diverse student identity development in college (Forber-Pratt & Aragon, 2013). In student affairs, identity is defined as one's beliefs about the self in relation to social groups and how one expresses that relationship (Torres, Jones, & Renn, 2009). This identity is shaped by the perception of different factors such as race, ethnicity, religion, sexual orientation, and abilities. Moreover, identity is constructed through social interactions within dominant cultural values and expectations. This interaction with the dominant culture shapes the view of self and contacts with others in different contexts.

However, the student affairs literature focusing on disability identity development seems to be scarce (Evans, Forney, Guido, Patton, & Renn, 2009). Students with disabilities are an important segment with institutions of higher education but often disregarded as part of diverse college students (NCD, 2015). Hence, student affairs practitioners should stretch themselves to understand how personal, physical, attitudinal, and educational barriers and challenges, in education and social settings, can influence the identity development of CSDs (Nichols & Quaye, 2009). In order to increase the understanding of the identity development of students with disabilities, some researchers and professionals have presented few models with this population in mind.

DISABILITY IDENTITY MODELS

Newer theoretical approaches focusing on marginalized groups, as well as societal structures that perpetuate oppression and discrimination, are emerging to provide a foundation on which to understand identity (Torres et al., 2009). Some of these models were developed using the experience of IWDs as part of the general population whereas most recent ones focused exclusively on CSDs. These disability identity models aim to conceptualize the impact of disabilities on an individual's personal, social, and environmental experiences and to describe how these forces may shape an individual's view of self.

Developing a disability identity as a student in higher education is a complex process because disabilities are often stigmatized and sometimes viewed as a political or as a social identity (Riddell & Weedon, 2014). Students with visible disabilities may lack an opportunity to reject a disability identity compared with those with invisible disabilities who can vary on disability identification. Having a visible or invisible disability can change the experience of students in higher education as society reacts differently to each condition. Similarly, disability tends to be negatively constructed as a mandate to meet governmental requirements by disability services in colleges (Hadley, 2011). This negative view of disability may inhibit a student from disclosing his or her conditions not only to students but to disability professionals, as well.

Disability Identity Integration Model

In 1997, Gill proposed a Disability Identity Integration Model (DIIM) for people with disabilities at the individual and group levels. As a result of civil rights movements, IWDs met with an opportunity to overcome social stigma and promote personal differences as integral parts of society. In an individual's quest for disability identity, there are potential risks and rewards of a growth process, potential shifts in personal attachments, redefinition of self, and the restructuring of relationships. Moreover, individuals born with disabilities and those who acquired them later in life must find a way to define the portion of their identity that involves their disabilities. The DIIM model aims to understand the integration process for people with disabilities into society in a process that involves identity development as part of the disabled minority group.

The DIIM (Gill, 1997) offers four types of integration: (a) coming to feel we belong, (b) coming home, (c) coming together, and (d) coming out. This integration process promotes personal empowerment and disability rights. In the first type, coming to feel we belong or integrating into society, the person with a disability develops an identity and establishes social roles within the dominant norm despite belonging to an ostracized group. This process involves recognizing that disability is a social construct reinforced by attitudinal and environmental barriers. The individual also asserts the right to inclusion in society including mainstream schooling and employment opportunities. The second type, coming home or integrating with the disability community, addresses the fact that sometimes IWDs may avoid any association with disabilities for a variety of reasons. The individual, for instance, may have a negative view of disabilities including special schools, disability segregation, or isolating institutions; have concerns about stigma contagion and being located within a group stereotype; and may espouse social ableism views of disabilities or a socially constructed devaluation of disabilities. However, Gill (1997) explained that IWDs eventually find others with disabilities in disability-related services or other settings that can facilitate the development of a sense of community, culture, or even family.

In the third type, coming together or internally integrating our sameness and differentness, IWDs need to separate and individuate from the majority culture that fears and devalues disability to create a positive disability identity (Gill, 1997). By excluding substantial aspects of possessing a disability, the person can develop a disintegrated identity and a view of self that can never be fully accepted. The final category, the coming out or integration of an individual with how he or she presents the self to others, describes IWDs who are comfortable identifying as a person with a disability in all situations. The individual feels that he or she no longer has anything to hide from self or others. This provides a foundation for free self-exploration of identity and confidence to reach out to others in the community. For a positive disability identity, an integration between self and the ideal image of others is needed to protect against internal conflict or social discomfort.

Gill (1997) explained that ethnic, cultural, and gender minorities experience a similar process of identity development. For members of marginalized minority groups, the trajectory of identity development begins with a desire to assimilate to the dominant culture, moves into a period of conflict and separation, and finishes with personal integrity, proud identification with the marginalized group, and a willingness to change others' misconceived views of the group. The disability identity process develops based on a personal craving for social integration to a search for group membership and personal integration to a relationship with society from a clear definition of self.

The Disability Identity Development Model

Gibson (2006) incorporated perceptions, experiences, and struggles of IWD. This model suggests that the discrimination and marginalization experience by IWD is not because of their disabilities or identities, but because of social constructions of able-bodied norms and exclusions of those who differ from this norm. This model consists of three stages: Passive Awareness, Realization, and Acceptance. IWD navigate through these three stages as they develop a disability identity in a fluid way.

In the Passive Awareness stage, the individual fails to recognize the disability and its related social implications. In a way, the person is in denial about his or her medical condition. In the arena of higher education, a student may focus on medical symptoms and implications of the condition and avoid any social connections with disabilities. Moving into the Realization stage, the student seeks to establish a relationship with society while experiencing negative feelings, such as hate and anger, toward the disability. Concurrently, the student may be concerned about how others perceive him or her while being preoccupied with his or her appearance. In the Acceptance stage, the individual is able to embrace the new identity as a person with a disability. In the social arena, the person feels comfortable connecting with other peers with disabilities, may become involved in disability advocacy and activism, and experience a sense of belonging within the disability community.

The Disability Identity Development Model (DIDM; Gibson, 2006) acknowledges disability as an identity that can fluctuate among three different stages in a nonlinear way. Gibson explained that other personal and social identities are also aspects of the individual's identity. Social and environmental factors can affect how students perceive their disabilities and the role that disability plays as part of their identity. At the same time, these factors can shape the fluidity of this model. For instance, the negative reaction of friends, classmates, faculty, or staff toward a disability can move an individual from the Acceptance to the Passive Awareness stage. Thus, the DIDM recognizes the impact of society and institutions on disability identity. Another characteristic of this model is that it focuses on an individual's experience and perspective of disability without disregarding the larger group identity. The DIDM offers a perspective to understand students with disabilities in different social settings, including on the college campus.

The Developmental Trajectory Into Disability Culture

The Developmental Trajectory Into Disability Culture (DTDC) model provides a way to understand the movement of students with physical disability into the disability culture (Forber-Pratt & Aragon, 2013). It incorporates consideration of the social and psychosocial identity development for postsecondary students with physical disabilities and the potential barriers and challenges encountered in college. Another important characteristic of this model is that it focuses on the experiences of students who have grown up with the ADA in place. Consequently, these students' experiences may be constructed in a different social and environmental context than prior generations. The DTDC propositions four phases: Acceptance, Relationship, Adoption, and Community into the disability culture.

The first stage of the Acceptance phase proposes that students with a congenital or acquired disability first go through the stages of grief presented by Kübler-Ross (1969) and Kübler-Ross and Kessler (2005) to reach acceptance of their disability. Within the social context, family, close friends, and other supports also accept the disability. This acceptance helps students to move forward and become active members of the disability culture. Consequently, in this stage, the person accepts his or her disability, whether congenital or acquired, and significant others also accept the disability.

The Relationship phase is the second stage of this model. In this stage, the student with disabilities meets and establishes relationships with others with disabilities. The individual develops a sense of belonging to a disability group and becomes part of the disability culture.

The third stage, the Adoption phase, requires that the student adopt and embrace the values of the disability group and culture. These include independence, social justice/equality, and engagement in giving back to the community. There is a sense of unity and understanding among members. Some of the issues and topics around which they are connected include topics that people without disability may not understand or feel uncomfortable addressing. A mutual sense of understanding among persons with disabilities about common issues and levels of comfort helps to establish a sense of independence. In addition, students learn from each other to advocate and request assistance in different settings. In addition, students grow in how they value equal access to education and social justice as well as develop a sense of social responsibility to new and current students in higher education.

Giving back to the Community phase, the fourth stage, involves the individual becoming a role model for others and actually giving back to the community. This stage is a parallel to Gill's (1997) integration phase of coming out where the individual feels comfortable with self in a variety of circumstances. By reaching out and becoming a model, students develop a sense of pride and find satisfaction in the performance of civic duty. In this stage, students develop a cohesive identity and embrace their disabilities. A student becomes a part of the disability culture with its different subgroups creating different facets of identity. However, some of the members of this disability culture may not understand the disability identity and it is up to each individual to become an accepted member of the disability culture. An individual who has not come to terms with his or her disability tends to be in denial or feels anger and self-pity while struggling with independence and accommodations.

DISABILITY IDENTITY IN STUDENT AFFAIRS SERVICES

Higher education often experiences changes that affect student affairs administrators, students, and communities. Even though there is some improvement in providing education to diverse students, significant achievement gaps still remain extant between minority and majority students (Task Force on the Future of Student Affairs [TFFSA], 2010). The field of student affairs has played a crucial role in identifying the disparities in educational opportunities for disadvantaged students (Sandeen & Barr, 2006). Thus, practitioners and professionals who work in the different areas of student support or services can be equipped to provide effective assistance for CSDs to participate in different aspects of the college experience.

Academic Services

Any student with disabilities entering an institution of higher education needs academic services to successfully engage in a positive college experience. In academic-advising services, counselors should notify students of services that can help with study skills and explain tutoring, especially for those students with learning and cognitive impairments. Student affairs professionals should become familiar with specific accommodations that can help to maintain academic standards for all types of disabilities (Burgstahler & Moore, 2009). Of special note, administrators and disability professionals may be more willing to accommodate students with mobility and sensory impairment than invisible conditions such as learning and psychiatric impairments (Sheppard-Jones, Krampe, Danner, & Berdine, 2002). In order to provide identical academic services, student affairs practitioners should educate themselves to be prepared to work equally with all CSDs regardless of their conditions.

Academic counselors can also work with CSDs to find a balance between their functional abilities and chosen majors. It is imperative for counselors to evaluate the impact of the disability on student's academic performance and coursework. Offices that address academic skills and tutoring can provide academic interventions with math, writing, reading, and any other academic subject for students with disabilities. Practitioners should also assess the quality of provision of academic accommodations, tutorial support, and an inviting climate for disability (Wilson, Getzel, & Brown, 2000).

For assessment services, it is imperative for practitioners to use appropriate accommodations to meet students' needs and to bear in mind that some traditional assessment methods may limit the opportunity of students with disabilities. Colleges and universities can use multiple assessment methods to support universal instruction design (Pliner & Johnson, 2004) and to reduce or even eliminate the need for accommodations for CSDs (Bowe, 2000). In addition, Higher Education Opportunity Programs can target to support students with disabilities with extensive academic support and services. These programs can provide support to some students who may not embrace their disability and help them to grow more comfortable with themselves and make them believe that they have the ability necessary to succeed in college.

Academic services practitioners can help CSDs to transition through stages of identity development, whether the practitioner uses the DIIM (Gill, 1997), the DIDM (Gibson, 2006), or the DTDC (Forber-Pratt & Aragon, 2013) models. By increasing their own comfort level in working with CSDs, staff members can help these students to come to feel they belong and to develop a path for coming together with others and coming out (Gill, 1997). Similarly, practitioners may facilitate the adjustment to college and the development of a disability identity for students by offering a welcoming environment for CSDs. Forber-Pratt and Aragon explained that college may be the first opportunity for CSDs to develop a sense of belonging to a larger culture and realize that other people have similar issues and experiences (2013). Therefore, student affairs professionals can help CSDs to transition into the disability culture and creating a disability identity. Finally, academic services counselors, administrators, and practitioners can help students to move from the Realization stage to the Acceptance stage in the DIDM (Gibson, 2006). When CSDs seek disability services and accommodations, they show at least a recognition of their disability. However, practitioners can work with these students to determine their level of acceptance and comfort by being an IWD.

Equity

Offices in Equity and Diversity in Student Affairs aim to promote social justice and the diversification of the student body in the higher education environment (Student Affairs Administrators in Higher Education, NASPA, 2016). Student affairs practitioners can benefit from understanding how students perceive their disability instead of attempting to define the student's experience and disability from their own perspective (McEwen, 2003). Equally important for professionals is to evaluate and identify their own attitudes and views of students with disabilities and how these views may affect their interactions with this student population. By engaging in self-evaluation, practitioners become more effective in working with CSDs while creating an inclusive environment that supports accountability for student learning success.

Disability support services may also provide accommodations and advocacy for students with developmental, physical, mental, intellectual, and learning disabilities. The disability services offices adhere to the mandates of federal and state legislation to guarantee equal education for CSDs. Student affairs professionals should work to provide a welcoming environment for CSDs, especially when evidence shows that CSDs may be hesitant to disclose their condition (Trammell, 2009). Students may feel that accommodations may give them an unfair advantage or negate an opportunity to create a positive student identity or lead others to see them as less competitive (Olney & Brockelman, 2005; Trammell & Hathaway, 2007).

Similarly, international student services, including study abroad programs, should include CSDs in their marketing efforts and offer cultural opportunities that are disability friendly. Having an opportunity to participate in an international education program can enhance the college experience of students with disabilities. In addition, the offices of multicultural services or students can also offer a safe and respectful environment that supports programs and groups of CSDs. Higher education institutions can also encourage student affairs practitioners to establish groups for CSDs and those with multiple cultural identities.

As some CSDs come to college without a refined disability identity and lack adequately mature skills to manage that identity (Trammell, 2009), equity and diversity practitioners can help students to form or navigate a positive disability identity. It can be of great benefit to individuals across student affairs and academic affairs when disability awareness training is offered. This can be especially useful in addressing invisible disabilities and in increasing disability support services personnel's sensitivity toward disabilities. Also important areas for education are knowledge and skills regarding legal issues, reasonable accommodations, universal design, and communication with CSDs and other departments (Burgstahler & Moore, 2009).

By improving the quality of services in disability services, practitioners can help CSDs to experience the feeling of coming home that can lead CSDs to feel that campus is a safe place for coming out (Gill, 1997). A similar sense of acceptance can be identified within the DTDC and DIDM models when students accept their disability and welcome their disability identity. For students to receive services at the university setting, they need to feel comfortable addressing their disabilities and needs (Forber-Pratt & Aragon, 2013).

In addition, international services can expand on the disability culture by allowing CSDs to give back to the community and become role models in international settings. Students with disabilities can have a sense of personal satisfaction while promoting social equity for other students with disabilities not only in the United States but also in other parts of the world with less legal or civil rights for IWDs. Another method of facilitating the development of a disability identity for college students is to incorporate collegewide programs that highlight disability and its personal, social, and political implications. The office of multicultural services, working collaboratively with other student affairs departments and students, can promote the understanding and increase awareness of disability while helping CSDs reach the final stage of the three models.

Multicultural service personnel can also strive to engage CSDs in diverse extracurricular and academic activities. Higher education and student affairs offices often fail to collect demographic data on categories related to disability and gender identity (Garvey, 2014). Without this type of data, it is challenging to support CSDs' educational outcomes and to evaluate their college experience (including admission, retention, attrition, performance, graduation). As a result, multicultural offices can help to support retention of CSDs by engaging them in collegial activities as well as to maintain data about CSDs receiving services. These services can also attend to the multidimensional aspects of identity and work with the different subgroups in the disability culture (Forber-Pratt & Aragon, 2013).

CASE VIGNETTE WRAP-UP: MELANIE

Although Melanie was born post-ADA, she still faced social and attitudinal challenges and barriers in college. After completing her core courses in the community college, she would be moving to a new educational setting with new accessibility concerns and social stigma. She would have to redefine her identity within a new context. Being born with a disability also allowed Melanie to integrate her disability into her identity not only as a student but also in other facets of her life.

The DIIM (Gill, 1997) presents an integration process to understand Melanie's view of her disability. Melanie has developed a social role and an identity within the dominant culture and recognized attitudinal barriers about her walker (coming to feel we belong). She has also requested accommodations and services from the disability office demonstrating that she has "come home." Even though Melanie might be hesitant about using her walker sometimes, she seemed comfortable with her disability identity by accepting accommodations and advocating for herself and others.

The DIDM (Gibson, 2006) can also describe Melanie's disability identity. Although Melanie showed some indication of the Realization stage by refusing to use her walker, she has accepted her disability identity. She has connected with other students with disabilities, participated in advocacy, and represented disability as a group. Therefore, contextual forces could push Melanie to the stages of Realization and Passive Awareness. Although unknown at this moment, the new university can fail to accommodate Melanie's positive identity, regressing her identity to the Passive Awareness stage.

Because Melanie has a physical disability, her disability identity development fits well with the DTDC (Forber-Pratt & Aragon, 2013). Melanie has gone through the Acceptance

(continued)

(continued)

phase as she felt comfortable to request services from the disability services office as well as the Relationship phase because she has connections with other CSDs. Melanie has participated in college clubs that promote inclusion and equal education for all students; thus, she has not only developed and accepted her identity, but she has given back to the community by becoming a role model for upcoming students. Melanie, from the DTDC view, has embraced her disability identity and has immersed herself in the disability culture. By having proper transition services from her community college to a university, combined with knowledgeable and skillful student affairs professionals, Melanie could successfully become a math teacher and a role model for students with disabilities from kindergarten to college years.

CASE VIGNETTE 1 FOR READER REFLECTION: PALOMA

Paloma, a self-identified Latina, has an incomplete spinal cord injury as a result of a car accident at the age of 19 years. She was driving to college when a car collided with her sending her into a coma for a few days. After her accident and receiving rehabilitation services, she has decided to apply for college next semester. She is also planning her wedding to her high school sweetheart and thinking about the possibility to being a mom in the future.

She explains that she has struggled with having a disability that limits her mobility because she has to rely on canes and sometimes a wheelchair. However, medical professionals and therapist have told her that she would be able to walk without assistance in the future. Paloma also shared that her counselors have helped her adjust well to her disability and identified ways to assist others in similar or worse situations.

Because of her traumatic personal experience, she has decided to become a counselor to help other people in difficult emotional situations. However, she is uncertain of the disability services on campus, her academic skills after the accident, and her reaction to students' view of her disability. It is a very new experience for her although she is comfortable with family members, significant others, and friends.

- *What are Paloma's greatest needs?*
- *What campus-based services might be most beneficial to her?*
- *What are some goals you would like to see her reach?*

CASE VIGNETTE 2 FOR READER REFLECTION: AURELIO

Aurelio, a biracial man, quickly began losing his hearing at the age of 30 years. Even though his friends have always teased him for looking "White," he identifies as a Black man. He is a graduate student at a local university actively pursuing a master's degree, taking two courses each semester, to move up in his career. Aurelio prefers traditionally delivered

(continued)

(continued)

courses over online courses because he truly enjoys listening to the lectures, participating in discussion, and presenting in class.

Aurelio is confused about having issues understanding or listening to sounds and information around him. He has not been formally evaluated for his hearing loss and is unsure how or where to go for services. He explains that he will take care of his hearing issues after the semester is over. He has no time to waste on doctors or testing because he has to do well in his class to get his dream job at work.

Aurelio is also very excited because he just recently began dating a young woman that he met in a religious fellowship group. He feels that the relationship has the potential to grow into marriage owing to the great trust, common values, and mutual respect they share. He wants to finish school, receive a promotion at work, and start a family soon. As far as college services, he has rarely used any of the services on campus. In fact, although he prefers face-to-face class settings, he actually handles most of his college business online because it is more efficient and his work, education, and new relationship keep him busy.

- *What are Aurelio's greatest needs?*
- *What campus-based services might be most beneficial to him?*
- *What are some goals you would like to see him reach?*

REFERENCES

Bowe, F. (2000). *Universal design in education: Teaching nontraditional students.* Westport, CT: Greenwood.

Burgstahler, S., & Moore, E. (2009). Making student services welcoming and accessible through accommodations and universal design. *Journal of Postsecondary Education and Disability, 21*(3), 155–174.

Evans, N. J., Forney, D. S., Guido, F. M., Patton, L. D., & Renn, K. A. (2009). *Student development in college: Theory, research, and practice.* San Francisco, CA: Jossey-Bass.

Forber-Pratt, A. J., & Aragon, S. R. (2013). A model of social and psychosocial identity development for postsecondary students with physical disabilities. In M. Wappett & K. Arndt (Eds.), *Emerging perspectives on disability studies* (pp. 1–22). New York, NY: Palgrave Macmillan.

Garvey, J. C. (2014). Demographic information collection in higher education and student affairs survey instruments. In D. Mitchell, C. Simmons, & L. Greyerbiehl (Eds.), *Intersectionality and higher education: Theory, research, and praxis* (pp. 201–216). New York, NY: Peter Lang.

Gibson, J. (2006). Disability and clinical competency: An introduction. *The California Psychologist, 39,* 6–10.

Gill, C. J. (1997). Four types of integration in disability identity development. *Journal of Vocational Rehabilitation, 9,* 39–46.

Hadley, W. M. (2011). College students with disabilities: A student development perspective. *New Directions for Higher Education, 2011*(154), 77–81.

Hutcheon, E. J., & Wolbring, G. (2012). Voices of "disabled" post-secondary students: Examining higher education "disability" policy using an ableism lens. *Journal of Diversity in Higher Education, 5*(1), 39–49. doi:10.1037/a0027002

Kaplan, D. (2000). The definition of disability: Perspective of the disability community. *Journal of Health Care Law and Policy, 3*(2), 352–364. Retrieved from http://digitalcommons.law.umaryland.edu/jhclp/vol3/iss2/5

Kübler-Ross, E. (1969). *On death and dying*. London, England: Routledge.

Kübler-Ross, E., & Kessler, D. (2005). *On grief and grieving: Finding the meaning of grief through the five stages of loss*. New York, NY: Scribner.

McEwen, M. K. (2003). New perspectives on identity development. In S. R. Komives, D. B. Woodard, Jr., & Associates, *Student services: A handbook for the profession* (4th ed., pp. 203–233). San Francisco, CA: Jossey-Bass.

National Center for Education Statistics, Institute of Education Sciences. U.S. Department of Education. (2014). Federal programs for education and related activities. In *Digest of Education Statistics: 2014* (Chap. 3). Retrieved from the National Center for Education Statistics website: http://nces.ed.gov/programs/digest/d14/ch_3.asp

National Council on Disability. (2015). Briefing paper: Reauthorization of the Higher Education Act (HEA): The implications for increasing the employment of people with disabilities. Washington, DC: Author. Retrieved from https://www.ncd.gov/publications/2015/05192015/#Endnote26

National Institute on Disability and Rehabilitation Research. (1998). Notice of proposed long-range plan for fiscal years 1999-2004. *Federal Register, 63*(206), 57189–57219. Retrieved from https://www2.ed.gov/legislation/FedRegister/announcements/1998-4/102698a.html

Nichols, A. H., & Quaye, S. J. (2009). Removing barriers to academic and social engagement for students with disabilities. In S. R. Harper & S. J. Quaye (Eds.), *Student engagement in higher education: Theoretical perspectives and practical approaches for diverse populations* (pp. 39–60). New York, NY: Routledge.

Olney, M. F., & Brockelman, K. F. (2005). The impact of visibility of disability and gender on the self-concept of university students with disabilities. *Journal of Postsecondary Education and Disability, 18*(1), 80–91.

Pliner, S. M., & Johnson, J. R. (2004). Historical, theoretical, and foundational principles of universal instructional design in higher education. *Equity & Excellence in Education, 37*(2), 105–113.

Riddell, S., & Weedon, E. (2014). Disabled students in higher education: Discourses of disability and the negotiation of identity. *International Journal of Educational Research, 63*, 38–46. doi:10.1016/j.ijer.2013.02.008

Rubin, S., & Roessler, R. (2008). *Foundations of the vocational rehabilitation process*. Austin, TX: Pro-ed.

Sandeen, A., & Barr, M. (2006). *Critical issues for student affairs*. San Francisco, CA: Jossey-Bass.

Scotch, R. (1989). Politics and policy in the history of the disability rights movement. *The Milbank Quarterly, 67*(Suppl. 2, Pt. 2), 380–400.

Sheppard-Jones, K., Krampe, K., Danner, F., & Berdine, W. (2002). Investigating postsecondary staff knowledge of students with disabilities using a web-based survey. *Journal of Applied Rehabilitation Counseling, 33*(1), 19–25.

Smart, J. (2015). *Disability, society and the individual*. Austin, TX: Pro Ed.

Student Affairs Administrators in Higher Education, NASPA. (2016). Equity and diversity. Retrieved from https://www.naspa.org/focus-areas/equity-and-diversity

Swain, J., & French, S. (2000). Towards an affirmation model. *Disability and Society, 15*(4), 569–582.

Task Force on the Future of Student Affairs. (2010). Envisioning the future of student affairs. Final report of the Task Force on the Future of Student Affairs appointed jointly by ACPA and NASPA. Retrieved from https://www.naspa.org/images/uploads/main/Task_Force_Student_Affairs_2010_Report.pdf

Torres, V., Jones, S. R., & Renn, K. (2009). Identity development theories in student affairs: Origins, current status, and new approaches. *Journal of College Student Development, 50*(6), 577–596.

Trammell, J. (2009). Postsecondary students and disability stigma: Development of the Postsecondary Student Survey of Disability-Related Stigma (PSSDS). *Journal of Postsecondary Education and Disability, 22*(2), 106–116.

Trammell, J., & Hathaway, M. (2007). Help-seeking patterns in college students with disabilities. *Journal of Postsecondary Education and Disability, 20*(1), 5–15.

U.S. Department of Education, Office for Civil Rights. (2012). Disability rights: Enforcement highlights. Washington, DC. Retrieved from https://www2.ed.gov/documents/news/section-504.pdf

Wilson, K., Getzel, E., & Brown, T. (2000). Enhancing the post-secondary campus climate for students with disabilities. *Journal of Vocational Rehabilitation, 14*(1), 37–50.

PART IV: FACTORS IMPACTING SELECTION OF MAJORS AND CAREERS

CHAPTER 16

COLLEGE MAJOR AND CAREER CHOICE

Wendy K. Killam, Suzanna M. Wise, and Bill Weber

CASE VIGNETTE: BROOKLYN

Brooklyn, a sophomore in college, is the daughter of two artists. Her father is a graphic designer at an athletic footwear manufacturing company and her mother is a self-employed photographer. Brooklyn's two younger twin brothers are in high school and are already exploring careers in video game development and graphic design. Brooklyn always enjoyed art but is wondering if she would prefer following a career path in the business world. When she brought this up with her parents, they have encouraged her to find a career that allows her to express her creative side and gives her maximum freedom and flexibility, as her parents both prize those opportunities in their own jobs. Brooklyn feels confused by the dissonance between her personal dreams and her parents' advice, as she always has prided herself on being a lot like her parents. Brooklyn determines that she would benefit from visiting the Career Center on campus.

MAJOR AND CAREER INDECISION

College is a time of significant exploration and new experiences that can present students with the opportunity to continue a successful path toward the future. Students may follow the path they began in high school or choose to reinvent themselves and start fresh. College is also a time of weighty decision making and future planning. Students may enter higher education with a strong set of ideals, firm models of career options, and certain confidence in their ultimate direction; however, it is not uncommon for students to begin college unprepared for life after graduation, let alone housing assignments and first semester coursework. Soon after the initial adjustments to college life, the responsibility to choose one's major looms large. Some students make a choice easily, while others struggle to decide the right decision for their future. This chapter focuses on the difficulties surrounding the major choice, the factors that influence decision making, career theories in student affairs, and campus and community resources available to assist students in gathering important data about their major and career choices.

When students initially select their undergraduate major, it is not uncommon for them to change academic focus a few times during the course of college, to be uncertain about future career goals, or to know how their chosen major connects to the world of work. Compelling coursework, peer experiences, and the impact of internship, athletic, and volunteer experiences may all influence this shift from one program area to the next. The student who does not change majors at least once might actually be quite rare. At universities where career education is an institutional value and practice, students become accustomed to the process of career exploration early and begin building skills, knowledge, and abilities for the working world. The career exploration journey is one that requires the convergence of multiple resources across campus and in the community. In most cases, this journey is not linear, but calls for adaptive and flexible consideration of options, creativity when expectations do not meet reality, and a willingness to try new things.

According to Porter and Umbach (2006), selecting a major is one of the most critical decisions a college student will ever make, yet the decision is being made at a time when the student is still trying to figure things out during a period of life known as emerging adulthood (Arnett, 2000). Given the typical developmental struggles faced during this time, such as individuation, autonomy, and identity differentiation (Johnson, Schamuhn, Nelson, & Buboltz, Jr., 2014), it makes sense that the decision-making process is so complex (Arnett, 2000). Additionally, the selection of undergraduate major and initial career path will have implications in many areas of a person's life, such as financial, geographical, and relational (Eun, Sohn, & Lee, 2012), so even though the college major may not be directly related to one's ultimate career path, choosing a major should not be taken lightly and requires careful consideration. Without specific guidance, such as a career planning course, or a series of workshops focused on career-related information, college students often lack sufficient knowledge about career options and the job market when they are making career decisions (Amit & Gati, 2013).

DEVELOPMENTAL FACTORS

In childhood, career aspirations are often identified through modeling by parents, celebrities, fantasy characters, and imagination. Bandura's Social Learning Theory (1969) certainly provides a framework for how this process takes place through early development, and later provides the foundation for the formation of self-efficacy, an essential element of the early career decision-making process (Lent & Brown, 1996). In addition, aspirations are frequently reflective of gender-based norms and gender-typical careers gleaned through media and public representation, or norms handed down from parents, family, and community members (L. S. Gottfredson, 2005). As they continue to grow and develop, children gain insight into other possibilities, but without shadowing careers, or engaging in career education, they do not fully understand the day-to-day activities involved in most jobs (Bubic, 2014).

Many children are first exposed to potential career choices through the media. Television shows and movies often paint a very unrealistic picture of what people really do at work. This leads to inaccurate expectations regarding careers, and a lack of knowledge regarding what the real world of work is like. For example, the vast majority of individuals who dream about being a professional athlete rarely have the skills, talent, or connections required for access to that opportunity, but because of media depictions of the money and fame attached to pro athletes, this aspiration appears as attainable and desirable (Burns, Jasinski, Dunn, & Fletcher, 2013). Student athletes are not the only individuals who might think in this way; any student with a narrow focus on major and career, and little flexibility for other options, will need a backup plan in case they do not succeed under the original plan. Developing a backup might be seen as a foreclosure on their initial dream, but with guidance and support, and exploration of alternatives, the student could see it as good groundwork for the future and a pragmatic choice (Johnson et al., 2014).

FACTORS INFLUENCING DECISION MAKING

This lack of realistic knowledge and overall preparedness can lead to unclear expectations about jobs in general, as well as the training needed to obtain certain jobs. Increasingly, students receive career information starting in middle school, and take basic career assessment inventories at various periods in their secondary school experience, but often are not provided with comprehensive interpretation of those assessments, or information regarding current market demand for jobs and associated salaries; thus, a student may select a college major and initial career path with little concern for realistic aspects of working, such as employment outlook, remuneration and benefits, or daily work tasks (Herndon, 2012). Furthermore, if the student accepts federal or private loans to cover the cost of higher education, he or she may financially struggle for many years to repay the debt, which can put greater pressure on making an informed major decision that will then lead to a viable career opportunity. In fact, when it comes to the selection of a college major, there are several factors that can influence the choice of college major and ultimately the career choice of an individual (Wright, Perrone-McGovern, Boo, & White, 2014).

Family Influence

As noted previously, the first exposure children have to the world of work is through their parents (Herndon, 2012). At a young age, children watch what their parents do to gain insight into the world of work (Bubic, 2014), and develop early notions of what jobs are for. Bandura's theory (1969), followed up by Lent and Brown (1996), highlights how readily children pick up on verbal and nonverbal modeling by parents, which extends to family stressors like money and work. The messages transmitted between parents, or in overheard conversations, often have an implicit or explicit influence over a child's future decisions and self-efficacy. Additionally, in some families, there is a strong cultural desire or expectation for children to follow in the footsteps of a parent, and again, these messages are both spoken and unspoken. For example, KuzMina (2014) notes that in families where one or both parents are doctors, attorneys, or college professors, the choice not to attend college with the goal of a lucrative career is likely not considered an option, and the initial selection of major is heavily influenced by parents regardless of the student's ability.

When circumstances such as those described earlier are in place, they present substantial issues and challenges for the individual who lacks sufficient interest, ability, and skills to follow a predetermined path. Such a mismatch can also contribute to a negative and unproductive college experience. It can potentially lead an individual to leave college for lack of authentic direction, as well. The need for individual discernment of interests, skills, and abilities in the selection of a college major cannot be overlooked; however, the influence of family is often strong and, for some, a deciding factor (L. S. Gottfredson, 2005). For those students whose parents did not attend college, making them first-generation college students, the road ahead becomes more difficult given the lack of precollege preparation and orientation to what college is, in addition to a potential lack of other tangible supports, such as financial and other assistance (Tate et al., 2015). Davis-Kean (2005) points out that in addition to the career attainment of an individual's parents, their culture, degree level, and values about education are also an instrumental influence.

Cultural Variables

KuzMina (2014) found that individuals from families with high income were more likely to select college majors that would result in careers with high incomes. Perhaps surprisingly, individuals from lower incomes were also more likely to select majors that would result in lower incomes. However, L. S. Gottfredson's theory of Circumscription and Compromise (2005) explains this phenomenon through the lens of access and opportunity. Together with the concept of modeling, in terms of observing and emulating what those around you do and have, society also provides a structure of privilege that applies only to certain groups. Therefore, much of the world of monetary success and ambition is simply not visually and representationally available for minority groups. As these institutional barriers are broken down over time, students will have a much broader picture of what occupations and opportunities are available. Gender and sexual minority groups, racial/ethnic groups, and immigrant groups are among those that lack full access to the world of work and opportunity.

Examples of the role that binary gender plays in the selection of a college major are found in statistics that indicate that women earn 85% of the nursing degrees and 80% of the degrees in education, yet women earn only 19% of the degrees granted in physics and engineering (Snyder & Dillow, 2012). This may be due to numerous social factors, such as how girls and women are taught science and math (Shumow & Schmidt, 2013), as well as healthy and supported development of self-efficacy (Lent & Brown, 2005). England and Li (2006) cite that in order for gender equity to occur with college majors, about one third of either gender would have to switch majors; however, it is interesting to note that women continue to enter fields where males tend to dominate. As the balance of women outweighs men in a workplace, the average salary decreases, which illustrates the strength of institutional oppression. Although there are more opportunities for all genders to obtain degrees and work in fields that are dominated by another gender, the evidence is clear that there are still rigid and expected gender roles within society (L. S. Gottfredson, 2005). For those females and minorities who select certain specific majors, there can be challenges in finding mentors and feelings of being isolated (Syed, 2010). Social expectations related to certain jobs can also affect the choice of a college major and subsequent career (Betz, 2002). However, even the selection of college plays a significant role in the choice of major and eventual career attainment.

College Selection

People are often drawn to organizations that fit well with their values. The same is true when students are selecting a college. People desire to work in a place where they feel comfortable and where their values are respected. Feeling connected to others has been identified as a major factor in college retention and success. Clinciu (2013) found that males tended to have an easier time adjusting socially to the college setting, given the existing supports in place that privilege male students. Enochs and Roland (2006) found that social adjustment for college students could be affected by freshman experience programs, and the quality of programming made a difference in how acclimated students became to the college campus. Social connection on campus was even more important to college adjustment for females because the aforementioned supports for male students are not as prevalent for female students (Betz, 2002; Tajlili, 2014) and nonbinary students (Schneider & Dimito, 2010). College personnel would be wise to take note and implement programs that can contribute to the college success of all students, regardless of identity. If a college student finds a fit that feels good, the college adjustment process and overall experience tends to be less stressful and increases the likelihood that the student will complete college (Balsamo, Lauriola, & Saggino, 2013). The selection of a college major can also encourage individuals to get more involved on campus and to forge meaningful connections with peers and faculty, especially when there are direct links among majors, internships, college activities, and future employment opportunities. Thus, part of the challenge for colleges is creating an infrastructure that supports academic and career planning.

The selection of a college major has been linked to having a higher level of persistence and a student's decision to remain in college (Willcoxson & Wynder, 2010). Minority students may select majors that are viewed as compatible with their ethnicity or race and prefer a field that contributes to social advancement (Syed, 2010). This highlights the need for career services to be available as students begin their college journey to assist them with finding the right fit based on individual factors. Helping students to identify areas of interest when selecting a college major can positively influence their achievement levels, as well as whether or not they complete college and obtain a degree (Pabler & Hell, 2012).

For some students, attending a college far away from home might not be ideal; for others, however, it would be an adventure and provide a fresh start. Some students might be drawn by a college with a strong alumni network or one that has a winning sports record. Others may want to attend the same college that a relative attended even if it limits the selection of college majors. The selection of a college is a highly personal and individual decision and is shaped to a large degree by the available majors and degree programs, as well as the rankings of those programs. Career services representatives can help college students to consider the labor market information about careers they are considering (Herndon, 2012), because it is very frustrating for students to graduate and then be unable to obtain a job in their selected fields. Although finding a good fit is important, one needs to consider the cost of a college education and how many years of debt students and families will incur.

Although many people believe that a college degree is important for college success, it is also becoming less and less affordable. However, some might overestimate the cost of a college degree and not attend based on inaccurate estimates and inaccurate information (Herndon, 2012). Students need to be informed about financial aid options and the actual cost of a college education. Some students fear having high levels of debt on graduation and thus opt to work throughout their college education (Humphrey, 2006). Working during college can sometimes result in delayed graduation depending on the number of hours a student is required to work each week. However, it can also allow a student to gain valuable experience regarding what it is like to actually work and to develop time management skills. Determining what one wants to do long term can be a daunting task especially given the potential long-term impact of challenges and choices faced in emerging adulthood. Thus, there is a clear need for career theories and campus services to be used to assist college students in making these decisions.

Campus and Community Resources

Several crucial resource offices exist on most college campuses, the comprehensiveness of which depends on funding and institutional value systems. A career services office is generally the hub of career information available on campus, and this type of office will serve current students and alumni. One of the most important functions of a career services office is the responsibility to host career and internship fairs, workshops to prepare for those fairs, and resume review. Larger career services offices also have space for local and regional employers to recruit students and alumni, and host events to share workplace information with potential employees. Internship and employment databases housed on campus are a crucial tool for students to locate available opportunities, post their resumes, and apply for positions, and these systems are even more lucrative for students when they are campus bound and not national, so that students are only competing with each other for positions and not a much larger applicant pool.

In addition to the resource-rich career services office, offering opportunities for career education is an excellent method for students to earn academic credit while learning how to map their career planning process. These courses are often connected to career services offices for the resources already described, and others exist in counseling departments, where the focus may include career counseling and more intentional one-on-one support for students who are struggling to define their interests, skills, abilities, and direction. Career education offers extensive access to career assessment instruments and theoretical information that help guide students in creating a path forward that best fits their personality, desires, and goals.

CAREER THEORIES AND ASSESSMENTS

The choice of the wrong major and wrong college can significantly influence the decision to leave college (Willcoxson & Wynder, 2010). So, how can students be sure they are making the right choice? The use of career theories can help students determine the best major choice. One theory that is frequently used is Holland's theory of person–environment interaction fit (G. D. Gottfredson & Johnstun, 2009), which provides an explicit link between various personality characteristics and corresponding job titles. This theory uses six personality types, each identified by a letter (Realistic, Investigative, Artistic, Social, Enterprising, and Conventional), and through a formal inventory helps students determine their one- to three-letter Holland code, which corresponds to aspects of their personality, and how their personality may fit into typical work environments. This could be beneficial in assisting them in selecting an appropriate major (Chen & Simpson, 2015), because it highlights occupational interests that connect to the workplace, positioned against actual workers who share those interests.

One challenge students often face is the lack of information about how specific majors link to career options (Herndon, 2012). A student's interest level in a particular major can positively influence the capacity to gain specific abilities during college even if academic achievement prior to college was less than ideal. The interest level in one's major has been linked to a higher likelihood of college completion (Pabler & Hell, 2012). Helping students gain insight into appropriate majors can be a major factor in college success. One of the most popular assessment interests using Holland's theory is the Strong Interest Inventory, which discerns an individual's interests, and if the College Profile version is chosen, the individual's interests will then be linked not only to potential career options, but also majors, and extracurricular activities that may enrich a student's college experience. Thus, the benefits of finding an area of interest when it comes to a major would highly support the ongoing use of Holland's theory with college students. Personality type is one such factor that can be considered when selecting a major, as students tend to make selections that fit with their personality (Chen & Simpson, 2015). The challenge, however, is that students might lack insight into their own personality type and what specific majors and careers would be the best fit.

In Chapter 8, we explored the Myers–Briggs type indicator (MBTI) in some depth. This personality assessment could help students to determine if their personality type would be a good fit for a particular occupational environment. For instance, a person who is not very outgoing and extremely introverted might want to select a college major that would allow one to frequently work independently and to require little engagement with the public on a regular basis. Research has been conducted that has linked certain personality types to specific careers. For example, people with strong leadership tendencies often major in prelaw, military science, and communication studies (Porter & Umbach, 2006). Understanding oneself is important and the use of personality and career assessments can be beneficial, though they must be interpreted by trained professionals to ensure authentic information transfer. The Strong Interest Inventory has also been used by college centers to assist students with the selection of college majors and is based on Holland's theory (Chen & Simpson, 2015). The use of multiple assessments can be highly beneficial in assisting students in selecting the most appropriate college major.

CONCLUSION

During the college years, students are grappling with multifaceted and weighty decisions as they try to seek a balance between autonomy and independence while still trying to make decisions that will please their families. It can be a time of great challenges, opportunities, and growth. Too often students do not realize and recognize the campus resources available to assist them as they struggle with decisions related to major selection and career options. Selecting a college major and making career decisions are not easy, and require self-knowledge, self-examination, and research on what is available in the world of work. There are many factors that can both negatively and positively affect the process (Eun, Sohn, & Lee, 2012), including cultural variables, access, support services, and family influence. Essential to student success is the ability of student affairs professionals to accurately recognize when students are struggling and make an appropriate referral for career counseling, academic support services, or personal counseling. In the next chapter, we examine Holland's theory of career development in detail, and highlight how career assessment can be helpful in this process of discernment.

CASE VIGNETTE WRAP-UP: BROOKLYN

When Brooklyn appeared at the Career Counseling Center on her campus, she was experiencing distress about her inability to make up her mind on how to map out her education for the next few years. During her first appointment, her assigned counselor listened to Brooklyn express the competing desires to follow her parents' suggestion to find a career that would allow her to be creative and her own desire for a business-based career. The counselor set up an appointment for Brooklyn to take several career assessments and to interview individuals in careers that attracted her. Brooklyn was connected with a marketing team that worked with a local charity foundation and was invited to shadow the team leader to learn what his role entailed. Brooklyn reported to the career counselor that the philanthropic mission of the organization really inspired her, and the use of theory to generate and implement creative ideas also made intuitive sense to her. Brooklyn was encouraged to follow her instincts and begin moving toward a major in marketing and business.

CASE VIGNETTE 1 FOR READER REFLECTION: MELISSA

Melissa is a first-generation college student whose single father never completed high school. She cannot remember her mother, who died from a drug overdose when Melissa was an infant. Melissa's father worked extra hours to build up his savings to ensure his daughter went to college, and Melissa recognizes that this step is significant not just for her, but for her father, as well. Unfortunately for Melissa, she feels pressured to choose a major to please her father, and he would like her to be a teacher. He believes that education is the key to a better world, and he would like Melissa to "unlock the dreams of others," as he has described it. Melissa, however, has strong interest in pursuing an engineering degree

(continued)

(continued)

because the financial compensation for a female engineer would be much greater than what she could earn as a teacher.

Melissa shows up at your office to discuss her choice of a major. As her academic advisor, you are concerned about the fit between her aspirations and her capabilities. You have reviewed her records and know that throughout high school, her grades in math and science were below average.

- What would you want to address with Melissa immediately?
- What resources would you want to encourage Melissa to use on campus?

CASE VIGNETTE 2 FOR READER REFLECTION: SANJAY

Sanjay is a senior biology major who is hoping to pursue his doctoral degree in this field. You are on duty in the campus counseling center's walk-in clinic the day that he shows up for help. Sanjay shares that his parents are eager for him to earn his doctoral degree in biomedical engineering and work in research and development in this field. Sanjay, however, shares with you that his dream is to become a nurse or a nurse practitioner as he derives great satisfaction from helping others in a practical, one-on-one manner. He is afraid to share this dream with his parents and is trying to find a way to pursue his plans to enter nursing school without his parents finding out. Sanjay also reveals that he believes that he may be gay and is unsure if this affects his career choice.

- As Sanjay's counselor, what issue do you feel would be the most important to address during his first walk-in session?
- What are the areas of exploration that you feel would be most relevant to Sanjay's circumstances and what other campus resources might you suggest he explore?

REFERENCES

Amit, A., & Gati, I. (2013). Table or circles: A comparison of two methods of choosing among career alternatives. *The Career Development Quarterly, 61*, 20–63.

Arnett, J. J. (2000). Emerging adulthood: A theory of development from the late teens through the twenties. *American Psychologist, 55*(5), 469–480.

Balsamo, M., Lauriola, M., & Saggino, A. (2013). Work values and college major choice. *Learning and Individual Differences, 2*, 110–116.

Bandura, A. (1969). Social-learning theory of identificatory processes. In D. A. Goslin (Ed.), *Handbook of socialization theory and research* (pp. 213–262). Skokie, IL: Rand McNally.

Betz, N. (2002). Explicating an ecological approach to the career development of women. *The Career Development Quarterly, 50*, 335–338.

Bubic, A. (2014). Decision making characteristics and decision styles predict adolescents' career choice satisfaction. *Current Psychology, 33*, 515–531.

Burns, G. N., Jasinski, D., Dunn, S., & Fletcher, D. (2013). Academic support services and career decision-making self-efficacy in student athletes. *The Career Development Quarterly, 61*, 161–167.

Chen, P. D., & Simpson, P. A. (2015). Does personality matter? Applying Holland's typology to analyze students' self-selection into science, technology, engineering, and mathematics majors. *The Journal of Higher Education, 86*, 725–750.

Clinciu, A. I. (2013). Adaptation and stress for the first year university students. *Procedia—Social and Behavioral Sciences, 78*, 718–722.

Davis-Kean, P. E. (2005). The influence of parent education and family income on child achievement: The indirect role of parent expectations and the home environment. *Journal of Family Psychology, 19*, 294–304.

England, P., & Li, S. (2006). Desegregation stalled: The changing gender composition of college majors, 1971–2002. *Gender and Identity, 20*, 657–677.

Enochs, W. K., & Roland, C. (2006). Social adjustment of college freshmen: The importance of gender and living environment. *College Student Journal, 40*, 63–72.

Eun, H., Sohn, Y. W., & Lee, S. (2012). The effect of self-regulated decision making on career path and major-related career choice satisfaction. *Journal of Employment Counseling, 50*, 98–109.

Gottfredson, L. S. (2005). Applying Gottfredson's theory of circumscription and compromise in career guidance and counseling. In S. D. Brown & R. W. Lent (Eds.), *Career development and counseling: Putting theory and research to work* (pp. 71–100). Hoboken, NJ: Wiley.

Gottfredson, G. D., & Johnstun, M. L. (2009). John Holland's contributions: A theory-ridden approach to career assistance. *The Career Development Quarterly, 58*, 99–107.

Herndon, M. C. (2012). Improving consumer information for higher education planning. *New Directions for Institutional Research, 153*, 63–74.

Humphrey, R. (2006). Pulling structured inequality into higher education: The impact of work on English university students. *Higher Education Quarterly, 60*, 270–286.

Johnson, P., Schamuhn, T. D., Nelson, D. B., & Buboltz, W. C., Jr. (2014). Differentiation levels of college students: Effects on vocational identity and career decision making. *The Career Development Quarterly, 62*, 70–80.

KuzMina, I. V. (2014). The direct and indirect effect of family factors on the choice of college major. *Russian Education and Society, 56*, 53–68.

Lent, R. W., & Brown, S. D. (1996). Social cognitive career approach to career development: An overview. *The Career Development Quarterly, 44*(4), 310–321.

Lent, R. W., & Brown, S. D. (2005). Integrating person and situation perspectives on work satisfaction: A social-cognitive view. *Journal of Vocational Behavior, 69*, 236–247.

Pabler, K., & Hell, B. (2012). Do interests and cognitive abilities help explain college major choice equally well for women and men. *Journal of Career Assessment, 20*, 479–496.

Porter, S. R., & Umbach, P. D. (2006). College major choice: An analysis of person–environment fit. *Research in Higher Education, 47*, 429–449.

Schneider, M. S., & Dimito, A. (2010). Factors influencing the career and academic choices of lesbian, gay, bisexual, and transgender people. *Journal of Homosexuality, 57*(10), 1355–1369.

Shumow, L., & Schmidt, J. A. (2013). Academic grades and motivation in high school science classrooms among male and female students: Associations with teachers' characteristics, beliefs and practices. *Journal of Education Research, 7*(1), 53–71.

Snyder, T. D., & Dillow, S. A. (2012). *Digest of education statistics 2011* (NCES 2012-001). Washington, DC: National Center for Education Statistics, Institute of Education Sciences, U.S. Department of Education.

Syed, M. (2010). Developing an integrated self: Academic and ethnic identities among ethnically diverse college students. *Developmental Psychology, 46*, 1590–1604.

Tajlili, M. H. (2014). A framework for promoting women's career intentionality and work-life integration. *The Career Development Quarterly, 62*, 254–267.

Tate, K. A., Caperton, W., Kaiser, D., Pruitt, N. T., White, H., & Hall, E. (2015). An exploration of first-generation college students' career development beliefs and experiences. *Journal of Career Development, 42*(4), 294–310.

Willcoxson, L., & Wynder, M. (2010). The relationship between choice of major and career, experience of university and attrition. *Australian Journal of Education, 54*, 175–189.

Wright, S. L., Perrone-McGovern, K. M., Boo, J. N., & White, A. V. (2014). Influential factors in academic and career self-efficacy: Attachment, supports, and career barriers. *Journal of Counseling and Development, 92*, 36–46.

CHAPTER 17

HOLLAND'S THEORY OF CAREER DEVELOPMENT

Kevin Stoltz

CASE VIGNETTE: TYREKA

Tyreka, a 20-year-old African American student, entered the career center at her university with a slow stride and a listless demeanor. She was there at the insistence of her mother to try to choose a major and narrow her career focus. Tyreka was finishing her second year at college and feeling the pressure to choose a major. Her mother was insisting that Tyreka "make a choice and stop wasting time." As a matter of routine, the career center staff gave Tyreka the link to the Self-Directed Search (SDS; Holland & Messer, 2013) to complete online. Also, she was given an appointment with a career counselor. When Tyreka returned for her appointment, she was still listless and appeared sleepy and distracted. She met with the career counselor and they began talking about her reasons for coming to the career center.

Tyreka explained that her mother was pressuring her into making a choice about a career. This led to a discussion about her responses to the SDS. The counselor noted that Tyreka scored low in every category, resulting in a low flat profile of Holland codes generated by the assessment. Additionally, she did not show much interest in talking with the counselor about her future. This worried the counselor, and he asked about other aspects of Tyreka's life. She shared that her father had died 7 months ago and that she missed his guidance and support. She went on to explain that he was the person who inspired her and helped her to feel competent and interested in new ideas.

Since he died, Tyreka felt lost and directionless. The career counselor screened for grief and depression, and Tyreka's responses indicated she was at risk for experiencing significant depression. At this time, the career counselor explained to Tyreka the debilitating effects of depression and grief on career decision making (Walker & Peterson, 2012). Tyreka agreed that she felt depressed, but she thought the mood would pass naturally. The career counselor asked if she would be willing to work with him on her career issues and with a referral counselor to address her depression. Tyreka agreed that getting help for the depression, in addition to her career search, would be a good approach.

(continued)

(continued)

Before leaving, the career counselor went over the SDS again with Tyreka explaining that her depressed mood might be affecting her scoring (Bullock & Reardon, 2005; Fuller, Holland, & Johnston, 1999). He asked her to be patient in making a choice about her major, and they planned a time, a few weeks later, when she would retake the SDS. Tyreka agreed and began seeing a mental health counselor at the university counseling center for the depression.

OVERVIEW OF HOLLAND'S THEORY

The Self-Directed Search (Holland & Messer, 2013) is an assessment founded in Holland's theory of worker personalities and workplace environments (Spokane, Luchetta, & Richwine, 2002). Based on Parson's (1909) theory of matching the self to appropriate work environments through logical reasoning, Holland devised a theory of worker personalities that corresponds to specific work environments. He stressed that assessing interests resulted in measuring aspects of personality. This is often an overlooked aspect of the theory (Holland, 1997). Interest assessment was an emerging technique for career assessment, but Holland added the personality perspective as an addition to career theory.

Holland theorized six distinct worker personalities (Realistic, Investigative, Artistic, Social, Enterprising, and Conventional). This is often referred to as RIASEC. The ordering of the acronym is important and is presented later in this chapter. The theory includes six work environments that correspond to the same personality types (Realistic, Investigative, Artistic, Social, Enterprising, and Conventional). Although people possess aspects of each type, the general thesis of the theory is that salient types (work personalities) will emerge in each individual. These salient personality types are matched with corresponding work environments that produce higher amounts of work satisfaction and productivity (De Fruyt, 2002; Holland, 1997).

The Realistic (R) type is described as frank, genuine, humble, and practical and prefers activities that include machines, tools, and manipulating things (Holland, 1997). The R-type values practical, productive, and concrete results. The Investigative (I)-type characteristics include analytical, cautious, intellectual, and rational. Investigative personalities engage in activities of exploring, and understanding the natural or theoretical world. These individuals value learning and investigation. Artistic (A) types express attributes of emotionality, imagination, and creativity. Often described as nonconforming and original, the A-type individual engages in reading, listening to music, writing, and other artistic activities. A types value aesthetics and creative ideas. Cooperative, friendly, tactful, and patient are descriptors of the Social (S) type. These individuals enjoy activities of helping others, teaching, counseling, and other social services. The S type values social welfare and community concerns. Enterprising (E) types are characterized as adventurous, ambitious, domineering, and self-confident. These people enjoy selling, persuading, and influencing others. The E-type person values power, influence, and responsibility. Individuals identifying as Conventional (C) types are conscientious, conforming, and orderly. C types prefer routine activities with clear standards and objectives. These individuals value orderliness and clarity in outcomes.

Generally, individuals completing the SDS will have variability in scoring and usually have results that indicate preferences for two or three types. To aid the counselor in helping the client learn more about himself or herself, three constructs are important for exploring the match between the person and work environments (Holland, 1997; Spokane et al., 2002). Consistency is directly related to the client's internal self (identity) and is a measure of how aligned the personality types are when arranged on the Holland hexagon. As mentioned earlier, the order of the personality types around the hexagon is an important element of the theory. Types closer to one another share more traits (overlap) and those opposing tend to have opposite or conflicting traits. More congruent personality types (e.g., Investigative, Artistic, and Social: IAS; or Enterprising, Conventional, Realistic: ECR) tend to have less conflicted interests and values (high consistency), while those with opposite types (e.g., Conventional, Social, Artistic: CSA; or Investigative, Social, Conventional: ISC) may have greater variety and conflicts in interests and values (moderate to low consistency). Persons with inconsistencies indicated in scoring may feel conflicted when exploring career options due to the conflicting traits associated with differing types. The ordering of the code assists the individual in increasing self-understanding of strengths associated with personality characteristics. This type of self-knowledge is a cornerstone of successful career counseling dating back to Parsons (1909).

Congruence is a measure of personality fit to the work environment (Holland, 1997; Spokane et al., 2002). When scored, the SDS offers an ordering of the personality coding with higher scored codes indicating more resemblance to those personality traits and lower scores indicating less. When ordered, the results include the top two or three codes ordered from highest to lowest (e.g., ASE, ISR). This ordering matches with the ordered coding for different work environments. This match of ordering between the person's code and the work environment code optimizes the interests and values between the two. The matching process is the crux of the theory, thus optimizing the person's interests, values, and career identity with an appropriate work environment. Matching occurs between the various work environments and the individual's personal code derived from the instrument. Congruence aids the counselor and client in piquing exploration of the various work environments based on the coding combinations. Increased understanding of options and exploratory behaviors is associated with greater career satisfaction and productive work habits (De Fruyt, 2002; Holland, 1997).

Salience is a measure of the degree of preference (Holland, 1997; Spokane et al., 2002). To calculate salience, subtract the lowest coding score from the highest coding score. This variability or distance between these two scores represents the amount of differentiation of the profile scores. Conceptually, those individuals with high salience numbers possess highly defined preferences. Those with lower salience scores have less definition of specific preferences and interests as measured by the instrument. This information helps the student understand specific areas of interest and personal characteristics that aid in career decision making. Often clients must determine a hierarchy of values and preferences in career decision making and knowing the strength of interests and personal characteristics can assist the student in establishing priorities.

Holland (1997) proposed a fourth construct he called identity. Identity relates to the values of consistency and differentiation and represents the strength of the person's goals and interests. Identity is an internal formation that unifies the individual's interests, behaviors, attitudes, and values. Holland developed the My Vocational Situation (MVS; Holland, Diager, & Power, 1980) inventory to measure aspects of identity.

In summary, the codes generated by the SDS help in understanding aspects of the student's personality. The ordering and strength of each code aids in the career counseling process. Specifically, the code ordering and strength assist individuals in exploring different aspects of their personality and matches with various work environments. These constructs provide indicators of the unity of the individual through the construct of identity.

HISTORY AND DEVELOPMENT OF HOLLAND'S THEORY

Holland stated that his theory grew from his work with clients (Holland, 1997). He noted that clients expressed different interests, values, and activities and that similar personality types appeared to have similar interests. Following the suggestion of Darley (1938), Holland began organizing these client-expressed traits into a stereotyped structure of six types (RIASEC). Guilford, Christensen, Bond, and Sutton (1954) later published factor analytic results of career interests and personality traits that corresponded with Holland's types. Although many researchers claimed that measuring vocational interests was limited to work preferences and choices, Holland posited that vocational interests were an expression of aspects of the individual's personality. His research indicated that vocational interests emerged from an individuals' life experiences and personality (Holland, 1997) and, thus, Holland equated measuring interests with measuring significant aspects of personality. From these theoretical underpinnings, Holland developed the RIASEC structure and subsequent assessments (e.g., Self-Directed Search, MVS).

The theory and system that grew from Holland's work represents a major contribution to the understanding of career development and personality. Holland's theory is used across the United States and in many countries to help inform students about their personality and possible work preferences. The U.S. government (Department of Labor/Employment and Training) uses aspects of Holland's theory to provide career information to users of O*NET (O*NET Resource Center, 2016). Users can search the online system by using the *Interests* tab that references Holland's definitions of the RIASEC codes. By entering their code derived from the SDS, users can view a list of occupations that share the same code providing additional career information and promoting exploration.

Tracey (1997, 2002a) continued study of worker types and added new aspects to Holland's theory. Similar to Gottfredson (1996), Tracey and Rounds (1996) identified prestige as a factor in career decision making. Their analysis indicated that people identify occupational preferences based on prestige when completing interest inventories. These results indicate that job prestige is an important consideration when individuals respond to and deliberate career choice decisions. Tracey (2002b) included prestige as a significant dimension in his spherical structure of interests, recognizing that prestige is an area that career counselors need to include when discussing specific career options and decisions. Including the student's personal perceptions of job prestige is a valuable addition to Holland's model and represents emerging research concerning career decision making and development.

Additionally, Tracey, and Sodano (2013) noted that self-efficacy influences the results of interest inventories. This interaction described in the Social-Cognitive Career Theory (Lent, Brown, & Hackett, 1994) outlines how self-efficacy leads to interest development. Tracey and Sodano described that interests and self-efficacy comingle to enhance one another. Interests create purposeful activity in focused areas and successful activity (increased efficacy) leads to increased interest. This convergence of interests and self-efficacy is well documented (e.g., Lent, Tracey, Brown, Soresi, & Nota, 2006) and highlights the need for career counselors to include assessment of both interests and self-efficacy in career counseling practice.

Overall, the theory and resulting assessment systems derived from Holland's work are useful in career counseling and college student affairs practice. The process of assessing a student's interests (aspects of personality) aid the student in self-understanding and exploring careers as outlets for personality attributes and self-expression. Additionally, the system helps to promote career exploration eventually narrowing the student's search for alternative occupations. By adding prestige and self-efficacy constructs to the theory and practice, counselors and student affairs professionals help students understand personal preferences for the social status of work titles and activities and how interests are formed and furthered. Of specific interest is the application of the theory in institutions of higher education as purposeful interventions for student development, major selection, and college completion.

Application of the theory to relevant areas in student affairs is the focus of this book. This particular theory is often relegated to the career center on campus. However, career interventions are becoming recognized as applicable to several initiatives on college and university campuses (Barclay & Stoltz, 2016).

Often students arrive on campus with little idea of choice for a college major or need support to be successful in the transition to college (Solberg et al., 1998). Universities have a long tradition of developing college introductory courses that help the student orient to the expectations of college rigor, aid the student in selecting a major, and assist the student in navigating the college experience (Folsom & Reardon, 2003). A common component of these classes is the use of interest and personality inventories to help the students learn about aspects of their personalities and how those attributes may be applied to work environments. Many aspects of these course experiences are based on Holland's model of person and work environment matching.

Another area of application of Holland's model is academic support and retention (Folsom & Reardon, 2003). Colleges and universities have long studied and attempted to address the problem of retaining students (Braxton et al., 2014). Programs organized to track, report, and influence college student completion are varied. Many include the recognition that college students may not complete college due to a lack of self-knowledge concerning academic and career interests. Many of these retention programs include experiences where students have the opportunity to learn about their interests and skills engaging in assessment and interpretation sessions that are based on Holland's concepts.

The application of Holland's work to institutions of higher education is important. As the workplace continues to require continual updating of skills, higher education will be a place where people come to learn additional knowledge and skills. Helping individuals to learn about themselves to capitalize on personal interests, values, and skills will become more critical in the evolving economy of the 21st century.

CONCLUSION

Holland's work represents a significant contribution to career development and counseling. Understanding Holland's focus on interests as expressions of personality aids career counselors and student development specialists in helping students gain critical self-understanding. Exploring the match between personalities and work environments is a fundamental aspect of applying this theory to student development. Helping students to explore and learn about different careers that may be of interest to them is congruent with the goals of higher education institutions and student development theories.

CASE VIGNETTE WRAP-UP: TYREKA

Applying Holland's theory to Tyreka was complicated by her experience of depression. Depression can interfere with career decision making (Walker & Peterson, 2012) and may affect estimates of self-efficacy (Rottinghaus, Jenkins, & Jantzer, 2009). Thus, continuing to work with Tyreka without addressing the depressive symptoms would be difficult and may prove unproductive.

After a few weeks of treatment for her depression, Tyreka returned to the career center. She exhibited signs of greater interest and happiness in her demeanor. On meeting with her career counselor, she stated that she was feeling better and believed she was ready to focus on her choice of major and career decision. The career counselor had her complete the SDS again and when she returned for her third appointment, Tyreka showed signs of engagement and excitement.

Her SDS scores indicated a profile of IRC (Investigative, Realistic, Conventional). The code indicated that Tyreka preferred working with ideas, data, and things (Prediger, 2002). The I code (44) was highest followed by the C code (32) and the R code (23). Her scores indicated high consistency in her personality. Her lowest code was E (11). This created a salience number of 33 indicating a strong degree of salience in her scores. Overall, this signaled that Tyreka had a pronounced interest in investigative and conventional careers.

Her first reaction was amazement when the career counselor began explaining her results. Tyreka agreed with several of the descriptors concerning investigative and conventional types. She was very interested in learning about insects and plants when she was young. Additionally, she enjoyed being outdoors and learning about life sciences. She related that she grew up in a rural area and would spend much time with her father outdoors. Her father, a pest exterminator (work environment code RC), engaged in collecting and categorizing insects as a hobby. When younger, Tyreka

(continued)

(continued)

would join him in hunting for and gathering specimens. As she got older, she engaged in identifying and categorizing the collection. She enjoyed her science classes in high school and often commented that she would like to go into science. She shared that her father often encouraged her to go into science, but she did not have any role models and had very little information concerning scientific careers. Her mother was not supportive of her interests and often suggested careers that included office work (C) or teaching (S).

The confirmation from the test results helped Tyreka to narrow her major choices. She admitted that until this time, she was influenced by social pressures to be involved in traditionally feminine work. Tyreka indicated that she wanted to have a position that was important and that could contribute to society in a positive way. She admitted that the social value (prestige) of the position was important to her. She wanted people to ask her about her work and she needed to feel proud of her accomplishments. Science seemed to be a way for her to accomplish these goals.

After working with her mental health counselor and engaging in the career counseling sessions, she began to recognize that she really enjoyed science and wanted to explore careers in agriculture, especially regarding "green" initiatives. The memories concerning her father served to support her manifest interests indicating that her internal self may match with specific job titles described in the listings of O*NET.

As she reviewed the list of careers generated by O*NET, she noticed the job titles of agricultural technician, biomass plant technician, and environmental engineering. These interested her and she began further investigation of the knowledge, skills, and abilities related to these titles. As she and the career counselor searched through the databases and talked about options, she began to express more interest in her future and capabilities (self-efficacy). These outcomes indicated that her depression continued to lift and that she was gaining the confidence to make life decisions without depending on her father for support.

The case of Tyreka demonstrates that career decision making can be complicated by mental health factors. Additionally, the case shows how the Holland coding system can capture aspects of the person's personality, helping the individual to align aspects of the identity with work environments. Of particular importance in this case is that Tyreka was able to access memories of special activities that she enjoyed in her youth. These memories were in concert with her assessed interests indicating good person and environment fits with IRC job titles and descriptions.

An especially important caveat of Holland's theory is that it may be viewed as a simplification of the process of career counseling. Researchers have made reference to the "test'em and tell'em" approach to career assessment, meaning that career counselors may rely more on test scores than counseling approaches to inform clients (Pope, 2003). This case highlights that the client's narrative is an important aspect of career counseling. The stories of Tyreka and her father served to relate the test scores to her actual lived experiences and personal joy. Rottinghaus and Miller (2013) emphasized that both assessment and counseling processes are important aspects of career counseling in identifying personality and work fit. They stressed the integration of these approaches to create a more holistic framework for career counseling.

CASE VIGNETTE 1 FOR READER REFLECTION: BRENT

Brent is a 19-year-old White, male, first-year college student. He was experiencing difficulty with math and was enrolled in remedial math courses. He came to the career center experiencing increasing frustration with his failure in math. He was interested in architecture as a career, but began questioning his ability based on his math performance.

Brent completed the SDS and scored highest in A (58). His next highest scores were R (38) and E (36). The career counselor asked Brent to discuss why he wanted to choose architecture as a profession. Brent smiled and said, "I have always been attracted to art, and I really enjoyed my perspective drawing classes in high school. I drew house plans and buildings in class all the time. I guess it was the only profession that I thought I could use my interest in art and make a decent living." The career counselor introduced aspects of Holland's theory to Brent. She explained that interests are an expression of personality and that people generally have multiple outlets for specific interests. Going on, she explained the concept that people in careers often share critical personality traits, values, and interests. Brent stated this all made sense to him. After confirming that Brent was seeking tutoring with math to improve his performance, the career counselor asked Brent if he would be willing to explore other careers that shared similar Holland coding (ARE and AER career). Because the R and E where so close in scores, the coding can be reordered to offer a wider selection of careers and represent the differences in traits indicated by the scoring.

As they reviewed the lists of careers, Bent admitted that he was amazed at the number of feasible careers available. He also discussed his opposite interests (A, R, E). Brent's code indicated low consistency with varied interests and values. He admitted that he often felt conflicted when thinking about careers because he had such varied and wide interests. Over the course of the next few weeks, Brent and his counselor continued to explore careers and compare and contrast values, work environments, and activities. This increased Brent's career information knowledge so that he could make a more informed choice based on his performance in math classes and other indicators of skills, values, and interests.

- *If Brent were your student/client, what activities might you encourage him to use to explore careers and compare and contrast values, work environments, and work activities?*
- *How might you help Brent use his wide variety of interests and values as potentially helpful in determining the best fitting career path?*

CASE VIGNETTE 2 FOR READER REFLECTION: DEMETRIUS

Demetrius, a 22-year-old African American male, came to the career center to discuss different career ideas. Demetrius was in the engineering program and double majoring in business administration and marketing. He and his father, a chemical engineer working for a large multinational corporation, designed Demetrius's program of study. Demetrius explained that his father had a position waiting for him in South America at one of the company's branches. Demetrius was excited about the travel and was very competent in his classes. Recently, he began to question his commitment to this career path. As he thought of his opportunities, he began to realize that he would be making many sacrifices. He especially was reminiscing about his friends and family. He was also connected

(continued)

(continued)

strongly to an outreach project at his church. He was working with young children from the African American community, encouraging them to maintain interest in school and sports activities.

After listening to Demetrius discuss his thoughts, the career counselor asked if he would be interested in completing an assessment designed to indicate personality preferences related to work environments. The counselor explained about Holland's theory, and Demetrius became fascinated with taking the assessment.

After completing the instrument, Demetrius's scores showed high interests across all codes except C. There was a lack of salience in his scoring and the career counselor discussed this aspect of his results. The lack of salience with high scores in several categories demonstrates vast interests. Additionally, the career counselor noted Demetrius's enthusiasm and self-efficacy for capitalizing on opportunities. After a few sessions of exploring different opportunities, Demetrius decided to continue with his present career plan that he and his father devised. He reasoned that if the plan did not take him in a direction he enjoyed, he would simply make adjustments or change the plan. He noted that understanding and seeing his results helped him to realize that he had many interests and choices in his life that he could actualize into a career.

- *As Demetrius's career counselor, how might you move forward with career exploration using the results of the initial assessment?*
- *What other exploration activities might you suggest for Demetrius as he struggles with his conflict?*

REFERENCES

Barclay, S. R., & Stoltz, K. B. (2016). The life-design group: A case study assessment. *Career Development Quarterly, 64*, 83–96. doi:10.1002/cdq.12043

Braxton, J. M., Doyle, W. R., Hartley, H. V., Hirschy, A. S., Jones, W. A., & McLendon, M. K. (2014). *Rethinking college student retention*. San Francisco, CA: Josey-Bass.

Bullock, E. E., & Reardon, R. C. (2005). Using profile elevation to increase the usefulness of the Self-Directed Search and other inventories. *Career Development Quarterly, 54*, 175–183.

Darley, J. G. (1938). A preliminary study of relations between attitudes, adjustment, and vocational interests. *Journal of Educational Psychology, 29*, 467–473.

De Fruyt, F. (2002). A person-centered approach to P-E fit questions using a multiple-trait model. *Journal of Vocational Behavior, 60*, 73–90. doi:10.1006/jvbe.2001.1816

Folsom, B., & Reardon, R. (2003). College career courses: Design and accountability. *Journal of Career Assessment, 11*, 421–450. doi:10.1177/1069072703255875

Fuller, B. E., Holland, J. L., & Johnston, J. A. (1999). The relation of profile elevation in the Self-Directed Search to personality variables. *Journal of Career Assessment, 7*, 111–123.

Gottfredson, L. S. (1996). Gottfredson's theory of circumscription and compromise. In D. Drown, L. Brooks, & Associates (Eds.), *Career choice and development* (3rd ed.). San Francisco, CA: Jossey-Bass.

Guilford, J. S., Christensen, P. R., Bond, N. A., & Sutton, M. A. (1954). A factor analysis of human interests. *Psychological Monographs, 68*, 1–38.

Holland, J. L. (1997). *Making vocational choices: A theory of vocational personalities and work environments* (3rd ed.). Odessa, FL: Psychological Assessment Resources.

Holland, J. L., Daiger, D. C., & Power, P. G. (1980). *My vocational situation*. Palo Alto, CA: Consulting Psychologists Press.

Holland, J. L., & Messer, M. A. (2013). *Self-Directed Search®* (5th ed.). Lutz, FL: PAR.

Lent, R. W., Brown, S. D., & Hackett, G. (1994). Toward a unifying social cognitive theory of career and academic interest, choice, and performance. *Journal of Vocational Behavior, 45,* 79–122. doi:10.1006/jvbe.1994.1027

Lent, R. W., Tracey, T. G., Brown, S. D., Soresi, S., & Nota, L. (2006). Development of interests and competency beliefs in Italian adolescents: An exploration of circumplex structure and bidirectional relationships. *Journal of Counseling Psychology, 53,* 181–191. doi:10.1037/0022-0167.53.2.181

O*NET Resource Center. (2016). About O*NET. Retrieved from http://www.onetcenter.org/overview.html

Parsons, F. (1909). *Choosing a vocation.* New York, NY: Houghton Mifflin.

Pope, M. (2003). Career counseling in the twenty-first century: Beyond cultural encapsulation. *Career Development Quarterly, 52,* 54–60.

Prediger, D. J. (2002). Abilities, interests, and values: Their assessment and their integration via the World-of-Work Map. *Journal of Career Assessment, 10,* 209–232. doi:10.1177/1069072702010002006

Rottinghaus, P. J., Jenkins, N., & Jantzer, A. M. (2009). Relation of depression and affectivity to career decision status and self-efficacy in college students. *Journal of Career Assessment, 17,* 271–285. doi:10.1177/1069072708330463

Rottinghaus, P. J., & Miller, A. D. (2013). Convergence of personality frameworks within vocational psychology. In W. B. Walsh, M. L. Savickas, & P. J. Hartung (Eds.), *Handbook of vocational psychology: Theory, research, and practice* (4th ed.). New York, NY: Routledge.

Solberg, V. S., Gusavac, N., Hamann, T., Felch, J., Johnson, J., Lamborn, S., & Torres, J. (1998). The Adaptive Success Identity Plan (ASIP): A career intervention for college students. *Career Development Quarterly, 47,* 48–95.

Spokane, A. R., Luchetta, E. J., & Richwine, M. H. (2002). Holland's theory of work personalities in work environments. In D. Drown & Associates (Eds.), *Career choice and development* (4th ed.). San Francisco, CA: Jossey-Bass.

Tracey, T. J. G. (1997). The structure of interests and self-efficacy expectations: An expanded examination of the spherical model of interests. *Journal of Counseling Psychology, 44,* 32–43.

Tracey, T. J. G. (2002a). Development of interests and competency beliefs: A 1-year longitudinal study of fifth- to eighth-grade students using the ICA-R and structural equation modeling. *Journal of Counseling Psychology, 49,* 148–163. doi:10.1037/0022-0167.49.2.148

Tracey, T. J. G. (2002b). Personal Globe Inventory: Measurement of the spherical model of interests and competence beliefs. *Journal of Vocational Behavior, 60,* 113–172. doi:10.1006/jvbe.2001.1817

Tracey, T. J. G., & Rounds, J. (1996). The spherical representation of vocational interests. *Journal of Vocational Behavior, 48,* 3–41. doi:10.1006/jvbe.1996.0002

Tracey, T. J. G., & Sodano, S. M. (2013). Structure of interests and competence perceptions. In W. B. Walsh, M. L. Savickas, & P. J. Hartung (Eds.), *Handbook of vocational psychology: Theory, research, and practice* (4th ed.). New York, NY: Routledge.

Walker, J. I., & Peterson, G. W. (2012). Career thoughts, indecision, and depression: Implications for mental health assessment in career counseling. *Journal of Career Assessment, 20,* 497–506. doi:10.1177/1069072712450010

CHAPTER 18

BRONFENBRENNER'S ECOLOGICAL SYSTEMS THEORY

Nathan C. D. Perron

CASE VIGNETTE: JOSE

Jose is a 20-year-old Mexican American student who attends a midwestern university that is 4 hours away from his hometown. Jose approached his academic advisor expressing tremendous levels of stress and anxiety over his college experience. He has been unable to sleep well since a poor grade on his midterm in his Introduction to Biology class 2 weeks ago. Although Jose excelled in high school academically and had a high grade point average (GPA) and a robust scholastic aptitude test (SAT) score, he finds that his grades are slipping in his first semester at college. Unsure how to proceed, he made an appointment with his advisor to explore his options.

Excited to pursue his bachelor's degree in biology at this well-known university, Jose had wished his family and friends back home good-bye to set out on his 4-year adventure in pursuit of his dreams to become a marine biologist. This was the first time he had left home for any substantial period of time. Jose had been used to very regular contact with his family. He is the third out of four children, and two of his siblings still live in his hometown. The second oldest child, his sister Hannah, is attending college 1 hour from home, the oldest child settled down in town after finding a job and getting married 2 years after graduating high school, and his younger sister is a junior in high school. Jose's family extends far beyond his parents and his three siblings, and he enjoyed close connections with his cousins and relatives, especially on his mother's side of the family. Three grandparents who are still living had regular contact with him. His closest friend was Miguel, his first cousin of the same age, the son of his mother's brother. Three other cousins his age attended his former high school, and four others attended schools nearby.

Jose also enjoyed regular contact with a group of friends from high school before moving to college. He played on the soccer team for all 4 years of high school, and was generally well liked by his peers. Jose enjoyed being one of the starting players on the soccer team, and he also was considered one of the smart kids in his high school of

(continued)

(continued)

700 students. In fact, he graduated in the top four of his graduating class of 128 students. Jose also held a regular job as a cook at a local pizza restaurant, where he had a good working relationship with his boss and coworkers.

On arriving at the university, he initially experienced the thrill of a new setting and new experiences. Jose began playing with the soccer team, but he did not begin as a starter as he had hoped. He found himself hanging out with friends after soccer games and regularly going to parties on campus. He avoided irresponsible use of alcohol but admitted drinking on occasion during these parties. Jose indicated that he has been speaking with his family less and less each week. In fact, he went from talking every 1 to 2 days with his parents to about once a week. Jose admits feeling more disconnected from his family than ever before. He has spent much of his time with friends and is having great difficulty focusing his attention on homework. In high school, Jose had a structured routine that helped him maintain good study habits, mostly because his mother would ask for details about his assignments. Now he has difficulty sleeping, concentrating, and practicing routines on his own. He admits feeling sad much of the time, despite acting happy with friends when he is out with them. Other than the group of friends with whom he spends time he is fairly isolated. Jose approached his advisor in a desperate plea for help, and he is uncertain how to proceed because he admits feeling overwhelmed in general.

OVERVIEW AND DESCRIPTION OF BRONFENBRENNER'S THEORY

Many adults understand the pressures of having multiple responsibilities that require attention in a variety of life circumstances. Whether giving attention to work, friends, school, religious activities, romantic relationships, family, or even recreation, adulthood requires the ongoing ability to multitask a variety of expectations and responsibilities. Before reaching adulthood, each person has experienced influences that affect how we think, feel, and react to life's circumstances. This chapter offers professionals and educators one model for understanding these influences and their impact on college students who oftentimes are transitioning to a new world of adult responsibilities for the first time. As academia becomes increasingly diverse, recognizing early influences remains crucial for supporting successful development and growth for students pursuing a college education.

Ecological theory originally developed out of the work of Urie Bronfenbrenner (1977) within the field of developmental psychology. The first of two core propositions in ecological theory purported that human development moves through a "process of progressively more complex reciprocal interactions" (Bronfenbrenner, 1994, p. 4) between a changing biopsychological human being and the immediate dynamic environment in which that human being exists. Bronfenbrenner originally defined these interactions as *proximal processes*. The second proposition emphasized how the impact of the proximal processes varies greatly based on the unique function of the developing person, the changing environment, and the developmental factors under consideration. These propositions provided a common foundation among professionals for understanding psychological development across cultures and experiences.

Bronfenbrenner (1994) proposed that four major environmental subsystems influence human behavior and development, including: *microsystems* (interaction with immediate environmental settings), *mesosystems* (interrelations among major settings), *exosystems* (systems with no direct interaction but extend from the mesosystem in ways that impinge on the individual), and *macrosystems* (overarching institutional patterns). These basic concepts, derived from developmental psychology, have provided meaningful application in a variety of ways, including multicultural counseling and psychology (Lau & Ng, 2014), international counseling (Perron, Tollerud, & Fischer, 2016; Tang et al., 2012), and student development (Renn, 2003).

The unique environmental subsystems provided a helpful template for understanding human behavior throughout the developmental life span of individuals across cultures. Further development of the theory integrated elements of time and genetics for understanding the behavioral attributes that individuals acquire. Each of these elements was seen as influential on human growth; however, ecological theory also depicts the notion that human behavior results within a dialectic between person and environment (Cook, Heppner, & O'Brien, 2005). Oftentimes, college students are at a unique developmental age where the influences of environment, biology, and time provide a substantial backdrop to a number of meaningful life-altering decisions. The weight of such monumental decisions can result in stress for individuals in college (Misra & McKean, 2000), whether they are in early adulthood or returning to education in later adult years (Merriam, Caffarella, & Baumgartner, 2012). Ecological theory helps remind professionals that decisions made among college students also inevitably shape and influence the environments in which they exist in a reciprocal manner.

Environmental Subsystems

Ecological theory can help professionals develop insight and understanding related to the ways in which early experiences impact current development. The focus on relationships in the early years provides a helpful lens for understanding how current relationships may influence continued development and success in college. The environmental subsystems demonstrate an impact both on relationships and the contexts in which they exist.

Microsystem

Berk (2001) described the *microsystem* as "the innermost level of the environment" and "activities and interaction patterns in the person's immediate surroundings" (p. 26). Bronfenbrenner (1977) continued to emphasize the bidirectional nature of this concept in child development. Although children are influenced by caregivers and their environments, they may elicit certain reactions from their caregivers or environments that in turn come back to influence the young person. Microsystem interactions are most evident with parent and family interactions, especially throughout early development (Danforth, Barkley, & Stokes, 1990), but also may be demonstrated within close friendships, romantic relationships, or family once an individual enters college.

Young adults in college may experience a major shift in microsystems from which they were accustomed through earlier development. This is often the time when they begin to seek a mate or even begin a family of their own outside their family of origin. The selection of a mate or family beginnings may involve parents and extended family depending on cultural norms. Potential expectations to move toward "settling down," whether the young person is ready or not, may be communicated. Friends also may become closer through shared experiences in adulthood, along with experiences with mentors, coaches, bosses, colleagues, and professional relationships.

Mesosystem

Bronfenbrenner's *mesosystem* referred to "connections between microsystems that foster development" (Berk, 2001, p. 26). Entering into emerging adulthood and beyond, various elements of the mesosystem may include the workplace, social and recreational connections (e.g., football team, choir, fraternity), religious involvement, the academic environment, friends, leisure activities, and family (e.g., spouse, children, parents). The bidirectional nature of these interactions remains important to understand, as individuals may continue to affect others in profound ways.

College students frequently are experiencing a heightened degree of conflicting themes that emerge among their interactions (e.g., sports teams conflicting with work, friends conflicting with family). Although students entering college may be escaping the oversight of parental supervision, they now experience the challenge of deciding their own paths while experiencing the influence of many microsystem interactions that vie for their attention. Renn (2003) emphasized, "Micro- and mesosystem environments may conflict or converge in their developmental influences" (p. 389). Although there is great opportunity and freedom in this unique time of development, there also is the potential for great anxiety and confusion through mesosystem interactions. This might be characterized by the psychosocial theme of adolescence described in Erikson's (1968) developmental theory, where he depicts a crisis of *identity versus role confusion* for individuals through middle and late adolescence.

Exosystem

"Social settings that do not contain the developing person but nevertheless affect experiences" (Berk, 2001, p. 26) may be understood as the *exosystem*. These influences may include a number of factors that intersect with an individual's life through a variety of sources. Such entities may include policy changes from administration at an individual's place of employment, a parent's job stability, local disasters that affect the community, or a friend who must move to another state for work or school. Exosystems develop from influences that are not in direct contact with the student within the college setting as well, such as university policies and curricula, faculty decisions, parental financial stability, and so on (Renn, 2003).

Macrosystem

The *macrosystem* "consists of the values, laws, customs, and resources of a particular culture" (Berk, 2001, p. 26). The influence of an overarching culture impacts the world of each individual at this level of Bronfenbrenner's (1977) model. This influence may include areas of emphasis that occur within the state and federal levels of government. For individuals in college, the culture's value will be reflected by resources and opportunities that become available due to legislation and policies. The macrosystem may include the value placed on education from federal or state funding, or the types of opportunities available for a variety of programs and for a variety of individuals with socioeconomic status (Renn, 2003). Additionally, the culture of one's professional field may function as a form of macrosystem that impacts the decisions and processes that occur among individuals growing in their careers.

Although macrosystems involve more distant levels of influence with cultural values over whole universities, states, or countries, college students conversely have influenced these systems in a bidirectional manner. This reality has often taken the shape of advocacy and protesting for laws or causes that are fairer and more just than those that currently exist. Such experiences have been evident among college students dating back to protests as early as the University of Paris strike of 1229 against student brutality (Frederic & Krey, 1912), the United States' protests throughout the 1960s for racial equality and in opposition to the war (Van Dyke, 2003), the Tiananmen Square Protests/Massacre of 1989 for freedom of citizens and governmental accountability (Vogel, 2011), and the Central Universities India Joint student protests of 2016 against student maltreatment and injustices (Bengali & Parth, 2016). These historical events serve as meaningful examples of the power that college students exercise through their influence over macrosystems, which have threatened to perpetuate injustice.

Additional Influences

Bronfenbrenner's ecological theory adapted new concepts over the years as additional research was conducted. Bronfenbrenner (1986) introduced the aspect of time and how it impacts the developmental process. He described this phenomenon as the *chronosystem*, which highlighted the significance of time on the development of individuals through various environmental subsystems. In later expansions of the theory, Bronfenbrenner (1986) also went on to recognize genetic factors that contribute to an accurate understanding of individuals' development through various contexts.

Chronosystem

Chronosystem models for understanding the mesosystem were described by Bronfenbrenner (1986) in saying, "the passage of time has been treated as synonymous with chronological age; that is, as a frame of reference for studying psychological changes within individuals as they grow older" (p. 724). Evaluation of one's chronosystem focused on life transitions that occurred as either normative or non-normative for ecological theory. The normative transitions occurred within culturally expected events, such as entering school, losing teeth, experiencing puberty, starting to date, going off to college, getting married, and others. Nonnormative transitions involved unexpected disruptions affecting the developmental progress through time and may include events such as the death of a loved one, divorce, moving, major changes in income, unexpected pregnancy, and many others.

Genetics

It was later on that Bronfenbrenner (1986) recognized genetic inheritance as a formal element of ecological theory. Bronfenbrenner even began to characterize his later work as a *bioecological model*, where a person's biology exhibited influence with ongoing developmental factors (Berk, 1998). The scientific community can no longer ignore the relevance of biological links to parental and ancestral conditions. Just as individuals are seen to inherit appearances, attributes, and diseases from parents, they are also seen within this model as adopting a number of traits influencing personality, mental health, and behavioral tendencies.

HISTORY AND DEVELOPMENT OF BRONFENBRENNER'S THEORY

Bronfenbrenner's work with ecological theory grew in response to a majority of researchers that "viewed the environment fairly narrowly—as limited to events and conditions immediately surrounding the individual" (Berk, 2001, p. 25). Bronfenbrenner's theory was introduced in the 1970s as a response to what Bronfenbrenner (1994) described as "the restricted scope of most research then being conducted by developmental psychologists" (pp. 37–38). The progression of developmental psychology was seen by some to lack a proper foundation before moving into the experimental phase in the profession (Miller, 1999).

The more ecological theory became recognized as an important theoretical construct, the clearer the potential became for influencing social and political policy. Influences observed by Bronfenbrenner (1977, 1994) and other contextualists began to highlight the great importance for supporting positive, healthy, and safe social environments because of the substantial influence they have on behavior. Although important studies have continued to develop from laboratory environments, proponents of the theory now value a greater collaboration of both laboratory and ecological considerations in order to have a better understanding of influences on development (Miller, 1999).

Bronfenbrenner (1994) expanded the notion that dynamic environments themselves become contexts of development in which young people experience the world. Ecological theory provided an important conversation for enhancing the awareness of environments and ecological realities that influence developmental progress. Still, this influence has been perceived as reciprocal due to the recognition that individuals also continue to influence their environments.

Based on the growing body of research evaluating environmental subsystems throughout the 1970s, Bronfenbrenner (1977) quickly emphasized the importance of time by introducing the chronosystem. This emphasis recognized a number of realities, including: life as constantly changing over time, the time period in which one lives influences one's approach, and chronological age influences expectations and assumptions about development. Renn (2003) explained, "The nested systems represent one moment of a life, yet individuals' environments change over time in response to developmental presses and personal decisions" (p. 390). These concepts structured further rationale that led to a clearly defined model that included person, process, context, and time—the PPCT model. Within a decade of Bronfenbrenner's first theoretical assertions, this model became widely known and highly developed through research, application, and analysis.

A number of medical and biological advances over the years led to the recognition that genetic factors offered tremendous importance by the early 1990s. Much of the heritability among research participants demonstrated substantial variance depending on the intensity of the proximal processes occurring and the nature of the environmental systems in which they existed, but the influence of genetics became undeniable for Bronfenbrenner (1994). From these observations came a shift from recognizing ecological theory proper to redefining this integration of genetic concepts as *bioecological theory* (Bronfenbrenner & Ceci, 1993). This biological concept combined with previous ecological theory and evolved into a more developed notion of the PPCT model (Bronfenbrenner & Morris, 2007).

BRONFENBRENNER'S THEORY APPLIED TO STUDENT DEVELOPMENT

The concepts described in Bronfenbrenner's ecological theory offer a number of important implications for supporting students in a college setting. The following examples offer only a sample of the ways in which the theory has been applied and may continue to inform strategies for helping college students toward successful outcomes in their own developmental journeys. Ongoing application of ecological theory with student development since its development in the early 1970s appears in the concepts of self-discovery, academic success, and multicultural awareness. Each of these concepts also exhibit interrelated notions for understanding student development in college in particular.

Self-Discovery

As described earlier, college-age students are experiencing an internal dilemma characterized by Erikson's (1968) psychosocial stages as *identity versus role confusion*. The opportunity to explore one's identity and pursue a sense of self is arguably never more realized than during this transition from high school to college. Adult learners also return to college and fulfill other needs that may be evident in Erikson's later adulthood stages (i.e., generativity vs. stagnation), or other factors previously impeded the experience of identity formation during adolescence (e.g., financial problems, having children) and they are now determined to overcome those barriers. One might argue that any return to college at any age assumes an element of identity reformation that may be occurring for a variety of reasons, so these concepts of self-discovery also may be applied with older learners in college.

Magolda (2009) compared the concepts of ecological theory to the notion of meaning making among students, where they experience the influence of their environment (both old and new) yet they also influence the environment with which they interact. In this way, Magolda highlighted comparisons with holistic approaches for understanding student realities that impacted student engagement both before entering college and after they have undergone the experience. In this way, ecological theory offers a framework for understanding the challenges students face, because the various holistic factors demonstrate microsystem and mesosystem realities that may be identified and analyzed more carefully.

The nature of the chronosystem also helps provide insight and understanding into how the various cultural expectations play into the responsibilities of this age, and how early experiences influence future development. College students may be exposed more than ever before with challenges to their own early experiences and perspectives along with the pressure to develop conclusions on their own values, beliefs, and identity. Students may gain greater insight when they experience the freedom to explore these challenges and their early relationships can be explored to understand how current relationships have been impacted (i.e., "Do I want to continue the same interactional patterns of my parents in my adult relationships?"). These areas of exploration have the potential to support continued development, learning, and success through the college experience. In comparing Bronfenbrenner's concepts of individuality, environment, and development, Renn (2003) expressed,

> The elements of person, process, context, and time (PPCT) create a developmental environment unique to an individual, though organizations such as college[s] and universities provide shared settings where the unique developmental environments of hundreds or thousands of students overlap significantly and are influenced by institutional policy and programs. (p. 387)

Academic Success

College students engage academia as an environmental subsystem that impacts their growth throughout the educational experience and beyond. This may be challenged on the level of the microsystem (if new knowledge and relationships become intimately identified), the mesosystem (with competing systems functioning with various levels of influence and interaction, such as academics and social life), the exosystem (administrative changes within one's program, or professors on strike), and even the macrosystem (recognizing the value placed on education through local, state, and federal opportunities). The ability for any student to adapt to the potential alterations on each environmental level may impact a student's ability to experience success.

Additionally, the influence of one's microsystemic experiences may become most pronounced when beginning the journey of higher education. For example, the value placed on learning and education in the home through early development was found to affect future success (Grolnick & Slowiaczek, 1994). Dennis, Phinney, and Chuateco (2005) explained, "The fact that the parents of first-generation college students lack first-hand knowledge of the college experience may pose another obstacle for these students. Their parents typically cannot help them directly with college tasks" (p. 223). Students from ethnic and socioeconomic minority backgrounds were also found to experience greater challenges. Success in college was further estimated by Dennis et al. as the result of personal traits that included mental ability, academic skills, motivation, goals, and the characteristics of the environment. The authors found that even among students with both individualistic and collectivistic motivations, individually oriented motivations were highly predictive of the student's level of satisfaction with the college environment and successful completion of the first year. This, again, may reinforce the importance of adaptability when striving for academic success amidst competing factors.

Multicultural Awareness

Branching out into college life often provides greater exposure to other cultures, customs, and beliefs than ever before. True awareness of diversity is described by Pederson and Carey (2003) as the end result of a development process they define as the Cross-Cultural Continuum. It cannot be presumed that students have progressed through the previous six stages of this model to reach a state of diversity awareness, so recognizing this developmental concept can be helpful for understanding and supporting further student growth along the continuum. The need to attend to acculturation and well-being becomes evident with students of diverse backgrounds as they gather in a common space for education (Schwartz et al., 2013). There remains much to be accomplished in supporting greater multicultural awareness and acceptance among campuses in the United States.

Renn (2003) applied Bronfenbrenner's ecology model in suggesting that universities enhance curricula to support student identity, align curricula to other forms of learning identity development, and setting appropriate boundaries among peer groups. College students have enhanced opportunities to solidify their own identity through various systemic experiences to which they are exposed. The intrinsic search for identity occurs through racial, ethnic, and cultural experiences that introduce challenges that might not otherwise exist outside the diversity of a college setting. The positive gain from this identity search may result in a tremendous source of motivation for success and achievement when students do reach a place of congruence between their identity and behavior (Oyserman & Destin, 2010).

> ### CASE VIGNETTE WRAP-UP: JOSE
>
> *Jose finds himself in a very difficult situation with declining grades and a lack of satisfaction through a superficial social life. The narrative of his life at college is very different from his experiences in high school where he enjoyed greater success and greater social support through his family. Applying ecological concepts to Jose's life quickly reveals the nature of competing systems at the microsystem and mesosystem levels. Jose grew up with close connections through the family and friends in his hometown, but now his greatest support is evident with the friends he spends much of his time. In many ways Jose's microsystem is lacking severely because these friends almost function at the mesosystem level, as distractions from his academic responsibilities although they provide some enjoyment. Although he states that his grades are important, he feels he lacks the discipline to change his current pattern. His grades are suffering tremendously, and he now admits his struggle with apathy.*
>
> *The chronosystem evident in Jose's life is congruent with the kinds of changes Jose is experiencing in his late adolescence into early adulthood. Jose experienced relative*
>
> *(continued)*

(continued)

success in the different roles he experienced throughout high school life. Because life is dynamic and changing, Jose experienced a shift that is common in the transition to college. Jose's closest relationships with family (his microsystem), changed in ways he did not imagine they would (less contact). He does not enjoy the regular contact he had when living in his hometown, and he feels embarrassed to admit his sense of loss. With all the time he spends with friends he does not feel they satisfy the closeness he experienced with family. Because of Jose's lack of openness with his friends, they are unaware he needs a greater depth of relationship overall.

Jose's advisor has an opportunity to address Jose's concerns by sharing thoughts and resources that might support his progress from his current state of stagnation. The advisor helps Jose go and see a counselor to explore the loss he is experiencing related to the dysregulation of his microsystem and mesosystem realities. A counselor may explore concepts related to communication strategies to help him address concerns with family, or even to share more freely with the college friends he keeps at a distance. He may be encouraged to discover coping mechanisms for managing reactions to the disconnection with family, and to relieve anxiety about his poor academic performance. Jose could work with the counselor to determine goal-setting techniques to organize himself in light of his difficulty focusing, and establishing a routine could help support change that would stabilize his anxiety and potential depression. Simply hearing from his advisor and his counselor that some elements of his reactions are typical experiences for college students may help normalize the anxiety, reduce the tension he feels, and possibly even help him engage others more openly.

Further information might be explored to determine if there are any factors related to the exosystem or macrosystem affecting his current reality. Discovering if there are any factors outside his control with his family that has caused a disconnection from them may be important, and understanding his perception of the stressors he is facing can reveal if there are exosystems available to help (financial aid) or macrosystems that result in negative effects on his experience as a whole.

CASE VIGNETTE 1 FOR READER REFLECTION: PHET

A 43-year-old Vietnamese American woman named Phet began a master's degree in social work after working for 20 years in the retail industry. Phet demonstrated tremendous potential for supporting others with her caring demeanor, but has begun having doubts about her potential role as a social worker. She approached her professor in her sociology class because she is now thinking about the challenges she faces in her program for the first time. The emotions that arise with discussing multicultural issues become very triggering for her to the point that she has excused herself from class crying on two occasions in the past month.

Phet grew up in a suburban middle-class town, despite the fact that her family arrived under refugee status in the late 1970s. Involvement with a local church was a big part of her family's life while growing up, especially since a Christian ministry helped her family relocate and settle in the United States. Phet lived with both parents and an older sister before going to college and receiving her bachelor's degree in visual arts. Phet did begin working in her field of study as a graphic designer at a large corporation, but she intended to pursue her master's degree in social work within 2 years of graduation. During those

(continued)

(continued)

2 years Phet met and married the father of her now 20-year-old daughter. She remained married for 5 years before ending the marriage for undisclosed reasons. Now that her daughter has been away at college for more than 1 year, she was inspired to return to her original dream to pursue social work.

Phet has been working successfully in retail for most of her adult life. She advanced to the position of assistant manager of a well-known department store, and says she prides herself on her excellence at work. Now that she has become more triggered in relation to the core content of multicultural issues in her classes, she is doubting whether she is capable of pursuing this degree. She asks her professor for direction on how to proceed, and wants to make a decision before the end of the week because her job is considering promoting her to a full manager.

- *What are Phet's greatest needs?*
- *What campus-based services might be most beneficial to her?*
- *What are some goals you would like to see Phet reach?*

CASE VIGNETTE 2 FOR READER REFLECTION: ASHLEY

Ashley, a 22-year-old White student, is a sophomore who is studying for her bachelor of science in business. She was referred to the department chair because faculty want to explore placing her on a remediation plan. Ashley has had many conflictual interactions with both students and university faculty, and she has not heeded opportunities to change her behavior. This meeting with the department chair will determine what steps need to be taken.

At the meeting, Ashley states multiple reasons why she feels she is a victim of circumstances beyond her control. Further discussion reveals a childhood that appears rather disconnected from close family ties. Ashley grew up as the oldest child of three children. She lived with her single mother and her two younger brothers, although she had very little contact with her father. Her mother never remarried, but had several serious boyfriends throughout her childhood. Ashley reports not feeling close with her mom, who burdened Ashley with many responsibilities for watching over her brothers while she worked and socialized.

Throughout her childhood, Ashley was actively involved in cheerleading and dance. She explains that these were great sources of relief for her until she turned 15 years and took her first job as a waitress. Ashley worked about 20 hours a week during her senior year in high school and maintains roughly the same work schedule now that she is in college. She does not have many long-term friendships. She names only one friend from high school with whom she still maintains contact, but says she did not have time to spend with friends and they "always created drama anyway." Now Ashley wants to get the meeting with the program chair over so she can move on and finish her degree. She expresses little concern for how people have reacted to her behavior in class, or about conflicts she starts.

- *What are Ashley's greatest needs?*
- *What campus-based services might be most beneficial to her?*
- *What are some goals you would like to see Ashley reach?*

REFERENCES

Bengali, S., & Parth, M. N. (2016, February 15). An attack on student demonstrators and reporters in India unfolds on social media. *Los Angeles Times*. Retrieved from http://www.latimes.com/world/asia/la-fg-india-student-protest-social-media-20160215-htmlstory.html

Berk, L. E. (2001). *Development through the lifespan* (2nd ed.). Boston, MA: Allyn & Bacon.

Bronfenbrenner, U. (1977). Toward an experimental ecology of human development. *American Psychologist, 32*(7), 513–531. doi:10.1037/0003-066X.32.7.513

Bronfenbrenner, U. (1986). Ecology of the family as a context for human development: Research perspectives. *Developmental Psychology, 22*(6), 723.

Bronfenbrenner, U. (1994). Ecological models of human development. *Readings on the Development of Children, 2*, 37–43.

Bronfenbrenner, U., & Ceci, S. J. (1993). Heredity, environment, and the question of "how?": A new theoretical perspective for the 1990s. In R. Plomin & G. E. McClearn (Eds.), *Nature, nurture, and psychology* (pp. 313–324). Washington, DC: American Psychological Association.

Bronfenbrenner, U., & Morris, P. A. (2007). The bioecological model of human development. *Handbook of Child Psychology, 1*(14), 793–828. doi:10.1002/9780470147658.chpsy0114

Cook, E. P., Heppner, M. J., & O'Brien, K. M. (2005). Multicultural and gender influences in women's career development: An ecological perspective. *Journal of Multicultural Counseling and Development, 33*, 165–179.

Danforth, J. S., Barkley, R. A., & Stokes, T. F. (1990). Observations of parent-child interactions with hyperactive children: Research and clinical applications. *Clinical Psychology Review, 11*, 703–727.

Dennis, J. M., Phinney, J. S., & Chuateco, L. I. (2005). The role of motivation, parental support, and peer support in the academic success of ethnic minority first-generation college students. *Journal of College Student Development, 46*(3), 223–236.

Erikson, E. H. (1968). *Identity: Youth and crisis*. New York, NY: W. W. Norton.

Frederic, D., & Krey, A. C. (1912). *Parallel source problems in medieval history*. London, UK: Harper & Brothers. Retrieved from https://archive.org/stream/parallelsourcepr00dunciala#page/n3/mode/2up

Grolnick, W. S., & Slowiaczek, M. L. (1994). Parents' involvement in children's schooling: A multidimensional conceptualization and motivational model. *Child Development, 65*, 237–252.

Lau, J., & Ng, K. M. (2014). Conceptualizing the counseling training environment using Bronfenbrenner's ecological theory. *International Journal for the Advancement of Counselling, 36*(4), 423–439.

Magolda, M. B. B. (2009). The activity of meaning making: A holistic perspective on college student development. *Journal of College Student Development, 50*(6), 621–639.

Merriam, S. B., Caffarella, R. S., & Baumgartner, L. M. (2012). *Learning in adulthood: A comprehensive guide*. San Francisco, CA: Wiley.

Miller, P. H. (1999). *Theories of developmental psychology* (3rd ed.). New York, NY: Worth.

Misra, R., & McKean, M. (2000). College students' academic stress and its relation to their anxiety, time management, and leisure satisfaction. *American Journal of Health Studies, 16*(1), 41.

Oyserman, D., & Destin, M. (2010). Identity-based motivation: Implications for intervention. *The Counseling Psychologist, 38*(7), 1001–1043.

Pederson, P. B., & Carey, J. C. (2003). *Multicultural counseling in schools: A practical handbook* (2nd ed.). Boston, MA: Allyn & Bacon.

Perron, N. C. D., Tollerud, T., & Fischer, T. (2016). International counseling traits: Identifying counseling traits ranked most important by international counseling professionals through Q sort analysis. *International Journal for the Advancement of Counselling, 38*(2), 159–176. doi:10.1007/s10447-016-9264-9

Renn, K. A. (2003). Understanding the identities of mixed-race college students through a developmental ecology lens. *Journal of College Student Development, 44*(3), 383–403.

Schwartz, S. J., Waterman, A. S., Umaña-Taylor, A. J., Lee, R. M., Kim, S. Y., Vazsonyi, A. T., & Zamboanga, B. L. (2013). Acculturation and well-being among college students from immigrant families. *Journal of Clinical Psychology, 69*(4), 298–318.

Tang, M., Conyne, R., Heppner, P. P., Horne, S., Norsworthy, K., Romano, J. L., . . . Merchant, N. (2012). Implications of the international counseling experiences of pioneering U.S. professionals: Considered from an ecological perspective. *International Journal for the Advancement of Counseling, 34*, 242–258. doi:10.1007/s10447-012-9154-8

Van Dyke, N. (2003). Crossing movement boundaries: Factors that facilitate coalition protest by American college students, 1930–1990. *Social Problems, 50*(2), 226–250.

Vogel, E. F. (2011). *Deng Xiaoping and the transformation of China*. Cambridge, MA: Belknap Press–Harvard University Press.

CHAPTER 19

BRINGING STUDENT GROUPS TOGETHER: UNDERSTANDING GROUP THEORY

Lucy Parker

CASE VIGNETTE: KAELYN

Kaelyn recently graduated from a community college. While studying there, she was a motivated student who was involved in community and student organizations. Now that she has moved on to a 4-year university, Kaelyn would like to meet people there. In addition to social interests, Kaelyn has many career aspirations. She is undecided about her ultimate choice of career after college. As a student, Kaelyn has supported herself by working as a server, at an hourly wage, and using student loans. It is hard for her to support herself and cope with the stressors of school—mental, financial, and emotional. Despite school-associated stress, Kaelyn loves to learn. She has always been interested in learning, especially in culinary art. She is also highly interested in community involvement projects, such as charity bake sales. Community involvement had been a great outlet while she was a student at the community college. In fact, she reported that much of her school stress was lowered by "having the distraction to help others in a group." When hearing Kaelyn's story, what groups do you think will help Kaelyn grow in all her academic, professional, and personal identities?

Kaelyn exhibits a significant level of development as well as current potential for intrapersonal growth. In fact, many theories, including the transitions and developments from Chickering, Erikson, and others can be used to conceptualize Kaelyn's experience. Another salient way to conceptualize Kaelyn's intrapersonal and interpersonal growth is to understand her development within group settings. This chapter provides a discussion of group theory in relation to various salient student development theories.

OVERVIEW AND DESCRIPTION OF GROUP THEORY

Student developmental models that can be used to understand various students in groups and their development include identity models, such as Chickering and Reisser's model, as well as Levinson's model; psychosocial models, such as Erikson's model; intellectual and ethical developmental models, such as Perry's model; moral developmental models, such as Kohlberg's model; cognitive models, such as Piaget's and Vygotsky's models; and experiential models, such as Kolb's model (Chickering, 1969; Evans, Forney, Guido, Patton, & Renn, 2010). For a broad and universal understanding, these and other student developmental theories are integrated into the group theory focus of this chapter.

To best understand student development theories, it is important to note various conceptualizations of students in group environments. According to M. S. Corey and Corey (2010), prominent theorists in group work, groups tend to be an inclusive and effective supplementary approach to helping students of varying ages. Groups offer much power for both intra- and interpersonal development and complement many contemporary student development approaches in today's academic settings (Chen & Rybak, 2004; M. S. Corey & Corey, 2010).

Contributing to the power of a group are various components including group norms, established trust, respectful conflict, intermember feedback, and leader interventions and interpersonal communications (Chen & Rybak, 2004; G. Corey, 1995). As M. S. Corey and Corey (2010), Yalom (2005), and other group theorists suggest, a group of students is, in itself, an interacting organism of various members. This group organism often develops in a parallel similarity to the development of students (Evans et al., 2010; Lacoursiere, 1980). Just as Chickering and other student developmental theorists suggest, development for students is sometimes slow and subtle, so too can be the changes within and from a group of student members (Evans et al., 2010).

Similarities Between Group and Student Development

Just as student developmental theorists work within the interactionist model framework, group theorists similarly believe that a multiplicity of environmental factors and interactions affect students (Bronfenbrenner, 1979; Chen & Rybak, 2004). In fact, Evans et al. (2010) referenced the $B = f(PXE)$ equation as one conceptual metaphor for describing student development (p. 29). This equation was originally created by theorist Kurt Lewin in 1936, and this equation describes the potential and various interactions that influence students (Evans et al., 2010; pp. 29–36). The attempt to quantify and make sense of the forces on student development provides support to the diverse nature of influences.

In this equation, B represents a student group member. The $f(PXE)$ is representative of a function of the student's or person's interaction(s) with their environment. For broad conceptualization's sake, group theorists also look at B. For both student development and group theorists, B is representative of the whole summation of a person and/or group, along with its development and internal and external influences (Bronfenbrenner, 1979; G. Corey, 1995; Lacoursiere, 1980).

In other words, both students and groups of students should be viewed in a holistic manner and conceptualized with all of their influences, interactions, circumstances, and conditions. For example, specific ecological student developmental models emphasize that size, relationships, and other factors influence a student's development; so too are groups affected by similar internal and external associated influences.

To understand the holistic conceptualization needed for both groups and students, envision a student support group with a focus on stress management. The group comprises several students who voluntarily attend such a support group after class for peer support. Thus, not only does the stress from school influence each student within the group, but also influences the entire group holistically. Each member may be experiencing stress due to individual factors, which may or may not be similar to those of other members. This intersectionality of members also adds complexity to a group. Thus, in order to understand student development within groups, an in-depth understanding both of groups and of members is needed. Salient factors that commonly and directly affect both individual members and the group overall include a group's size, closed- versus open-group status, length of time as a group, duration of meetings, location of a group, and other environmental factors (Yalom, 2005).

When considering the multiplicity of relationships among student group members and groups, leaders must remember that they will never be able to gather all of the data. Just as it is highlighted in student development theories, each individual and each group is varied and similarities or differences cannot be assumed (Evans et al., 2010). This generates the need for a respectful, holistic, and in-depth multicultural lens to be used for successfully facilitating both student and group development (Chen & Rybak, 2004; M. S. Corey & Corey, 2010; Evans et al., 2010). A brief introduction about the need for inclusion and multicultural awareness for students and student groups is addressed later in this chapter.

Despite many group member differences, however, student group members may also experience similar co-occurring phenomena, which are common to all people collectively. M. S. Corey and Corey (2010), as well as Yalom (2005), recognized that there is universality, or shared universal experience, that is present across individuals in any group. Universality is a broad construct that may look different from student to student in a group. However, the summative existence and presence of this construct from students and the group add cohesion and relatability to a group's experience and development.

One concrete example of understanding and experiencing universality includes an experience many of us have had in our own past student roles. Imagine the times that you have walked into a school setting as a first time student. Did you ever experience nervousness? If so, what did you do? Many of us may have "broken the ice" by talking to a seemingly relatable classmate. In fact, if you did this, and your new peer disclosed that they too, were nervous, their similar feeling and expression may have normalized your own new classroom anxiety. This relatability with another classmate is an example of universality in a group. Universality extends to all humans as we all experience various similar existential commonalities, such as, death, anxiety, and others (Yalom, 2005). Thus, in both students and student groups, universality is important.

Along with the experience of universality in a group, students may also experience other common phenomena found in effective groups. These common experiences, feelings, and behaviors of all groups of students are often called *therapeutic factors* (Chen & Rybak, 2004; G. Corey, 1995; Yalom, 2005). To facilitate an effective student-led or student participant group, a facilitator must ensure that therapeutic factors are fostered within the group. These factors include student self-disclosure, respectful confrontation, meaningful and authentic feedback, cohesion and universality, hope, risk taking and trust being continuously recognized and built, caring and acceptance, recognition of power dynamics, catharsis, cognitive stimulation, commitments for some change, appropriate freedom of experimentation, and timely and appropriate usage of humor (M. S. Corey & Corey, 2010; Yalom, 2005).

When considering both group developmental and student developmental theories with diverse students, various considerations of the group type, group leader, group members, and group process also become salient. The following sections include aspects for understanding successful student group development regarding group types, group leader guidelines, group processes, and learning reflection of student groups through a multicultural lens.

Group Types

There is a wide variety of group types that vary based on purpose. These include task groups, psychoeducational groups, counseling and psychotherapy groups, as well as others (Chen & Rybak, 2004; M. S. Corey & Corey, 2010). Task groups are described as groups where goals are aimed toward some types of task completion. Real-life examples of these groups may range from trivia teams to intimate trauma survivor groups. Psychoeducational groups are groups where students will learn about the education of their prescribed psychological well-being (M. S. Corey & Corey, 2010). Oftentimes, psychoeducational groups are partnered with academic settings and various mental health agencies. Counseling and psychotherapy groups are also important for students, especially for students on diverse campuses, as these groups are growing in number to offer therapeutic services to students of varying typologies in education (Chen & Rybak, 2004; Evans et al., 2010). Other increasingly researched group types, which are inferred by their titles, include groups for children, involuntary groups, support groups, groups for the elderly, and various other cultural groups (M. S. Corey & Corey, 2010).

Just as student development theories acknowledge that students present various identities and developments, so, too, do group theories. Group types not only differ based on goal differences, but may also differ based on member population. For example, a task group of African American students may bring different presenting concerns, issues, topics, and goals, than a task group of Caucasian women (Bronfenbrenner, 1979; Chen & Ryak, 2004).

Group Leader Guidelines

Just as various student development theories recognize that external factors and others influence individual students, group members are also highly impacted by their co-group members and their group leader, or facilitator, during and after their group experience (Yalom, 2005). The group facilitator creates the setting in which the work of the group can be accomplished. Following is a discussion addressing the skills necessary to be an effective group leader for student groups.

First, it is important to acknowledge that the group leader's power is so distinct that many group theorists have recommended the intentional de-emphasizing of power of the group leader. In other words, Yalom (2005) stated that in all groups, "the leader must fall." Though some structure and hierarchy may be needed more for some student groups than others, intentions of having a more egalitarian approach should remain emphasized. In addition to being respectful, egalitarian, and authoritative, an effective group leader for student groups must also have courage, goodwill, a caring nature, awareness of oneself and others, stamina, presence, openness, personal autonomy, and a willingness to explore (M. S. Corey & Corey, 2010).

With the presence of effective leadership, a group leader may benefit members by also using a variety of theoretical group skills, including linking members' ideas to one another, suggesting activities for members, facilitating authentic discussion, summarizing common themes of student members, blocking monopolizing students, and leading the termination of the student group. In addition to addressing these tasks, group leaders must also remind members about their co-constructed definition of their own goals and foci. Intentionality of the facilitator and a semistructured group session is the best group option to foster both students' short-term and long-term goals (Braaten, 1974; Chen & Rybak, 2004; Evans et al., 2010). Intentionality of goal pursuit must be modeled by the group facilitator.

For example, one important goal that exists across all groups, and for which the responsibility lies with the facilitator, is an informed consent and an encouraged confidentiality agreement (Chen & Rybak, 2004; G. Corey, 1995; M. S. Corey & Corey, 2010). Although the informed consent of the facilitator may look a bit different, it nonetheless should include limits to the group experience, real-life applications for the group, psychoeducation about feelings and respect for others, transparency, multicultural recognition, and limits, but also the encouragement of confidentiality (Chen & Rybak, 2004; G. Corey, 1995). Furthermore, although the leader cannot guarantee confidentiality in a group, the group leader must remind student members of their consent to be in the group and to encourage sensitivity and confidence from talking about others or the group experiences outside of the group.

The group facilitator may also address that exceptions to confidentiality can occur for the safety of all group members. These exceptions, which may influence collaboration as well as disclosure outside of a group, may include instances in which student members' are suspected of harm to self or others (Chen & Rybak, 2004). Overall, this reference of confidentiality along with a leader's appropriate transparency and personhood is most effective for safe and transformative student groups (Yalom, 2005). This group leader modeling is hoped to provoke the authentic development of both individual students and the student group as a whole as well.

Group Member Identity

When considering individual students in a group, it is important to remember each of their individual and unique developmental identities (Evans et al., 2010). Although groups are made of unique individuals, each of whom could be conceptualized through various student development models, these members also share generalized commonalities, such as experienced universality and therapeutic factors. Other common feelings expressed by student members in a group can include fears (e.g., including the fear of rejection), anxiety, and a want for connection(s) (M. S. Corey & Corey, 2010). Developmental theorist Erik Erikson (1968) referenced various developmental transitions and their importance for students. These transitions also affect students' contact with others, and knowledge of these can enhance group effectiveness (Evans et al., 2010). For example, a group of middle school students may initially have more fear of judgment within a group than a group of college seniors (Evans et al., 2010). In other words, factors, such as students' ages, are important to not assume, but to consider in understanding how a student group may function.

Group Norms

For many students, during the practice of reflecting on common experiences, issues, goals, and feelings, a facilitator can provoke increased trust, therapeutic factors, universality, and cohesiveness in a student group (M. S. Corey & Corey, 2010). With this continued universality and cohesiveness, student members can more effectively set group norms and goals. Group norms can include norms for individuals inside and outside of the student group. For example, a student group emphasizing learning coping skills for stress management in school may use aspects from Kolb's Experiential Model to actively engage members to become aware and share the irrational fears they may experience (e.g., social anxiety about speaking with a professor or from receiving assistance from a tutor) when in school (Chen & Rybak, 2004; Evans et al., 2010). Members' meaningful feedback and connection can generate student development physically, cognitively, intrapersonally, interpersonally, emotionally, mentally, and in other ways. Again, because of the robust potential that various groups may directly and/or indirectly have on student development, it is important to understand group theory in supplementation to the various student developmental theories.

Theory knowledge and application competence are important to ensure smooth running and problem prevention in groups. Some challenges that may occur in a student-oriented group may include not enough, or too much, unintended silence; monopolizing or defensive behaviors from student members; advice giving; dependency; disrespect; and scapegoating, among others (Chen & Rybak, 2004; M. S. Corey & Corey, 2010).

Group Processes

Just as students develop in varying phases and stages, so, too, do groups. *All* effective groups move through various stages. The four main developmental stages that are exhibited by most groups include the initial, transitional, working, and termination stages (Chen & Rybak, 2004). Specifically, for theorists focusing on student development, such as Erikson and Piaget, this model is easily understood because of its emphasis on phasic conceptualization (Evans et al., 2010). Just as student developmental theorists acknowledge that no two students develop exactly the same, groups will never develop along the exact same path. Because group development processes are not always sequential, a much generalized model of the four main stages of a group is provided.

The first stage begins when the group first forms and is called the initial or forming stage (G. Corey, 1995; M. S. Corey & Corey, 2010). During this early period, students may feel the most risk in deciding to participate and group members rely heavily on the group leader to keep the discussions moving forward. The initial meetings usually open with structured activities to foster initial contact and interpersonal student development (M. S. Corey & Corey, 2010; Evans et al., 2010). As student group members begin to converse and connect, they may eventually transition into a more unified "whole" group.

As group identity forms, the group moves into the transition stage, which may occur sequentially or not, occur once, or be repeated (Chen & Rybak, 2004; M. S. Corey & Corey, 2010). During this stage, significant levels of growth occur for the members of the group, as well as the group itself. Some authors call this stage the storming stage of a group due to the intense activity and engagement characteristic of this period (Bratten, 1979; Chen & Rybak, 2004). During this stage, trust is questioned, but also generated and the beginning of commonalties, therapeutic factors, and universality typically arise (Yalom, 2005).

Following the transition stage, the working stage evolves (Chen & Rybak, 2004). This stage is vital for the further development of both the group and its student members. During this developmental period, members experience challenges, risks, and self-disclosures that increase the impact and authenticity of the group experience. Though the leader may choose to implement specific interventions, members are more interdependent on one another than dependent on the leader (Chen & Rybak, 2004; M. S. Corey & Corey, 2010). During this working stage, healing may also take place as members learn to work together, use respectful confrontation, and be together as an in-depth whole.

The last stage of group is the ending or termination stage. During the termination stage, student members and the group leader process what it will be like for them as the group ends regarding their feelings and thoughts. Additionally, a group facilitator may also reinforce the personal and interpersonal work that members in the group have done to get to this ending stage. One technique that student affairs professionals may find helpful includes offering members the technique of sentence completion (M. S. Corey & Corey, 2010). At the end of a student group, a facilitator may state, "Please finish this sentence ... 'My hope after group is ...' or 'What I took from my group is ...'" (Chen & Rybak, 2004; M. S. Corey & Corey, 2010).

LOOKING AT STUDENT AND GROUP DEVELOPMENT THROUGH A MULTICULTURAL LENS

Because space does not permit a full exploration of the role of culture and intersectionality in group work, this is merely a topic introduction and reminder to continue to seek multicultural competence for both students and student groups. One practical way to facilitate culturally enriching and facilitative student groups is by becoming a diversity-sensitive group leader (M. S. Corey & Corey, 2010). To be a diversity-sensitive group leader, an individual must encourage continuous cultural exploration for students inside and outside of the group. In fact, many group theorists assert that group work cannot be effective without some consideration of student group and student members' cultures (M. S. Corey & Corey, 2010; Evans et al., 2010; Yalom, 1995).

One way to introduce the consideration of culture(s) in student groups is for the facilitator to openly recognize and acknowledge his or her own cultural identities. A facilitator's modeling of this type of openness and disclosure can assist student members to become aware of their own biases, stereotypes, and prejudices (M. S. Corey & Corey, 2010). With continued awareness, reflection, and transparency, active dialogue about differences can occur. Members should be reminded about the need for respectful confrontation and recognition of boundaries if defensiveness or emotional saturation of members arises (Chen & Rybak, 2004). Group leaders must also reinforce ethical considerations and remind student members of the safety of their vulnerability and disclosures about their own worldviews and identities (Chen & Rybak, 2004; M. S. Corey & Corey, 2010). To ensure a positive outcome of any discussion of students' values, beliefs, family, community, religions, spirituality, ethnicity, race, gender, sexual identity, and other cultural components, it must occur in a safe, accepting, and authentic space. In discussions of these topics, it is likely that some discomfort may arise. Through openness and respect, however, cultural understanding between students may occur, as well as between students and the group leader. Ultimately, if successfully processed, multicultural components can create a new level of depth and cohesion for students. Please refer to the Helpful Resources section at the end of this chapter, which addresses techniques for facilitating a multiculturally sensitive group.

HISTORY AND DEVELOPMENT OF GROUP THEORY

The earliest group theorists include those such as Carl Jung, Carl Whitaker, and Irvin Yalom (Yalom, 2005). It is only recently, however, that group theory was embraced by practitioners, such as student affairs professionals, once group counseling and group work received public credibility. One of the practical reasons the group milieu became popular in American society was due to the ability of clinicians to serve more than one client at a time. However, there are strengths inherent in group work that are not available in the one-on-one setting. Advantages of group work include the direct exposure to interpersonal relationships, the provided here-and-now experience, and exposure to a variety of diverse perspectives in a nonthreatening situation.

One of the most salient movements for recognizing group counseling and theory was the creation of the Association for Specialists in Group Work (ASGW). The best practices guidelines of the ASGW were released and formally recognized in 1998. These practices emphasized that "professional competence in group work is not a final product, but a continuous process" (M. S. Corey & Corey, 2010; Wilson, Rapin, & Haley-Banez, 2000). Groups since this time have been recognized for not only serving people in a variety of ways, including student and client groups, but also with counseling, supervision, and consultation services. The ASGW not only serves as a valuable source for those seeking to gain an understanding the rich history, but also the current resources and new developments, within the field of group work and theory (Chen & Rybak, 2004; M. S. Corey & Corey, 2010).

APPLICATION OF GROUP THEORY WITHIN STUDENT AFFAIRS

Many benefits arise for student affairs practitioners who understand how to integrate multiple student development theories as well as group theory. Facilitators are not only more competent, but more confident when applying these frameworks to actual real-life students and student groups, when they believe they have understood the material (Chen & Rybak, 2004). Three salient concerns for bridging any gaps from theory to actual practice of using student developmental theory and group theory include: (a) the continued need for inclusion and multicultural awareness; (b) the ability to intuitively "do more, with less," and (c) the ability to remain adaptable and increasingly competent in the current research for both effective applications of group and student development.

Of these, the most crucial area for continued development for *all* professionals, not only student affairs professionals, covers the increased need for inclusion both within and outside of the student's direct classroom. Please bear in mind that the need for continued inclusivity and multicultural awareness is vital due to the frequently experienced circumstances in which some nonmajority groups in our macro-societal overarching group are often invalidated and/or dismissed in various contexts (Chen & Rybak, 2004; M. S. Corey & Corey, 2010). Furthermore, work is needed to better understand and more effectively facilitate groups for women and students of color; groups addressing academic dishonesty or other taboo-related support groups for students; facilitating student behavioral change groups; facilitating other social justice and advocacy groups; and continuing various types of here-and-now learning groups (Chen & Rybak, 2004).

Due to current fiscal variability within the United States, unfortunately, student affairs professionals must know how to "do more with less" in all student development settings (Evans et al., 2010). In fact, knowing how to do more with less is also consistent for groups. One technique that allows facilitators to do more with less time is to provide student group members with creative "homework" activities for outside of their group sessions (Chen & Rybak, 2004; M. S. Corey & Corey, 2010). For example, imagine that you are asked to run a student group focusing on bullying prevention. Due to there being inadequate time available to allow students to share all of their thoughts, feelings, or experiences about bullying, a group facilitator may ask students to provide a few sentences of disclosure and reflection about their group experience with a follow-up reflection journal completion task at home. Then, after completion, a facilitator may collate all of the students' journals and find themes and differences. This can then save time and later guide discussion for the group during a future session. This is only one example of a way for student group development leaders to do more with less, which is a very practical need for student affairs professionals and group leaders currently.

Another practical-needs area of student affairs professionals includes continuous engagement with current research, both in terms of academic research findings and their own personal, informal research. Only through keeping abreast of the ongoing and everyday research can professionals learn about the situational and real-life influences of student development within groups (Chen & Rybak, 2004; M. S. Corey & Corey, 2010; Evans et al., 2010). Methods of gaining the most current information about student development groups include professional development attendance, networking with other professionals in the field, and researching peer-reviewed articles, such as those included in the Helpful Resources section at the end of this chapter.

CASE VIGNETTE WRAP-UP: KAELYN

As we mentioned in the beginning of this chapter, Kaelyn exhibits much development and current potential for intrapersonal growth. Nearly all of the student development theories, including those addressed throughout this text, may be supplemented with effective student group involvement for Kaelyn. Different groups will influence Kaelyn to grow interpersonally (e.g., a task-oriented group), while others may foster more intrapersonal development (e.g., a support group for students facing both personal and academic issues) for Kaelyn. It is important for a group facilitator to recognize that not only will the group affect Kaelyn, but Kaelyn will also influence others. Looking in depth at and empathizing with Kaelyn's many circumstantial, internal, and external influences are necessary for Kaelyn to grow and bring her most authentic and present-minded self to any group. With successful group facilitation to supplement Kaelyn's self-reflection and willingness to receive and give feedback and to change, she will grow. In fact, many types of groups would and do benefit students of all types in many of their various life transitions and developments.

CASE VIGNETTE 1 FOR READER REFLECTION: AHMED

Ahmed recently graduated from a university in Saudi Arabia and moved to the United States for graduate school. Ahmed always loved learning, and expresses gratitude as he recently received a scholarship to study electrical engineering in the United States. Now that Ahmed has moved, and now lives on the northeast coast of the United States, he feels alone and fearful. In addition to feeling isolated, Ahmed also has struggled to learn a lot of the norms of American college culture. He expresses interest to learn about the culture and people here, in America. Despite his uncertainty and loneliness, Ahmed is beginning with a great academic start. As a student, Ahmed is currently earning a 3.80 grade point average (GPA) in his first few weeks of graduate school. Ahmed was fearful of conversing with others at first, but after the first few weeks he has opened up about the aforementioned addressed issues to some of his professors. His professors speak with you about helping Ahmed. They think that a group setting would be best as Ahmed does not want individual counseling or any individual focus, as he states these experiences are "too much" for him right now.

- *When hearing Ahmed's story, what groups do you think will help him?*
- *Which groups or techniques within groups may help Ahmed feel supported in American culture, but continue to help him preserve his intrinsically preferred identity?*
- *What other multicultural aspects are salient to help Ahmed feel connected in a group?*

CASE VIGNETTE 2 FOR READER REFLECTION: JUDY

Judy is a high school graduate who recently began taking classes at the local university. Specifically, Judy aspires to teach philosophy in a college setting. Furthermore, one may notice when meeting her that Judy is highly intelligent, open minded, and self-driven. However, what many others may not know is that Judy is a nontraditional student. Judy jokes with her peers that "though I look 20 years old, I am certainly 40 years old." Furthermore, she jokes, that she appreciates her peer's compliments of underestimating her appearance, but that though she may look young, her worldview, now, is much different than when she was in her early 20s. Judy elaborates with her peers about the importance of education, as she states that she had had a child by the age of 20 years, and without a formal higher education experience, she felt that she had done a disservice to herself and her son financially. Judy also describes that though she really appreciates all of her classmates, she sometimes feels like "the wise old mom" in a classroom of youngsters. One of her college goals is to participate and interact with more students. She also talks to her classmates about her desire to get back into the dating world, as she has been single since the birth of her now adult son.

- *How do you think a student group can help Judy?*
- *Which student groups do you think would be most congruent to meet Judy's interpersonal and/or intrapersonal needs?*
- *Additionally, how do you think a facilitator can help Judy to not shame herself for her differences in her nontraditional student status?*

HELPFUL RESOURCES

Baxter Magolda, M. B. (2001). *Making their own way: Narratives for transforming higher education to promote self-development*. Sterling, VA: Stylus.

Coe, D. M., & Zimpfer, D. G. (1996). Infusing solution-oriented theory and techniques into group work. *Journal for Specialists in Group Work, 21*, 49–57.

Corey, G., Corey, M. S., & Haynes, R. (2014). *Groups in action: Evolution and challenges* (2nd ed.). Pacifica Grove, CA: Brooks/Cole.

Laube, J., & Trefz, S. (1994). Group therapy using a narrative theory framework: Application to treatment of depression. *Journal of Systemic Therapies, 13*, 29–37.

Manning, K., Kinzie, J., & Schuh, J. H. (2006). *One size does not fit all: Traditional and innovative models of student affairs practice*. New York, NY: Routledge.

Patton, L. D., McEwan, M., Rendón, L., & Howard-Hamilton, M. F. (2007). Critical race perspectives in theory in student affairs. In S. R. Harper & L. D. Patton (Eds.), *Responding to the realities of race on campus. New directions for student services* (No. 120, pp. 39–53). San Francisco, CA: Jossey-Bass.

Reason, R. D., & Kimball, E.W. (2012). A new theory-to-practice model for student affairs: Integrating scholarship, context, and reflection. *Journal of Student Affairs Research and Practice, 49*(4), 359–376. doi:10.1515/jsarp-2012–6436.

Renn, K. A. (2003). Understanding the identities of mixed-race college students through a developmental ecology lens. *Journal of College Student Development, 44*(3), 383–403.

Schuh, J. H., Jones, S. R., & Harper, S. R. (Eds.). (2011). *Student services: A handbook for the profession* (5th ed.). San Francisco, CA: Jossey-Bass.

Stage, F. K. (1994). Fine tuning the instrument: Using process models for work with student development theory. *College Student Affairs Journal, 13*(2), 21–28.

Tanaka, G. (2002). Higher education's self-reflexive turn: Toward an intercultural theory of student development. *Journal of Higher Education, 73*(2), 263–296.

Torres, V., Jones, S. R., & Renn, K. A. (2009). Identity development theories in student affairs: Origins, current status, and new approaches. *Journal of College Student Development, 50*(6), 577–596.

REFERENCES

Braaten, L. J. (1974). Developmental phases of encounter groups: A critical review of models of a new proposal. *Interpersonal Development, 75,* 112–129.

Bronfenbrenner, U. (1979). *The ecology of human development: Experiments by nature and design.* Cambridge, MA: Harvard University Press.

Chen, M., & Rybak, C. J. (2004). *Group leadership skills: Interpersonal process in group counseling and therapy.* Belmont, CA: Brooks/Cole.

Chickering, A. W. (1969). *Education and identity.* San Francisco, CA: Jossey-Bass.

Corey, G. (1995). *Theory and practice of group counseling.* Pacific Grove, CA: Brooks/Cole.

Corey, M. S., & Corey, G. (2010). *Groups: Process and practice* (7th ed.). [PowerPoint]. Wadsworth, CA: Thomson Learning.

Erikson, E. (1968). Womanhood and the inner space. In E. Erikson, *Identity, youth, and crisis* (pp. 261–294). New York, NY: W. W. Norton.

Evans, N. J., Forney, D. S., Guido, F. M., Patton, L. D., & Renn, K. A. (2010). *Student development in college: Theory, research, and practice* (2nd ed.). San Francisco, CA: Jossey-Bass.

Lacoursiere, R. (1980). *The life-cycle of groups: Group development and stage theory.* New York, NY: Human Sciences.

Wilson, F. R., Rapin, L. S., & Haley-Banez, L. (2000). Association for Specialists in Group Work: Professional standards for the training of group workers. *Journal for Specialists in Group Work, 25*(4), 327–342.

Yalom, I. D. (2005). *The theory and practice of group psychotherapy.* New York, NY: Basic Books.

CHAPTER 20

THEORY AS THE LANGUAGE OF STUDENT AFFAIRS PROFESSIONALS

Adam Gregory

CASE VIGNETTE: AKIO

Akio is a promising college student of Japanese descent. His family came to the United States when he was just 4 years old. His parents have high expectations for him, and he earned a full scholarship to Winington University. Akio is majoring in engineering and although he is able to do the academic work, he struggles to get along with others. In fact, when he lost two points on an assignment he argued with a professor for more than 2 hours. He will argue if he feels he is right even if it is just one point that will not lower his A in a course. His classmates are often frustrated with him because he asks numerous questions in class. In addition, Akio seems to be socially awkward when it comes to relating to peers, and this resulted in bullying by a roommate last year. Akio feels like no one really understands him. Because he does top-notch work and is extremely detail oriented, other students want to work with him on group projects. However, his tendency to see the world in black and white leaves little room for understanding or appreciating opinions and views that differ from his own. This has created conflict and frustration in many different situations. Often Akio gets upset about even little details that have no major impact, such as the color of a tablecloth used at a meeting of the professional organization that he joined. In fact, he points out every single flaw no matter how small and looks for someone to blame. Akio has also made a few comments that were perceived by other students as veiled threats, although they were said to them in a "joking" manner. Students have brought their concerns about his comments to program faculty. Akio will be starting an internship soon and faculty members are concerned about his ability not only to do the job but also to get along with others. They are reluctant to offer recommendations for an internship unless Akio seeks assistance in learning better interpersonal skills.

His faculty advisor meets with Akio to discuss the concerns about his interpersonal skills. The meeting is tense and Akio is defensive and upset. He does not feel as if he is understood but agrees to seek assistance from the Career Services Office. Although very

(continued)

(continued)

reluctant to see a counselor, Akio agrees that it could be helpful to discuss his feelings with someone at least once. Because he is so distraught and had made a few comments during the meeting about fellow students that could be perceived as threats, the faculty advisor walks Akio to the counseling center for an emergency appointment. He tells Akio that this is not a big deal; it is just to make sure he is okay and able to process the information. Nonetheless, the advisor is somewhat concerned and nervous, because of recent shootings and other incidents of interpersonal violence on college campuses.

THE ROLE OF STUDENT AFFAIRS

Traditionally, there has been a division of labor in higher education between academics and student affairs. As evidenced throughout the previous chapters, the term *student affairs* is an umbrella term used within the higher educational setting and typically used in reference to the department(s) or division(s) of said educational institutions where the primary focus is that of student development, growth, and well-being (Long, 2012; McClellan & Stringer, 2011). Origins of student affairs frameworks can be dated back even before the United States became a sovereign nation with the formation of dining halls and dormitories in Colonial colleges (Komives & Woodard, 2003; Thelin, 2011). By the mid-1800s, American universities began to adopt European influence when it came to the extent that extracurricular activist emerged with opportunities for students to participate in a variety of clubs, societies, and associations focused on students' development of mind, body, and personality (Geiger & Bubolz, 2000). In fact, early American higher education institutions took on such parental responsibilities of students that the doctrine of *in loco parentis* (translated from Latin as "in place of parent") was in place for centuries by colleges and universities (Lee, 2011).

REVIEW OF THE HISTORICAL CONTEXT OF STUDENT AFFAIRS

The 1900s saw an expansion in the field of student affairs due in part to the education-seeking veteran returning from both World Wars, and the resulting need for additional higher education staff specializing in student personnel issues (Long, 2012). Over the next several decades, numerous advancements and changes were made in the field of student affairs due in part to, but not limited to, the revision of the *Student Personnel Point of View* report in the 1940s (Sandeen et al., 1987); the decisions of 1961's *Dixon vs Alabama State Board of Education* (*Dixon v. Alabama*, 1961); the 1972 report *Student Development in Tomorrow's Higher Education: A Return to the Academy* (Brown, 1972); the deviations that captured a nation's attention via Kent State University and the tragedies of Virginia Tech; movements involving civil rights, women's rights, and rights of the gay, lesbian, bisexual, and transgender communities, just to name a few. Over the years, the field of student affairs has also been referred to by a number of pseudonyms (e.g., student development, student personnel, student services), but despite the many names and innumerable changes, the field of student affairs has been, and continues to be, committed to the betterment of all students' higher educational experiences. Just as the field of student affairs has borne witness to a number of changes and responsibilities, since its earliest beginnings, so has the profession and subsequent proficiencies of the student affairs personnel.

Although this chapter is designed to focus on the plausibility of using theory to facilitate communication across the many departments and divisions of higher education, it is important to remember that the student affairs profession "grew from the campus up, not from theory down" (Cowley, 1934, p. 4). Early institutions of higher education followed the Oxbridge model with historically based residential living systems in which educators resided in residence halls with the students (Duke, 1996). This concept of faculty–student integration remains a valuable component in student success today, and is discussed in greater detail in a subsequent section of this chapter. The original student affairs personnel were deans of men and deans of women, whose primary responsibilities differed from those of a typical educator and attended to the students' personal matters (Brubacher & Rudy, 1997). The men and women who held these positions were typically those with a formal education within a liberal arts discipline because of the fact that at the time there was no formal institution-based preparation or area of study specific to the practice of student affairs (Sandeen et al., 1987). It was not until the early 20th century that the first formal educational specialty was created in the area of student affairs, resulting in a vocational guidance program offered at Columbia University's Teachers College (Nuss, 2003).

STUDENT AFFAIRS AND THEORY

By the 1960s, college student personnel had solidified a strong standing as professionals in colleges and universities and, in 1979, the Council for Advancement of Standards in Higher Education was formed in order to hold graduate programs reasonable for consistent preparation and governance (Dungy & Gordon, 2011). During the next few decades, student affairs practitioners completed graduate studies programs and subsequent training from colleges and universities typically located within departments of education and higher education programs. In recent years, there has been added pressure placed on student affairs graduate programs to focus on the whole student. Rogers and Love (2004) credited this modification to the increasing demand of students who were looking for more than simple academic preparation, and, instead, preparation to deal with more holistic issues related to self-realization and the larger meaning of life for individuals. Because of this relatively recent trend, more and more student affairs graduate programs are placing emphasis in administration, student development models, and counseling theory (Patton et al., 2016; Rhatigan, 2000). So to reiterate, while Cowley (1934) stated that the profession of student affairs "grew from the campus up, not from theory down" (p. 4), one can see how theoretical application has begun to trickle down from the ivory towers.

As previously mentioned, dining halls and residential dormitories were essentially the first areas or departments that developed because of the Oxbridge model adopted from the educational institutions in Europe (Mann, 2010). Today, the Council for the Advancement of Standards in Higher Education (CAS) identifies 45 functional areas in the profession of student affairs, all of which are intended to promote and enhance student development, learning, and success. For these programs to achieve such a task, it is often important for these separate divisions or departments to work together, foster communication, and often share office space or be located in similar geographical locations on university or college campuses (Dungy, 2003). O'Connor, Polnariev, and Levy (2016) moved this notion a step further by predicting that programs are more likely to produce positive outcomes with extensive collaboration between staff and faculty from the initial stages of development to the final stages of implementation.

USING THEORY AS A LANGUAGE

In the article titled *The Case for Promoting Partnerships Between Academic and Student Affairs,* Joe Cuseo, a professor of psychology at Marymount College, credited increases in student retention, increased student learning, and the promotion of personal development of students to collaborative communication between a variety of student affairs areas and academic faculty (Cuseo, n.d.). Often, counselor educators and those trained in the counseling-related fields have a particular advantage in assisting with these goals because of their skills training and competencies in the areas of student development and counseling theory (Jacob & Greggo, 2001). Knowledge of student development theories serves as a valuable tool for student affairs professionals to use when developing programming and events, communicating with other professionals, and as an important framework to use when conceptualizing and working with their college and university students (Torres, Jones, & Renn, 2009). Typically, or perhaps even ideally, this gives staff and faculty a 4-year window to help mold and cultivate not only student learning but also the development of the identities that students will embody throughout their lives. Abes, Jones, and McEwen (2007), using analytical feminist literature, purported that college and university student development theory can function as a "framework of intersectionality that recognizes how socially constructed identities are experienced simultaneously, not hierarchically" (p. 2). Using this framework, one can suggest that student affairs professionals can use student development and identity development simultaneously when planning programs and events.

It seems clear that a reciprocal relationship among the different divisions and aspects of student affairs as hypothetical agents of change for specific student development and identity development frameworks exists on many campuses. Long (2012) illustrated that Kohlberg's theory of moral development has greatly affected the ways in which student affairs practitioners working in student conduct offices handle disciplinary issues. Mathiasen (2005) identified and validated the potential for emphasis on and growth of moral development as a by-product of involvement in the typical events, programs, and traditions supported by student affairs personnel working in the Greek life specialty area. It is also apparent that minority development frameworks, such as Cass's sexual orientation identity development model, racial identity development, Cross's Black racial identify development, and Gibson's model of disability identity development, can influence and enrich the work of student affairs professionals working in lesbian, gay, bisexual, transgender, and queer (LGBTQ) programs, multicultural student programs, and disability services, respectively (Patton et al., 2016; Quaye & Harper, 2014).

Similarly, to show Dungy's (2003) indicated overlap among student affairs departments, a comparable assertion can be made in terms of theories of student development and identity development. These overlaps can, in turn, create unique collaboration opportunities for student affairs professionals. Empirical evidence has indicated the rich communication and collaboration opportunities that can arise from Schlossberg's theory of transition when utilized across various areas of student affairs including, but not limited to, international student programs, housing and residence life, veterans and military programs, academic advising, commuter and off-campus living programs, athletic departments, and career services (Aune, 2000; Erb, Sinclair, & Braxton, 2015; Jacoby & Garland, 2004; Kortegast & Yount, 2016; Pearson & Petitpas, 1990).

CURRENT TRENDS IN STUDENT AFFAIRS

College student retention rates continue to be of grave concern year after year across the United States at a growing number of college campuses in a variety of degree levels (Baker & Robnett, 2012; Brooks & DuBois, 1995; Friedman & Mandel, 2011; Hippel, Lerner, Gregerman, Nagda, & Jonides, 1998; Popiolek, Fine, & Eilman, 2013). Retention rates directly affect almost every student affairs area across a university or college from admissions offices, to learning assistance programs, to housing and dining, and financial aid.

In relation to the concerns of student retention, a number of different variables have been explored. Numerous research studies have shown that college students experience significant levels of anxiety, depression, and stress while attending higher education institutions (Anxiety Disorder Association of America, 2010; Floyd, Mimms, & Yelding, 2007; Mahmoud, Staten, Hall, & Lennie, 2012). Because of this, college counseling services are frequently unable to keep up with the mental health demands of students. Students suffering from mental health concerns tend to exhibit lower levels of academic success (Brooks & DuBois, 1995; Van Heyningen, 1997). In fact, stress and anxiety are correlated with retention rates among college and university students (Brooks & DuBois, 1995). Thus, many educational institutions in the United States are attempting to combat the low retention rates that have plagued the university and colleges setting for decades, and in turn, student affairs programs and event collaborations have increased the frequency to which a variety of departments across campus are working together.

Empirical evidence has suggested that college and university students with increased student involvement have higher retention rates and academic success (Astin, 1984). These findings coincide with research that shows social support and student involvement decrease the likelihood of depression (Delistamati et al., 2006). Developing the social relationships associated with student involvement plays a positive role in terms of retention (Upcraft & Gardner, 1989) as well as academic success (Boyer & Sedlacek, 1988; Brooks & DuBois, 1995). Furthermore, student involvement in college and university activities can increase students' overall satisfaction and well-being when attending a higher education institution (Cooper, Healy, & Simpson, 1994). Developing innovative and effective ways of enhancing student engagement can require creativity and ingenuity, as college students are exposed to greater freedom and opportunities than in past decades.

TALKING ACROSS CAMPUS: MONTHLY "MOVIE NIGHTS"

One university that has been successful in increasing student engagement sponsors several events every semester encouraging and promoting student involvement on campus. With a student body of more than 40,000 students, this institution has initiated a monthly screening of popular films before they are released to DVD. This early screening, called "Real Late Reels," is free of charge for students, faculty, and other members of the community. Although the initial intent of the event was simply student entertainment, the screenings have grown into something more. Student organizations, student affairs departments, and faculty from a variety of disciplines are encouraged to attend this event thereby giving students the opportunity to network and connect with individuals who can provide assistance and support during their academic journey at the institution. One of the most unique elements of this event is that different student affairs entities are assigned to be the "hosts" each month, and they reach out to other relevant departments and/or campus organizations whose interests or involvement coincides with the film that is being shown. The event takes place on a Friday or a Saturday evening to avoid interference with regularly scheduled classes.

When attending this type of event, a unique socialization and convergence of individuals from a variety of roles (student, staff, faculty, administration, etc.) occurs and the sense of community is strengthened. There is little distinction among faculty, staff, and students during this shared exchange, almost as if the entire enculturated norms and characteristics of the normative university hierarchy have melted away. Students from a variety of cliques or social groupings converge as professors mingle with students from noticeably variant social circles. The location of the film screening provides space for banners, pamphlets, and promotional materials from a variety of university-related areas including Greek life, residence life, counseling services, health services, and the offices of compliance, equal opportunity and affirmative action. Conversations and discussions spring from the film topic, but reach far beyond the plot or characters in the film. This event provides an opportunity for students and others to find themselves in a "melting pot" of campus diversity.

Theoretical Exploration of the Movie Night Across Campus

Most of the individuals involved in the planning, delivery, and participation in the movie night event may recognize that "something good" is happening as a result of the gathering. Not everyone, though, will have the same perspective or same vocabulary or jargon, necessarily, to describe the engagement. The use of shared theory, however, can provide a shared language in which diverse stakeholders can have a meaningful and purposive conversation.

Using Erikson's Theory as a Means of Communication

One useful "language" for student affairs practitioners is found in Erikson's stages of psychosocial development. Erik Erikson pioneered a theoretical framework and proposes an eight-staged life-span model through which developing individuals permeate starting at birth and eventually ending with death (Erikson, 1950). Although all of the stages hold ample weight throughout the life span of an individual, the sixth stage encompasses the observed characteristics applicable to the attended event. As noted in Chapter 4, the Intimacy Versus Isolation stage occurs between the ages of 18 and 40 years, which would include the majority of the students who are attending the event. It is during this stage that individuals are driven to explore more meaningful and intimate relationships, some of which having the capacity to be enduring connections that exist beyond the family of origin or extended family. Successful navigation of this stage produces feelings of trust, care, and safety. Individuals will move from a more self-centered perspective as they open themselves to sacrifice or compromise their needs and desires in an effort to maintain the stability of these lasting relationships (Erikson, 1958). If individuals are not successful during this stage of development, they are expected to experience feelings of loneliness and isolation, which has the potential to propel them into a depressive state (Pittman, Keiley, Kerpelman, & Vaughn, 2011).

Aspects of this stage can be seen as being relevant to the example of the movie night event in terms of the formation of bonds and relationships between the individuals attending. As noted previously, students who are depressed exhibit lower rates of retention (Anxiety Disorder Association of America, 2010; Floyd et al., 2007; Mahmoud et al., 2012), whereas research shows that student involvement and social support can aid in decreasing the feeling of depression (Delistamati et al., 2006). Taken together, these findings suggest that the interactions at the "Real Late Reels" event combined with the budding of new and possible relationships described by Erikson could enhance retention. Even though these relationships are in very early and premature phases, the possibility exists for further growth.

One could also take notice of the different sizes of the groups that had formed. Some groups consisted of several individuals, whereas others had very few individuals. One could argue that with an increased number of social connections comes greater probability for relationship formation. Although rare, there were still particular individuals who came to the event solo and did not make attempts to join a social assemblage. If this behavior is common or the norm for these individuals, according to Erikson (1958), they could run the risk of isolation and loneliness. It is fortunate that the secluded students were few and far between at this event, therefore promoting student involvement and social interactions that could result in relationships, social support, and possibly even higher retention ratings.

Using Chickering's Theory as a Means of Communication

Although Erikson's stages of psychosocial development were applicable when observing and evaluating the movie night example, Chickering's theory of identity development would also be an appropriate theoretical framework through which to describe the events. One of the seven vectors described in this theory is termed *Developing Mature Interpersonal Relationships*. Similarly to Erikson's Intimacy Versus Isolation stage, Chickering's relevant vector describes students' efforts in forming more meaningful and mature relationships (Chickering, 1969). In the previous section, the use of the monthly film night as a means of forming meaningful relationships was explored as well as the importance of social support with its effect on retention rates (Anxiety Disorder Association of America, 2010; Delistamati et al., 2006; Floyd et al., 2007; Mahmoud et al., 2012). In applying the language of Chickering, the applied theoretical framework that will be used is cross-cultural tolerance, which is also a component found within this vector (Evans, Forney, Guido, Patton, & Renn, 2009). During this period, students begin to appreciate the differences between individuals and they also become more objective. This phenomenon was noted as occurring during the film series events. Students representing a diverse student body in terms of ethnicity, social groups, age, gender, and so on were not only coexisting, but also actively engaged in social interaction and expressive conversations with one another as well as faculty and staff. It was pointed out that there was a heightened sense of community at this point in the students' development. This was clearly visible as the students discussed issues ranging from the film, to the university's facilities, academic courses in which the students were enrolled, as well as topical political issues. One example of the depth of discussion and connection fostered by these events was evidenced in a discussion of the concerns over the "campus rape culture" between students and the university's Title IX coordinator.

As previously noted, faculty and staff were highly encouraged to attend this event and were also highly engaged in conversations, not only with one another, but with students as well. Chickering and Gamson's *Seven Principles for Good Practice in Undergraduate Education* (1987) conveyed the importance of contact between students and faculty both in and out of the class setting. They believed that open interactions encourage students to further engage in student involvement with college and university commitments as well as to aid with the provision of social support and motivation. Although the dialogue between many of the students was insightful and meaningful, the presence of faculty and administrators interjected a notably enhanced level of intellect that was not typical of the usual undergraduate conversations. Chickering and Gamson (1987) would likely have described this experience as one that "enhances students' intellectual commitment and encourages them to think about their own values and future plans" (p. 3).

Although this series of movie nights and discussions may first seem more about entertainment than engagement, it became evident that there was much more going on than expected. On closer examination, however, it is apparent that even a popular movie screening on a college campus can promote student development, communication across various areas of student affairs, and, hopefully, encourage students, faculty, staff, and community members to engage in shared campus activities. In turn, these activities can foster and facilitate student involvement and social support—and perhaps even enhance the psychological, emotional, and developmental health of students—as well as increase levels of retention.

FUTURE TRENDS

Although some student affairs professionals adamantly believe that student affairs education should occur in discrete academic programs, other professionals, notably counselor educators, may believe that these programs should be housed in counseling programs (Protivnak, Paylo, & Mercer, 2013). Regardless of where a student affairs program is located within the academic setting, there is an unquestionable need to provide aspiring student affairs professionals with a thorough grounding in relevant theories related to the multifaceted development of their future students. As research continues to expand the knowledge base for student affairs, new theoretical frameworks and approaches to student development and identity are likely to emerge. New technological advances will continue to challenge developmental landmarks, identity standards, and the role of globalization will expand within higher education and academia.

Existing theories of student development and student identity have narrowly focused on growth in the "offline world" (Junco, 2014). As the digital divide continues to narrow, with young individuals continuing to make greater use of new technology and innovations (Hutter, 2007), gone are the days of filtered information accessible only through authorities and gatekeepers of knowledge. Dissemination of information through a variety of mediated forms and social networks will continue to change the way that students develop and new research will be required to incorporate the evolution of those whose identities may have developed both online and off (Junco, 2014). Increasing communication through technological advances will also continue to revolutionize the student identity development of minorities as well (Torres et al., 2009). Minority status groups, as an entity, are continuing to increase. Colby and Ortman (2015) predicted that by the middle of the 21st century, minority groups will make up more than half of the American population.

Although it is unlikely that the impact of discrimination, prejudice, and privilege will be soon eliminated or no longer play a role in the development and identity of students, the increasing fluidity may provide a stimulus for identity evaluations that motivate change in development (King & Baxter Magolda, 2005). There is ample evidence of the ability for increased globalization to present students with opposing viewpoints and a variety of alternatives (Miller & Fernández, 2007) and it is predicted that this process will continue in the transformation of existing theoretical frameworks (Lorelle, Byrd, & Crockett, 2012). Further research on these and a variety of other possible impacts will need to be completed before one can fully understand the extent to which these implications will truly effect student development and identity development.

CASE VIGNETTE WRAP-UP: AKIO

When it comes to the impact that elements of the college and university experience can have on student development, the case of Akio highlights the need for faculty and staff to work together. Akio's faculty advisor walked Akio over to the counseling center because he recognized there could be major issues that needed to be addressed.

(continued)

(continued)

At the counseling center, a counselor named Jane talks with Akio about his concerns. During the conversation, Akio expresses his frustrations and discusses several instances where other students made fun of him because of his cultural heritage. This has led to a buildup of anger and frustration. Akio feels isolated and has been unable to make meaningful connections. With his consent, the counselor contacts the director of the Multicultural Student Office. They discuss the areas in which Akio is struggling in terms of Chickening's Vectors and discuss ways to help Akio connect with other students on campus, and Akio agrees to attend a diversity club meeting. At the meeting, he is able to connect for the first time with other students from diverse backgrounds. In addition, he keeps his appointment with the Career Services Office and, because he allows communication between Jane and the director of that office, the specialists in the Career Services Office work with Akio on understanding workplace norms in addition to basic interviewing skills. This case highlights the powerful impact that student affairs professionals can have when they work together for the good of a student. The use of theories to conceptualize and understand issues can help to enhance the communication.

CASE VIGNETTE 1 FOR READER REFLECTION: AMY

Amy is enjoying college and has been highly involved in several organizations. She will be graduating in the spring but is not sure what she wants to do. She will have a degree in psychology but does not want to go to graduate school. She is very outgoing and has a great personality. She thinks that starting out she should be able to make at least $60,000 as she has a bachelor's degree. Amy is unclear about what she wants to do in terms of her relationship with her long-term boyfriend who will also be graduating. He has a more realistic view of the future. He has told Amy that she needs to consider that she will not be making that much money right away with only a bachelor's degree in psychology. Her boyfriend, Ed, will be graduating in the summer (right after Amy) with a degree in engineering and will be doing an internship in the spring. She is upset that he will not be on campus during her last semester and thinks he should have finished school the same time as her. It bothers her significantly that Ed does not want to get married until he has a job and feels financially stable. She thinks they should get married in the summer and believes she would be able to support them both on the salary from her expected high-paying job. In fact, she has even thought about getting pregnant, hoping it will force Ed to marry her. In meeting with her academic advisor, she discusses her current struggles and indicates that she is not really even sure how to start searching for a job. Her advisor refers her to Career Services and to the Counseling Center.

- *How might using student development theory to explain Amy's situation be beneficial when referrals are made?*
- *What are some ways in which various areas of student affairs can help Amy to reach a resolution regarding decisions she needs to make that will impact her future?*

CASE VIGNETTE 2 FOR READER REFLECTION: JASMINE

Jasmine recently transferred from a junior college to Madison Bay University, a 4-year college a few hours from her home. She is classified as a college sophomore. She has a 5-year-old son whose father is not active in his life. Jasmine was excited about being able to attend a 4-year university with the help of a scholarship that covers a significant portion of her expenses. However, she was disappointed that the university did not have family housing and thus she had to live off campus. She could not afford an apartment close to campus and she has a 30-minute commute to campus. She has enrolled her son in day care, but feels the professors are not sympathetic when she has to miss class because he is sick. She also has not found time to socialize, connect, or make friends with other students. Everyone on campus during the day seems to be a full-time student, and she hasn't met any other students with children. Jasmine feels lonely and is struggling to adjust. Although she knew going away to college would be more difficult financially, the added expenses, including childcare, were more than she anticipated. Her older sister and mother had taken care of her son while she worked and went to junior college. The difficulty Jasmine is having in connecting with others is contributing to feelings of sadness, depression, and loneliness. She recently went to the student health center and was diagnosed with strep throat. The doctor at the health center noticed that she seemed depressed and started talking to her. She told him that it has not been easy, and shared her frustrations.

- *What services on campus might the doctor consider referring Jasmine to visit?*
- *What theory might be useful in helping student affairs professionals to conceptualize her case/situation?*
- *How might programs on campus be modified to meet the needs of single mothers?*

REFERENCES

Abes, E. S., Jones, S. R., & McEwen, M. K. (2007). Reconceptualizing the model of multiple dimensions of identity: The role of meaning-making capacity in the construction of multiple identities. *Journal of College Student Development, 48*, 1–22.

Anxiety Disorder Association of America. (2010). Facts. Retrieved from http://www.adaa.org/finding-help/helping-others/college-students/facts

Astin, A. W. (1984). Student involvement: A developmental theory for higher education. *Journal of College Student Personnel, 25*, 297–308.

Aune, B. (2000). Career and academic advising. *New Directions for Student Services, 2000*(91), 55–67.

Baker, C. N., & Robnett, B. (2012). Race, social support and college student retention: A case study. *Journal of College Student Development, 53*(2), 325–335.

Boyer, S. P., & Sedlacek, W. E. (1988). Noncognitive predictors of academic success for international students: A longitudinal study. *Journal of College Student Development, 29*, 218–223.

Brooks, J. H., & DuBois, D. L. (1995). Individual and environmental predictors of adjustment during the first year of college. *Journal of College Student Development, 36*, 347–360.

Brown, R. D. (1972). *Student development in tomorrow's higher education: A return to the academy.* Alexandria, VA: American College Personnel Association.

Brubacher, J. S., & Rudy, W. (1997). *Higher education in transition: A history of American colleges and universities.* New Brunswick, NJ: Transaction.

Chickering, A. W. (1969). *Education and identity.* San Francisco, CA: Jossey-Bass.

Chickering, A. W., & Gamson, Z. F. (1987, March). Seven principles for good practice in undergraduate education. *AAHE Bulletin*, pp. 3–7.

Colby, S. L., & Ortman, J. M. (2015). *Projections of the size and composition of the U.S. population: 2014 to 2060* (Report No. P25-1143). Washington, DC: U.S. Census Bureau.

Cooper, D. L., Healy, M. A., & Simpson, J. (1994). Student development through involvement: Specific changes over time. *Journal of College Student Development, 35*, 98–102.

Cowley, W. H. (1934). The history of student residential housing. *School and Society, 40*, 705–712.

Cuseo, J. (n.d.). The case for promoting partnerships between academic and student affairs [PDF]. Retrieved from http://cpe.ky.gov/NR/rdonlyres/FC5065E4-E5A0-4F3F-9B36-FA33FEF29929/0/TheCaseforPromotingPartnershipsBetween.pdf

Delistamati, E., Samakouri, M. A., Davis, E. A., Vorvolakos, T., Xenitidis, K., & Livaditis, M. (2006). Interpersonal Support Evaluation List (ISEL)-college version: Validation and application in a Greek sample. *International Journal of Social Psychiatry, 52*(6), 552–560.

Dixon v. Alabama, 294 F. 2d 150 (5th Cir. 1961).

Duke, A. (1996). *Importing Oxbridge: English residential colleges and American universities*. New Haven, CT: Yale University Press.

Dungy, G. (2003). Organization and functions of student affairs. In S. Komives, D. Woodard, Jr., & Associates (Eds.), *Student services: A handbook for the profession* (4th ed., pp. 339–357). San Francisco, CA: Jossey-Bass.

Dungy, G., & Gordon, S. A. (2011). The development of student affairs. In J. H. Schuh, S. R. Jones, S. R. Harper, & Associates (Eds.), *Student services: A handbook for the profession* (pp. 61–79). San Francisco, CA: Jossey-Bass.

Erb, N. M., Sinclair, M. S., & Braxton, J. M. (2015). Fostering a sense of community in residence halls: A role for housing and residential professionals in increasing college student persistence. *Strategic Enrollment Management Quarterly, 3*(2), 84–108.

Erikson, E. H. (1950). *Childhood and society*. New York, NY: Norton.

Erikson, E. H. (1958). *Young man Luther: A study in psychoanalysis and history*. New York, NY: Norton.

Evans, N. J., Forney, D. S., Guido, F. M., Patton, L. D., & Renn, K. A. (2009). *Student development in college: Theory, research, and practice*. San Francisco, CA: Jossey-Bass.

Floyd, P., Mimms, S., & Yelding, C. (2007). *Personal health: Perspectives and lifestyles*. Belmont, CA: Wadsworth.

Friedman, B. A., & Mandel, R. G. (2011). Motivation predictors of college student academic performance and retention. *Journal of College Student Retention: Research, Theory and Practice, 13*(1), 1–15.

Hippel, W. V., Lerner, J. S., Gregerman, S. R., Nagda, B. A., & Jonides, J. (1998). Undergraduate student-faculty research partnerships affect student retention. *The Review of Higher Education, 22*(1), 55–72.

Hutter, M. (2007). *Experiencing cities*. New York, NY: Pearson.

Geiger, R. L., & Bubolz, J. A. (2000). College as it was in the mid nineteenth century. In R. L. Geiger (Ed.), *The American college in the nineteenth century* (pp. 80–90). Nashville, TN: Vanderbilt University Press.

Jacob, E. J., & Greggo, J. W. (2001). Using counselor training and collaborative programming strategies in working with international students. *Journal of Multicultural Counseling and Development, 29*(1), 73–88.

Jacoby, B., & Garland, J. (2004). Strategies for enhancing commuter student success. *Journal of College Student Retention: Research, Theory & Practice, 6*(1), 61–79.

Junco, R. (2014). *Engaging students through social media: Evidence-based practices for use in student affairs*. New York, NY: Wiley.

King, P. M., & Baxter Magolda, M. B. (2005). A developmental model of intercultural maturity. *Journal of College Student Development, 46*, 571–592.

Komives, S. R., & Woodard, D. B., Jr. (2003). *Student services: A handbook for the profession*. New York, NY: Wiley.

Kortegast, C., & Yount, E. M. (2016). Identity, family, and faith: U.S. third culture kids transition to college. *Journal of Student Affairs Research and Practice, 53*(2), 230–242.

Lee, P. (2011). The curious life of *in loco parentis* at American universities. *Higher Education in Review, 8,* 65–90.

Long, D. (2012). The foundations of student affairs: A guide to the profession. In L. J. Hinchliffe & M. A. Wong (Eds.), *Environments for student growth and development: Librarians and student affairs in collaboration* (pp. 1–39). Chicago, IL: Association of College & Research Libraries.

Lorelle, S., Byrd, R., & Crockett, S. (2012). Globalization and counseling: Professional issues for counselors. *Professional Counselor, 2*(2), 115–123.

Mahmoud, J. S. R., Staten, R. T., Hall, L. A., & Lennie, T. A. (2012). The relationship among young adult college students' depression, anxiety, stress, demographics, life satisfaction, and coping styles. *Issues in Mental Health Nursing, 33*(3), 149–156.

Mann, B. J. (2010). Preserving the history of a student affairs association. *College Student Affairs Journal, 28*(2), 164.

Mathiasen, R. E. (2005). Moral development in fraternity members: A case study. *College Student Journal, 39*(2), 242–253.

McClellan, G. S., & Stringer, J. (2011). *The handbook of student affairs administration* (4th ed.). San Francisco, CA: Jossey-Bass.

Miller, A. T., & Fernández, E. (2007). New learning and teaching from where you've been: The global intercultural experience for undergraduates. In M. Kaplan & A. T. Miller (Eds.), *Scholarship of multicultural teaching and learning* (New Directions for Teaching and Learning, No. 111, pp. 55–62). San Francisco, CA: Jossey-Bass.

Nuss, E. M. (2003). The development of student affairs. In S. R. Komives & D. B. Woodard, Jr. (Eds.), *Student services: A handbook for the profession* (4th ed., pp. 65–88). San Francisco, CA: Jossey-Bass.

O'Connor, S., Polnariev, B. A., & Levy, M. A. (2016). Developing successful collaborative bridge programs. In M. A. Levy & B. A. Polnariev (Eds.), *Academic and student affairs in collaboration: Creating a culture of student success* (pp. 111–122). New York, NY: Routledge.

Patton, L. D., Renn, K. A., Guido, F. M., Quaye, S. J., Evans, N. J., & Forney, D. S. (2016). *Student development in college: Theory, research, and practice.* San Francisco, CA: Jossey-Bass.

Pearson, R. E., & Petitpas, A. J. (1990). Transitions of athletes: Developmental and preventive perspectives. *Journal of Counseling & Development, 69*(1), 7–10.

Pittman, F. J., Keiley, K. M., Kerpelman, L. J., & Vaughn, E. B. (2011). Attachment, identity, and intimacy: Parallels between Bowlby's and Erikson's paradigms. *Journal of Family Theory & Review, 3,* 32–46.

Popiolek, G., Fine, R., & Eilman, V. (2013). Learning communities, academic performance, attrition, and retention: A four-year study. *Community College Journal of Research and Practice, 37*(11), 828–838.

Protivnak, J. J., Paylo, M. J., & Mercer, J. C. (2013). The perceived value of counselor preparation for student affairs professionals. *Journal of Counselor Preparation and Supervision, 5*(1), 49–65.

Quaye, S. J., & Harper, S. R. (2014). *Student engagement in higher education: Theoretical perspectives and practical approaches for diverse populations.* New York, NY: Routledge.

Rhatigan, J. J. (2000). The history and philosophy of student affairs. *The Handbook of Student Affairs Administration, 2,* 3–24.

Rogers, J., & Love, P. (2004). Preparing professionals to respond to students' search for meaning. *Journal of College and Character, 7*(1), 1–10.

Sandeen, A., Albright, R. L., Barr, M. J., Golseth, A. E., Kuh, G. D., Lyons, W., & Rhatigan, J. J. (1987). *A perspective on student affairs: A statement issued on the fiftieth anniversary of the Student Personnel Point of View.* Washington, DC: National Association of Student Personnel Administrators.

Thelin, J. (2011). *A history of American higher education.* Baltimore, MD: Johns Hopkins University Press.

Torres, V., Jones, S. R., & Renn, K. A. (2009). Identity development theories in student affairs: Origins, current status, and new approaches. *Journal of College Student Development, 50*(6), 577–596.

Upcraft, M. L., & Gardner, J. N. (1989). A comprehensive approach to enhancing freshman success. In M. L. Upcraft & J. N. Gardner (Eds.), *The freshman year experience* (pp. 1–12). San Francisco, CA: Jossey-Bass.

Van Heyningen, J. J. (1997). Academic achievement in college students: What factors predict success? *Dissertation Abstracts International Section A: Humanities and Social Sciences, 58*(6-A), 2076.

INDEX

academic-advising services, 167–168
academic readiness, 6
academic success, and ecological systems theory, 204–217
accountability, of student, 40
activity systems, 15
   multivoicedness within, 16
adulthood, psychosocial development, 38, 42–43
affiliation, 39
Affirmative Model of Disability, 163
age, and support system, 26
American Indian identity development model, 129–131
   change in Indian consciousness, eras of, 130
   cultural consciousness, 131
   linguistic consciousness, 131
   political consciousness, 131
   race consciousness, 130–131
Americans with Disabilities Act (ADA), 4, 162
anticipated transitions, 25
Arnett, J., 94–95
arrested development, 40
Asian American identity development model, 127–129
Association for Specialists in Group Work, 218
Association of American Colleges and Universities (AACU), Core Commitments, 58
Association of College Unions International (ACUI), 18–19
autonomy
   and interdependence, 103
   versus shame and doubt, 37, 41

Bandura's Social Learning Theory, 176
behaviorism, 50
biculturalism, 114
bioecological model, 202, 203. *See also* Bronfenbrenner's ecological systems theory
biracial identity. *See* Black and biracial identity development theories
birth to 18 months, psychosocial development, 36, 40–41

Black and biracial identity development theories. *See also* racial identity development theories
   application of, 117–119
   case vignettes, 111, 119–120
   history and development of, 113–116
   Nigrescence model. *See* Cross Nigrescence model
   overview and description of, 111–113
Black nationalism, 114
Bronfenbrenner's ecological systems theory
   and academic success, 204–205
   application of, 203–205
   case vignettes, 197–198, 205–207
   chronosystem, 201, 202, 204
   exosystem, 200, 204
   genetic inheritance, 202
   history and development of, 202–203
   macrosystem, 200–201
   mesosystem, 200, 204
   microsystem, 199–200, 204
   and multicultural awareness, 205
   overview and description of, 198–202
   and self-discovery, 203–204
Brown v. Board of Education, 136

career choice. *See* college major and career choice
career services/counselors, 107, 179–180
care for others, 39–40, 44
Cass, V. C., 151–152
Chickering, A., 93
Chickering's theory
   advising, 106–107
   application of, 106–107
   autonomy and interdependence, 103
   case vignettes, 101–102, 107–109
   competence development, 102–103
   emotions regulation, 103
   history and development of, 105–106
   identity establishment, 104
   integrity development, 104
   interventions, 107
   mature interpersonal relationships development, 103–104

Chickering's theory (cont.)
  as a means of communication, 229–230
  overview and description of, 102–105
  programming, 106
  purpose development, 104
  seven factors of environmental influences, 105
children
  cognitive development of, 14
  of single mother students, care for, 7–8
chronic illness, impact on students, 4
chronosystem, 201, 202, 204
Circumscription and Compromise theory, 178
Civil Rights Act of 1964, 136
coeducation, 2
cognitive development, 14
  stages of, 67
cognitive functioning, and wellness, 4
college affordability, 5–6
college counseling centers, 4–5, 9, 107
  LGBTQ identity development, 155–156
  and mental health, 155–156
college major and career choice
  campus and community resources, 180
  career theories and assessments, 181
  case vignettes, 175, 182–183
  college selection, 179–180
  cultural influence, 178–179
  developmental factors, 176–177
  family influence, 177–178
  influencing factors, 177
  major and career indecision, 175–176
college student retention rates, 227
college students with disabilities (CSDs), 162. *See also* disability and identity development models
communities of practice, 16–18
community volunteering projects, 58
competency, 37–38, 42
  development of, 102–103
concrete operational phase, cognitive development, 67
conflict mediation, 58
conformists, 27
congruent personality types, 189
consistency, and self, 189
contextual relativism, 53, 55
conventional level, moral development
  Gilligan's theory, 69, 71–72
  Kohlberg's theory, 67–70
Convoy of Social Support, 26
coping resources, 28
cost of education, 5–6
Council for Advancement of Standards in Higher Education, 225–226
counseling groups, 214
counseling services, 4–5, 9
cross-campus collaboration, 8
Cross-Cultural Continuum, 205
Cross Nigrescence model, 113
  encounter stage, 113
  immersion–emersion stage, 113
  internalization–commitment stage, 114
  internalization stage, 113–114
  preencounter stage, 113
cultural development, 14
cultural historical activity theory, 15–16, 19
cultural identity development model, 96
Cuseo, J., 226

daughters of crisis, identity status, 94
Dean of Men, 2
developing mature interpersonal relationships, 230
developmental instruction model, 57
developmental psychology, 50–51
Developmental Trajectory Into Disability Culture (DTDC), 166
  acceptance phase, 166
  adoption phase, 167
  community phase, 167
  relationship phase, 167
devotion, 38
difficult dialogues, engagement in, 144
diffusion, identity status, 94, 150
direction in life, 37
disability and identity development models
  and academic services, 167–168
  Affirmative Model of Disability, 163
  application of, 167–179
  brief background, 163–164
  case vignettes, 161, 170–172
  Developmental Trajectory Into Disability Culture (DTDC), 166–167
  Disability Identity Development Model (DIDM), 165–166
  Disability Identity Integration Model (DIIM), 164–165
  and equity, 169–170
  medical model, 163
  minority model, 163
  overview, 161–162
  social model, 163
Disability Identity Development Model (DIDM), 165
  acceptance stage, 166
  passive awareness stage, 166
  realization stage, 166
Disability Identity Integration Model (DIIM), 164
  coming home, 165
  coming out, 165
  coming to feel we belong, 165
  coming together, 165
Disability Rights Movement, 163
disability support services, 169
diversity, in developmental model, 57
diversity-sensitive group leader, 217–218
dropout rate, 2
  and academic readiness, 6
dualism, 52–53, 55

ecological biracial identity development model, 116
ecological theory. *See* Bronfenbrenner's ecological systems theory

education cost, 5–6
ego development state, 27
emerging adulthood, 2–3, 39, 92, 94–95
emotions regulation, 103
environmental subsystems
    exosystem, 200, 204
    macrosystem, 200–201, 204
    mesosystem, 200, 204
    microsystem, 199–200, 204
equity, 169–170
Erikson, E., 93
Erikson's theory of psychosocial development, 200, 203, 215–216
    adulthood, heading toward, 38, 42–43
    application of, 40–45
    birth to 18 months, 36, 40–41
    case vignettes, 35–36, 45–47
    finding a partner and settling down, 39, 43–44
    maturity and giving back, 39–40, 44
    as a means of communication, 229
    overview of, 36
    preschool years, 37, 41–42
    primary school years, 37–38, 42
    time of review, 40, 44–45
    toddler years, 37, 41
escape, deflection from growth and development, 54
ethical development. *See* Perry's theory of moral development
Evans et al.'s equation of group and student development, 212
exercise, benefits of, 9
exosystem, 200, 204
experiential learning, 57
    Kolb's theory. *See* Kolb's theory of experiential learning
experiential reality, enhancement of, 144
extroverts, 84

Factor Model of Multiracial Identity (FMMI), 116
family support, and college success, 3
feeling individuals, 85
Ferdman and Gallegos, 124–125
fidelity, 38, 42–43
Filipino American identity development model, 127–128
    assimilation to dominant culture stage, 127
    ethnic awareness stage, 127
    ethnocentric realization stage, 128
    incorporation stage, 128
    Panethnic Asian American consciousness stage, 128
    social political awakening stage, 127–128
financial issues, 5–6
foreclosure, identity status, 93, 94, 150
formal operational period, cognitive development, 67
Four S System, 25–28, 29, 30
freshman orientation programs, 2

gay identity. *See* lesbian, gay, bisexual, trans, and queer identity development theories

gender
    and college major choice, 178–179
    identity, 96. *See also* lesbian, gay, bisexual, trans, and queer identity development theories
    and sexual minorities, 151
generativity versus stagnation, 39–40, 44
genetic inheritance, 202
Gibson, J., 165–166
Gill, C. J., 163–164
Gilligan, C., 65
Gilligan's theory, 69, 71–72
Gottfredson's theory of Circumscription and Compromise, 178
group theory
    application of, 219–220
    case vignettes, 211, 220–221
    diversity-sensitive group leader, 217–218
    ending or termination stage, 217
    group and student development, similarities between, 212–214
    group leader guidelines, 214–215
    group member identity, 215–216
    group norms, 216
    group processes, 216–217
    group types, 214
    history and development of, 218
    initial or forming stage, 216–217
    and multiculturalism, 217–218
    overview and description of, 212–217
    therapeutic factors, 213–214
    transition stage, 217
    universality, 213
    working stage, 217

Harvard University, 2
Helms, J. E., 114
Helms's model of White identity development, 138–141
    autonomy status, 140–141
    contact status, 138–139
    disintegration status, 139–140
    immersion/emersion status, 140
    pseudoindependence status, 140
    reintegration status, 140, 141
Higher Education Opportunity Programs, 168
Hispanic identity development model, 126
    Influences on Change category, 126
    Situating Identity category, 126
Holland's theory of career development
    application of, 191
    artistic personality, 188
    case vignettes, 187–188, 192–195
    conventional personality, 188–189
    enterprising personality, 188
    history and development of, 190–192
    investigative personality, 188
    overview, 188–190
    realistic personality, 188
    Self-Directed Search, 188–190
    social personality, 188

Holland's theory of person–environment
    interaction fit, 181
hope, 36, 40–41
Horse, P. G., 130

Ibrahim, F., 128
identity, 189
    achievement status, 94
    establishment, 104
    versus role, 38, 42–43, 93–94, 200, 203
identity development, defined, 150–151
identity development, in young adulthood
    case vignettes, 91–92, 97–99
    challenges to, 92
    influencing factors, 92
    psychosocial development theories, 93–95
    social identity development theories, 95–97
    theories, 93
income level, and college major choice, 178
Indianness, 129–131
    assimilated, 130
    bicultural, 130
    marginal, 130
    traditional, 129
    transitional, 129
Individuals With Disabilities Education Act
    (IDEA), 162
individuation, 38
industry versus inferiority, 37–38, 42
initiative versus guilt, 37, 41–42
instrument-relativist orientation, 67
integrity
    versus despair, 40, 44–45
    development, 104
intellectual competence, 102
interdependence, 103
international student services, for CWDs, 169
interpersonal competence, 102
interpersonal concordance, 68
intimacy, 103
    versus isolation, 39, 43–44
introverts, 84
intuitive individuals, 85

Johns Hopkins University, 2
joint enterprise, 18
Josselson, R., 93
Josselson's study on women's identity
    development, 94
Journal of College and Character, 58
Journal of Moral Education, 58
judging individuals, 85

K–12 education, sociocultural theories in, 18
Knefelkamp's model, 57
Kohlberg, L., 65
Kohlberg's theory of moral development,
    67–70, 226
Kolb's theory of experiential learning, 216
    application of, 78–79

case vignettes, 75, 79–81
history and development, 76–78
overview and description of, 75–76

Latinx racial identity orientations, 124–126
    Latinx-identified individuals, 125
    Latinx-integrated individuals, 125
    Latinx as "other," 125
    subgroup-identified individuals, 125
    undifferentiated orientation, 125
    White-identified orientation, 125–126
Lave, J., 16, 17
law and order phase, 68
leadership summits, 58
legitimate peripheral participation, 17
lesbian, gay, bisexual, trans, and queer (LGBTQ)
        identity development theories
    application of, 153
    case vignettes, 149–150, 156–158
    college counseling and mental health, 155–156
    heteronormative and gender-restrictive
        assumptions, 151
    identity development, 150–151
    multicultural student services and affairs,
        153–155
    theoretical foundations, 150–153
logical positivism, 50
lost and sometimes found, identity status, 94
love, 39, 43–44
Loving v. Virginia, 115

macrosystem, 200–201, 204
manual competence, 102
Marcia, J., 93
Marcia's model of identity development, 93–94
mattering, of student in transition, 24–25
mature interpersonal relationships development,
    103–104
maturity, 40
maturity and giving back years, psychosocial
    development, 39–40, 44
meaning making, and ecological theory, 203
mediation, 15–16
mental health, and college counseling, 155–156
mental health services, 107
mesosystem, 200, 204
microaggressions, recognition and reduction
    of, 143
microsystem, 199–200, 204
Millennial age group, 39
minorities
    and college major choice, 178–179
    development frameworks, 226
    identity development, 96, 165
    and remedial courses, 6
minority identity development theories
    application of, 131–132
    case vignettes, 123–124, 132–133
    Filipino American identity development model,
        127–128

Hispanic identity development model, 126
history and development of, 131
Indianness, categories of, 129–130
Latinx racial identity orientations, 124–126
Native American identity model, 130–131
overview and description of, 124–131
South Asian American identity development model, 128–129
monoracial identity development models, 115
moral development, 66–67, 226
conventional level, 67–68, 69, 70, 71
post-conventional level, 67, 68, 69, 70, 71–72
pre-conventional level, 67, 69–70, 71
moral development theories, 65–66
case vignettes, 65, 72
Gilligan's theory, 69, 71–72
Kohlberg's theory, 67–70
overview, 65
Perry's. *See* Perry's theory of moral development
moratorium, identity status, 93–94, 150
movie night across campus
Chickering's theory, as a means of communication, 229–230
Erikson's theory, as a means of communication, 229
theoretical exploration, 228
multicultural awareness, and ecological systems theory, 205
multiculturalism, 114
multicultural services, for CWDs, 169–170
multicultural student services and affairs, 153–154
on macrosystemic level, 154
on microsystemic level, 154
multiplicity, 52–53, 55
multivoicedness within activity system, 16
mutual engagement, 17
Myers–Briggs Type Indicator (MBTI), 181
application of, 86–87
case vignettes, 83, 88–89
overview and description of, 84–86
personality type assessment, 84

Nadal, K. L., 127
NASPA, 153
National Institute on Disability and Rehabilitation Research (NIDRR), 163
Native American Identity Model, 130–131
new student programming, and transition theory, 30
Nigrescence model. *See* Cross Nigrescence model
Noddings, N., 66–67
nonevents, and transition to college, 25
nontraditional college students, 6–8
development theory, 39–40, 44–45
single mothers, 7–8
transition of, 30–31
veterans, 7

Offices of Nontraditional Students/Veterans, 30–31
Ohnishi, H., 128

"One Drop Rule," 115
O*NET users, and Holland's theory, 190
online courses, 7

Pacific Islander identity development model, 127–129
parental divorce, impact on students, 3
parent–child relationship, 38
participation, in community of practice, 17
partner finding and settling down years, psychosocial development, 39, 43–44
pavers of the way, identity status, 94
peer effects, 58
peer mentoring/counseling services, 107
People of Color Racial Identity, 114
perceivers, 85
Perry's theory of moral development
application of, 54–57
case vignettes, 49, 56, 59–61
commitment in relativism, 53–54, 56
contextual relativism, 53, 55
deflections from growth and development, 54, 57
dualism, 52–53, 55
history and development of, 50–51
implications for practice, 58–59
implications for student affairs professionals, 57–58
multiplicity, 52–53, 55
overview and description of, 50, 51–52
Perry's development schema, 52–54
person, process, context, and time (PPCT) model, 202–203, 204
personal and demographic characteristics, and transitions, 26–27
personal challenges, of students, 2
personalism, 57
personality types. *See also* Myers–Briggs Type Indicator (MBTI)
assessment, 84–85
and college major selection, 181
combination of, 85–86, 188–189
extrovert and introvert, 84
Holland's RIASEC model, 188–189, 190
judging and perceiving, 85
sensing and intuitive, 85
thinking and feeling, 85
person's outlook, and transition, 27
philosophy, 51
physical competence, 102
physical health, 4, 8–9
Piaget, J., 65, 67
Plessy v. Ferguson, 115
post-conventional level, moral development
Gilligan's theory, 69, 71–72
Kohlberg's theory, 67, 68, 70
pre-conventional level, moral development
Gilligan's theory, 69, 71
Kohlberg's theory, 67, 69–70
preoperational period, cognitive development, 67

preschool years, psychosocial development, 37, 41–42
prestige, and career choice, 190
primary school years, psychosocial development, 37–38, 42
psychoeducational groups, 214
psychological resources, and transitions, 27
psychological services, 107
psychological theories, 50–51
psychosocial development theories, 93–95
    "emerging adulthood," 94–95
    Josselson's study on women's identity development, 94
    Marcia's model, 93–94
psychotherapy groups, 214
puberty, 37–38
punishment-and-obedience orientation, 67
purpose development, 37, 41–42, 104
purveyors of heritage, identity status, 94

racial identity development theories, 95–96, 111–113. *See also* Black and biracial identity development theories; White identity development theories
recreation, 8
Rehabilitation Act of 1973, 162
Reisser, L., 93
relativism, 53, 55
    commitment in, 53, 56
    contextual, 53–54, 55
religious and spiritual development, social identity, 96
religious beliefs, 5
religious needs, 59
remedial courses, 6
Renn, K. A., 115, 116
residence halls, 8
resilience, and transition, 27
responsibility, of students, 40
retention rates, 227
retreat, deflection from growth and development, 54
risk-taking behaviors, students' engagement in, 4, 92
Root, M. P., 115

salience, 189
Sandhu, D. S., 128
scaffolding learning, 15
Schlossberg, N. K., 23–24
Schlossberg's transition theory, 227
    application of, 30–31
    case vignettes, 23, 31–33
    history and development of, 28–30
    mattering, 24–25
    overview and description of, 23–28
    and self, 26–28
    and situation, 25–26
    and support system, 26

self, and transitions, 26–28
    personal and demographic characteristics, 26–27
    psychological resources, 27
self-control, 37
Self-Directed Search, 188–190
self-discovery, and ecological systems theory, 203–204
self-efficacy, 42
    and interest development, 190–191
    and transition, 27
self-protective people, 27
sensing individuals, 85
sensorimotor stage, cognitive development, 67
sexual identity, 96. *See also* gender
sexual orientation identity development, 151. *See also* lesbian, gay, bisexual, trans, and queer identity development theories
    linear stage model, 151–152
shared repertoire, 18
single mothers, nontraditional students, 7–8
situation, and transition to college, 25–26
Social-Cognitive Career Theory, 191
social-contract, legalistic phase, 68
social identity development theories, 95–97
social identity domains
    collective domain, 95–96
    individual/personal domain, 95, 96
    material domain, 95
    relational domain, 95
Social Learning Theory (Bandura), 176
sociocultural issues, 2
sociocultural theories
    application of, 18–19
    case vignettes, 13, 19–21
    communities of practice, 16–18
    cultural historical activity theory, 15–16, 19
    history and development of, 14–18
    overview and description of, 14
socioeconomic status (SES), 2
    and remedial courses, 6
South Asian American identity development model, 128–129
    dissonance stage, 129
    introspection stage, 129
    preencounter stage, 128
    resistance and immersion stage, 129
    synergistic articulation and awareness stage, 129
spirituality, 5
spiritual or religious centers, 107
strategies, and transitions, 28, 31
Strong Interest Inventory, 181
structure, in developmental model, 57
student affairs
    biracial/multiracial identity development theories, 115–116
    case vignettes, 223–224, 231–233
    Chickering's theory, 106–107
    current trends in, 227–228
    from developmental standpoint, 4

disability and identity development models, 167–170
Erikson's theory of psychosocial theory, 40–45
future trends, 231
group theory, 219–220
historical context, review of, 224–225
history of, 1–2
Holland's theory of career development, 191–192
Kolb's theory, 78–79
minority identity development theories, 131–132
and movie night across campus, 228–230
Myers–Briggs Type Indicator (MBTI), 86–87
overlap between, 227
Perry's theory of moral development, 54–57
role of, 224
Schlossberg's transition theory, 30–31
sociocultural theories in, 18
and theory, 225–226
using theory as a language, 226–227
White identity development theories, 141
student affairs professionals. *See also* student affairs
implications for, 8–9
Perry's theory of moral development implications for, 57–59
student development and group, similarities between, 212–214
student involvement, 227
and movie night across campus, 228–230
student needs, 2–3
supervised graduate training clinic, 107
support system, for transitions, 26, 31

task groups, 214
temporizing, deflection from growth and development, 54
theories, importance of, 9–10
thinking individuals, 85
time of review years, psychosocial development, 40, 44–45
toddler years, psychosocial development, 37, 41
tolerance, 103–104
Torres, V., 126
Training of Counselors of Adults, 28
transgender identity. *See* lesbian, gay, bisexual, trans, and queer identity development theories

transition, definition of, 24
transition theory of Schlossberg. *See* Schlossberg's transition theory
transition to college, 2
moving in phase, 24, 31
moving out phase, 24, 31
moving through phase, 24, 31
trust versus mistrust, 36, 40–41

unanticipated transitions, 25
universal–ethical–principle orientation, 68

veterans, nontraditional students, 7
volunteerism, 58
Voting Rights Act of 1965, 136
Vygotsky, L., 14–15

wellness, 3–5, 8
Wenger, Etienne, 16, 17
White identity development theories. *See also* racial identity development theories
application of, 141
case vignettes, 135, 144–146
enhancing one's own racial identity development and multicultural competences, 142
formal and informal models, 136–138
Helms's contributions, 138–141. *See also* Helms's model of White identity development
history and development of, 136
implications for helping professionals, 142–144
overview and description of, 136–141
promoting White racial identity development and healthy interracial interactions among students, 142–144
Whiteness, deconstruction of, 142–143
willpower, 37, 41
wisdom, 40, 44–45
women. *See also* gender
and college major choice, 178–179
identity development, 94
working during college years, 5–6
workplace learning, sociocultural theories in, 18

zone of proximal development, 14–15